EYEWITNESS TRAVEL

# PROVENCE
## & THE CÔTE D'AZUR

# EYEWITNESS TRAVEL

# PROVENCE
## & THE CÔTE D'AZUR

### MAIN CONTRIBUTOR: ROGER WILLIAMS

LONDON, NEW YORK,
MELBOURNE, MUNICH AND DELHI
www.dk.com

PROJECT EDITOR Jane Simmonds
ART EDITOR Jane Ewart
SENIOR EDITOR Fay Franklin
EDITORS Tom Fraser, Elaine Harries, Fiona Morgan
DESIGNERS Claire Edwards, Pippa Hurst, Malcolm Parchment

CONTRIBUTORS
John Flower, Jim Keeble, Martin Walters

PHOTOGRAPHERS
Max Alexander, John Heseltine,
Kim Sayer, Alan Williams

ILLUSTRATORS
Stephen Conlin, Richard Draper, Steve Gyapay,
Chris D Orr Illustration, John Woodcock

Reproduced by Colourscan (Singapore)
Printed and bound in China by
Toppan Printing Co. (Shenzhen Ltd)

First published in Great Britain in 1995
by Dorling Kindersley Limited
80 Strand, London WC2R 0RL

**Reprinted with revisions 1995, 1996, 1997, 1999,
2000, 2001, 2002, 2003, 2004, 2006, 2008, 2010**

Copyright 1995, 2010 © Dorling Kindersley Limited, London
A Penguin Company

*Front cover main image: fields of lavender by rustic farmhouse, Var.*

**The information in this DK Eyewitness Travel Guide
is checked regularly.**
Every effort has been made to ensure that this book is as up-to-
date as possible at the time of going to press. Some details,
however, such as telephone numbers, opening hours, prices,
gallery hanging arrangements and travel information are liable to
change. The publishers cannot accept responsibility for any
consequences arising from the use of this book, nor for any
material on third-party websites, and cannot guarantee that any
website address in this book will be a suitable source of travel
information. We value the views and suggestions of our readers
very highly. Please write to: Publisher, DK Eyewitness Travel
Guides, Dorling Kindersley, 80 Strand, London WC2R 0RL.

◁ Abbaye de Sénanque, Vaucluse

# CONTENTS

## HOW TO USE THIS
## GUIDE 6

Poppy field outside Sisteron

## INTRODUCING
## PROVENCE

### DISCOVERING
### PROVENCE 10

### PUTTING PROVENCE
### ON THE MAP 12

**Busy Pampelonne beach to the
south of fashionable St-Tropez**

Marseille fisherman and his catch

Tarascon's château by the Rhône

Goat cheese in chestnut leaves

**TRAVELLERS'
NEEDS**

One of the perfumes of Provence

Typical Provençal countryside
between Grasse and Castellane

Fondation
Maeght outside
St-Paul-de-Vence

# HOW TO USE THIS GUIDE

This guide will help you get the most from your stay in Provence. It provides both expert recommendations and detailed practical information. *Introducing Provence* maps the region and sets it in its historical and cultural context. *Provence Area by Area* describes the important

sights, with maps, photographs and detailed illustrations. Suggestions for food, drink, accommodation, shopping and entertainment are in *Travellers' Needs*, and the *Survival Guide* has tips on everything from the French telephone system to getting to Provence and travelling around the region.

## PROVENCE AREA BY AREA

In this guide, Provence has been divided into five separate regions, each of which has its own chapter. A map of these regions can be found inside the front cover of the book. The most interesting places to visit in each region have been numbered and plotted on a *Regional Map*.

**Each area** of Provence can be quickly identified by its colour coding.

**1 Introduction**
*The landscape, history and character of each region is described here, showing how the area has developed over the centuries and what it has to offer the visitor today.*

**A locator map** shows the region in relation to the whole of Provence.

**2 Regional Map**
*This gives an illustrated overview of the whole region. All the sights are numbered and there are also useful tips on getting around by car and public transport.*

**Features and story boxes** highlight special or unique aspects of a particular sight.

**3 Detailed information on each sight**
*All the important towns and other places to visit are described individually. They are listed in order, following the numbering on the Regional Map. Within each town or city, there is detailed information on important buildings and other major sights.*

**4** **Major Towns**
*An introduction covers the history, character and geography of the town. The main sights are described individually and plotted on a Town Map.*

**A Visitors' Checklist** gives contact points for tourist and transport information, plus details of market days and local festival dates.

**The town map** shows all main through roads as well as minor streets of interest to visitors. All the sights are plotted, along with the bus and train stations, parking, tourist offices and churches.

**5** **Street-by-Street Map**
*Towns or districts of special interest to visitors are shown in detailed 3D, with photographs of the most important sights. This gives a bird's-eye view of towns or districts of special interest.*

**A suggested route** for a walk covers the most interesting streets in the area.

**For all the top sights**, a Visitors' Checklist provides the practical information you will need to plan your visit.

**Fondation Maeght**

**6** **The top sights**
*These are given two or more pages. Important buildings are dissected to reveal their interiors; museums have colour-coded floorplans to help you locate the most interesting exhibits.*

**The gallery guide** explains the layout of the museum and gives details on the arrangement and display of the collection.

**Stars** indicate the works of art or sights that no visitor should miss.

# INTRODUCING
# PROVENCE

# DISCOVERING PROVENCE

This is a land for all the senses: the sight of timeless light-suffused landscapes, the scents of lavender and olive groves, the taste of sun-drenched produce and grapes, the sound of sea gently lapping and the feel of the sun – so good you can almost taste it.

**Famous regional lavender perfume**

From the glamorous resorts of the Riviera to tiny islands, from bustling cities to *villages perchés*, to magnificent Roman remains and to the picturesque rural Provence with its sun-baked villages and endless seas of purple lavender, this is also a land of startling contrasts.

Spectacular view of the Riviera from Nice

## RIVIERA AND ALPES MARITIMES

- Nice, Cannes and Monaco
- Sensual Grasse
- Vallée des Merveilles

The fabled Riviera has been the playground of painters, composers, writers and celebrities for more than a century. The beautiful landscapes enchanted all the major French Impressionists and still weave their magic for visitors on every budget.

Try to break the bank at **Monte Carlo**'s casino *(see pp92–3)*, go celebrity spotting at the **Cannes Film festival** *(see pp68–69)*, stroll along the Promenade des Anglais in **Nice** *(see pp80–1)*, the Riviera's largest city, follow in the footsteps of Picasso in the charming *vieille ville* of **Antibes** *(see p72)*, or relax in the warmth of **Menton** *(see pp98–9)*, the lemon capital which enjoys the best climate in France.

Inland, medieval towns stretch lazily over the hills,

such as the much photographed, gastronomic town of **Mougins** *(see p66)*. Among fragrant fields of roses and jasmine, discover the world perfume capital, **Grasse** *(see pp66–7)*, the birthplace of Chanel No 5.

The back country of the Alpes Maritimes is a scenic delight, largely undiscovered by tourists. Gorges plunge, rivers sparkle and mountain peaks glisten with snow. The crowning delight is the aptly named **Vallée des Merveilles** *(see p97)*, cradled among craggy peaks where ibex and goats roam.

## VAR AND ILES D'HYERES

- Stylish St Tropez
- Côtes de Provence vineyards
- Iles d'Hyères, Golden Islands

**St Tropez** *(see pp118–22)*, or St-Trop as the French call it, is the most glamorous resort on the Provence coast. Its gorgeous sandy beaches act as a magnet for stars and sybarites. Nearby, wonderful beaches seem to appear at the roadside out of nowhere. **Fréjus** *(see p125)* has safe swimming and pristine beaches, while **Bandol** *(see p112)* has sandy coves, sheltered by an arc of wooded hills.

Around Bandol the land is cloaked with the **Côtes de Provence** *(see pp108–9)* vineyards. These wines are excellent, especially the reds, and opportunities for tasting are plentiful. The jewel of the bay of Hyères is its islands, the **Iles d'Hyères** *(see pp114–5)*, known as the "*Iles d'Or*" or "Golden Islands". They are an intense green set amid a sea of brilliant blue, the best islands of the western Riviera.

St Tropez harbour, full of glitz and glamour

The hilltop village of Roussillon, known as the "red village"

## BOUCHES-DU-RHONE AND NIMES

- Amazing natural history in the **Camargue**
- Superb Roman ruins at **Nîmes** and **Pont du Gard**
- **Marseille** and smaller ports

The breathtaking, contrasting landscapes of this region have been immortalized on canvas by Van Gogh and Cézanne. To the west is the **Camargue** *(see pp136–9)*, one of France's greatest wildlife reserves. *Gardians* or Camargue cowboys herd the black bulls astride their white horses, birdwatchers twitch with pleasure at the rich variety of birdlife, and flora and fauna enthusiasts are rewarded with unique collections.

**Nîmes** *(see pp132–3)* is full of southern charm with a Spanish accent. It is the site of some of Europe's best preserved Roman buildings including their version of Rome's Colosseum, **Les Arènes** *(see p132)*. Nearby is the extraordinary feat of Roman engineering, the **Pont du Gard** *(see p131)* which, at 48 m (157 ft), is the highest bridge ever built by the Romans. Glorious **Arles** *(see pp144–6)* is, for many, the jewel of Provence.

This area is also home to **Marseille** *(see pp150–2)*, Provence's largest city, and France's biggest port and oldest city. It has recently

benefitted from a facelift and is more sparkling and dynamic than ever. Elegant, cultured **Aix-en Provence** *(see pp148–9)* should not be missed nor should the lovely little resort, **Cassis** *(see p153)*.

Colourful, fresh produce at Aix-en-Provence market

## VAUCLUSE

- *Villages perchés* of **Gordes** and **Roussillon**
- **Avignon**, Provençal jewel
- **Châteauneuf-du-Pape**

Dominated by the snow-capped peak of **Mont Ventoux** *(see p160)*, this lovely region is redolent of rosemary, sage, thyme, lavender and pine wherever you go. The hilltop villages can often only be reached by winding roads, but your efforts are well rewarded. **Gordes** *(see p169)* clings spectacularly to its mountaintop eyrie and **Roussillon** *(see p169)* basks in its ochre light.

**Avignon** *(see pp166–8)*, on the banks of the Rhone, is a gateway to Provence. This fascinating city of ramparts bursts with culture and

energy. In this extraordinarily fertile region, don't miss the Côtes-du-Rhone wines, especially from **Châteauneuf -du-Pape** *(see p164)*, nor melons from **Cavaillon** *(see p170)*, France's largest market garden.

## ALPES-DE-HAUTE-PROVENCE

- Secret Provence
- Striking **Gorges du Verdon**
- **Plateau de Valensole** lavender fields

Provence's least-known and least populated area has a climate blending Provençal warmth and clear, cool Alpine air. The terrain is sprinkled with dramatic gorges, deeply carved valleys, bizarre rock formations and sparkling lakes framed by the soaring Alps.

The **Gorges du Verdon** *(see pp184–5)* is one of France's top sights. This breathtaking gorge carves into the rock up to 700 m (2,300 ft) deep. The whole area is a paradise for lovers of the outdoors – walking, white-water canoeing and hang-gliding. In the north is the highest peak in the Provencal Alps, **Mont Pelat** *(see p179)*. In the south is France's most important lavender-growing area, the **Plateau de Valensole** *(see pp182–3)*. To see this vision of purple magnificence at its best, visit in the summer.

The distinctive mauve of lavender fields in the Plateau de Valensole

# Putting Provence on the Map

Provence is situated in the sun-blessed south-east corner of France, edged to the south by the Mediterranean. Its most illustrious stretch of coastline, roughly from Menton to Bandol, is also known as the Côte d'Azur, although the nearer to Italy it gets the more likely it is to be referred to as the Riviera. To the east are Italy and the Alps, to the west, the Rhône river. The region covers an area of over 30,000 sq km (18,650 sq miles) with a population of about 4.25 million.

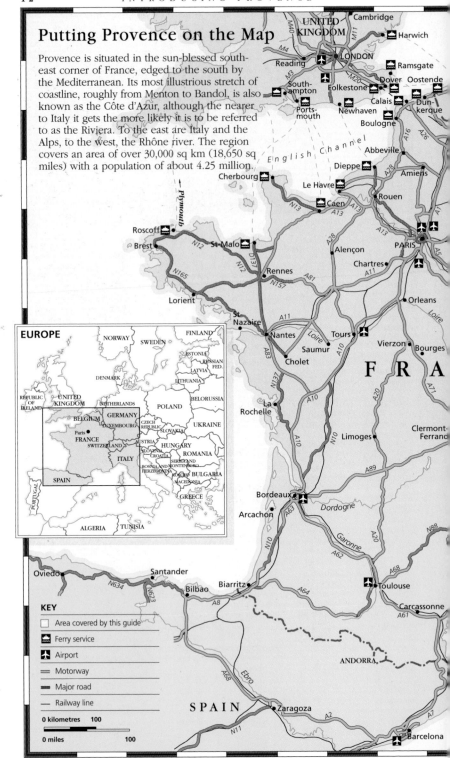

**EUROPE**

**KEY**

- ☐ Area covered by this guide
- ⛴ Ferry service
- ✈ Airport
- ═ Motorway
- ▬ Major road
- — Railway line

0 kilometres 100

0 miles 100

View of the impressive Palais des Papes in Avignon next to the Rhône

# A PORTRAIT OF PROVENCE

*I*n a comparatively short time, Provence has changed its face. A generation or two ago it was, to the French, a place of indolent southern bumpkins. To foreigners, it was an idyllic spot, but one reserved, it seemed to many, for the rich or artistic. Now, Provence, more than any other region, is where the French would choose to live and work, and its holiday routes buzz with traffic all year round.

The high-tech industry based here can attract top-flight staff, not just from France but from all over the world.

Still, Provence remains an essentially rural region. At its edges, it has a lively Latin beat: almost Spanish among the *gardians* of the Camargue in the west, Italian in Nice to the east. The rest of the region is mostly traditional and conservative. Only in games of *boules* or discussions about European bureaucracy does the talk become animated. But, once engaged in conversation, Provençals are the most generous and warmest of hosts. There is an all-pervading Frenchness, of course, which means that people are polite and punctilious.

**Monaco Grand Prix poster**

Shopkeepers always greet you as you enter, but will close at the stroke of noon. Other institutions open and close on the dot, too. Lunch, in Provence, is sacrosanct.

Traditions are important to the people of Provence. Local crafts are not quaint revivals, but respected, time-honoured occupations. Artists who came here for the light and the scenery found other inspirations, too. Picasso himself learned the potter's art at the wheel of a Provençal craftsman. Homes will have hand-turned local chestnut or oak furniture, *terre rouge* clay pots, Moustiers *faïence*, Biot glassware and furnishings using the traditional *indiennes* patterns of Arles and Nîmes.

A leisurely game of *boules* at Châteauneuf-du-Pape

◁ One of the many narrow, Italianate streets in the Old Town of Nice

A traditional bakery in Ville-sur-Auzon, in Vaucluse

The home is run as it has been for generations. Provençal kitchens, at the heart of family life, are famous. Combining simplicity with bounty, they mix the aroma of herbs with the generosity of wine. In the envious and admiring eyes of visitors, they are the epitome of taste.

Good taste is inbred. In this rural community, the familiarity of the weather, the seasons and the harvests are sources of constant discussion. Gardens, full of fruit trees, vegetables and flowers, are a matter of pride. Even city-dwellers know how the best produce should be grown, and may well have access to a country relation's plot. Market stalls are beautifully laid out and carefully scrutinized and, no matter how abundant the fruit, the vegetables or the wine, they are all grist for debate.

There are still heated discussions fuelled by the latest developments imposed by the European Union, whose legislation, farmers say, has in the past had a detrimental effect on productive Provençal land, when for example ancient vineyards were grubbed up and landowners' wealth sent into rapid decline.

The harvest cycle is close to the gods, whose benificence can affect the crops as surely as any EU bureaucrat. As Catholic as the rest of France, the people of Provence are also touched with a mystic sense that has been influenced by Mithraism and Islam, as well as by

A colourful fruit and vegetable market

pagan gods. Religious beliefs are so well mixed that it is often difficult to separate them. Carnival and Corpus Christi extend Easter, which has more importance here than in many other parts of Europe. Christmas, too, is an elaborate affair. The rituals begin as early as 4 December, St Barb's day, with the planting of grains of wheat, a pagan symbol of renewal and rebirth.

Superstitions linger in the countryside. An egg, salt, bread and matches, humble representations of elemental concepts, may be given to a newborn baby, while carline thistles may be seen nailed to front doors for good luck.

Provence has a typically Mediterranean landscape: the mountains drop down to the sea; communities perch on crags or cling to remote hillsides. It is little wonder that traditions live on here. For centuries, too, it was a place for outlaws from France, who could assume new identities here and carry on with their lives. Perhaps as a result, strangers were not to be trusted, and

Harvesting linden blossoms to make *tilleul* infusion

The dramatic, isolated crags of Les Pénitents des Mées, in Alpes-de-Haute-Provence

remained outsiders for ever. A seemingly trivial slight might spark a feud which could last for generations. There are still villages today where one family does not speak to another, even though each has long forgotten why. This attitude, and its tragic implications, was finely portrayed by Yves Montand, with Gérard Depardieu as the shunned outsider, in Claud Berri's films of Marcel Pagnol's *Jean de Florette* and *Manon des Sources*. The more cosmopolitan coast is the territory of *film noir*. Here, the tradition of silence and family ties has not always been beneficial. Jean-Paul Belmondo and Alain Delon romanticized it in *Borsalino;* Gene Hackman revealed its dark underside in *The French Connection*.

In 1982, the Antibes-based novelist Graham Greene published an exposé of corruption in nearby Nice. In 1994, Yann Piat, anti-drugs

Pavement café on cours Mirabeau, Aix

campaigner and member of parliament, was assassinated in Hyères.

The fact that Piat was a woman made no difference to her enemies, ironic in a region where women have not been treated as equals. Alphonse Daudet noted the Provençal male's "incurable contempt" for women, however, the Queen of Arles is elected for her virtues as an upholder of the traditional Provençal values. It was also this region that nurtured the 20th century's icon of French womanhood, Brigitte Bardot.

There are great rewards for the visitor who can appreciate the many facets of Provence – its traditions as well as its beauty and glamour. But, the more often you return, the more you will realize, as have some of the world's greatest artists and writers, that part of the endless allure of Provence lies within the very secrets that it refuses to surrender.

# The Natural History of Provence

**A two-tailed pasha butterfly**

A fascinating array of insects, birds, animals and flowers flourish in the varied habitats available in Provence, from the Mediterranean to coastal wetlands, rocky gorges and the remote peaks of the Alpes Maritimes. The area has the mildest climate in France: hot, mainly dry summers, and warm, mild winters near the coast. In early spring the myriad flowers are at their best, while numbers of unusual birds are at their highest in late spring. Many of the wilder areas have been made into reserves, often with routes marked out for exploration.

**The Luberon** (see pp170–72) *is a huge limestone range, rich in orchids, such as this military orchid. It is also a hunting ground for birds of prey.*

**Mont Ventoux**'s lower slopes are flower-covered in the spring *(see p160).*

**Les Alpilles***' limestone ridge (see p141) attracts birds of prey, including Bonelli's eagles, Egyptian vultures and eagle owls, as well as this more mild-mannered bee-eater.*

• Orange

Carpentras •

• Avignon

**VAUCLUSE**

*Rhône*

• Arles

**BOUCHES-DU-RHONE AND NIMES**

**The Camargue,** *at the delta of the river Rhône, is one of Europe's most important wetlands (see pp136–9). Water birds that thrive here include purple herons and the greater flamingo. Lizards, such as this ocellated lizard, can also be seen.*

• Marseille

**The Côte Bleue** is rich in marine life, such as octopuses, in the deeper waters.

**The Montagne Ste-Victoire** is a limestone range that attracts walkers and climbers. It was one of Cézanne's favourite subjects.

**The Plaine de la Crau** *is 50,000 ha (193 sq miles) of stony plains and steppe-like grasslands southeast of Arles, home to birds like this hoopoe, and the rare pin-tailed sandgrouse.*

**Les Calanques** *(see p153)* are narrow inlets bounded by cliffs. The rocky slopes are home to woodland birds such as owls.

**The Parc National du Mercantour** *is one of the finest Alpine reserves* (see p97), *containing wildlife such as this marmot, and chamois, ibex and mouflon* (wild sheep). *It is also good walking country.*

**The Haute Provence Geo- logical Reserve** near Digne *(see p180)* has a spectacular collection of giant ammo- nites embedded in rock.

**The Cime de la Bonette** *(see p179)* is a lofty pass where chamois roam.

**The Gorges du Verdon** *area, between the Alps and the Mediterranean, is a beautiful nature reserve with a dramatic canyon at its centre* (see pp184–5). *A footpath along the canyon floor allows detailed examination of the rock formations, rare plants and birds.*

Barcelonnette •

**ALPES-DE-HAUTE- PROVENCE**

Durance

Digne-les-Bains

Verdon

Var

**The Gorges de la Vésubie** *(see p95)* has viewpoints from which to spot migrating birds such as swallows.

**The Prealpes de Grasse**, known for their dramatic gorges, lie to the east of the Alpes Maritimes.

**THE RIVIERA AND THE ALPES MARITIMES**

Nice

**THE VAR AND THE ILES D'HYERES**

• Fréjus

**The Massif de l'Esterel's** *(see p124)* high rocky coves and scrubland are home to various species of snakes.

**In the Massif des Maures** (see pp116–17), *dense woods contain bee-eaters, wood- chat shrikes and hoopoes. They also provide sanctuary for the rare Hermann's tortoise.*

**The Massif de la Ste-Baume** has many broadleaved trees that are vividly coloured in autumn.

• Toulon

**KEY**

| | National park |
| | Regional natural park |
| | Protected site |
| | Reserve |

0 kilometres     25

0 miles          25

**The Iles d'Hyères** (see pp114–15), *scattered a ferry ride away from the most southerly point of Provence, are best known for their abun- dant sea life, including fish such as this wrasse. Geckos and rare birds like the great spotted cuckoo can be seen.*

# Perched Villages

Some of the most attractive architectural features of Provence are the *villages perchés* or perched villages. They rise like jagged summits on the hilltops where they were built for safety in the political turmoil of the Middle Ages. From their lofty heights they kept vigil over the hinterland as well as the coast. They were built around castle keeps and wrapped in thick ramparts, a huddle of cobbled streets, steps, alleys and archways. Few were able to sustain their peasant communities beyond the 19th-century agrarian reforms, and a century of poverty and depopulation followed. Today many of the villages have been restored by a new generation of artists, craftworkers and holiday-makers.

**The mountainous site** *of Peillon (see p95) is typical of the way perched villages blend organically with the landscape.*

GRANDE PLACE

RUE DE LA POURTOUNE

RUE CASSETT

RUE DES DORIERS

RUE DE LA CASTRE

RUE DES BAUQUES

RUE GRANDE

**ST-PAUL-DE-VENCE**
St-Paul is a typical *village perché*, with many of the key features preserved. The medieval ramparts were completely reinforced by Francis I in the 16th century. Today it is again besieged – as one of the most popular tourist sights in France *(see p75)*.

COURTINE ST PAUL

BASTION ST REMY

REMPARTS

**The chapel** was always the focal point of the village.

**Complicated entrances** confused invaders and provided extra security against attack.

**Side entrances** *were never obtrusive or elaborate, but were usually small and, as in Eze (see p88), opened onto narrow, winding lanes. Sometimes there were more gates or abrupt turns within the walls to confuse attacking soldiers, making the town easier to defend.*

**Castles and keeps** *(donjons), and sometimes fortified churches, were always sited with the best viewpoint in the village, and provided sanctuary in times of crisis. Many, like the castle at Eze (see p88), were often attacked and are now in ruins.*

**The chapel** *sustained the religious life of the community. As in Les Baux (see p142), it was usually built near the keep of the castle, part of a central core of communal buildings, and was often fortified. The bell would be rung to warn of impending attack.*

**Fountains** *were essential to the village, often being the sole source of water. Many, like this one in Vence (see p74), were elaborately embellished.*

**The arcades** *lent support to the buildings in the narrow, winding streets, as here in Roquebrune (see p98). They also gave shelter from sun and rain.*

Fountain

Arched and stepped streets

RUE DU HAUT FOUR

LE PONTIS

RUE GRANDE

RUE GRANDE

PLACE DE L'HOSPICE

REMPARTS OUEST

OUEST

A narrow gateway was easily secured.

Ramparts and bastions provided solid defences.

**The ramparts** *surrounded the entire village with thick stone walls, often with houses built into them. The defences, like those of St-Paul (see p75), were strengthened in the 16th century under Francis I and by Vauban, Louis XIV's military architect. Today they offer excellent panoramas.*

**Main gates** *were always narrow so they could be closed off and defended in times of attack. Some gates had the additional protection of portcullises. This example is one of four 12th-century gates built into the ramparts of the ancient village of Bargemon (see p106) in the Var.*

# Rural Architecture in Provence

**Shutters to keep out the sun and wind**

Traditional architectural features are reminders of how influential the weather is on living conditions in rural Provence. Great efforts are made to ease the biting gusts of the Mistral and the relentless heat of the summer sun. Thick stone walls, small windows and reinforced doors are all recognizable characteristics. Traditional farmhouses were built entirely from wood, clay, stone and soil, all locally found materials. Rows of hardy cypress trees were planted to act as a windbreak on the north side; plane and lotus trees provided shade to the south.

**Bories** (see p169) *are drystone huts built using techniques dating back to 2,000 BC.*

## THE PROVENÇAL MAS

Found across rural Provence, the *mas* is a low, squat stone farmhouse. Protection and strength are vital to its construction – walls are made of compact stone blocks and the wooden doors and shutters are thick and reinforced. Outbuildings often included a cellar, stables, a bread oven and dovecote.

**Chimneys** are stone-built, low and squat, and lie close to the roof.

**Canal roof tiling,** *or* tuiles romaines, *is typical of the south.*

**Dovecot**

**Roughly cut** stone bricks are used to make the walls.

**The most exposed** part of the roof is unthatched.

**The roof** is gently sloping and thatched with marsh reeds.

**The north wall** is rounded for protection against the Mistral.

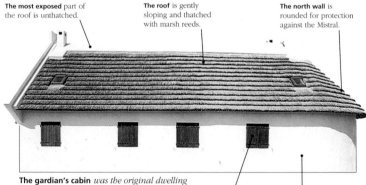

**The gardian's cabin** *was the original dwelling place of the bull herdsman or* gardian *of the Camargue. It is a small, narrow structure, consisting of a dining room and bedroom, divided by a reed screen and furnished simply.*

**The windows** are small and reinforced.

**Walls** are made of compressed clay and straw, known as cob.

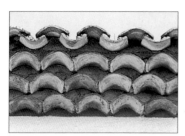

**The tiled roofs** *are gently sloping and are influenced by Roman design, with a decorative frieze (génoise) under the eaves. The tiles are made of thick, red terracotta and curved in shape – a double or triple layer of tiles are set in mortar and protrude beyond the wall.*

**Windows are built** *on three sides of the* mas *but none on the north to avoid the Mistral's full blast. They are kept small to prevent the winter winds coming in, but large enough to let light in.*

**Interlocking clay** tiles form canals, allowing rainwater to run down and drain off the roof.

**The Mistral** winds blow so fiercely that the *mas* was often built facing the southeast to minimize the wind's impact. Roofs are built low to the ground, covering the living quarters and annexes. The gentle slope prevents the tiles blowing and sliding off.

**The walls are** rendered smooth with plaster.

**Stone ice houses** *were built near the* mas *and used for storage during the winter months. Blocks of ice were cut and put in the huts, insulated with hay.*

## IRONWORK BELL TOWERS

Wrought-iron bell towers have been a speciality in Provence since the 16th century. Their light, open framework allows strong winds to blow through and the sound of the bells to carry for miles. The design and complexity depends on the size and purpose of the building. These examples illustrate the skills of local craftsmen across the region.

**Highly ornate bell tower in Aix**

**The bell tower of St-Jérôme in Digne**

**The Hôtel de Ville bell tower in Orange**

**Notre Dame's bell tower in Sisteron**

# Architectural Styles in Provence

From the imperial grandeur of Roman constructions to the modern domestic designs of Le Corbusier, Provence has a magnificent array of architectural styles. The Middle Ages saw a flourishing of great Romanesque abbeys and churches and from the 16th to the 18th centuries, as prosperity increased, châteaux and town houses were built. With the expansion of towns in the 19th century came an increase in apartment blocks and public buildings to accommodate the fast-growing population. Today, successful restoration has taken place, but often in haste. The demands of tourism have taken their toll, particularly on the coast, resulting in ugly developments.

An 18th-century fountain in Pernes-les-Fontaines

## ROMAN ARCHITECTURE (20 BC–AD 400)

The quality of Roman architecture is illustrated by the many extant amphitheatres, triumphal arches and thermal baths found across the region, all built with large blocks of local limestone.

Ornate high-relief

The triumphal arch of **Glanum** (pp140–41) *is the original entrance to the oldest Roman city in Provence. Carvings on the outer arch show Caesar's victory over the Gauls and Greeks.*

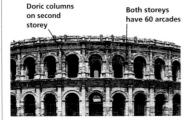

Doric columns on second storey

Both storeys have 60 arcades

Nîmes Arènes, built in the 1st century AD *(p132)*

Nîmes' well-preserved Maison Carrée *(p132)*

## ROMANESQUE ARCHITECTURE (11–12TH CENTURIES)

The high point of Provençal architecture came after the Dark Ages. It was a combination of Classical order and perfection, inspired by Roman design and new styles from northern and southern Europe. This style is characterized especially in religious buildings by elegant symmetry and simplicity.

Multiple arches

Elaborate religious carvings

This church entrance in Seyne (see p178) *is an example of 13th-century Romanesque architecture. The slight point of the multiple arches hints at a move away from strict Romanesque purity.*

Clustered pillar

Decorated capital with interlaced leaves

Capital from the Abbaye du Thoronet *(p108)*

The Abbaye de Sénanque, founded in 1148 *(pp164–5)*

## LATE MIDDLE AGES (13TH–16TH CENTURIES)

Feuding and religious wars led to people withdrawing to towns, protected by fortified walls and gates. Communication between houses was often by underground passages. Streets were roughly paved and water and sewage were carried away by a central gutter.

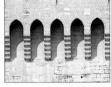

Tour de la Campana in the Palais des Papes *(pp44–5)*

Street in St-Martin-Vésubie *(p95)* showing central gutter

Crenellation or battlements

Portcullis used against invaders

**Aigues-Mortes** (see pp134–5) *was built by Louis IX in the 13th century, according to a strict grid pattern. This strategically placed fort overlooks both sea and land.*

## CLASSICAL ARCHITECTURE (17TH–18TH CENTURIES)

The severity and order of the Classical style was relieved by elaborate carvings on doorways and windows. Gardens became more formal and symmetrical.

Tablet with symbol of authority

Refined stone

Carved Regency doorway

Neo-Classical pillar

The 17th-century Barbentane château, fronted by formal gardens *(p130)*

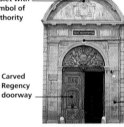

**The Musée des Tapisseries** *in Aix* (see p148) *has elaborately carved wooden entrance doors.*

Pavillon de Vendôme detail, Aix-en-Provence *(p149)*

## MODERN ARCHITECTURE (1890–PRESENT DAY)

The magnificent hotels and villas of the Belle Epoque have given way to more utilitarian housing and public buildings. But the numerous modern art galleries represent the highest standards of 20th-century architecture.

Le Corbusier's Cité Radieuse *(p152)*

Rounded pavilion

Cupola above a round corner tower

The palatial Négresco hotel in Nice *(p84)*

**The Musée d'Art Contemporain in Nice** (see p85) *was built in 1990. It is made up of square towers, linked by glass passageways.*

# Artists of Provence

Provence inspired many of the most original 19th-
and 20th-century painters. They were attracted by
the luminescent quality of the light here, and the
consequent brilliance of the colours. Cézanne,
who was a native, and Van Gogh, a convert, were
both fired by the vibrant shades of the landscape.
The Impressionists Monet and Renoir came early,
and followers included Bonnard, Signac and Dufy.
The two giants of 20th-century painting, Matisse
and Picasso, both settled here. The artistic tradition
is kept alive by small galleries in almost every town,
as well as major museums throughout the region.

**Jean Cocteau** *(1889–1963) spent
many years on the coast and created
his museum in Menton (see p99).
Noce imaginaire (1957) is one of his
murals from the Salle des Mariages.*

**Vincent Van Gogh** *(1853–90)
painted* Van Gogh's Chair *(1888)
in Arles (see pp144–6). His two
years here and in St-Rémy (see
pp140–41) were his most prolific.*

**Victor Vasarely** *(1908–
97) restored the château
in Gordes. His Kinetic and
Op Art can be seen in Aix-
en-Provence (see p149).*

**Hans Van Meegeren**
*(1889–1947), the Dutch
master-forger of Vermeer,
was living in Roquebrune
(see p98) when found out.*

**REGIONS OF
PROVENCE**

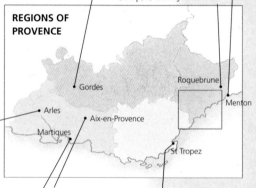

Gordes

Roquebrune

Menton

Arles

Aix-en-Provence

Martigues

St Tropez

Vallauris

**Paul Cézanne** *(1839–
1906), in his desire to
scour the "depth of reality",
often painted his native
Aix (see pp148–9).*

**Paul Signac** *(1863–1935)
came to St-Tropez in 1892,
painting it in his palette of
rainbow dots (see pp118–22).*

**Félix Ziem** *(1821–1911) was born in Burgundy
but was a great traveller. He adored Venice,
and found the same romantic inspiration by
the canals of Martigues (see p147), where he
painted* Camargue, Côté Soleil.

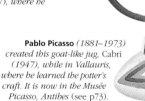

**Pablo Picasso** *(1881–1973)
created this goat-like jug,* Cabri
*(1947), while in Vallauris,
where he learned the potter's
craft. It is now in the Musée
Picasso, Antibes (see p73).*

0 kilometres    3

0 miles          3

**Marc Chagall** *(1887–1985),
Russian painter of light-hearted
and biblically inspired works,
lived in St-Paul-de-Vence
from 1949 (see p75).*

**Raoul Dufy** *(1877–1953)
appreciated the pleasures of the
coast. A twilight stroll beneath the
palm trees is fondly evoked in* La
Jetée, Promenade à Nice *(1928).*

• Vence

• Cagnes-sur-Mer

• Nice

• Biot

**Henri Matisse**
*(1869–1954) captured
the Riviera's light and colour
even in homely settings such as*
Intérieur au Phonographe
*(1924) (see pp82–3).*

**Pierre Auguste Renoir**
*(1841–1919) sought relief
from his rheumatism at
Cagnes in 1906 and found
new inspiration (see p78).*

**Fernand Léger** *(1881–
1955) is celebrated for his
vivid Cubist and industrial
works in oils and ceramics,
on show in Biot (see p74).*

Antibes

### ARTISTS IN PROVENÇAL HISTORY

Provence was home to great artists long
before the advent of modern art. In the
Middle Ages, the Schools of Avignon and
Nice flourished. The latter was dominated
by the Bréa family, whose works can be
seen in churches throughout the
region. Sculptor Pierre Puget
(1620–94) is called the
"Michelangelo of Provence".
His birthplace, Marseille,
has several of his works *(see
pp150–52)*. But Jean-Honoré
Fragonard (1732–1806)
is most Provençal
of them all – his Romantic
paintings are filled with
Grasse flowers *(see p66)*.

**Crucifixion (1512) by Louis
Bréa, monastery of Notre-
Dame, Cimiez (see p84)**

**Nicolas de Staël** *(1914–55) was born in
Russia. When successful, he bought a house
in the Luberon for his wife, but chose to live
with his mistress in Antibes (see p72). His*
Paysage Méditerranéen *was painted in 1953.*

# Writers in Provence

The Nobel Laureate Frédéric Mistral (1830–1914) was the champion of the Provençal language, but better known are the local writers who have captured the Provençal character: Alphonse Daudet, Jean Giono, Emile Zola and Marcel Pagnol. French writers such as Dumas and Hugo used Provençal backdrops for their fiction; foreign writers also found inspiration in the region.

Victor Hugo

*Alphonse Daudet*

*Frédéric Mistral*

An early edition of The Count of Monte Cristo

**1920** Consumptive New Zealand short story writer Katherine Mansfield recuperates in Menton *(see p99)* and writes *Miss Bull* and *Passion* among other pieces.

**1895** Jean Giono is born in Manosque *(see p182)*. Work like *The Man who Planted Trees* evokes the region.

**1892** The last part of *Thus Spake Zarathustra* by German Friedrich Nietzsche is published. He devised it after traversing the path in Eze *(see p88)* which was later named after him.

**1904** Frédéric Mistral wins the Nobel Prize with his poem, *Mirèio*.

**1869** Alphonse Daudet publishes *Collected Letters from my Windmill*, set in a windmill at Fontvieille *(see p143)*.

**1844** Alexander Dumas publishes *The Count of Monte Cristo*, set in the Château d'If, Marseille *(see p152)*.

**1870** Death in Cannes of Prosper Mérimée, author of *Carmen*, Bizet's opera.

| 1840 | 1855 | 1870 | 1885 | 1900 | 1915 |
|------|------|------|------|------|------|

| 1840 | 1855 | 1870 | 1885 | 1900 | 1915 |
|------|------|------|------|------|------|

**1862** *Les Misérables* by Victor Hugo is published. The early chapters are set in Digne-les-Bains *(see p180)*.

**1868** Edmond Rostand, author of *Cyrano de Bergerac* (1897) is born in Marseille *(see pp150–51)*.

**1887** Journalist Stéphen Liégeard introduces the term, *Côte d'Azur*.

**1907** Provençal poet, René Char, is born in L'Isle sur-la-Sorgue.

**1915** Edith Wharton, American author of *The Age of Innocence*, visits Hyères *(see p115)* with André Gide. A street is named after her.

*Edith Wharton*

*Somerset Maugham*

**1926** American author Ernest Hemingway sets *The Garden of Eden* in La Napoule. Britain's W Somerset Maugham buys the Villa Mauresque, Cap Ferrat, and writes *Cakes and Ale* (1930).

## EARLY WRITERS

For centuries, troubadour ballads and religious poems, or *Noels*, formed the core of literature in Provence. While certain unique individuals stand out, it was not until 1854, with Mistral's help, that Provençal writers found their own "voice".

**1327** Petrarch *(see p45)* falls in unrequited love with Laura de Noves in Avignon, inspiring his *Canzonière* poems.

**1555** Nostradamus, from St-Rémy, publishes *The Centuries*, prophecies outlawed by the Vatican.

**1764** Tobias Smollett "discovers" Nice. (He published his book, *Travels through France and Italy*, in 1766.)

**1791** Marquis de Sade, the original sadist, publishes *Justine*, written while imprisoned in the Bastille.

*Petrarch's Laura de Noves*

**1885** *Germinal* published by Emile Zola, boyhood friend of Cézanne, as part of his 20-novel cycle, *The Fortunes of the Rouge* (1871–93), set partly round Aix.

*Emile Zola*

**1932** Briton Aldous Huxley writes *Brave New World* in Sanary-sur-Mer *(see p112)*, the setting for *Eyeless in Gaza* (1936).

*Marcel Pagnol*

**1974** Death of film director and writer Marcel Pagnol, whose *Marseille Trilogy* explored his Provençal childhood.

**1933** Thomas Mann, who wrote *Death in Venice* (1913) and brother Heinrich, flee Germany for Sanary *(see p112)*.

**1981** British actor Dirk Bogarde moves to Provence and publishes his first novel, *A Gentle Occupation*.

*Lawrence Durrell*

**1985** The last volume of Briton Lawrence Durrell's *Avignon Quintet* is published.

*St-Exupéry's poignant fable,* Le Petit Prince

**1989** Briton Peter Mayle's book *A Year in Provence* generates interest in the Luberon.

**1944** Antoine de St-Exupéry, aviator and author of *Vol de Nuit* (1931) and *Le Petit Prince* (1943), goes missing. His last flight passed his sister's house at Agay.

| 30 | 1945 | 1960 | 1975 | 1990 | 2005 |
|---|---|---|---|---|---|
| 30 | 1945 | 1960 | 1975 | 1990 | 2005 |

**1978** Marseille-born Sébastien Japrisot publishes the award-winning *L'Eté Meurtrier*, set in a Provençal village.

**1985** Patrick Süskind's novel *Perfume*, in which much of the action takes place in Grasse, is published.

*Le Clézio*

**1954** Françoise Sagan, aged 18, writes *Bonjour Tristesse* (1954) about the Esterel coast.

**1994** Jean-Marie Gustave Le Clézio (born 1940 in Nice) wins the award for best living French writer.

*Albert Camus*

**1993** Briton Anthony Burgess, the author of *A Clockwork Orange* (1962), writes his final work, *Dead Man in Deptford*, in Monaco.

**1957** Albert Camus buys a house in Lourmarin *(see p171)*, where he writes his autobiography, not published until 1994.

*Graham Greene*

*The Fitzgeralds*

**1982** Britain's Graham Greene writes *J'Accuse – The Dark Side of Nice.*

**1934** American author F Scott Fitzgerald's South of France-based *Tender is the Night* is published. Scott and his wife Zelda stay in a villa at Juan-Les-Pins in 1926.

# The Beaches of Provence

From the untamed expanses of the Rhône delta to the hot spots of the Riviera, via the cliffs and coves of the Var, the coastline of Provence is extremely varied. Resort beaches around the towns of the Riviera, such as Menton, Nice and Monte-Carlo, are crowded and noisy in the height of summer. They often charge a fee, but are usually well-kept and offer good watersports facilities. It is, however, possible to seek out quieter corners away from the crowds if you know where to look.

*The Côte d'Azur beaches offer warmth and sunshine all year long, as advertised in this 1930s poster by Roger Broders.*

**The Camargue beaches** (see pp136–8) *at the mouth of the Rhône delta, are often deserted. The long, flat sands are ideal for horse riding, but there is a shortage of amenities.*

**The Côte Bleue** *is dotted with fishing ports and elegant summer residences. Pine trees line the beaches.*

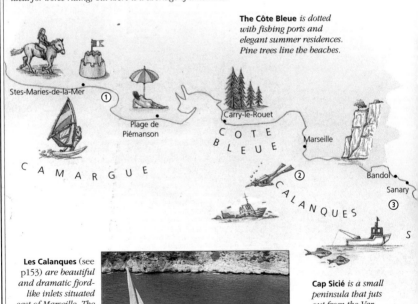

Stes-Maries-de-la-Mer ①

Plage de Piémanson

Carry-le-Rouet

C O T E
B L E U E

Marseille

C A M A R G U E

C A L A N Q U E S ②

Bandol

Sanary ③

S

**Les Calanques** (see p153) *are beautiful and dramatic fjord-like inlets situated east of Marseille. The sheer white cliffs, some 400 m (1,312 ft) high, drop vertically into the tempting, blue water.*

**Cap Sicié** *is a small peninsula that juts out from the Var mainland. It is famed for its strong winds and waves, ideal for experienced windsurfers.*

## PROVENCE'S TEN BEST BEACHES

**Best sandy beach ①**
Plage de Piémanson, east of the Camargue, is remote enough for nudist bathing.

**Best deep-sea diving ②**
The deep Calanques waters are ideal for exploring.

**Best sea fishing ③**
Bandol and Sanary are charming resorts, where the tuna boats make their daily catch.

**Best small resort beach ④**
Le Lavandou offers all amenities on a small scale.

**Best trendy beach ⑤**
Tahiti-Plage in St-Tropez is the coast's showcase for fun, sun, fashion and glamour.

**Best family beaches ⑥**
Fréjus-Plage and the beach of St-Raphaël are clean, safe and have excellent facilities.

**Best star-spotter's beach ⑦**
Cannes' beautiful setting, with its scenic harbour, casino and stylish beaches, attracts the rich and famous.

**Best teen and twenties beach ⑧**
The all-night bars, cafés and nightclubs of Juan-les-Pins make this a lively resort.

**Best activity beach ⑨**
Watersports fanatics gather at the Ruhl-Plage in Nice for the jet-skiing and parasailing.

**Best winter beach ⑩**
Menton is the warmest resort on the Riviera and the sun shines all year round, ideal for relaxing winter holidays.

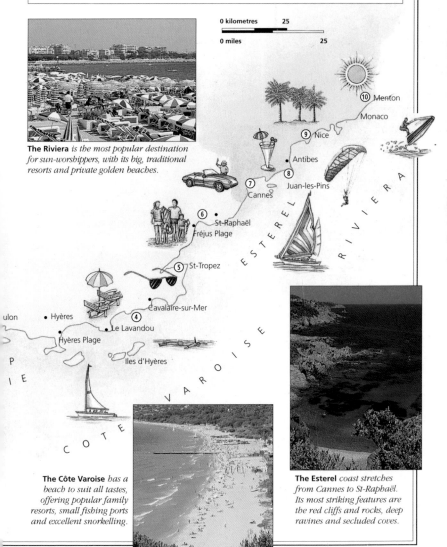

**The Riviera** *is the most popular destination for sun-worshippers, with its big, traditional resorts and private golden beaches.*

0 kilometres 25
0 miles 25

⑩ Menton
Monaco
⑨ Nice
Antibes
⑧
Juan-les-Pins
⑦
Cannes
ESTEREL
RIVIERA
⑥ St-Raphaël
Fréjus Plage
⑤ St-Tropez
Cavalaire-sur-Mer
ulon
Hyères
④ Le Lavandou
Hyères Plage
Iles d'Hyères
P
I E
COTE VAROISE

**The Côte Varoise** *has a beach to suit all tastes, offering popular family resorts, small fishing ports and excellent snorkelling.*

**The Esterel** *coast stretches from Cannes to St-Raphaël. Its most striking features are the red cliffs and rocks, deep ravines and secluded coves.*

# PROVENCE THROUGH THE YEAR

Provence is at its prettiest in spring, when flowers bring livelihoods to perfume-makers and pleasure to passers-by. It can also be surprisingly cold as this is when the Mistral blows its strongest.

Summer fruit and vegetables are both abundant and beautiful, filling the local markets. The midsummer heat is added to by the fires of St Jean and the Valensole plains are striped with lavender, the indelible colour of the region.

Medieval-style grape harvest or *vendange*

To entertain the thousands of holidaymakers, July and August are filled with music festivals. Come autumn, vineyards turn to copper and the grapes are harvested. Snows blanket the mountains from December and skiers take to the slopes. Throughout the year, every town and village celebrates with a *fête*, often with traditional costume and lively activities. For information, contact the local tourist office (*see p237*).

Women at the Feria Pascale in Arles

## SPRING

By the time March begins, lemons have already been harvested and the almond blossom faded. The landscape is brightened with pear, plum and apricot blossom and the first vegetables of spring are ready for the markets: beans, asparagus and green artichokes known as *mourre de gats*. By May, fruit markets are coloured with the first ripe cherries and strawberries of the year.

Southern mountain slopes warm to the sunshine and come alive with alpine flowers but the northern slopes remain wintery. Broom turns hillsides deep yellow and bees start to make honey from the sweet-smelling rosemary flowers. Flocks of sheep begin the journey of transhumance up to the summer pastures, and on the vast plains maize, wheat and rape push their way up through the softening earth.

## MARCH

**Exposition International de la Fleur** (*end-March-April*), Cagnes-sur-Mer (*p78*). Flower festival to celebrate spring.
**Festin des Courgourdons** (*last Sun*), Nice (*pp84–5*). Folklore and sculpted gourd *fête*.

## APRIL

**Procession aux Limaces** (*Good Friday*), Roquebrune-Cap-Martin (*p98*). The streets are lit with shell lamps and a parade of locals dressed as disciples and legionnaires recreate the entombment of Christ.
**Fête de la St-Marc** (*end April*), Châteauneuf-du-Pape (*p164*). Wine contest. (The year's vintage is blessed on the 1st weekend in August.)
**Fête des Gardians** (*last Sunday in April*), Arles (*pp144–6*). The town is taken over by the *gardians* or cowboys who look after the Camargue cattle herds.
**Feria Pascale** (*Easter*), Arles (*pp144–6*). Arletans turn out in their traditional costume for a

*feria.* The *farandole* is danced to the accompaniment of the *tambourin* drum and *galoubet* flute to mark the beginning of the famous bullfighting season.

## MAY

**Pèlerinage des Gitans avec Procession à la Mer de Sainte Sarah** (*24–25 May*), Stes-Maries-de-la-Mer (*pp228–9*).
**Festival International du Film** (*two weeks in May*), Cannes (*pp68–9*). The most prestigious annual film festival.
**La Bravade** (*16–18 May*), St-Tropez (*see p228*).
**Fête de la Transhumance** (*mid–late May*), St-Rémy (*p140*). Celebrates the ancient custom of moving sheep to higher ground for the summer.
**Grand Prix Automobile de Formule 1** (*weekend after Ascension*), Monaco (*p94*). The only Grand Prix raced on public roads laps up an impressive 3,145 km (1,954 miles).
**Feria** (*Pentecost*), Nîmes (*see pp132–3*). The first major bullfighting event of the year.

Rodeo-style horse games at the Fête des Gardians in Arles

## AVERAGE DAILY HOURS OF SUNSHINE

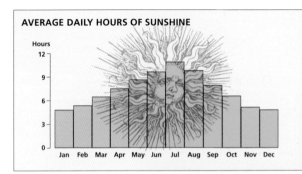

Hours
12
9
6
3
0

Jan Feb Mar Apr May Jun Jul Aug Sep Oct Nov Dec

**Sunshine Chart**
*The summer months are guaranteed to be hot, with the intensity climaxing in July. Even in the winter, coastal towns can have up to 150 hours of sunshine a month, but be warned: it is often the icy Mistral that blows the clouds away in early spring.*

## SUMMER

The Côte d'Azur is essentially a playground in summer, particularly in August when the French take their holidays. Rafters take to the rivers and scuba divers explore the varied sea-life. For laid-on entertainment, there are music festivals throughout the region.

Three national celebrations are also manifest: fireworks and bonfires brighten the skies on the **Fête de St-Jean** (June 24). **Bastille Day** (July 14) is celebrated with fireworks while **Assumption Day** (August 15) is a time for great feasting.

Celebrating the Fête de St-Jean with fireworks over Marseille harbour

### JUNE

**Fête de la Tarasque** *(last w/e)*, Tarascon *(p140)*. According to local legend, the Tarasque monster once terrorized the region. An effigy of the monster is paraded through the town.
**Festival d'Art Lyrique** *(June and July)*, Aix-en-Provence *(pp148–9)*. Extensive programme of classical music concerts and opera is staged in the courtyard theatre of the Archbishop's Palace.

The legendary Tarasque

### JULY

**Festival de la Sorgue** *(weekends in July)*, Fontaine-de-Vaucluse & l'Isle-sur-la-Sorgue *(see p165)*. Concerts, shows, boat races and floating markets on the river Sorgue.
**Festival d'Avignon** *(mid- to late July)*, Avignon *(see p229)*.
**Chorégies d'Orange** *(all*

*month)* Orange. This long-established opera season is held in the acoustically perfect Roman theatre *(pp162–3)*.
**Jazz à Juan** *(mid- to late July)*, Juan-les-Pins *(p72)*. One of the top jazz festivals in Provence.
**Festival du Jazz** *(mid-month)*, Toulon *(p112–13)*. A week of free concerts in different squares every day throughout the town.
**Rencontres Internationales de la Photographie** *(Jul–Sep)*, Arles *(pp144–6)*. The National School of Photography was set up in 1982 as a result of this festival, and each year the town is transformed into a photographic arena.

### AUGUST

**Corso de la Lavande** *(first weekend)*, Digne-les-Bains *(see p229)*.
**Les Journées Médiévales** *(biennial, weekend before Assumption)*, Entrevaux

*(p187)*. The quiet streets come to life with a 16th- and 17th-century music *fête*.
**Fête du Jasmin** *(first weekend)*, Grasse *(pp66–7)*. Floats, music and dancing in the town.
**Procession de la Passion** *(5 Aug)*, Roquebrune-Cap-Martin *(p98)*. Over 500 locals take part in staging Christ's passion, enacted since the Virgin saved the town from plague in 1467.
**Le Festival de Musique** *(all month)*, Menton *(pp98–9)*. Chamber music in the square.

Holiday-makers on the crowded beaches of the Côte d'Azur

## AVERAGE MONTHLY RAINFALL

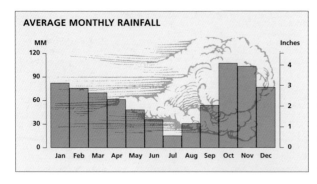

MM: 120, 90, 60, 30, 0

Inches: 4, 3, 2, 1, 0

Jan Feb Mar Apr May Jun Jul Aug Sep Oct Nov Dec

**Rainfall Chart**
*Spring and autumn are the wettest times, with the amount of rainfall increasing as you head inland. November rain is the most violent, often with storms and flooding. Summer is virtually rain-free, causing drought in some forest areas.*

## AUTUMN

When summer is over it is time for the *vendange*, the grape harvest. In the Camargue, rice is ready to be brought in. Walnuts are picked and, in the Maures, sweet chestnuts are collected. The woods also yield rewards for mushroom hunters, while in Vaucluse and the Var truffles are harvested from oak woods and sold on the market stalls, notably at Richerenches.

The hunting season begins in November. Small birds, such as thrushes, and ducks fall from flight into the pot and wild boar are bagged, their feet kept as talismans. Sheep are brought down to their winter pastures.

On the hunt for truffles in the woods of Haute Provence

### SEPTEMBER

**Fête des Prémices du Riz** *(early Sep)*, Arles *(pp144–6)*. This festival of the rice harvest coincides with the last Spanish-style bullfights of the year.

A grape picker at work during the autumn harvest

**Féria des Vendanges** *(second week)*, Nîmes *(pp132–3)*. An enjoyable combination of wine, dancing and bullfights.
**Festival de la Navigation de Plaisance** *(mid-Sep)*, Cannes *(pp68–9)*. Yachts from around the world meet in the harbour.
**Fête du Vent** *(mid-Sep)*, Marseille *(pp150–2)*. Kites from all over the world decorate the sky for two days down on the Plages du Prado.

### OCTOBER

**Fête de Sainte Marie Salomé** *(Sunday nearest 22 Oct)*, Stes-Maries-de-la-Mer. A similar festival to the Gypsy Pilgrimage held in May *(see p228–9)* with a procession through the town's streets to the beach and the ritual blessing of the sea.
**Foire Internationale de Marseille** *(end of Sep–early Oct)*, Marseille *(pp150–52)*. Thousands of visitors pour into the city to enjoy the annual fair. Various activities and sports are organized with crafts, music and folklore entertainment from over 40 different countries.

### NOVEMBER

**Fête du Prince** *(19 Nov)*, Monaco *(pp90–94)*. The second smallest independent state in Europe celebrates its national day with a firework display over the harbour.
**Festival International de la Danse** *(biennial, late-Nov or early Dec)*, Cannes *(pp68–9)*. A festival of contemporary dance and ballet with an impressive programme of international performances.

Performers at the Festival International de la Danse in Cannes

## AVERAGE MONTHLY TEMPERATURE

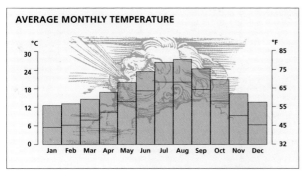

**Temperature Chart**
*The Mistral has a substantial effect on the temperature. During the winter and early spring, it can drop 10°C (18°F) in only a few hours. The summer heat can be uncomfortable, but the evenings cool down and are perfect for sitting outside.*

## WINTER

There is an old saying in Provence used to describe winter: *"l'hiver a ges d'ouro,"* "winter has no hours". It is a time to open the jams of the summer, to make the geese and duck *confits* and to turn the olive harvest into oil.

Snow soon cuts off mountain passes and, at weekends, locals and visitors take to the many ski resorts, warmed by juniper or wild strawberry liqueurs.

Christmas is heralded by the sale of *santons*, the figurines used to decorate Provence's distinctive cribs. Epiphany is another important festival, when the Three Kings are fêted with crown-shaped pastries.

## DECEMBER

**Foire aux Santons** *(all month)*, Marseille *(pp150–52)*. The largest fair honouring the symbolic clay figures that are an integral part of Christmas.
**Fête du Vin** *(early December)*, Bandol *(p112)*. Every wine-grower in the town has their own stand and there is free wine-tasting. A different theme is chosen every year with activities and much merriment.
**Noël and midnight mass** *(24 Dec)*, Les Baux-de-Provence *(pp142–3)*. A traditional festive feast of the shepherds before mass.

## JANUARY

**Rallye de Monte-Carlo** *(late Jan, pp92–3)*. A major event in the motor sporting calendar.
**Festival du Cirque** *(end of month)*, Monaco *(p94)*. Circus shows from around the globe.

**Relaxing in the winter sun in the Alpes-de-Haute-Provence**

## FEBRUARY

**Fête du Citron**, *(late Feb–early Mar)*, Menton *(pp98–9)*. Floats and music fill the town during the lemon festival.
**Fête du Mimosa** *(third Sunday)*, Bormes-les-Mimosas

*(pp116–17)*. The annual festival in celebration of the perched village's favourite flower.
**Carnaval de Nice**, *(all month)*, Nice *(see p228)*.

## PUBLIC HOLIDAYS

**New Year's Day** (1 Jan)
**Easter Sunday and Monday**
**Ascension** (sixth Thursday after Easter)
**Whit Monday** (second Monday after Ascension)
**Labour Day** (1 May)
**VE Day** (8 May)
**Bastille Day** (14 Jul)
**Assumption Day** (15 Aug)
**All Saints' Day** (1 Nov)
**Remembrance Day** (11 Nov)
**Christmas Day** (25 Dec)

**The Taj Mahal re-created at the Fête du Citron in Menton**

# THE HISTORY OF PROVENCE

Few regions of France have experienced such a varied and turbulent history as Provence. There is evidence, in the form of carvings, tools and weapons, of nomadic tribes and human settlements from 300,000 BC. The introduction of the vine, so important today, can be credited to the Phoenicians and Greeks who traded along the coast. Perhaps more crucially, Provence was the Romans' "Province" and few regions of their vast empire have retained such dramatic buildings; the theatre at Orange, the arenas of Arles and Nîmes, the Pont du Gard and the imposing trophy of La Turbie are all testimony to past Roman power.

**Virgin and Child, Aix-en-Provence**

The Middle Ages proved a stormy period of feuding warlords and invasions; the many well-fortified hilltop villages that characterize the region were a desperate attempt at defence. The presence of the papacy dominated the 14th century, and the magnificent palace that the popes built in Avignon remains today. The arts flourished too, especially under King René in his elegant capital of Aix. Following his death in 1480, Provence lost its independence and its history became enmeshed with that of France. Religious war took its toll and the Great Plague killed tens of thousands in 1720.

A beguiling climate and improved transport in the 19th century began to attract artists and foreign nobility. Tiny fishing villages grew into glamorous Riviera resorts. The allure remains for millions of tourists while economic investment means it is also a boom area for the technology industry.

**16th-century map of Marseille and its harbour**

◁ **Detail of an illuminated 13th-century manuscript showing a troubadour playing to a royal audience**

# Ancient Provence

Rock carvings, fragments of paintings and remains from primitive settlements suggest that Provence was first inhabited a million years ago. Carvings in the Grotte de l'Observatoire in Monaco and the decorated Grotte Cosquer near Marseille are among the oldest of their kind in the world. Nomadic tribes roamed the land for centuries, notably the Celts from the north and the Ligurians from the east. Not until the arrival of the Phoenicians and the Greeks did trade flourish in a more structured way and Provençal society become more stable.

**Stone fertility figurine (1,000,000 BC)**

**"Double Head" Carving**
*This stone figure (3rd century BC) probably decorated a Celtic sanctuary.*

**The bories** at Gordes date back to 3,500 BC.

**Celtic Doorway**
*(3rd century BC) The niches in the pillars held the embalmed heads of Celtic heroes.*

**The Grotte des Fées** at Mont de Cordes contain prehistoric carvings often associated with modern astrological symbols.

## THE FOUNDATION OF MARSEILLE

When Greek traders arrived in 600 BC, their captain, Protis, attended a feast in honour of the local chief's daughter, Gyptis. She chose Protis as her husband. The chief's dowry to Protis and Gyptis was the strip of land on which Marseille grew.

**St-Blaise**, once a heavily fortified Greek trading centre, has only minimal remains.

**The Grotte Cosquer**, with paintings dating to 30,000 BC, is accessible only from the sea.

**Wine jars**, bound for Greece from 1,000 BC onwards, were found in Les Calanques near Marseille.

## TIMELINE

**1,000,000 BC** Earliest human presence in Provence at Grotte de l'Observatoire in Monaco; use of bone as a tool

**400,000 BC** Fire first used in Nice

**60,000 BC** Neanderthal hunters on the Riviera

| 1,000,000 BC | 5,000 | | 4,000 | 3,500 |
|---|---|---|---|---|

**30,000 BC** Appearance of *Homo sapiens* (modern man); cave painting at Grotte Cosquer

*Cave painting from Grotte Cosquer*

**3,500 BC** First *borie* villages

**Vallée des Merveilles**
*About 36,000 carvings date from 2,000 BC. Among them are strange, witch-like figures known as* orants.

**The Vallée des Merveilles** carvings suggest that nearby Mont Bégo was a focus for worship.

## WHERE TO SEE ANCIENT PROVENCE

Many museums, such as the Musée Archéologique, Nîmes (*see p132*), have excellent collections of ancient artifacts. The well-preserved *bories* in the Luberon (*p169*) illustrate early village communities; the Grotte de l'Observatoire in Monaco (*p94*) is an example of an even more primitive settlement.

**Borie Village at Gordes**
*These dry-stone dwellings (p169) have for centuries been used by nomadic shepherds.*

The Grotte de l'Observatoire in Monaco yielded evidence of symbolic human burials from prehistoric times.

**Grotte de l'Observatoire**
*Skeletons uncovered here have characteristics linking them with southern African tribes.*

The "Fairy Stone", *Peïro de la fado* in Provençal, is the only true prehistoric dolmen in Provence.

## ANCIENT SITES OF PROVENCE

Most sites lie along the coast, but there are some pockets of settlement inland near Tende, in the Luberon, and in the inaccessible Vallée des Merveilles, which stands at about 2,500 m (8,200 ft).

**Standing Stone**
*Prehistoric stelae, like this carved stone from the Luberon, are scattered throughout Provence.*

---

**2,500–2,000 BC**
Carvings at Vallée des Merveilles

*Hannibal crossing the Alps*

**218 BC** Hannibal passes through region to reach Italy

| 3,000 | 2,500 | 2,000 | 1,500 | 1,000 | 500 BC |
|-------|-------|-------|-------|-------|--------|

**2,000 BC** Tombs carved at Cordes

**600 BC** Greek traders settle at St-Blaise. Founding of Marseille

**380 BC** Celtic invasions of Provence

# Gallo-Roman Provence

**Mosaic from Vaison-la-Romaine (40 BC)**

The Romans extended their empire into Provence towards the end of the 2nd century BC. They enjoyed good relations with the local people and within 100 years created a wealthy province. Nîmes and Arles became two of the most significant Roman towns outside Italy; colonies at Glanum and Vaison-la-Romaine flourished. Many fine monuments remain and museums, for instance at Vaison-la-Romaine, display smaller Roman treasures.

Christ's followers are reputed to have brought Christianity to the region when they landed at Les-Saintes-Maries-de-la-Mer in AD 40.

**Pont Julien** *(3 BC)*
*This magnificently preserved triple-arched bridge stands 8 km (5 miles) west of Apt.*

**Two temples**, dedicated to the emperor Augustus's adopted sons, Caius and Lucius, date from 30 BC.

**Marble Sarcophagus** *(4th century)*
*The Alyscamps in Arles (see p146), once a vast Roman necropolis, contains many carved marble and stone coffins.*

**Triumphal Arch at Orange**
*Built in about 20 BC this is, in spite of much restoration, one of the best preserved Roman triumphal arches. Carvings depict the conquest of Gaul and sea battle scenes.*

**The fortified gate** was built by the original Greek community that occupied Glanum from the 4th century BC.

## ROMAN GLANUM
The impressive ruined site at Glanum reveals much earlier Roman and Greek settlements. This reconstruction shows it after it was rebuilt in AD 49.

## TIMELINE

**118 BC** Provincia founded – first Gallo-Roman Province

**125 BC** Roman legions defend Marseille against Celto-Ligurian invaders

*Consul Marius*

**49 BC** Emperor Julius Caesar lays siege to Marseille for supporting his rival, Pompey. Romans rebuild Glanum

**40 BC** Vaison-la-Romaine ranks among Roman Gaul's wealthiest towns

| 100 BC | AD 1 | 100 |

**123 BC** Romans make Entremont first Provençal settlement

**121 BC** Foundation of Aquae Sextiae, later to become Aix-en-Provence

**102 BC** Consul Marius defeats invading German tribes; over 200,000 killed

**14 BC** Emperor Augustus defeats Ligurians in Alpes Maritimes. Trophy at La Turbie erected *(see p89)*

**AD 40** "Boat of Bethany" lands at Les-Saintes-Maries-de-la-Mer

**3 BC** Pont Julien built

*2nd-century BC Venus d'Arles*

**Les-Stes-Maries-de-la-Mer**
*Mary Magdalene, Mary Salome and Mary Jacobea reputedly sailed here in AD 40. The town where they landed is named in their honour and continues to attract pilgrims (see p138).*

(see p138)

## WHERE TO SEE GALLO-ROMAN PROVENCE

Arles *(see pp144–6)* and Nîmes *(pp132–3)*, with their amphitheatres and religious and secular buildings, offer the most complete examples of Roman civilization. Orange *(p161)* and Vaison-la-Romaine *(p158)* contain important monuments, and the Pont du Gard *(p131)* and Le Trophée des Alpes *(p89)* are unique.

**Théâtre Antique d'Orange**
*Built into a hill, this Roman theatre would have held up to 7,000 spectators (pp162–3).*

**Cryptoporticus**
*The foundations of Arles' forum, these horseshoe-shaped underground galleries were probably used as grain stores (p146).*

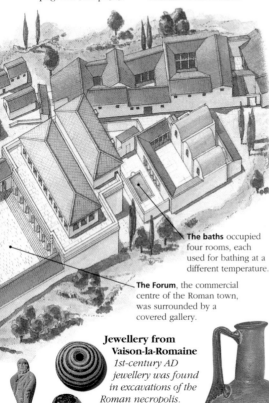

**The baths** occupied four rooms, each used for bathing at a different temperature.

**The Forum**, the commercial centre of the Roman town, was surrounded by a covered gallery.

**Jewellery from Vaison-la-Romaine**
*1st-century AD jewellery was found in excavations of the Roman necropolis.*

**Roman Flask**
*Well-preserved ancient Roman glassware and everyday items have been found in many areas of Provence.*

---

# Medieval Provence

**13th-century manuscript illustration**

With the fall of the Roman Empire, stability and relative prosperity began to disappear. Although Provence became part of the Holy Roman Empire, the local counts retained considerable autonomy and the towns became fiercely independent. People withdrew to hilltops to protect themselves from attack by a series of invaders, and *villages perchés (see p20–21)* began to develop. Provence became a major base for Christian Crusaders, intent on conquering Muslim territories in Africa and Asia.

**The Great Walls**, finally completed in 1300, 30 years after Louis IX's death, were over 1.6 km (1 mile) long and formed an almost perfect rectangle.

**St-Trophime Carving**
*The monumental 12th-century portal at St-Trophime in Arles (see p144) is adorned with intricate carvings of saints and scenes from the Last Judgment.*

**Louis IX's army** consisted of 35,000 men plus horses and military equipment.

**Louis IX**

**St Martha and the Tarasque**
*The 9th-century legend of St Martha and the Tarasque, a dragon, proved the strength of Christianity. The beast is said to have fled at the sight of her crucifix.* (See p140.)

## THE SEVENTH CRUSADE

Hoping to drive the Muslims out of the Holy Land, Louis IX (St Louis) of France set sail from his new port, Aigues-Mortes *(see p134–5)*, in 1248. It was a spectacular occasion, with banners waving and his army singing hymns.

## TIMELINE

**536** Provence ceded to the Franks

**737–9** Anti-Frankish rebellions in Avignon, Marseille and Arles brutally suppressed by Charles Martel

**855** Kingdom of Provence created for Charles the Bald, grandson of Charlemagne

**949** Provence divided into four counties

| 600 | 700 | 800 | 900 |
|---|---|---|---|

*Saracen warrior and Provençal maiden*

**800** First wave of Saracen invasions

*Charles the Bald*

**924** Hungarians sack Nîmes

**Troubadour Ivory** *(c. 1300)*
*The poetry of Provençal
troubadours tells how
knights wooed virtuous
women through patience,
courtesy and skill.*

**Notre-Dame-de-
Beauvoir Chapel**
*At the top of a path from
Moustiers (see p186), the
chapel has a fine Roman-
esque porch and nave.*

**1500 ships** set sail
for the Holy Land on
28 August 1248.

**WHERE TO SEE
MEDIEVAL PROVENCE**

The highlights are undoubtedly the Romanesque abbeys
and churches, especially the
"three sisters": Silvacane
*(p147)*, Le Thoronet *(p108)*
and Sénanque *(p164)*. Fortified *villages perchés*, such as
Gordes *(p169)* and the spectacular 11th-century citadel at
Les Baux-de-Provence *(p142)*,
testify to the unrest and hor-
rific violence that scarred this
period of Provence's history.

**Les Pénitents des Mées**
*These are said to be 6th-century
monks turned to stone for gaz-
ing at Saracen women (p181).*

**St Christopher Fresco**
*The Tour Ferrande in Pernes-
les-Fontaines (see p164)
contains religious frescoes
from 1285. They are among
the oldest in France.*

**Silvacane Abbey** *(1175–1230)*
*This beautiful, austere Cister-
cian abbey was Provence's last
great Romanesque abbey.*

---

**974** Saracens
defeated at La
Garde-Freinet

*Seal of
Simon
de Montfort*

**1213** Battle of Muret: de Montfort defeats
count of Toulouse and King of Aragon

**1209** French military
leader Simon de Mont-
fort marches on Provence

**1246** Charles of Anjou marries
Béatrice, heiress of Provence, to
become Count of Provence

**1248** Louis IX embarks on Seventh
Crusade from Aigues-Mortes

| **1000** | **1100** | **1200** | **1300** |
|---|---|---|---|

**1032** Provence
becomes part of Holy
Roman Empire

**1096–1099**
First Crusade

**1112** Raymond-Bérenger III,
Count of Barcelona, marries
the Duchess of Provence

**1186** Counts of
Provence declare
Aix their capital

**1125** Provence shared
between Barcelona
and Toulouse

**1187** Remains of St Martha
discovered at Tarascon

**1274** Papacy acquires
Comtat Venaissin

**1295** Death of
Guiraut Riquier, the
"Last Troubadour"

**1280** Relics of Mary
Magdalene found at St-
Maximin-la-Ste-Baume

# Papal Avignon

**14th-century carving, Palais des Papes**

When the papacy temporarily abandoned war-torn Italy, Avignon became the centre of the Roman Catholic world. From 1309 until 1377 seven French popes ruled unchallenged. When a new Italian pope, Urban VI, was elected, the French cardinals rebelled. In 1378 they chose a rival pope, Clement VII, thus causing a major schism that lasted until 1403.

During the 14th century the papal court in Avignon became a wealthy centre for both learning and the arts, extending its influence across the region.

**The Palais Vieux** (1334–42), built by Benedict XII in typically austere Cistercian style, is more of a fortress than a church.

Benedict XII's cloister

Grand Tinel

Consistory Hall

**Bargème, Northern Var**
*Instability across Provence led to villages like Bargème building strong fortifications.*

**Papal Throne**
*The Pope's Room in the Palais des Papes contains copies of the original 14th-century furniture, like this carved wooden throne.*

Great Courtyard

**Prophets Fresco** *(1344–5)*
*Matteo Giovanetti from Viterbo was the principal fresco-master of Clement VI. His realism contrasts with earlier medieval artists.*

## TIMELINE

*Coin of Pope Innocent VI*

**1327** Petrarch first catches sight of Laura of Avignon, his muse

**1316–34** Reign of John XXII

**1342–52** Reign of Clement VI

**1352–62** Reign of Innocent VI

| 1310 | 1320 | 1330 | 1340 | 1350 |

**1309** Papacy moves to Avignon

**1334–42** Reign of Benedict XII

**1348** Clement VI acquires Avignon

**1349** Jews take refuge in the Comtat Venaissin, part of the Papal lands

*Pope John XXII*

### Death of Clement VI
*Clement VI came to Avignon to "forget he was pope". In 1348 he bought the town for 80,000 florins and built the splendid Palais Neuf.*

**Pope's Room**

**Stag Room Frescoes**
*The hunting scenes are a reminder that monastic life was not only about learning and prayer.*

**Stag Room**

**The Great Chapel**, covering 780 sq m (8,400 sq ft), contains the restored papal altar.

**The Palais Neuf** was built by Clement VI in 1342–52.

**Great Audience Hall**

## PALAIS DES PAPES
The maze of corridors and rooms in the Palais des Papes *(see p168)*, built over 18 years (1334–52), were richly decorated by skilled artists and craftsmen introduced from Italy. The building's scale is overwhelming.

**Petrarch** *(1304–74)*
*The great Renaissance poet Petrarch considered papal Avignon to be a "sewer" and a place of corruption.*

1362–70 Reign of Urban V

1370–78 Reign of Gregory XI

1378–94 Reign of anti-pope Clement VII

1403 Benedict XIII flees Avignon

| 1360 | 1370 | 1380 | 1390 | 1400 |
|---|---|---|---|---|

**1363** Grimaldis recapture Monaco

*Effigy of Urban V*

**1377** Papacy returns to Rome

**1394–1409** Reign of anti-pope Benedict XIII

*Anti-Pope Benedict XIII*

# René and the Wars of Religion

Pietà, Notre-
Dame-de-
l'Assomption

The end of the 15th century saw the golden age of Aix *(see pp148–9)*, then Provence's capital. Under the patronage of King René, art and culture flourished and the Flemish-influenced Avignon School was formed. After René's death, Provence was annexed by the French king, Louis XI. Loss of independence and subsequent involvement with French politics led to brutal invasions by Charles V. The 16th-century Wars of Religion between "heretic" Protestants and Catholics resulted in a wave of massacres, and the wholesale destruction of churches and their contents.

**Detail of the Triptych**
*René's favourite château of Tarascon (p140) on the Rhône is realistically painted.*

**King René**,
himself a poet, painter and musician, was a great influence on Provençal culture.

**Nostradamus**
*Born in St-Rémy (pp140–41), the physician and astrologer is best known for his predictions,* Les Centuries *(1555).*

**Massacres of Protestants and Catholics**
*The religious wars were brutal. Thousands of Protestants were massacred in 1545, and 200 Catholics died in Nîmes in 1567.*

## BURNING BUSH TRIPTYCH

Nicolas Froment's painting (1476) was commissioned by King René. The star of the Cathédrale de St-Sauveur, Aix, it depicts a vision of the Virgin and Child surrounded by the eternal Burning Bush of Moses.

## TIMELINE

*King René*

**1434–80** Reign of Good King René

*Retable from Avignon*

**1486** Union of Provence with France

**1501** Parliament de Provence created

| 1425 | 1450 | 1475 | 15• |
|---|---|---|---|

**1481** Charles du Maine, Count of Provence and René's nephew, gives Provence to King of France

**1496** Military port built at Toulon

### The Annunciation
*The Master of Aix, one of René's artistic circle, painted this Annunciation. Dark symbolism, including the owl's wings of the angel Gabriel, undercuts this usually joyful subject.*

**The Bush,** burning but unconsumed, was a pagan and Christian symbol of eternal life.

### Holy Roman Emperor, Charles V, by Titian
*Between 1524 and 1536, Charles V (Charles I of Spain) attacked Provence frequently as part of his war against France.*

**The saints** John the Evangelist, Catherine of Alexandria and Nicolas of Myra are behind Queen Jeanne.

**Moses** is seen receiving the word of God from an angel.

**Queen Jeanne,** René's second wife, is shown kneeling in adoration.

## WHERE TO SEE 15TH- AND 16TH-CENTURY PROVENCE

Architecture from this period can be seen today in the fine town houses and elegant streets of Aix *(pp148–9)* and Avignon *(pp166–8)*. The Musée Granet, also in Aix, contains several interesting examples of religious paintings. A collection of period furniture is exhibited in the Musée Grobet-Labadié in Marseille *(p151)*.

**Château at Tarascon**
*This 13th-century château (p140) was partly rebuilt by Louis II and then completed by King René, his son.*

### Rhinoceros Woodcut by Albrecht Dürer
*In 1516, Marseille's Château d'If (p152) was briefly home to the first rhinoceros to set foot in Europe. It was in transit as a gift for the Pope, but died later in the journey.*

**1524** Invasion of Charles V

**1545** Massacre of Protestants in Luberon villages

**1577** First soap factory in Marseille

**1598** Edict of Nantes signals end of Wars of Religion

| 1525 | 1550 | 1575 | 1600 |
|---|---|---|---|

**1525** Jews in Comtat Venaissin forced to wear yellow hats

**1562** Wars of Religion commence

*Protestant martyrdom*

# Classical Provence

Provence in the 17th and 18th centuries saw a decrease in regional allegiance and growth of national awareness. Towns grew and majestic monuments, town houses (*hôtels*) and châteaux proliferated. But despite economic development in the textile industry and the growth of the ports of Toulon and Marseille, the period was bleak for many, culminating in the devastating plague of 1720. The storming of the Bastille in Paris in 1789 sparked popular uprisings and revolutionary marches on Paris.

**Pavillon de Vendôme**
*Jean-Claude Rambot made the Atlantes for this building (1667) in Aix (see pp148–9).*

**The death toll** was over 100,000 in the last plague in Europe.

**Boat-Building in Toulon**
*Toulon, a strategic port, was famous for its boat-building. Galley slaves, chained to their oars, were a great tourist attraction in the 17th century.*

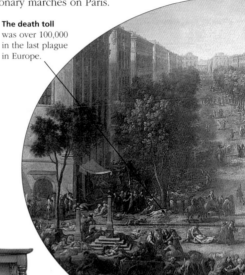

**Corpses** were hauled in carts to mass graves.

**Santon Crib Scene**
*The santon ("little saints" in Provençal) cribs were first made after the Revolution, when the churches were shut. They soon became a very popular local craft.*

## THE GREAT PLAGUE
*Vue du Cours pendant la Peste* by Michel Serre depicts the 1720 plague in Marseille, brought by a cargo boat from Syria. Over half of Marseille's population died. All contact with the city was banned and huge walls were built to halt the epidemic, but it still spread as far as Aix, Arles and Toulon.

**TIMELINE**

**1622** Louis XIII visits Arles, Aix and Marseille

**1660** Louis XIV, the "Sun King", enters Marseille

*Sun King emblem*

**1696** France returns Nice to Savoy

**1707** English siege of Toulon fails

| 1625 | 1650 | 1675 | 1700 |
|---|---|---|---|

**1646** Jews confined to ghettos, notably in Carpentras

**1666** Work begins on the Canal du Midi

**1679** Vauban starts work on new port at Toulon

**1691** Nice occupied by the French

**1707** Provence invaded by Eugène of Savoy

*Louis XIII*

## Napoleon Seizes Toulon

*Junior officer Napoleon Bonaparte first made his name when he took Toulon from occupying English troops in 1793.*

**Cours Belsunce**, built in 1670 in the Italian style, was lined with trees and Baroque palaces.

**Monks**, led by the devout Jean Belsunce, the Bishop of Marseille, gave succour to the dying.

## Marshal Sébastien Vauban

*Louis XIV's brilliant military architect, Vauban, fortified towns and ports including Toulon and Antibes.*

### Moustiers Faïence

*Brought to France from Italy in the 17th century, traditional faïence features pastoral scenes in delicate colours.*

## WHERE TO SEE CLASSICAL PROVENCE

Avignon *(see pp166–8)* and Aix *(pp148–9)* have period town houses with fine doorways and staircases. Jewish synagogues and remains of Jewish enclaves can be found in Cavaillon *(p170)*, Forcalquier *(p182)* and Carpentras *(p164)*. The 18th-century Jardin de la Fontaine in Nîmes *(pp132–3)* can still be visited.

**Pharmacy at Carpentras**
*The 18th-century Hôtel-Dieu (hospital) houses a chapel and a pharmacy containing faïence apothecary jars.*

**Fontaine du Cormoran**
*The best known of the 36 fountains in Pernes-les-Fontaines (p164) is the 18th-century carved Cormoran fountain.*

| | | | | |
|---|---|---|---|---|
| **1713** Treaty of Utrecht cedes Orange to France | | **1791** Avignon and Comtat Venaissin annexed to France | | **1793** Breaking of siege of Toulon catapults Napoleon Bonaparte to fame |
| **1718** Nice becomes part of new Kingdom of Sardinia | | **1779** Roman mausoleum at Aix demolished | | |
| **1725** | **1750** | **1775** | **1800** | |
| **1720** Great Plague strikes Marseille and spreads throughout Provence | | **1771** Aix parliament suppressed | **1787** Provençal silk harvest fails | |
| *The Great Plague, Marseille* | | **1789** Storming of the Bastille, Paris; Provençal peasants pillage local châteaux and monasteries | **1792** Republicans adopt Rouget de Lisle's army song: *La Marseillaise* | |

# The Belle Epoque

**Marseille soap advert, 1880**

From the start of the 19th century the beguiling climate, particularly the mild winters, of coastal Provence attracted foreign visitors, from invalids and artists to distinguished royalty and courtesans. Railways, grand hotels, exotic gardens, opulent villas and the chic promenade des Anglais in Nice were built to meet their needs. Queen Victoria, the Aga Khan, King Leopold of Belgium and Empress Eugénie – Napoleon III's wife and doyenne of Riviera royalty – all held court. Artists and writers came in droves to revel in the light and freedom.

**Homage à Mistral**
*Frédéric Mistral created the Félibrige group in 1854 to preserve Provençal culture.*

**Printing in Marseille**
*Cheap labour, ample paper supplies and good communications fostered the development of printing.*

**Casino tables** were sometimes draped in black mourning when a gambler succeeded in breaking the bank with a major win.

**Grasse Perfume**
*More modern methods of cultivation and distillation played an important role in the expanding 19th-century perfume-making industry.*

## MONTE-CARLO CASINO INTERIOR

From being the poorest state in Europe in 1850, Monaco boomed with the opening of the first Monte-Carlo casino in 1856, as seen in Christian Bokelman's painting. The fashionable flocked to enjoy the luxury and glamour, while fortunes were won and lost *(see pp92–4).*

## TIMELINE

**1814** Napoleon lands at Golfe-Juan

**1830** Beginnings of tourism around Nice

**1861** Monaco sells Roquebrune and Menton to France

**1860** Nice votes for union with France

**1820**    **1840**    **1860**

*Paul Cézanne*

**1839** Marseille-Sète railroad begun. Birth of Cézanne

**1854** Founding of Félibrige, the Provençal cultural school

**1859** Mistral publishes his epic poem, *Mirèio*

### Vineyard blight
*Ravaged by phylloxera, vines in Provence and across France were replaced by resistant American root stocks.*

### Tourism
*By the late 19th century, sun and sea air were considered beneficial to health.*

**Belle Epoque decor** had interiors lavish with ornate chandeliers, gilt and coloured marble.

**High society** included famous courtesans as well as their rich and royal lovers.

### Van Gogh's Provence
*Van Gogh produced turbulent works in the Clinique St-Paul in St-Rémy (see pp140–41).*

## WHERE TO SEE BELLE EPOQUE PROVENCE

Although many have been destroyed, villas and hotels built in the extravagant Belle Epoque style still survive on the Côte d'Azur. The Négresco in Nice *(see pp84–5)* is especially fine. Other period pieces include the Cathédrale Orthodoxe Russe, also in Nice, and, on glamorous Cap Ferrat, the Musée Ephrussi de Rothschild *(pp86–7)*. In Beaulieu the Villa Kerylos, Rotunda and lush exotic gardens are all typical of the era *(p88)*.

**Hôtel Carlton, Cannes**
*Built in 1911, this ostentatious Riviera landmark is still an exclusive hotel overlooking the beach (see pp68–9).*

**Monte-Carlo Opéra**
*Charles Garnier designed this opera house (see pp92–3), as well as the Casino.*

**1879** Monte-Carlo Opéra opens

*Casino at Monte-Carlo*

**1909** Earthquake centred on Rognes in the Bouches-du-Rhône causes widespread damage.

| 1880 | 1900 | 1920 |
|---|---|---|

**1869** Opening of Suez Canal brings trade to Marseille; railway extended to Nice

**1888–90** Van Gogh works in Provence

**1904** Mistral wins Nobel prize for Literature for *Mirèio*

# Provence at War

After the economic drain caused by World War I, Provence enjoyed increasing prosperity as the tourist industry boomed. While much of the interior remained remote and rural, the vogue for sea-bathing drew crowds to resorts such as Cannes and Nice from the 1920s onwards. Provence continued to build on its image as a playground for the rich and famous, attracting visitors from Noël Coward to Wallis Simpson. The 1942–44 German occupation brought an end to the glamorous social life for many, and some towns, including St-Tropez and Marseille, were badly damaged by Germans and Allies.

**Tourism**
*As swimming in the sea and sun-bathing became fashionable pursuits, resorts along the Riviera attracted many new visitors. In the 1930s a nudist colony opened on the Ile du Levant.*

**Monaco Grand Prix**
*This race around the principality's streets was started on the initiative of Prince Louis II in 1929. It is still one of the most colourful and dangerous Formula 1 races.*

**Precious ammunition** and arms were dropped from Allied planes or captured from the Nazis.

**Antoine de Saint-Exupéry**
*France's legendary writer-pilot disappeared on 31 July 1944 while on a reconnaissance flight (see p29).*

## LA RÉSISTANCE

After 1942 the Résistance (or *maquis* after the scrubland that made a good hiding place) was active in Provence. The fighters were successful in Marseille and in preparing the coastal areas for the 1944 Allied invasion.

**TIMELINE**

| | | **1930** Novelist DH Lawrence dies in Vence |
|---|---|---|
| *Coco Chanel* | **1925** Coco Chanel arrives on the Riviera | |
| **1920** | **1925** | **1930** |
| **1924** Scott and Zelda Fitzgerald spend a year on the Riviera | **1928** Camargue National Park created | |
| *F Scott Fitzgerald* | **1930** Pagnol begins filming *Marius, Fanny* and *César* trilogy in Marseille | |

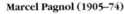

**Many who joined** the Résistance had scarcely left school. Training was often only by experience.

**Marcel Pagnol (1905–74)**
*Pagnol immortalized Provence and its inhabitants in his plays, novels and films, depicting a simple, rural life (see p29).*

## WHERE TO SEE 1920s TO 1940s PROVENCE

The now slightly seedy suburbs of Hyères *(see p115)* retain evidence of graceful living after World War I. Toulon harbour's bristling warships *(pp112–13)* are a reminder of the French navy's former power. The activities of the Résistance are well documented in the Musée d'Histoire 1939–45 in Fontaine-de-Vaucluse *(p165)*.

**Allied Landings**
*On 14 August 1944, Allied troops bombarded the coast between Toulon and Marseille and soon gained ground.*

**Les Deux Garçons, Aix**
*This still chic café was frequented by Churchill and Cocteau among others (pp148–9).*

**Citadelle, Sisteron**
*Rebuilt after the Allied bombing in 1944, the citadel has displays on its turbulent history (p178).*

**Marseille Exhibition**
*The 1922 exhibition was an invitation to enjoy the cosmopolitan delights of Marseille.*

**1942** Nazis invade southern France; French fleet scuttled in Toulon harbour

**1940** Italians occupy Menton

**1943** *Maquis* resistance cells formed

| 1935 | 1940 | 1945 |
|---|---|---|

**1939** Cannes Film Festival inaugurated, but first festival delayed by war

*Liberation of Marseille*

**1944** American and French troops land near St-Tropez; liberation of Marseille

# Post-War Provence

**Scooter rider in St-Tropez**

Paid vacations, post-war optimism, and the St-Tropez sun cult all made the Riviera the magnet it has remained for holiday-makers. The region still offers a rich variety of produce – olive oil, wine, fruit, flowers and perfume – though industry, especially in the high-tech sector, grows apace. The environment has suffered from overdevelopment, pollution and forest fires. The 1960s saw massive North African immigration, and today unemployment creates racial and political tension.

**Port-Grimaud**
*The successful "Provençal Venice", a car-free leisure port, was built by François Spoerry in 1966 in regional village style (see p123).*

**Bus Stop by Philippe Starck**
*The modern architecture of Nîmes typifies many bold projects in the region.*

**Beach at Nice**
*Though many are pebbly, the Riviera beaches still attract dedicated sun-worshippers.*

**Fires**
*The devastating forest fires which ravage the region are fought with planes scooping up sea water.*

## TIMELINE

**1952** Le Corbusier's Cité Radieuse built

**1946** Picasso starts painting in the Grimaldi Castle, Antibes

**1954** Matisse dies

**1956** Roger Vadim films *And God Created Woman*, starring Brigitte Bardot, in St-Tropez

*Grace Kelly*

**1956** Grace Kelly marries Monaco's Prince Rainier III

**1959** Floods in Fréjus

**1950**

**1961** Art festival of new Ecole de Nice

**1962** Lower Durance engineered to develop hydro-electric power

**1962** Algerian Independence – French North Africans (*pieds-noirs*) settle in Provence

**1970** Sophia-Antipolis technology park opens near Antibes

**1960**

*Picasso*

**1970** Autoroute du Soleil completed

**1973** Picasso dies at Mougins

**1971** The "French Connection" drug ring is exposed

**1970**

**1977** First section of Marseille underground railway opened

**1982** Princess Grace is killed in car accident

**1980**

## Winter Sports

*Skiing has become increasingly popular (see p96). Isola 2000, near Nice, a purpose-built, futuristic resort, was built in 1972.*

**Colombe d'Or, St-Paul**
*Once an artists' café, this is now one of many chic venues for the rich and famous (see p75).*

## CANNES FILM FESTIVAL

First held in 1946, the festival *(see p68)* has become the world's annual film event, a glamorous jamboree of directors, stars and aspiring starlets. *And God Created Woman*, starring Brigitte Bardot, became a *succès de scandale* in 1956.

**Brigitte Bardot**     **Kim Novak**

## WHERE TO SEE MODERN PROVENCE

Some of the most striking modern architecture includes Le Corbusier's Cité Radieuse in Marseille (see p152), the Musée d'Art Contemporain in Nice (p85) and the Norman Foster-designed Carré d'Art in Nîmes (p132). Large-scale rebuilding programmes in towns such as St-Tropez (pp118–22) and Ste-Maxime (p123) have concentrated on new buildings that blend well with the existing ones.

**St-Tropez**
*Successful post-war restoration means it is often difficult to tell new buildings from old.*

**Fondation Maeght**
*The building reflects the modern use of traditional Provençal style and materials (see pp76–7).*

**1992** Floods in Vaison-la-Romaine

**1998** Jacques Médecin dies in Uruguay, self-exiled after a year in jail in France

**2001** TGV Méditerranée link with Paris launched

**2005** Prince Rainier III dies and is succeeded by his only son, Prince Albert II

*Prince Albert II*

| 1990 | 2000 | 2010 | 2020 |
|---|---|---|---|

**1990** Jacques Médecin, Mayor of Nice, flees to Uruguay to avoid trial for corruption and tax arrears

*TGV train*

**2002** Euro replaces Franc as legal tender

**2009** J.M.G. Le Clézio wins the Nobel Prize for Literature

# PROVENCE
# AREA BY AREA

# Provence at a Glance

From natural wonders and historic architecture to the cream of modern art, Provence is a region with something for everyone. Even the most ardent sun-worshipper will be tempted into the cool shade of its treasure-filled museums and churches. Visitors who come in the footsteps of the world's greatest artists will be equally dazzled by the wild beauty of the Gorges du Verdon and the Camargue. In a region packed with delights, those shown here are among the very best.

Papal Avignon's medieval architectural splendour (see pp166–7)

The beautifully preserved Roman theatre at Orange (see pp162–3)

• Avignon

VAUCLUSE

BOUCHES-DU-RHONE AND NIMES

La Camargue

Marseille •

Wildlife in its natural habitat in the Camargue (see pp136–7)

The massive basilica of St-Maximin-la-Ste-Baume, housing relics of St Mary Magdalene (see pp110–11)

0 kilometres   20

0 miles          20

Unspoiled and tranquil, the Iles d'Hyères (see pp114–15)

Outstanding modern art at the Fondation Maeght, St-Paul-de-Vence *(see pp76–7)*

Musée Matisse, in the artist's beloved Nice *(see pp82–3)*

Musée Ephrussi de Rothschild, a "dream villa" among the pines of Cap Ferrat *(see pp86–7)*

Monaco

St-Paul-de-Vence

Nice

ALPES-DE-HAUTE-PROVENCE

THE RIVIERA AND THE ALPES MARITIMES

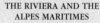

See inset above

Nice

Monaco

THE VAR AND THE ILES D'HYERES

Cannes

*Illes de Lérins*

St-Tropez

Toulon

The dramatic Gorges du Verdon *(see pp184–5)*

*Illes d'Hyères*

St-Tropez's Musée de l'Annonciade, displaying its art collection in a former chapel *(see pp120–21)*

# THE RIVIERA AND THE ALPES MARITIMES

*The French Riviera is, without doubt, the most celebrated seaside in Europe. Just about everybody who has been anybody for the past 100 years has succumbed to its glittering allure. This is the holiday playground of kings and courtesans, movie stars and millionaires, where the seriously rich never stand out in the crowd.*

There is a continual complaint that the Riviera is not what it used to be, that the Cannes Film Festival is mere hype, that grand old Monte-Carlo has lost all sense of taste and that Nice isn't worth the trouble of finding a parking space. But look at the boats in Antibes harbour, glimpse a villa or two on Cap Martin, or observe the baubles on the guests at the Hôtel de Paris in Monte-Carlo. Money and class still rule.

The Riviera is not just a millionaire's watering hole: a diversity of talent has visited, seeking patrons and taking advantage of the luminous Mediterranean light. This coast is irrevocably linked with the life and works of Matisse and Picasso, Chagall, Cocteau and Renoir. It lent them the scenery of its shores and the rich environment of hill villages like St-Paul-de-Vence. St-Paul has echoed to the voices of such luminaries as Bonnard and Modigliani, F Scott Fitzgerald and Greta Garbo. Today, its galleries still spill canvases on to its medieval lanes.

The Alpes Maritimes, which incorporates the principality of Monaco, is renowned for its temperate winter climate. The abundance of flowers here attracted the perfume industry and the English - who created some of the finest gardens on the coast. Inland, the mountainous areas of Provence offer a range of skiing activities in superb mountain scenery, and a chance to try traditional Alpine food.

Relaxing on the promenade des Anglais, Nice

◁ View of Roquebrune village from the castle

# Exploring the Riviera and the Alpes Maritimes

The rocky heights of the pre-Alps lie in tiers, running east to west and tumbling down to the Riviera's dramatic, Corniche-hemmed coast. On bluffs and pinnacles, towns and villages keep a watchful eye on the distant blue sea. Towards the Italian border, the Alpine ridges run from north to south, cut by torrents and gorges which provide snowy winter slopes for skiers. Much of the higher ground is occupied by the Parc National du Mercantour *(see p97)*, home of the ibex and the chamoix. Its jewel is the prehistoric Vallée des Merveilles, less than two hours from the contrasting bustle of the Riviera.

D2205
Saint-Étienne-de-Tinée
Auron
Entraunes
Var
LE PARC
D2202
Valberg
Beuil
Guillaumes
GORGES DU CIANS
1
D902
PUGET-THÉNIERS 2
D6202
Digne-les-Bains
Touë-sur-Va
ALPES
Mont Cheiron 1777m
Sisteron
Le Logis-du-Pin
D2
D6085
Loup
GOURDON 4
St-Vallier-de-Thiey
Grottes de St-Cézaire
GRASSE 5
3 ST-CÉZAIRE-SUR-SIAGNE
D6185
MOUGINS
CANNES
Draguignan
La Napou

## GETTING AROUND

The A8 from Italy runs inland, parallel to the coast. Between this highway and the sea, from Nice to Menton, are three corniches. The Grande Corniche follows the Roman road, Julia Augusta, via La Turbie. The Moyenne Corniche passes through Eze, and the Corniche Inférieure visits all coastal resorts. The inland roads are narrow and winding, so allow more time for your journey. Grasse and Cannes are linked by a regular bus service, and bikes can be hired at some railway stations. Other bus links are also good. The largest airport in the region and second busiest in France, is at Nice, west of the city.

**Expensive yachts in the colourful harbour at Antibes**

## SIGHTS AT A GLANCE

Antibes 10
Beaulieu 20
Biot 12
Cagnes-sur-Mer 16
*Cannes pp68–9* 7
Cap Ferrat 18
Eze 21
Forêt de Turini 28
Gorbio 33
Gorges du Cians 1
Gourdon 4
Grasse 5
*Iles de Lérins pp70–71* 8
Juan-les-Pins 9
La Turbie 22
Lucéram 26
Menton 35
*Monaco pp90–94* 23
Mougins 6
*Nice pp80–81* 17
Parc National du Mercantour 29
Peille 25
Peillon 24
Puget-Théniers 2
Roquebrune-Cap-Martin 34
St-Cézaire-sur-Siagne 3
St-Paul-de-Vence 15
Saorge 31
Sospel 32
Tende 30
Vallauris 11
Vallée de la Vésubie 27
Vence 14
Villefranche 19
Villeneuve-Loubet 13

***SEE ALSO***

- ***Where to Stay*** pp194–7
- ***Where to Eat*** pp210–12

0 kilometres 10

0 miles 10

For additional map symbols *see back flap*

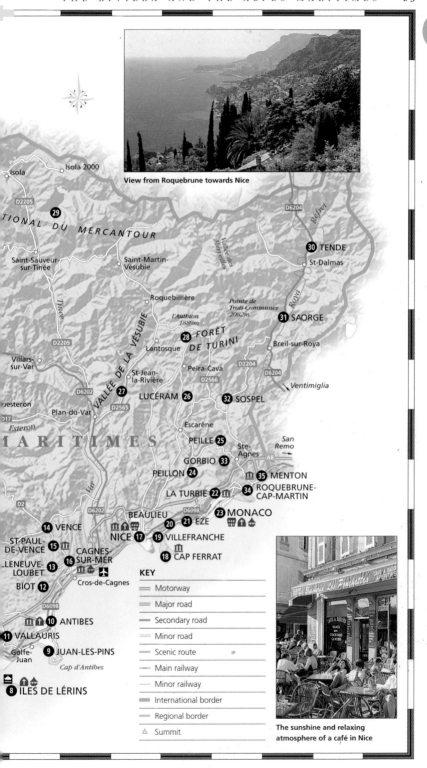

**View from Roquebrune towards Nice**

Isola

Isola 2000

D2205

**29** TIONAL DU MERCANTOUR

D6204

Réfret

Saint-Sauveur-sur-Tinée

Saint-Martin-Vésubie

Vallée des Merveilles

**30** TENDE

St-Dalmas

Tinée

Roquebillière

Pointe de Trois-Communes 2082m

Roya

**31** SAORGE

l'Authion 1889m

**28** FORÊT DE TURINI

D2205

Lantosque

Breil-sur-Roya

Villars-sur-Var

VALLÉE DE LA VÉSUBIE

St-Jean-la-Rivière

Peïra-Cava

D2204

D6204

D2566

Ventimiglia

D6202

**27**

D2565

**26** LUCÉRAM

**32** SOSPEL

uesteron

Plan-du-Var

Escarène

017

Esteron

San Remo

**25** PEILLE

Ste-Agnes

A8

MARITIMES

**33** GORBIO

**24** PEILLON

**35** MENTON

Var

**22** LA TURBIE

**34** ROQUEBRUNE-CAP-MARTIN

D2

BEAULIEU

D6098

**23** MONACO

**14** VENCE

**20**

**21** ÈZE

ST-PAUL-DE-VENCE

**15**

A8

NICE **17**

**19** VILLEFRANCHE

LENEUVE-LOUBET

**13**

**16** CAGNES-SUR-MER

**18** CAP FERRAT

BIOT **12**

Cros-de-Cagnes

## KEY

D6098

**10** ANTIBES

**11** VALLAURIS

Golfe-Juan

**9** JUAN-LES-PINS

Cap d'Antibes

**8** ÎLES DE LÉRINS

| | |
|---|---|
| ═══ | Motorway |
| ═══ | Major road |
| ─── | Secondary road |
| ┈┈┈ | Minor road |
| ─·─ | Scenic route |
| ┄┄┄ | Main railway |
| ─── | Minor railway |
| ▬▬▬ | International border |
| ▬▬▬ | Regional border |
| △ | Summit |

**The sunshine and relaxing atmosphere of a café in Nice**

**Upstream view of the upper Gorges du Cians**

## Gorges du Cians ❶

🚶 Nice. 🚌 Touët-sur-Var. 🚌 Nice, Touët-sur-Var, Valberg. 🛈 pl du Quartier, Valberg (04 93 23 24 25).

Among the finest natural sights in the region, these gorges are a startling combination of deep red slate and vivid mountain greenery. They follow the course of the river Cians, which drops 1,600 m (5,250 ft) in 25 km (15 miles) from Beuil to Touët-sur-Var. At Touët, through a grille in the floor of the church nave, you can see the torrent below.

Approaching from the lower gorges, olives give way to scrubland. It is not until Pra d'Astier that the gorges become steep and narrow: at their narrowest, the rock walls entirely obliterate the sky. Higher still up the gorge, you may spot saffron lilies in June.

At the upper end of the gorges, overlooking the Vallée du Cians, is the 1,430-m (4,770-ft) eyrie of Beuil. Now a military sports centre, it was first fortified by the counts of Beuil, members of the aristocratic Grimaldi family (see p91). They lived here until 1621, despite staff revolt: one count had his throat cut by his barber and another was stabbed by his valet. The last, Hannibal Grimaldi, was tied to a chair and strangled by two Muslim slaves. Stones from their château were used to build the Renaissance chapel of the White Penitents in the 1687 Eglise St-Jean-Baptiste.

## Puget-Théniers ❷

**Road map** E3. 🚶 1,700. 🚍 🚌
🛈 RD 6202 (04 93 05 05 05).

This attractive village lies at the foot of a rocky peak, nestling at the confluence of the Roudole and the Var beneath the ruins of a château that belonged to the Grimaldi family (see p91). The old town has some fine manorial homes with overhanging roofs, but the chief attraction is the 13th-century parish church **Notre-Dame de l'Assomption** built by the Templars. The delightful altarpiece, Notre-Dame de Secours (1525), is by Antoine de Ronzen. Inside the entrance, the altarpiece of the Passion (1515–20) is by Flemish craftsmen, possibly working with the architect and sculptor Matthieu d'Anvers.

Beside the main road, the striking statue of a woman with her hands tied is called L'Action Enchaînée, by Aristide Maillol (1861–1944). It commemorates the local revolutionary and master of insurrection, Louis-Auguste Blanqui. He was born in the town hall in 1805 and became one of the

**L'Action Enchaînée, in Puget-Théniers square**

socialist heroes of the Paris Commune in 1871. A year later he was imprisoned for life and served seven years, having already spent 30 years in jail.

## St-Cézaire-sur-Siagne ❸

**Road map** E3. 🚶 3,200. 🚌
🛈 3 rue de la République (04 93 60 84 30). 🕑 Tue & Sat.
**www**.saintcezairesursiagne.com

Dominating the steep-sided Siagne valley, St-Cézaire has been occupied since pre-Roman times. The walls and towers of the village are reminders of its feudal past. At its heart is the 13th-century **Chapelle du Cimetière**, which houses a Gallo-Roman tomb discovered nearby – a fine example of Provençal Romanesque design. From the medieval part of the village, a path leads to a viewpoint.

To the northeast of the village are the **Grottes de St-Cézaire-sur-Siagne** – iron-rich caves filled with beautiful rock crystallization. Dramatic stalactites and stalagmites have formed on the cave ceilings and floors,

**Antoine Ronzen's altarpiece Notre-Dame de Secours (1525), Puget-Théniers**

creating enchanting shapes, reminiscent of flowers, animals and toadstools. If touched, the stalactites become remarkably resonant, but leave this to the guide. Red oxide in the limestone gives a rich colour to the caves' chambers: the Fairies' Alcove, Great Hall, Hall of Draperies and Organ Chamber, all connected by narrow underground passages, one of which ends abruptly, 40 m (130 ft) below ground, at the edge of an abyss.

### 🦇 Grottes de St-Cézaire-sur-Siagne
*Tel* 04 93 60 22 35. ⬜ daily (Feb, Mar: pm only; Jan, Nov: Sun pm). ⬤ Dec. 🖼 🎫 obligatory. 📷 🍴 🚻 www.lesgrottesdesaintcezaire.com

The village of Gourdon, on the edge of a rocky cliff

**Inside the remarkable Grottes de St-Cézaire-sur-Siagne**

## Gourdon ❹

**Road map** E3. 🏛 *437.*
🛈 pl Victoria (04 93 09 68 25).
**www.**gourdon-france.com

For centuries, villages were built on hilltops, surrounded by ramparts. Gourdon is a typical *village perché (see pp20–21)*, its shops filled with regional produce, perfume and local art. From the square at its precipitous edge, there is a spectacular view of the Loup valley and the sea with Antibes and Cap Roux in the distance.

There are good views, too, from the terrace of the **Château de Gourdon**, built in the 12th century by the *Seigneurs* du Bar, overlords of Gourdon, on the foundations of what was once a Saracen fortress. Its vaulted rooms are remnants of Saracen occupation. The terrace gardens were laid out by André Le Nôtre when the château was restored in the 17th century. Although it is still privately owned, it has two museums. The **Musée Historique** has an Aubusson tapestry, a writing desk belonging to Marie-Antoinette, and a self-portrait by Rembrandt. There is also an adjoining **Musée d'Arts Décoratifs et de la Modernité** with 1930s furniture, lamps by Jacques Le Chevallier and Paul Dupré-Lafon, and some Salvador Dali sculptures.

### 🏛 Château de Gourdon
*Tel* 04 93 09 68 02. ⬜ Jun–Sep: daily; Oct–May: Wed–Sun pm only.
🖼 **www.**chateau-gourdon.com

### JOURNEY IN THE GORGES DU LOUP

The village of Gourdon is on the edge of the Gorges du Loup, the most accessible of many dramatic gorges running down to the coast. The route up to the Gorges du Loup begins at Pré-du-Loup, just east of Grasse, and leads to Gourdon. From Gourdon, the D3 goes up into the gorge and offers the best views, turning back down the D6 after 6.5 km (4 miles).

Descending on the left bank, the road passes the great pothole of Saut du Loup and the Cascades des Demoiselles, where the river's lime carbonate content has partly solidified the vegetation. Just beyond is the 40-m (130-ft) Cascade de Courmes, which has a treacherously slippery stairway under it.

The D2210 continues to Vence, passing via Tourrettes-sur-Loup, an art and craft centre on a high plateau. The 15th-century church has a triptych by the Bréa School and a 1st-century altar dedicated to the Roman god Mercury.

**The 40-m (130-ft) Cascade de Courmes**

## Grasse ❺

**Road map** E3. 🏛 *45,000*. 🚌 ℹ️
*22 cours Honoré Cresp (04 93 36 66
66).* 🚌 *Tue–Sun.* **www**.grasse.fr

Once known for its leather
tanning industry, Grasse
became a perfume centre
in the 16th century. The
tanneries have vanished, but
three major perfume houses
are still in business. Today,
perfume is mainly made from
imported flowers, but each
year, this attractive, fragrance-
filled town holds a Jasmine
festival *(see p31).* The best
place to find out more is the
**Musée International de la
Parfumerie**. It also displays
*bergamotes*, decorated
scented *papier-mâché* boxes.
At **Molinard** there is also a
museum and visitors have
the opportunity to create
their own perfume.

Grasse became fashionable
after 1807–8 when Princess
Pauline Bonaparte recuperated
here. Queen Victoria often
wintered at the Grand Hotel.
Artist Jean-Honoré
Fragonard (1732–1806) was
born here and the walls of
the **Villa-Musée Fragonard** are
covered with his son's murals.
The artist's *Washing of the
Feet* hangs in the 12th-century
**Ancienne Cathédrale Notre-
Dame-du-Puy**, in the old town.
The cathedral also houses
three works by Rubens. The
**Musée d'Art et d'Histoire de
Provence** has Moustiers ware.
18th–19th century Provençal
costumes and jewellery can be
seen at the **Musée Provençal
du Costume et du Bijou**.

🏛 **Musée International de la
Parfumerie**
2 bd du Jeu de Ballon. ℹ️ *04 97 05
58 00.* ◻️ *daily (Oct–May: Wed–
Mon).* ⬤ *public hols.* 🎦 🚹 🅿️

🏛 **Molinard**
60 bd Victor Hugo. **Tel** *04 93 36 01
62.* ◻️ *daily (Oct–May: Mon–Sat).*
⬤ *1 Jan, 25 Dec.* 🎦

🏛 **Villa-Musée Fragonard**
23 bd Fragonard. **Tel** *04 97 05 58 00.*
◻️ *daily (Oct–May: Wed–Mon).*
*pub hols, Nov.* 🎦 🅿️ *by appt.* 🅿️

🏛 **Musée d'Art et d'Histoire
de Provence**
2 rue Mirabeau. **Tel** *04 97 05 58 00.*
◻️ *daily (Oct–May: Wed–Mon).*
*pub hols, Nov.* 🎦 🅿️ *by appt.* 🅿️

Exterior of the Musée International
de la Parfumerie in Grasse

## Mougins ❻

**Road map** E3. 🏛 *19,000*. 🚌 ℹ️
*15 av Charles Mallet (04 93 75 87 67).*
**www**.mougins-coteazur.org

This old hilltop town *(see
pp20–21),* huddled inside
the remains of 15th-century
ramparts and fortified Saracen
Gate, is one of the finest in
the region. Mougins is a smart
address: it has been used by
royalty and film stars as well
as Yves St Laurent and Picasso,
who spent his last years in a
house opposite the Chapelle
de Notre-Dame-de-Vie.

Mougins is also one of the
smartest places in France to
eat. Among its many high-class
restaurants, is Roger Vergé's
**Moulin de Mougins** *(see
p211),* set in an old mill just
outside the village. Diners
can also browse through his
quality kitchen equipment
shop, open until midnight.

The **Musée de la Photo-
graphie** has a fine permanent
collection of Picasso's
photographs. The radiator-
shaped **Musée de l'Auto-
mobiliste**, some 5 km
(3 miles) south of Mougins,
has a classic car collection,
notably Bugattis, on show.

🏛 **Musée de la Photographie**
Porte Sarrazine. **Tel** *04 93 75 85 67.*
◻️ *daily.* ⬤ *1 May, Nov, 25 Dec.*

🏛 **Musée de l'Automobiliste**
Aire des Breguières, autoroute A8.
**Tel** *04 93 69 27 80.* ◻️ *Tue–Sun.*
⬤ *mid-Nov–mid-Dec.* 🎦 🚹 🅿️
**www**.musauto.fr.st

Jacques-Henri and Florette Lartigue, Musée de la Photographie, Mougins

# The Perfumes of Provence

For the past 400 years, the town of Grasse has been the centre of the perfume industry. Before that it was a tannery town, but in the 16th century, Italian immigrant glove-makers began to use the scents of local flowers to perfume soft leather gloves, a fashion made popular by the Queen, Catherine de' Médici. Enormous acres of lavender, roses, jonquils, jasmine and aromatic herbs were cultivated. Today, cheaper imports of flowers and high land prices mean that Grasse focuses on the creation of scent. The power of perfume is evoked in Patrick Süskind's disturbing novel, *Perfume*, set partly in Grasse, in which the murderous perfumer exploits his knowledge of perfume extraction to grisly effect.

Catherine de'Médici, 1581

**Picking early morning jasmine**

**Jasmine waiting to be processed**

## CREATING A PERFUME

Essences are extracted by various methods, including distillation by steam or volatile solvents, which separate the essential oils. *Enfleurage* is a costly and lengthy method for delicate flowers such as jasmine and violet. The blossoms are layered with lard which becomes impregnated with scent.

**Steam distillation** *is one of the oldest extraction processes originally developed by the Arabs. It is now used mainly for flowers such as orange blossom. Flowers and water are boiled together in a still and the essential oils are extracted by steam in an essencier, or oil decanter.*

**Vast quantities** *of blossoms are required to create the essence or "absolut" perfume concentrate. For example, almost a ton of jasmine flowers are needed to obtain just one litre of jasmine essence.*

**The best perfumes** *are created by a perfumer known as a "nose" who possesses an exceptional sense of smell. The nose harmonizes fragrances rather like a musician, blending as many as 300 essences for a perfume. Today, scents can be synthesized by using "head-space analysis" which analyzes the components of the air above a flower.*

# Cannes ❼

Lord Brougham, British Lord Chancellor, put Cannes on the map in 1834 when he stopped on his way to Nice. He was so entranced by the climate of what was then a tiny fishing village that he built a villa and started a trend for upper-class English visitors. Today, Cannes may not attract blue blood but it has become a town of festivals, the resort of the rich and famous. It is busy all year round, its image reinforced by the Film Festival (see p32). With its casinos, fairs, beach, boat and street life, there is plenty to do, even though Cannes lacks the great museums and monuments of less glamorous resorts.

**Cannes beach and Hôtel Carlton**

### Exploring Cannes

The heart of the city is built around the Bay of Cannes and the palm-fringed seafront boulevard de la Croisette. Here there are luxury boutiques and hotels and fine views of La Napoule Bay and the Esterel heights. The eastern end of the bay curves out to Pointe de la Croisette and the summertime Palm Beach Casino, built on the ruins of the medieval Fort de la Croix, which has a nightclub, restaurant and swimming pool. The town's other gaming house is **Casino Croisette**, which is open all year.

Brougham persuaded King Louis-Philippe to donate two million francs to build the Cannes harbour wall. Between La Pantiero and rue Félix Faure are the allées de la Liberté. Shaded by plane trees and surveyed by a statue of Lord Brougham, this open space is ideal both for *boules* and the colourful morning flower market. It provides a fine view of the harbour, which is filled with pleasure craft and fishing

boats. Behind the allées is the rue Meynadier, where you can buy delicious pasta, bread and cheese. This leads you to the sumptuous **Marché Forville**. Succulent regional produce turns up here fresh every day except Monday. The small streets and lanes meander up from the *marché* to the old Roman town of Canoïs Castrum. This area was named after the reeds that grew by the seashore, and is now known as Le Suquet. The church in the centre of the old town, **Notre-Dame de l'Espérance**, was completed in 1648.

The Cannes Film Festival has been held here every May since 1946. The main venue is the **Palais des Festivals**, but there are cinemas all over town, some of which are open to the public and film screening starts as early as 8:30am. The beach has been a focus for paparazzi since 1953, when Brigitte Bardot's beautiful pout put her on the world's front pages.

**Famous handprint**

The main hotels in Cannes have their own beaches with bars and restaurants, where prices match their standing. Celebrities are most likely to be seen at the Carlton, Majestic and Martinez. There is a small charge to enter most beaches in Cannes, where imported sand covers the natural pebbles, and sun-loungers cost extra. Just next to the festival building there is also a free public beach.

### 🎪 Palais des Festivals et des Congrès

1 la Croisette. **Tel** 04 93 39 01 01.
📠 04 92 99 84 22.
www.palaisdesfestivals.com

Built in 1982, this unmistakable modern slab, known as The Bunker, stands beside the Vieux Port at the west end of the promenade. It is the chief venue for the *Palmes d'Or* and other internationally recognised awards sufficiently prestigious for the film business to take them seriously, and much business goes on, so that the festival is not all hype and publicity. Some 78,000 official tickets are distributed to professionals only. Apart from its use for the great Film Festival, the building also houses a casino and a nightclub, and is a regular conference venue. In the nearby allée des Stars, handprints of such famous celebrities as the film director Roman Polanski are immortalized in pavement cement.

**Carla Bruni, the French First Lady, and Karen Mulder at the Film Festival**

Cannes Old Town, known locally as Le Suquet, overlooking the harbour

### 🏨 Hôtel Carlton

58 la Croisette. *Tel 04 93 06 40 06.*
See **Where to Stay** p195.
This ultimate symbol of comfort and grace contains 338 rooms and apartments. It was designed and built in 1911 by the architect, Henri Ruhl. The huge Rococo-style dining room, where the colonnades rise to an ornately decorated ceiling with finely wrought cornices, is unchanged. The hotel's wedding-cake exterior is studded with tiny balconies, and the window frames, cornices and attic pediments are decorated with stucco. The hotel's twin black cupolas are said to be modelled on the breasts of the notorious Belle Otéro, a half-gypsy courtesan who captivated Ruhl. The Carlton was so revered that in World War II, a *New York Times* journalist asked a commanding officer to protect what he considered the world's finest hotel.

**The height of luxury**

## VISITORS' CHECKLIST

**Road map** E4. 🏠 69,000.
🚉 *rue Jean-Jaurès.* 🚌 *pl de l'Hôtel de Ville.* 🛈 *Palais des Festivals (04 92 99 84 22).*
🗓 *Tue–Sun.* 🎬 *Film Festival (May).* **www**.*cannes.fr*

### 🏛 Musée de la Castre

Château de la Castre, Le Suquet. *Tel 04 93 38 55 26.* 🕐 *Tue–Sun.* 🔴 *some pub hols.* 📷 🎫 *by appt.* 🚫
The old Cannes castle, erected by the Lérins monks in the 11th and 12th centuries, houses this museum. Set up in 1877, it contains some fine archaeological and ethnographical collections from all over the world, ranging from South Sea Island costumes to Asian art and African masks. Also housed in the Cistercian St-Anne chapel is a collection of superb musical instruments. The 11th-century **Tour de la Castre** is worth climbing for the view.

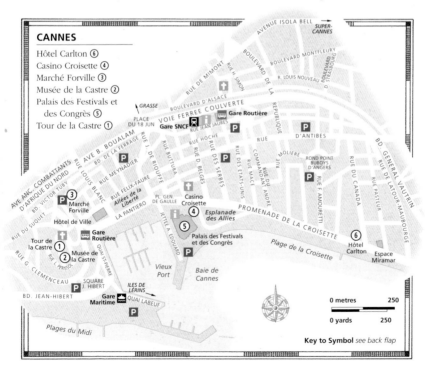

## CANNES

Hôtel Carlton ⑥
Casino Croisette ④
Marché Forville ③
Musée de la Castre ②
Palais des Festivals et
  des Congrès ⑤
Tour de la Castre ①

0 metres 250
0 yards 250

**Key to Symbol** *see back flap*

# Iles de Lérins ❽

Lerina liqueur

Although only a 15-minute boat ride from the glitter of Cannes, the Iles de Lérins reflect a contrasting lifestyle, with their forests of eucalyptus and Aleppo pine and their tiny chapels. The two islands, separated only by a narrow strait, were once the most powerful religious centres in the south of France. St-Honorat is named after the Gallo-Roman, Honoratus, who visited the smaller island at the end of the 4th century and founded a monastery. Ste-Marguerite was named after his sister, who set up a nunnery there. Its fort is well known as the prison of the mysterious 17th-century Man in the Iron Mask, who spent 11 years here.

★ **Fort Ste-Marguerite**
*Built under Richelieu and strengthened by Vauban in 1712, its ground floor has a maritime museum.*

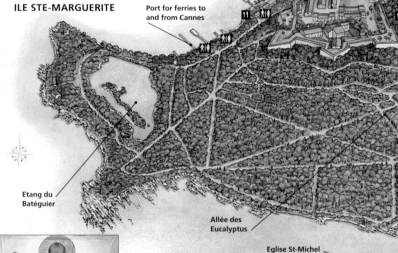

**ILE STE-MARGUERITE**

Port for ferries to and from Cannes

Etang du Batéguier

Allée des Eucalyptus

Eglise St-Michel

**ILE ST-HONORAT**

Chapelle St-Sauveur

**St-Honorat et les Saints de Lérins**
*This icon of St-Honorat can be found in the Abbaye de Lérins.*

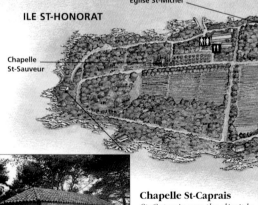

**Chapelle St-Caprais**
*St-Caprais was the disciple of St-Honorat during his first visit to Provence.*

| 0 metres | 1000 |
|---|---|
| 0 yards | 1000 |

*For hotels and restaurants in this region see pp194–7 and pp210–12*

### The Man in the Iron Mask

*The mystery man was imprisoned in Fort Royal from 1687 to 1698, then moved to the Bastille, where he died in 1703.*

**Remains on Ste-Marguerite**
*Excavations on the coast near the fort have revealed houses, mosaics, wall paintings and ceramics which date back to around the 3rd century BC.*

## VISITORS' CHECKLIST

**Road map** D5. 🚢 Cannes: quai Labeuf for Ste-Marguerite *(04 92 98 71 36)*; for St-Honorat *(04 92 98 71 38)*. **Fort Ste-Marguerite/ Musée de la Mer** *Tel* 04 93 43 18 17. ⬜ daily *(Oct–May: Tue–Sun)*. ⬤ 1 Jan, 1 May, 1 & 11 Nov, 25 Dec. 🅿 **Monastère Fortifié** *Tel* 04 92 99 54 00. ⬜ daily. **www**.abbayedelerins.com

Allée du Grand Jardin

**Allée de la Convention**
*Both the islands have many paths leading through the densely wooded interior as well as round the coast.*

Chapelle St-Cyprien

La Chapelle de la Trinité

**Abbaye de Lérins**
*The old church and monks' quarters were incorporated in the 19th-century building.*

### ★Monastère Fortifié

*Built in 1073 by Abbot Aldebert, to protect the monks from Saracen pirates, this "keep" gives views as far as Esterel.*

## STAR SIGHTS

★ Fort Ste-Marguerite

★ Monastère Fortifié

## Juan-les-Pins ❾

**Road map** E3. 🕵 *78,000
(Commune of Antibes).* 🚌 🚍
🚉 *57 bd Guillaumont (04 97 23 11
10).* **www**.antibesjuanlespins.com

To the east of Cannes is the
hammerhead peninsula of
Cap d'Antibes, a promontory
of pines and coves where
millionaires' mansions grow.
Its finest beach is tucked in
the west side of the cape in
Golfe-Juan, where Napoleon
came ashore from Elba in 1815.
This is a 20th-century resort,
promoted by American railroad heir Frank Jay Gould,
who attracted high society in
the 1920s and 1930s when
writers F Scott Fitzgerald and
Ernest Hemingway stayed.

Today, in the high season,
it is filled with a young
crowd. The area at the
junctions of boulevards
Baudoin and Wilson is filled
with colourful bars. Action
centres round the 1988 casino,
the Palais des Congrès, and
Penedés pine grove, which
reaches down to the shore and
gives shelter to the World Jazz
Festival *(see p33)* in July.

**Nightlife in Juan-les-Pins**

## Antibes ❿

**Road map** E3. 🕵 *70,000.* 🚌 🚍
🚊 🚉 *11 place du Gen de Gaulle
(04 97 23 11 11).* 🗓 *Tue–Sun.*
**www**.antibesjuanlespins.com

Originally the ancient Greek
trading post of Antipolis,
Antibes became heavily
fortified over the centuries,
notably by Vauban in the 17th
century, who built the main
port and Fort Carré, where
Napoleon lived and was
temporarily imprisoned.

There are some pleasant
lanes splashed with colourful
flowers in the old town, and a

**Spectacular pleasure yachts in Antibes harbour**

picturesque market place in
cours Masséna. The town's
high points include the 12th-
century towers of the church
and Grimaldi castle on the site
of Antipolis. The **Cathédrale
Notre-Dame**, which took over
the town's watchtower as a
belfry, has a wooden crucifix
from 1447, a 16th-century
Christ and a fine Louis
Bréa altarpiece
depicting the Virgin
Mary, dating from
the same period.

The Château
Grimaldi nearby
houses the **Musée
Picasso**, in which
over 50 drawings,
paintings, prints and ceramics
by the artist when he used
the museum as a studio
during 1946 are displayed.
Also on show is Antoine
Aundi's *La Vierge de Douleur*
(1539), with one of the
earliest views of Antibes.

The modern art collection
includes works by Ernst, Léger,
Miró and Nicolas de Staël in
the last two years of his life.

Further south, the **Musée
d'Histoire et d'Archéologie** in
the fortified Bastion St-André
houses Greek and Etruscan
finds, including a 3rd-century
BC inscription to the spirit of
Septentrion, a boy who danced
at the Antipolis theatre.

🏛 **Musée Picasso**
Château Grimaldi. **Tel** *04 92 90 54
26.* 🗓 *Tue–Sun.* ⬤ *1 Jan, 1 May,
1 Nov, 25 Dec.* 📷 ♿ 🎥 ⊘ 🛈

🏛 **Musée d'Histoire et
d'Archéologie**
Bastion St-André. **Tel** *04 92 90 54
37.* 🗓 *Tue–Sun.* ⬤ *1 Jan, 1 May,
1 Nov, 25 Dec.* 📷 ♿ 🛈

## Vallauris ⓫

**Road map** E3. 🕵 *24,000.*
🚍 🚉 *square 8 mai 1945
(04 93 63 82 58).* 🗓 *Tue–Sun.*
**www**.vallauris-golfe-juan.fr

In summer, the wares of
potters spill on to the avenue
of this pottery capital.
Picasso revitalized
this industry, the
history of which
is traced in the
**Musée Magnelli**,
together with some
fine Pre-Columbian
ceramics. In the
square is *L'Homme
au Mouton* (1943).
*La Guerre et la Paix*
(1951) is on the ceiling of
the **Musée National Picasso**.

**Local pottery from
Vallauris**

🏛 **Musée Magnelli**
Pl de la Libération. **Tel** *04 93 64 16 05.*
🗓 *Wed–Mon.* ⬤ *1 Jan, 25 Dec.* 📷
🏛 **Musée National Picasso**
Pl de la Libération. **Tel** *04 93 64 71
83.* 🗓 *Wed–Mon.* ⬤ *1 Jan, 1
May, 1 & 11 Nov, 25 Dec.* 📷 🛈

**78-year-old Pablo Picasso with a
man-sized dalmatian companion**

# Pablo Picasso (1881–1973)

Picasso, the giant of 20th-century art, spent most of his later life in Provence, inspired by its luminous light and brilliant colours. He came first to Juan-les-Pins in 1920, and returned to Antibes in 1946 with Françoise Gilot. He was given a studio in the seafront Grimaldi palace, where, after wartime Paris, his work became infused with Mediterranean light and joyful images. No other artist has succeeded with so many art forms, and the Antibes collection is a taste of his versatility. He died at Mougins, aged 92.

**Violin and Sheet of Music** *(1912), now in Paris, is a Cubist collage from the period when Picasso experimented with different forms.*

**Les Demoiselles d'Avignon** *(1907), now in New York, was the first Cubist painting. Its bold style shocked the art world of the day.*

**La Joie de Vivre** *(1946), is one of Picasso's main works from the Antibes period, using favourite mythological themes. He is the bearded centaur playing the flute, and Françoise Gilot is the Maenad who dances while two fauns leap about and a satyr plays a panpipe.*

**The Goat** *(1946), also in Antibes, is one of his best-known images. In 1950 he made his famous goat sculpture using a wicker basket as the ribcage.*

**L'Homme au Mouton** *(1943) was sculpted in an afternoon. It stands in the main square of Vallauris, also home of* La Guerre et la Paix *(1951).*

# Biot ⑫

**Road map** E3. 🏘 8,200. 🚆 🚌
ℹ 46 rue St-Sébastien (04 93 65
78 00). 🚌 Tue & Fri. www.biot.fr

The picturesque village of
Biot, which has 12 themed
walks (available at the tourist
office), was the main pottery
town in the region until Pablo
Picasso revived the industry in
Vallauris after World War II.
Today, Biot is renowned for its
bubble-flecked glassware, with
eight glass works. Visitors to
**La Verrerie de Biot** can marvel
at master craftsmen at work.

Biot was once the domain
of the Knights Templar (*see
p123*), and some fortifications
remain, such as the 1566 Porte
des Migraniers (grenadiers).

The church has two fine
16th-century works: *L'Ecce
Homo*, attributed to Canavesio,
and *La Vierge au Rosaire*,
attributed to Louis Bréa.

The modern **Musée
National Fernand
Léger**, built on
land the artist
bought as a studio,
contains many
of his works.

🏛 **Musée National
Fernand Léger**
Chemin du Val-de-
Pome. **Tel** 04 92 91
50 30. ◻ Wed–Mon.
● Jan, 1 May, 25 Dec.
🛇 🛇 🗑 🗑 🗑

🏛 **La Verrerie de Biot**
Chemin des Combes. **Tel** 04 93 65
03 00. ◻ daily. ● Sun pm, public
hols pm, 25 Dec. 🛇 🗑 🗑

Detail of Léger mosaic from the eastern façade of the museum, Biot

# Villeneuve-Loubet ⑬

**Road map** E3. 🏘 13,000. 🚌
ℹ 16 av de la Mer (04 92 02 66 16).
🚌 Wed & Sat. www.ot-villeneuve
loubet.org

This old village is dominated
by a restored medieval castle
which belonged to the
Villanova family. It is
also where France's
most celebrated
chef, Auguste
Escoffier, (1846–
1935) was born. The
man who
invented the
*bombe Néro* and
*pêche Melba* was
*chef de cuisine*
at the Grand
Hotel, Monte-
Carlo before Mr
Ritz persuaded him to become
head chef at the Savoy in
London. The **Musée de l'Art
Culinaire**, in the house of his
birth, contains many show-

**Chef Auguste Escoffier,
born in Villeneuve-Loubet**

pieces in almond paste and
icing sugar, and over 1,800
menus, some dating back to
1820. The **Marineland** leisure
park includes a children's
farm and shark-filled aquarium.

🏛 **Musée de l'Art
Culinaire**
3 rue Escoffier. **Tel** 04 93 20 80 51.
◻ Sun–Fri. ● Nov; pub hols. 🛇 🗑

🦈 **Marineland**
306 av Mozart. **Tel** 04 93 33 49 49.
◻ daily. 🛇 🛇 🗑 🍴

# Vence ⑭

**Road map** E3. 🏘 17,000. 🚌 ℹ
place du Grand-Jardin (04 93 58 06
38). 🚌 Tue & Fri. www.ville-vence.fr

A delightful old cathedral
town on a rocky ridge,
Vence has long attracted
artists. English writer DH
Lawrence died here in 1930.

The old town is entered by
the Porte de Peyra (1441),
beside the place du Frêne,
named after its giant ash tree
planted to commemorate the
visits of King François I and
Pope Paul III. The 16th-
century castle of the lords
of Villeneuve, seigneurs of
Vence, houses the museum
and the **Fondation Emile
Hughes**, named after an
illustrious former mayor.

The town's cathedral, one
of the smallest in France,
stands by the site of the forum
of the Roman city of Vintium.
Vence was a bishopric from
the 4th to the 19th centuries.
Its notable prelates included
Saint Véran (d AD 492), and
the former wit and ladies'
confidant, Bishop Godeau
(1605–72). The 51 oak and
pear choir stalls are carved

---

## THE CREATION OF BIOT GLASSWARE

Biot is the capital of glassblowing on the coast. Local
soils provide sand for glass-
making, and typical Biot
glass is sturdy, with tiny air
bubbles (known as *verre à
bulles*). The opening of
Léger's museum led to an
increased interest in all local
crafts, and to the arrival of
the Verrerie de Biot workshop in 1956. This revived
old methods of making oil
lamps, carafes and narrow-
spouted *porrons*, from which
a jet of liquid can be poured
straight into the mouth.

with satirical figures. Marc Chagall designed the mosaic of *Moses in the Bulrushes* in the chapel (1979).

Henri Matisse *(see pp82–3)* decorated the **Chapelle du Rosaire** between 1947 and 1951 to thank the Dominican nuns who nursed him through an illness. The stations of the cross are reduced to black lines tinted with stained glass.

**Ⅲ Fondation Emile Hughes**
Château de Villeneuve.
*Tel 04 93 58 15 78.* ◯ *Tue–Sun.*
◉ *1 Jan, 1 May, 25 Dec.* 🎟 🚻
www.museedevence.com

**⛪ Chapelle du Rosaire**
Av Henri Matisse. *Tel 04 93 58 03 26.* ◯ *Tue & Thu: am; Mon–Thu & Sat: pm* ◉ *mid-Nov–mid-Dec, publ hols.* 🎟

## St-Paul-de-Vence ⑮

**Road map** E3. 🏠 *2,900.* 🚉 *Vence.*
🛈 *2 rue Grande (04 93 32 86 95).*
www.saint-pauldevence.com

This classic medieval *village perché (see pp20–21)* was built behind the coast to avoid Saracen attack. In 1537 it was re-ramparted, under François I, to stand up to Savoy, Austria and Piedmont. A celebrity village, it was first "discovered" by Bonnard, Modigliani and other artists of the 1920s. Since that time, many of the rich and famous literati and glitterati have flocked to St-Paul. A photographic display in the local museum includes Simone de Beauvoir, Jean-Paul Sartre, F Scott Fitzgerald, Catherine Deneuve, Sophia Loren and the elusive Greta Garbo.

Simone Signoret and Yves Montand in St-Paul-de-Vence

Most famously, these personalities slept, dined, and, in the case of Yves Montand and Simone Signoret, even had their wedding reception at the **Colombe d'Or** *auberge (see p211).* Today it has one of the finest 20th-century private art collections, built up over the years in lieu of payment of bills. The priceless dining-room décor includes paintings by such world-famous artists as Miró, Picasso and Braque. In the 12th-century Gothic church, there is a painting, *Catherine of Alexandria,* attributed to Tintoretto. There are also gold reliquaries and a fine local 13th-century enamel Virgin. The **Musée d'Histoire Locale de St-Paul** nearby features waxwork costumed tableaux of scenes from the town's rich past, and the old castle keep opposite is now used as the town hall.

The main street runs from the 13th-century entrance gate of Porte Royale and past the Grande Fontaine to Porte Sud. This gives on to the cemetery, a resting place for Chagall, the Maeghts, Escoffier and many locals. It also offers wonderful views.

Just outside St-Paul, on La Gardette Hill, is Josep Lluis Sert's striking concrete and rose **Fondation Maeght** *(see pp76–7),* one of Europe's finest modern art museums.

**Ⅲ Musée d'Histoire Locale de St-Paul**
Pl de la Mairie. *Tel 04 93 32 41 13.*
◯ *Mon, Wed–Sat.* ◉ *public hols; 2 wks Nov.* 🎟

Entrance to Chapelle du Rosaire in Vence, decorated by Henri Matisse

# Fondation Maeght

Nestling amid the umbrella pines in the hills above St-Paul-de-Vence, this small modern art museum is one of the world's finest. Aimé and Marguerite Maeght were Cannes art dealers who numbered the likes of Chagall, Matisse and Miró among their clients and friends. Their private collection formed the basis for the museum, which opened in 1964. Like St-Paul itself, the Maeght has been a magnet for celebrities: Duke Ellington, Samuel Beckett, André Malraux, Merce Cunningham and, of course, a galaxy of the artists themselves have mingled at fundraising events. The museum now receives over 250,000 visitors each year.

★ **Cour Giacometti**
*Slender bronze figures by Alberto Giacometti, such as L'Homme Qui Marche I (1960), inhabit their own shady courtyard or appear about the grounds as if they have a life of their own.*

**La Vie** *(1964)*
*Marc Chagall's painting is full of humanity: here is love, parenthood, religion, society, nature; all part of a swirling, circus-like tableau of dancers and musicians, acrobats and clowns.*

**Les Poissons**
is a mosaic pool designed by Georges Braque in 1962.

**Les Renforts** *(1965)*
*One of many works of art that greet arriving visitors, Alexander Calder's creation is a "stabile" – a counterpart to his more familiar mobiles.*

**L'Eté** *(1909)*
*Pierre Bonnard settled in Provence for the last 22 years of his life, becoming a close friend of Aimé Maeght. Matisse called Bonnard "the greatest of us all".*

**Cowled roofs**
allow indirect light to filter into the galleries. The building was designed by Spanish architect Josep Lluis Sert.

**La Partie de Campagne** *(1954)*
*Fernand Léger lends his unique vision to the classic artistic scene of a country outing.*

### ★ **Labyrinthe de Miró**
*Joan Miró's l'Oiseau Lunaire (1968) is one of the many statues in this multi-levelled maze of trees, water and gargoyles.*

**Oiseau dans le Feuillage** *(1961)*
*Georges Braque's bird nestles amongst "foliage" made of newsprint. Braque was highly influential in the creation of the Fondation, but died before he could see the museum finally opened to the public.*

## GALLERY GUIDE

*The permanent collection is comprised entirely of 20th-century art. The only items on permanent view are the large sculptures in the grounds. The indoor galleries display works from the collection in rotation but, in summer, only temporary exhibitions are held.*

**Chapelle St-Bernard**
was built in memory of the Maeghts' son, who died in 1953 aged 11. The altarpiece is a 15th-century Christ; above it is a stained-glass window by Braque.

**Main entrance and information**

## STAR SIGHTS

★ Cour Giacometti
---
★ Labyrinthe de Miró

**Renoir's studio at Les Collettes**

## Cagnes-sur-Mer ⓰

**Road map** E3. 🏠 45,000. 🚌
🚇 🛈 6 bd Maréchal Juin (04 93
20 61 64). 🕭 Tue–Sun. 🎵 Country
Music (Aug); Medieval (Aug).
www.cagnes-tourisme.com

There are three parts to
Cagnes-sur-Mer: Cros-de-
Cagnes, the fishing village
and beach; Cagnes-Ville, the
commercial centre; and Haut-
de-Cagnes, the upper town.

Haut-de-Cagnes is the place
to head for. This ancient hilltop town is riven with lanes,
steps and vaulted passages. It
is dominated by the **Château
Grimaldi** but also has some
fine Renaissance houses and
the church of St-Pierre, where
the Grimaldis are entombed.

East of Cagnes-Ville is Les
Collettes, built in 1907 among
ancient olive trees by Pierre-
Auguste Renoir (1841–1919).
He came here, hoping that
the climate would relieve his
rheumatism and stayed for the
rest of his life. A picture of
Renoir in his last year shows
him still at work, a brush tied
to his crippled hand.

Now the **Musée Renoir** at
Les Collettes is almost exactly
as it was when the artist died.
In the house are 11 of Renoir's
paintings, as well as works by
his friends Bonnard and Dufy.
Renoir's beloved olive groves
are the setting for the bronze
*Venus Victrix* (1915–16).

🏛 **Musée Renoir**
19 chemin des Collettes.
**Tel** 04 93 20 61 07. ☐ Wed–Mon.
☐ 1 Jan, 1 May, last wk Nov,
1st wk Dec, 25 Dec. 🚫 🚻 🅿

# Château Grimaldi

In the Middle Ages the Grimaldi family held sway over
many of the Mediterranean coastal towns. The castle
that towers over Haut-de-Cagnes was built by Rainier in
1309 as a fortress-prison; in 1620 his descendant, Jean-
Henri, transformed it into the handsome palace which
shelters behind its dramatic battlements. Mercifully, the
château survived the worst ravages of the Revolution and
later occupation by Piedmontese troops in 1815. It now
houses an eclectic mixture of
museums, from olives to
modern art.

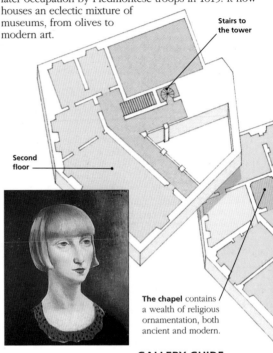

**Stairs to
the tower**

**Second
floor**

**The chapel** contains
a wealth of religious
ornamentation, both
ancient and modern.

## GALLERY GUIDE
*The olive tree museum is on
the ground floor, along with
exhibits about life in the medieval castle. The Suzy Solidor
collection is displayed in a
former boudoir on the first
floor. Selections from the permanent collection of modern
Mediterranean art, as well as
temporary exhibitions, are on
the first and second floors.*

**★ Donation Suzy Solidor**
*This 1930s chanteuse was
painted by 244 artists during
her lifetime. The 40 works
on display include portraits
by Jean Cocteau (above)
and Kisling (top).*

### KEY TO FLOORPLAN
☐ Donation Suzy Solidor
☐ Musée d'Art Modern
  Méditérranéen
☐ Musée de l'Olivier
☐ Permanent collection
☐ Temporary exhibition space
☐ Non-exhibition space

**Renaissance Courtyard**
*Filled with lush greenery and dappled sunlight, this central space rises past two levels of marble-columned galleries to the open sky.*

## VISITORS' CHECKLIST

Pl Grimaldi, Cagnes-sur-Mer.
**Tel** 04 92 02 47 30. ☐ 10am–
noon, 2–6pm Wed–Mon (Nov–
Apr: to 5pm). ● 1 Jan, 1 May,
mid-Nov–2 Dec, 25 Dec. ⚙

**First floor**

**Ground floor**

**★ La Chute de Phaëton attributed to Carlone**
*The Piedmontese soldiers occupying the château in the 19th century had little respect for this spectacular 1620s illusionistic ceiling – and used it for target practice.*

**Musée de l'Olivier**
*A massive wooden oil mill, vast terracotta jars and other arti-facts illustrate the time-honoured Provençal tra-dition of olive cultivation.*

🚹

**To place du Château**

**Main entrance and ticket office**

## STAR SIGHTS

★ La Chute de Phaëton attributed to Carlone

★ Donation Suzy Solidor

# Street-by-Street: Nice ⑰

A dense network of pedestrian alleys, narrow buildings and pastel, Italianate façades make up the Old Town. Its streets contain many fine 17th-century Italianate churches, among them St-François-de-Paule, behind the Opéra, and l'Eglise du Jésus in the rue Droite. Most of the seafront, at quai des Etats-Unis, is taken up by the Ponchettes, a double row of low houses with flat roofs, a fashionable walk before the promenade des Anglais was built. To the east of this lies the Colline du Château, occupied in the 4th century by Greeks who kept fishing nets on the quay.

**★ Cathédrale Ste-Réparate**
*Built in 1650 by the Nice architect J-A Guiberto in Baroque style, this has a fine dome of glazed tiles and an 18th-century tower.*

**Palais de Justice**
*This awesome building was inaugurated on 17 October 1892, replacing the smaller quarters used before Nice became part of France. On the same site was a 13th-century church and convent.*

**★ Cours Saleya**
*The site of an enticing vegetable and flower market, it is also a lively area at night.*

**Opera House**
*Built in 1855, the ornate and sumptuous Opéra de Nice has its entrance just off the quai des Etats-Unis.*

## Chapelle de la Miséricorde

*Designed in 1740 by Guarino Guarinone, this Baroque masterpiece has a fine Rococo interior. The Nice altarpieces are by Louis Bréa and Jean Miralhet.*

## VISITORS' CHECKLIST

**Road map** F3. 349,000.
7 km (4.5 miles) SW. av Thiers. 5 blvd Jean Jaurès. quai du Commerce. 5 prom des Anglais (08 92 70 74 07). Tue–Sun. Carnival (before Lent), Nice Jazz Festival (July). www.nicetourisme.com

### ★ Palais Lascaris

*18th-century statues of Mars and Venus flank the staircase. The trompe l'oeil ceiling is by Genoese artists.*

### Tourist Train

*It passes the market, old town and castle gardens.*

## KEY

– – – Suggested route

0 metres 100
0 yards 100

### Les Ponchettes

*One of Nice's most unusual architectural features is the row of low white buildings along the sea-front once used by fishermen, now a mix of galleries and ethnic restaurants.*

## STAR FEATURES

★ Cathédrale Ste-Réparate

★ Palais Lascaris

★ Cours Saleya

# Musée Matisse

Henri Matisse (1869–1954) first came to Nice in 1916, and lived at several addresses in the city before settling in Cimiez for the rest of his life. His devotion to the city and its "clear, crystalline, precise, limpid" light culminated, just before his death in 1954, with a bequest of works. Nine years later they formed the museum's core collection, sharing space with archaeological relics in the Villa des Arènes, next to the Cimiez cemetery, which holds the artist's simple memorial. Since 1993 the entire villa, complete with its new extension, has been devoted to celebrating his life, work and influence.

★ **Nu Bleu IV** *(1952)*
*The celebrated "cut-outs" were made in later life when Matisse was bedridden.*

**Matisse in his Studio** *(1948)*
*The museum's photographic collection offers a unique insight into the man and his work. Robert Capa's picture shows him drafting the murals for the Chapelle du Rosaire at Vence (see pp74–5).*

First floor

To stairs up to villa

Ground floor

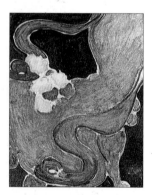

★ **Fauteuil Rocaille**
*A gilded Rococo armchair, painted by Matisse in 1946, is among many of his personal belongings that are on display in the museum.*

Main Entrance

## STAR EXHIBITS

- ★ Nature Morte aux Grenades
- ★ Fauteuil Rocaille
- ★ Nu Bleu IV

## GALLERY GUIDE

*The ground and first floors of the villa are used to display works from the museum's ever-expanding permanent collection. The new subterranean wing is used for changing thematic exhibitions devoted to Matisse and his contemporaries.*

## KEY TO FLOORPLAN

- ☐ Permanent collection
- ☐ Temporary exhibition space
- ☐ Non-exhibition space

**Liseuse à la Table Jaune** *(1944)*
*The tranquillity of this work belies the troubles that beset Matisse in World War II, including a major operation and the arrest of his wife for Resistance work.*

**VISITORS' CHECKLIST**

164 av des Arènes de Cimiez, Nice. **Tel** *04 93 53 40 53.*
◻ *10am–6pm Wed–Mon.*
● *1 Jan, Easter, 1 May, 25 Dec.*
▨ ▨ ▨ ▨ ▨
**www**.musee-matisse-nice.org

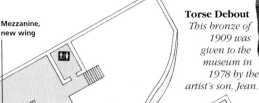

**Mezzanine, new wing**

**Children's workshop**

**Torse Debout**
*This bronze of 1909 was given to the museum in 1978 by the artist's son, Jean.*

**Lower ground floor, new wing**

**Exit**

**The upper floors**
of the villa hold a library and resource centre for students and researchers.

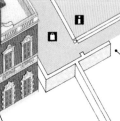

**Trompe l'Oeil Façade**
*The decorative stonework that adorns the 17th-century Villa des Arènes is, in fact, a masterful disguise of plain walls, only visible close up.*

**★ Nature Morte aux Grenades** *(1947)*
*Ripe pomegranates feature in a favourite setting: an interior with a window to "skies… as brilliantly blue as Matisse's eyes", as the poet Aragon put it.*

# Exploring Nice

Nice is France's largest tourist resort and fifth biggest city. It has the second busiest airport in France and more banks, galleries and museums than anywhere else outside the capital. Each year, Nice hosts a lavish pre-Lent carnival, ending with a fireworks display and the Battle of the Flowers *(see p228)*. The city has its own dialect and its own cuisine of *socca*, chickpea pancakes, but the ubiquitous pizza ovens lend a rich Italian flavour.

**Beach and promenade des Anglais**

### A glimpse of the city

Nice lies at the foot of a hill known as the Château, after the castle that once stood there. The flower and vegetable market (Tue–Sun) in the cours Saleya is a shoppers' paradise. The fashionable quarter is the Cimiez district, on the hills overlooking the town, where the old monastery of **Notre-Dame** is worth a visit. Lower down, next to the **Musée Matisse** *(see p82–3)*, are the remains of a Roman amphitheatre and baths. Artifacts are on show at the nearby archaeological museum.

The city's most remarkable feature is the 19th-century promenade des Anglais, which runs right along the seafront. It was built in the 1820s, using funds raised by the English colony. Today it is an eight-lane 5-km (3-mile) highway. Until World War II, Nice was popular with aristocrats. Queen Victoria stayed here in 1895, and in 1912, Tsar Nicholas II built the onion-domed **Cathédrale Orthodoxe Russe** in St-Philippe. The old town is now gentrified, although it once had a bad reputation. In 1982 English author Graham Greene criticized Jacques Médecin, the city's right-wing mayor, who was eventually imprisoned for corruption and died in exile.

### 🏨 Hotel Négresco

37 promenade des Anglais. *Tel 04 93 16 64 00.* See *Where to Stay* p196. This palatial hotel was built in 1912 for Henri Négresco, once a gypsy-violin serenader, who went bankrupt eight years later.

**The fountain in place Masséna**

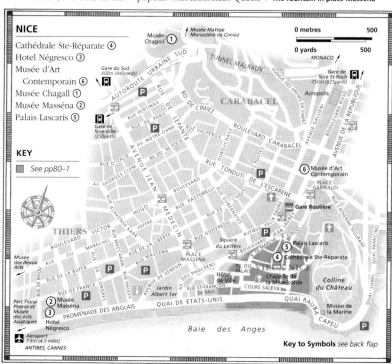

## NICE

Cathédrale Ste-Réparate ④
Hotel Négresco ③
Musée d'Art
   Contemporain ⑥
Musée Chagall ①
Musée Masséna ②
Palais Lascaris ⑤

### KEY

🟦 See pp80–1

In the *salon royale* hangs a Baccarat chandelier made from 16,000 stones. The infamous American dancer Isadora Duncan spent her last months here in 1927. She died tragically outside the hotel when her trailing scarf caught in the wheel of her Bugatti and broke her neck.

### � Musée Masséna

65 rue de France. *Tel 04 93 91 19 10.* ◯ *Wed–Mon.*

This 19th-century Italianate villa belonged to the great-grandson of Napoleon's Nice-born Marshal. Its Empire-style main hall has a bust of the Marshal by Canova. Among its exhibits are religious works, paintings by Niçois primitives, white-glazed faïence pottery *(see p186)* and Josephine's gold cloak.

### ⓕ Musée Chagall

36 av Dr Ménard. *Tel 04 93 53 87 20.* ◯ *Wed–Mon.* ◉ *1 Jan, 1 May, 25 Dec.* 🎫 👥 📷 📀 *in summer.*

This museum houses the largest collection of Marc Chagall's work. There are 17 canvases from his Biblical Message series, including five versions of *The Song of Songs*. Three stained-glass windows depict the *Creation of the World*, and the large mosaic reflected in the pool is of the prophet Elijah.

### 🔓 Cathédrale Ste-Réparate

Place Rossetti. *Tel 08 92 70 74 07 for guided tours.* ◯ *daily.*

This 17th-century Baroque building has a handsome tiled dome. The interior is lavishly decorated with plasterwork, marble and original panelling.

### ♣ Palais Lascaris

15 rue Droite. *Tel 04 93 62 72 40.* ◯ *Wed–Mon.* ◉ *1 Jan, Easter, 1 May, 25 Dec.*

This salon of this stuccoed 17th-century palace has a *trompe l'oeil* ceiling, said to be by Carlone. An 18th-century pharmacy has been re-created on the ground floor.

### ⓕ Musée des Arts Asiatiques

405 prom des Anglais. 📱 *04 92 29 37 00.* ◯ *Wed–Mon.* ◉ *1 Jan, 1 May, 25 Dec.* 👥 📷 📀

This museum has outstanding examples of ancient and 20th-century art from across Asia in Kenzo Tange's uncluttered white marble and glass setting.

### ⓕ Musée des Beaux-Arts

33 av des Baumettes. *Tel 04 9215 28 28.* ◯ *Tue–Sun.* ◉ *1 Jan, Easter, 1 May, 25 Dec.* 👥 📷 📀 **www.** musee.beaux-arts-nice.org

**Russian Orthodox cathedral**

Once home to a Ukranian princess, this 1878 villa houses a collection begun with a donation by Napoleon III. Three centuries of art cover work by Jules Chéret, Carle Van Loo, Van Dongen, and Impressionists and Post-Impressionists such as Bonnard, Dufy and Vuillard.

### ⓕ Musée d'Art Contemporain

Promenade des Arts. *Tel 04 97 13 42 01.* ◯ *Tue–Sun.* ◉ *1 Jan, Easter, 1 May, 25 Dec.* 👥 📷 📀

Housed in a strikingly original building with marble-faced towers and glass passageways, the collection reflects the history of the *avant-garde*, including Pop Art by Andy Warhol and work by Ecole de Nice artists such as Yves Klein.

Hillside view over Cap Ferrat

## Cap Ferrat ⑱

**Road map** F3. 🚉 *Nice.* 🚌 *Beaulieu.* 🚕 *St-Jean-Cap-Ferrat.* 🛈 *St-Jean-Cap-Ferrat (04 93 76 08 90).* **www.**saintjeancapferrat.fr

The Cap Ferrat peninsula is a playground for the rich, with exclusive villas, luxury gardens and fabulous yachts in the St-Jean marina.

King Léopold II of Belgium started the trend in the 19th century, when he built Les Cèdres on the west side of the cape overlooking Villefranche. Today the 14-ha (35-acre) park is open to the public, and a 3-ha (7-acre) lake on Leopold's estate has been turned into the **Parc Zoologique**. In 1906 he built the Villa Mauresque for his personal priest; it was bought by Somerset Maugham 20 years later. The Duke and Duchess of Windsor rented a villa here in 1938, and post-war residents have included David Niven and Edith Piaf. High hedges and gates protect these exotic villas, but one of the finest, **Musée Ephrussi de Rothschild** *(see pp86–7)*, is open to the public.

There is a superb view from the little garden around the 1837 lighthouse at the end of the cape. A pretty shoreside walk leads around the Pointe St-Hospice, east of the port at **St-Jean-Cap-Ferrat**, a former fishing village with old houses overlooking the harbour.

### 🐾 Parc Zoologique

117 blvd Général de Gaulle, Cap Ferrat. *Tel 04 93 76 07 60.* ◯ *daily.* 🎫 👥 📷 📀

Yves Klein's *Anthropométrie* (1960) in the Musée d'Art Contemporain

# Musée Ephrussi de Rothschild

Béatrice Ephrussi de Rothschild (1864–1934) could have led a life of indolent luxury, but her passions for travel and fine art, combined with an iron will, led to the creation of the most perfect "dream villa" of the Riviera, Villa Ile-de-France. Despite interest shown by King Léopold II of Belgium for the land, she succeeded in purchasing it and later supervised every aspect of the villa's creation. It was completed in 1912 and, although she never used it as a primary residence, Béatrice hosted garden parties and soirées here until 1934. The villa remains a monument to a woman of spirit and vision.

**★ Fragonard Room**
*The fine collection of working drawings by Jean-Honoré Fragonard (1732–1806) includes this sketch, wryly named* If he were as faithful to me.

**Béatrice, Aged 19**
*Her meek appearance belies a woman who, a contemporary once observed, "commands flowers to grow during the Mistral".*

**The Salon Louis XV** looks out on to the French garden, combining the pleasures of a sea breeze with the comfort of elegant surroundings.

**Béatrice's Boudoir**
*Béatrice's writing desk is a beautiful piece of furniture dating from the 18th century. It once belonged to Marie-Antoinette.*

## STAR SIGHTS

- ★ Fragonard Room
- ★ Salon Louis XVI
- ★ Gardens

**Villa Ile-de-France**
*Béatrice christened her villa following a pattern established by another villa she owned named "Rose de France". Its stucco walls are coloured in a lovely shade of rose pink.*

*For hotels and restaurants in this region see pp194–7 and pp210–12*

**Covered Patio**

*Combining Moorish and Italian elements, this airy space rises the full height of the villa. The marble columns, mosaic flooring and diffused light complement the Renaissance religious works and 15th–16th-century tapestries on the walls.*

**VISITORS' CHECKLIST**

1 av Ephrussi de Rothschild, St-Jean-Cap-Ferrat. 04 93 01 45 90. 10am–6pm daily (until 2pm weekdays Nov–Feb). 1st floor collections only (obligatory). ground floor only. **www**.villa-ephrussi.com

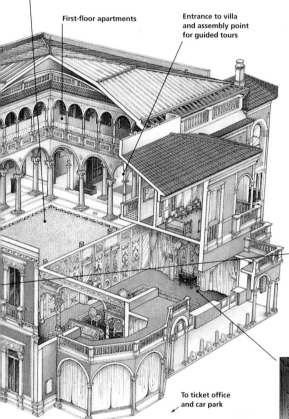

First-floor apartments

Entrance to villa and assembly point for guided tours

To ticket office and car park

**Cabinet des Singes**

*Béatrice's love of animals is epitomized by this tiny room. Its wooden panels are painted with monkeys dancing to the music of the diminutive 18th-century Meissen monkey orchestra.*

**★ Gardens**

*The main garden is modelled on a ship's deck – Béatrice employed extra staff to wander around in sailors' uniforms. There are nine themed gardens, including Japanese and Florentine gardens.*

**★ Salon Louis XVI**

*Like every room in the villa, the decor here is lavish, with wood ornamentation from the Crillon in Paris, Savonnerie carpets, and chairs upholstered in 18th-century Aubusson tapestries.*

## Villefranche ⑲

**Road map** F3. 👥 6,650. 🚊 🚌
🛈 *Jardin François Binon (04 93 01 73 68).* 🐟 *Sat & Sun.*
**www**.villefranche-sur-mer.com

This unspoilt town overlooks a beautiful natural harbour, deep enough to be a naval port, with a lively waterfront lined by bars and cafés.

The medieval **Chapelle St-Pierre** on the quay, once used for storing fishing nets, was renovated in 1957, when Jean Cocteau added lavish frescoes. Steep lanes climb up from the harbour, turning into tunnels beneath the tightly packed buildings. The vaulted rue Obscure has provided shelter from bombardment as recently as World War II. The Baroque **Eglise St-Michel** contains a 16th-century carving of St Rock and his dog and a 1790 organ.

Within the sturdy grey walls of the 16th-century Citadelle de St-Elme are the chapel, open-air theatre and museums.

Fishing in the natural harbour at Villefranche

🏛 **Chapelle St-Pierre**
Quai Amiral Courbet.
**Tel** *04 93 76 90 70.*
⭘ *Tue–Sun.* ⬤ *25 Dec.* 🖼 ♿

## Beaulieu ⑳

**Road map** F3. 👥 3,700. 🚊 🚌
🛈 *pl Clemenceau (04 93 01 02 21).*
🐟 *Mon–Sat.*
**www**.otbeaulieusurmer.fr

Hemmed in and protected by a rock face, this is one of the Riviera's warmest resorts in winter, with two beaches: the Baie des Fourmis and, by the port, Petite Afrique. The casino, formal gardens and the Belle Epoque Rotunda, now a conference centre and museum, add to Beaulieu's old-fashioned air. Among its hotels is La Réserve, founded by Gordon Bennett, the owner of the *New York Herald*. As a stunt, in 1871, he sent journalist HM Stanley to rescue the Scottish missionary and explorer Dr Livingstone, who was looking for the source of the Nile.

Beaulieu is the site of the **Villa Kerylos**. Built by archeologist Théodore Reinach, it resembles an ancient Greek villa. Authentic techniques and precious materials were used to create lavish mosaics, frescoes and inlaid furniture. There are also numerous original Greek ornaments, and a new antique sculpture gallery.

🏛 **Villa Kerylos**
Imp. Eiffel. **Tel** *04 93 76 44 09.*
⭘ *daily.* ⬤ *25 Dec.* 🖼 🅿
**www**.villa-kerylos.com

## Eze ㉑

**Road map** F3. 👥 3,100. 🚊 🚌 🛈
*pl Général de Gaulle (04 93 41 26 00).*

Eze is a dramatic *village perché (see pp20–21)*, a cluster of ancient buildings some 427 m (1,400 ft) above the sea. At its summit are the bat-filled ruins of a 14th-century castle. Around it is the **Jardin Exotique**, offering views as far as Corsica.

The flower-decked, car-free streets lead to an 18th-century church. Its bust of Christ is made from olive wood that survived the terrible fires that raged close by in 1986.

🌿 **Jardin Exotique**
Rue du Château. **Tel** *04 93 41 10 30.* ⭘ *daily.* ⬤ *Christmas wk.* 🖼

Steps of the elegant Belle Epoque Rotunda (1886), Beaulieu

*For hotels and restaurants in this region see pp194–7 and pp210–12*

# La Turbie ②

**Road map** F3. 🏘 *3,200.* 🚌
ℹ *2 pl Decras (04 93 41 21 15).*
🗓 *Thu.* **www**.ville-la-turbie.fr

High above Monte-Carlo is one of the finest views on the Riviera, reached by a stretch of the Grande Corniche which crosses ravines and tunnels through mountains. The village of La Turbie, scented with bougainvillea, has two medieval gateways. Its oldest houses, dating from the 11th–13th centuries, are on the Roman Via Julia.

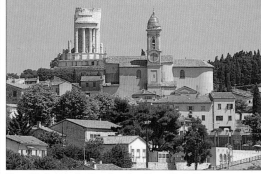

**View of Le Trophée des Alpes from the village of La Turbie**

## 🏛 Musée du Trophée des Alpes

Cours Albert 1er. **Tel** 04 93 41 20 84. ◻ *Tue–Sun.* ◐ *1 Jan, 1 May, 1 & 11 Nov, 25 Dec.* 📷 ♿ *by appt.* 🛍

The most spectacular feature of La Turbie is the Trophée des Alpes, a huge Roman monument, built out of white local stone, which marked the division between Italy and Gaul. Its construction was ordered in 6 BC by the Roman Senate to honour Augustus's

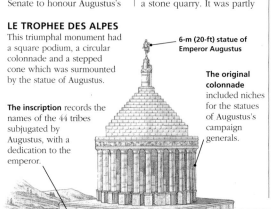

**Monument detail**

victory in 13 BC over 44 fractious Ligurian tribes. The original trophy was 50-m (164-ft) tall and had niches with statues of each of the campaign's victors. There were stairs leading to all parts of the structure.

When the Romans left, the trophy was gradually dismantled. In the 4th century, St Honorat chipped away at the monument because it had become the object of pagan worship. Later it served both as a fort and as a stone quarry. It was partly destroyed on the orders of Louis XIV, who feared it would fall into enemy hands during the invasion of Provence by Savoy in 1707. Restoration was first begun in 1905, and continued in 1923 by an American, Edward Tuck. Today, the triumphal inscription of Roman victory has been restored to its original position.

A small museum on the site documents the history of the trophy, with fragments of the monument, pieces of sculpture, inscriptions, drawings and a small-scale model.

The spectacular panorama from the terraces of the trophy takes in Cap Ferrat and Eze. Monaco, at 480 m (1,575 ft) below, seems breathtakingly close, like an urban stage set seen from a seat in the gods.

Among visitors impressed with La Turbie and its trophy, was the poet Dante (1265–1321), and his comments are inscribed on a plaque in rue Comte-de-Cessole. From the end of this street there is a fine view of the monument.

## 🔒 Eglise St-Michel-Archange

◻ *daily.* ♿

The 18th-century Nice Baroque church was built with stones plundered from the trophy. Inside there is an altar of multi-coloured marble and a 17th-century onyx and agate table, which was used for communion. Its religious paintings include two works by the Niçois artist Jean-Baptiste Van Loo, a portrait of St Mark attributed to Veronese, and a Piéta from the Bréa School.

## LE TROPHEE DES ALPES

This triumphal monument had a square podium, a circular colonnade and a stepped cone which was surmounted by the statue of Augustus.

**6-m (20-ft) statue of Emperor Augustus**

**The original colonnade** included niches for the statues of Augustus's campaign generals.

**The inscription** records the names of the 44 tribes subjugated by Augustus, with a dedication to the emperor.

# Monaco ❷

**Grimaldi family crest**

If you come to Monaco by car, you may well travel in on the Moyenne Corniche, one of the world's most beautiful coastal highways. Arriving amid the skyscrapers of present-day Monaco, it is hard to imagine its turbulent history, much of it centred on Monaco-Ville. The palace, cathedral and museums are all in this old part of town, set on the Rock, a sheer-sided, flat-topped finger of land extending 792 m (2,600 ft) into the sea. First a Greek and later a Roman colony, it was bought from the Genoese in 1309 by François Grimaldi. In spite of family feuds and at least one political assassination, the Grimaldis, whose crest shows two sword-waving monks, remain the world's oldest ruling monarchy.

**Modern Monaco**
*Lack of space has led to vertical building, and a striking skyline of skyscrapers and apartment blocks.*

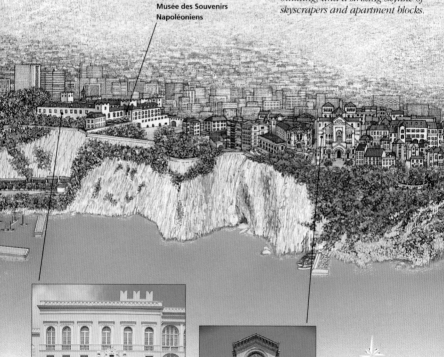

**Musée des Souvenirs Napoléoniens**

**Palais Princier**
*The Grimaldis have ruled from here since the 14th century. The palace dates from the 16th–17th centuries but its towers are Genoese of 1215. The constitution insists it is guarded by French carabiniers. (See p94).*

**Cathédrale**
*This Neo-Romanesque construction in cream-coloured stone sits on a rocky spur. Among its treasures are two early 16th-century screens by Bréa,* La Pietà *and* St-Nicolas. *(See p94).*

### Musée Océanographique

*Erected on a sheer cliff, high above the Mediterranean, it has one of the best aquaria in Europe. It is also used as a scientific research institute. (See p94).*

## VISITORS' CHECKLIST

**Road map** F3. 35,000.
15 km (9 miles) SW Nice.
pl Ste Dévote (08 36 35 35 35)
2a bd des Moulins (00 377 92 16 61 16). daily. Festival du Cirque (Jan); Grand Prix (May); Fête Nationale (19 Nov).
www.visitmonaco.com

### Théâtre du Fort Antoine

*This ancient fort has been converted into a theatre which shows a wide range of productions in summer.*

**Monte Carlo Story** is a multi-visual history in film and photographs, recorded in different languages.

**Typical Old Town Villa**
*Hidden in a labyrinth of passages are fountains, tiny squares and elegant façades.*

### THE ROYAL FAMILY

Monaco was ruled from 1949 by the businesslike Prince Rainier Louis Henri Maxence Bertrand de Grimaldi. He was the 26th ruling prince, a descendant of the Grimaldi who, disguised as a monk, entered the Monaco fortress in 1297. At that time the territory extended to Antibes and Menton. Prince Rainier's wife, the former film star Grace Kelly, whom he married in 1956, died tragically in 1982. Their son, Albert, inherited the $200 million throne on Rainier's death in 2005 but it is his beautiful, sometimes wayward, sisters Stephanie and Caroline who have taken up most media attention in recent years.

**Prince Rainier III and Grace Kelly at their engagement party in 1956**

# Monte-Carlo

**Art Deco entrance, Le Café de Paris**

The dramatic heights of Monte-Carlo are the best-known area of Monaco. People flock to the annual car rally in January and many of the world's greatest singers perform here in the opera season. Monte-Carlo is named after Charles III, who opened the first casino in 1856, to save himself from bankruptcy. Such was his success that in 1883 he abolished taxation. Although Queen Victoria thought Monte-Carlo a den of iniquity, her view was not shared by other aristocrats, including Edward VII, who were regular visitors. The stunning Casino and Opera House were built by Charles Garnier, architect of the Paris Opéra. Between Monaco-Ville and Monte-Carlo lies La Condamine, a shopping and commercial centre surrounding the luxury yachts.

**View of Monte-Carlo**
*It is worth pausing at La Turbie (see p89) to admire the panorama.*

Palais Princier

**Jardin Exotique**
*Plants normally grown in balmy climates flourish here, and its grottoes housed prehistoric animals and humans 200,000 years ago (see p94).*

**La Condamine**
*The quays are pleasant yacht-watching promenades laid out by Albert I. The current prince added a watersports pool, and it is also a popular setting for funfairs.*

**La Turbie**

## VISITORS' CHECKLIST

**Road map** F3. 🚌 *pl Ste Dévote*
ℹ️ *2a bd des Moulins* (00 377
92 16 61 16). **Grimaldi Forum**
*(cultural centre)* **Tel** 00 377 99
99 3000. ⭕ *daily*. 🎪 *Monte-
Carlo Rally (Jan); Festival
International de Feux d'Artifice
(fireworks) (Jul–Aug).* 🚢 *daily.*

### Le Café de Paris
*Ladies' man Edward VII
was a regular visitor to this
renovated Art Deco triumph.
The dessert* crêpe suzette *was
named after one companion.*

**Eglise Ste-Dévote**

**Hôtel Hermitage**

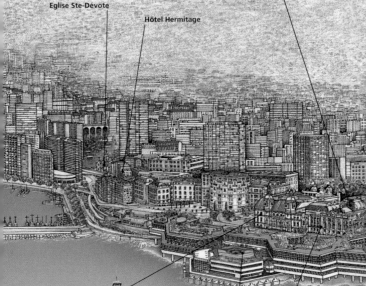

**Centre de Congrès**

### Salle Garnier
*Designed by Charles Garnier
in 1878, this was where ballet
innovators such as Diaghilev
and Nijinksy congregated.*

### Casino
*In a 3-day gambling
spree in 1891, Charles
Deville Wells turned
$400 into $40,000
and inspired the tune,*
The Man Who Broke
the Bank at Monte-
Carlo *(see p94).*

# Exploring Monaco

After the Vatican, Monaco is the world's smallest sovereign state. It covers 1.95 sq km (0.75 sq miles), about half the size of New York City's Central Park. Its inhabitants, 20 per cent Monégasque citizens, pay no taxes and enjoy the world's highest per capita income. Monégasque, a dialect of Provençal, is reflected in street names, such as *piaca* for place, *carrigiu* for rue. But the official language is French, the euro is used here and most of France's laws apply. Monaco's road network is complicated, so drivers should plan routes with care.

**Marine explorer Jacques Cousteau**

**Monaco Grand Prix route**

### ♣ Palais Princier

Pl du Palais. *Tel* 00 377 93 25 18 31. ◯ Apr–Oct: daily. 🖾
Monaco's seat of government is an attractive castle-palace, protected by cannons donated by Louis XIV, and sentries who change daily at 11:55am. The palace, with its priceless furniture and frescoes, is only open in the summer. Concerts are held in the Cour d'Honneur.

### 🏛 Musée des Souvenirs Napoléoniens et Archives Historiques du Palais

Pl du Palais. 📠 00 377 93 25 18 31. ◯ Tue–Sun. ● 1 Jan, 1 May, Grand Prix, Nov, 25 Dec. 🖾 📷
The palace museum combines local history with Napoleonic memorabilia. A large family tree traces links between the Bonapartes and the Grimaldis, while the ground floor is, appropriately to the nature of the man, devoted to Napoleon, with numerous busts of him.

### ♠ Casino

Pl du Casino. *Tel* 00 377 92 16 23 00. ◯ from noon daily. 🖾
www.casino-montecarlo.com
Renovated in 1878 by Charles Garnier *(see p51)*, the casino sits on a terrace with superb

views of Monaco. Its interior is still decorated in Belle Epoque style. Roulette is played in the opulent Salon Europe, blackjack in the Salons Privés. American games are played in the Sun Casino, which is decorated in a circus theme.

### 🏛 Musée National (Poupées et Automates)

17 av Princesse Grace. *Tel* 00 377 93 30 91 26. ◯ daily. ● 1 Jan, Grand Prix, 1 May, 19 Nov, 25 Dec. 🖾 📷
Charles Garnier built this villa, set in a rose garden with sculptures including the *Young Faun* by the Carpeaux School. It has dolls from the 18th–19th centuries. The automata are set in motion daily: some are opened to show their inner workings.

### ⛪ Cathédrale

4 rue Colonel Bellando del Castro. *Tel* 00 377 93 30 87 70. ◯ daily. 🖾
The 12th-century church of St-Nicolas was replaced by this 19th-century Neo-Romanesque building in La Turbie stone. Its old altarpiece, by Louis Bréa, is by the ambulatory, with its tombs of princes and bishops. The much-mourned Princess Grace is buried here.

### 🏛 Musée Océanographique

Av St-Martin. *Tel* 00 377 93 15 36 00. ◯ daily. ● 1 Jan, 25 Dec. 🖾 🖾 📷 🍴 *Cinema*. www.oceano.mc
Founded by Prince Albert I in 1910, this clifftop museum has an aquarium filled with rare marine plants and animals, a collection of shells, coral and pearls, and a life-sized model of a giant squid. Marine explorer Jacques Cousteau was director here for 30 years until 1988. The roof terrace offers a superb coastal view.

### ♣ Jardin Exotique

62 bd du Jardin Exotique. *Tel* 00 377 93 15 29 80. ◯ daily. ● 1 Jan, 19 Nov, 25 Dec. 🖾 📷 🖾 restricted.
These gardens are among the finest in Europe, with a vast range of tropical and sub-tropical plants. Off the gardens is the **Grotte de l'Observatoire**, where prehistoric animals lived 200,000 years ago. The **Musée d'Anthropologie Préhistorique**, accessible via the garden, displays prehistoric tools, figurines and bones.

**Roulette tables in the Salle Europe of the Casino**

*For hotels and restaurants in this region see pp194–7 and pp210–12*

## Peillon  ㉔

**Road map** F3. 🚶 *1,200.* ℹ️ *La Mairie (04 93 79 91 04; pm only).*

At a level of 373 m (1,225 ft), this pretty *village perché* is said by locals to mark the extremity of the inhabited world. Its streets are stepped and narrow, with houses that have scarcely changed since the Middle Ages. There is an attractive cobbled square with fine views, and the 18th-century parish church has an unusual octagonal lantern. But most impressive of all are Giovanni Canavesio's frescoes in the Chapelle des Pénitents Blancs. Peillon is ideally placed for woodland walks leading to both Peille and La Turbie.

The Gorges de la Vésubie in the pine-forested Vallée de la Vésubie

Ancient arch across Peillon street

## Peille ㉕

**Road map** F3. 🚶 *2,000.* 🚌 ℹ️ *La Mairie (04 93 91 71 71).*

Peille is a charming medieval village with a view from its war memorial across the Peillon Valley and as far as the Baie des Anges. Behind the village looms the vast Pic de Baudon, rising to 1,264 m (4,160 ft).

The town is full of cobbled alleys and covered passages. At the end of place A-Laugier, beyond a Gothic fountain, two arches beneath a house rest on a Romanesque pillar.

The Counts of Provence were lords of the castle, and the 12th-century church of Ste-Marie has a picture of Peille in the Middle Ages. There is also a fine 16th-century altarpiece

by Honoré Bertone. The Hôtel de Ville is in the domed 18th-century former Chapelle de St-Sébastien, and there is a museum in rue de la Turbie.

## Lucéram ㉖

**Road map** F3. 🚶 *1,000.* 🚌 ℹ️ *pl Adrien Barralis (04 93 79 46 50).*

In the midst of this pretty, Italianate village is the tiled roof of the 15th-century Eglise Ste-Marguerite, which contains art by Nice's Primitive masters, notably Louis Bréa, the artist of the 10-panelled altarpiece, who made Lucéram a centre for religious painting. Other treasures include a silver statue of the Tarascon dragon and Ste Marguerite *(see p140).* The church is the setting for a Christmas service, where shepherds, accompanied by flutes and tambourines, bring lambs and fruit as offerings.

Italian-style houses in Lucéram, set between two ravines

## Vallée de la Vésubie ㉗

🚶 *Nice.* 🚌 *St-Martin-Vésubie.* ℹ️ *St-Martin-Vésubie (04 93 03 21 28).*

Some of the most attractive landscape around Nice can be uncovered and enjoyed in the valley of the river Vésubie, with its dense pine forests, alpine pastures, peaks and cascades. The river rises high in the snowy Alps near the Italian border, courses past Roquebillière to the west of the Parc National du Mercantour *(see p97)* and dives through the Gorges de la Vésubie before entering the river Var, 24 km (15 miles) north of Nice airport.

The Vésubie is created from the Madone de Fenestre and the Boréon torrents, which meet at St-Martin-Vésubie. This popular summer mountaineering centre is surrounded by waterfalls, summits and lakes. In its fine 17th-century church is a 12th-century statue of Notre-Dame-de-Fenestre. Each year this statue is carried to the Chapelle de la Madone de Fenestre, in a craggy alpine setting, 12 km (8 miles) to the east, for a three-month stay.

The Gorges de la Vésubie begins at St-Jean-la-Rivière, and there is a spectacular panorama at la Madonne d'Utelle, above the fortified village of Utelle. In places, the dramatic gorge, etched with coloured rock, runs up to 244 m (800 ft) deep. Sadly, the road beside it has few stopping places from which to admire the view.

# Skiing in the Alpes d'Azur

Provence offers a wide range of skiing activities in the Alpes d'Azur. Around one hour from the coast, in breathtaking mountain scenery, there are more than 20 resorts, with over 250 ski-runs. The *après-ski* includes ice-skating, riding on a snowmobile and a chance to sample traditional Alpine food such as delicious melted cheese *raclette*. In summer, Auron and Isola 2000, resorts in the Parc National du Mercantour, offer swimming, cycling and horse-riding in dramatically contrasting surroundings to the Côte d'Azur.

Snowbound Valberg, a winter resort since 1935

## AURON

**ALTITUDE** *1,600 m (5,250 ft) – 2,100 m (6,890 ft).*
**LOCATION** *97 km (60 miles) from Nice via RN 202 and D 2205.*
**SKI RUNS** *9 black, 15 red, 16 blue, 2 green.*
**SKI LIFTS** *21 including 9 chair lifts and 3 cable cars.*

## ISOLA 2000

**ALTITUDE** *2,000 m (5,250 ft) – 2,310 m (7,584 ft).*
**LOCATION** *90 km (56 miles) from Nice via RN 202, D 2205 and D 97.*
**SKI RUNS** *4 black, 11 red, 22 blue, 9 green.*
**SKI LIFTS** *22 including 2 cable cars and 9 chairlifts. Funicular railway.*

## VALBERG

**ALTITUDE** *1,430 m (4,690 ft) – 2,100 m (6,890 ft).*
**LOCATION** *86 km (51 miles) from Nice via RN 202, CD 28, CD 202 or CD 30.*
**SKI RUNS** *4 black, 30 red, 15 blue, 9 green.*
**SKI LIFTS** *26 including 6 chair lifts.*

Climbing a frozen waterfall, or frozen fall climbing, in one of the many alpine resorts

Getting ready for a few hours of snow-shoe trekking

| Auron | Isola 2000 | Valberg | ALPINE ACTIVITIES |
|---|---|---|---|
| • | • | • | Cross-country skiing |
|   | • |   | Disabled skiing |
|   |   | • | Horse riding |
| • |   | • | Horse-driven buggy rides |
|   | • |   | Ice circuit driving |
| • | • | • | Ice skating |
|   | • |   | Kart Cross on ice |
|   | • | • | Mono-skiing |
|   | • |   | Night skiing |
|   | • |   | Ski-jo-ring |
|   | • |   | Ski jumping |
| • | • | • | Ski school |
| • |   | • | Ski touring |
| • | • | • | Snowboarding |
|   | • |   | Snow scooter circuits |
| • | • | • | Snow-shoe trekking |
|   | • |   | Speed ski school |
| • | • |   | Aquatic centre (17 km), sauna and jacuzzi |

Snowboarding in the alpine resort of Isola 2000

## Forêt de Turini 28

🚉 l'Escarène, Sospel. 🚌 Moulinet, Sospel. 🛈 La Bollène (04 93 03 60 54).

Between the warm coast and the chilly Alps, from the Gorges de la Vésubie to the Vallée de la Bévéra, lies this humid, 3,497-sq km (1,350-sq mile) forest. Beech, maple and sweet chestnut thrive here, and pines grow to great heights.

At the forest's northeastern edge is the 1,889-m (6,197-ft) mountain of l'Authion, site of heavy fighting in the German retreat of 1945. Casualties are recorded on a war memorial.

The neighbouring Pointe des Trois-Communes, at 2,082 m (6,830 ft), offers superb views of the pre-Alps of Nice and the peaks of the Mercantour national park.

## Le Parc National du Mercantour 29

**Road map** E2 & F2. 🚉 Nice. 🚌 St Etienne de Tinée, Auron. 🛈 Maison du Parc (04 93 04 73 71). www.parc-mercantour.fr

Scoured by icy glaciers and bristling with rocky summits, this sparsely populated park covers 70,000 ha (270 sq miles). Among its unusual wildlife are the chamois, the ibex and the *mouflon*, a sheep which originated in Corsica. Sometimes visible in the mornings is the marmot, a rodent which is prey to golden eagles, and the exotic lammergeier, a bearded vulture with orange-red feathers and black wings. There are also many brightly coloured butterflies and alpine flowers.

**Tower at Tende**

## Tende 30

**Road map** F2. 🏠 2,200. 🚉 🛈 av du 16 Sep 1947 (04 93 04 73 71). 🚌 Wed. www.tendemerveilles.com

Sombre Tende once guarded the mountain pass connecting Piedmont and Provence, now bypassed by a tunnel. Its tall, balconied, green schist buildings appear piled on top of each other. Only a wall

A street scene in the old border town of Tende

remains of the castle of Lascaris' feudal lords, near the terraced cemetery above the town. Tende's unusual towers include that of the 15th-century church of **Notre-Dame-de-l'Assomption**. Lions support the pillars around the Renaissance doorway and there are green schist columns inside.

The **Vallée des Merveilles**, the most spectacular part of Mercantour national park, can be visited with a guide. For information, contact the tourist office at Tende or St-Dalmas. The most direct route is from Lac des Mesches. A two-hour walk leads to Lac Long and Le Refuge des Merveilles. The Mont Bégo area has 36,000 engravings, dating from 2,000 BC, carved into the rock face. They reveal a Bronze Age culture of shepherds and farmers. In Tende, the **Musée des Merveilles** is worth a visit.

Southeast of Tende, there are fine paintings in the church at La Brigue. Jean Canavasio's 15th-century frescoes of *La Passion du Christ*, and the lurid *Judas pendu* are in the nearby 13th-century **Chapelle Notre-Dame-des-Fontaines**.

🏛 **Musée des Merveilles**
Av du 16 Septembre 1947 **Tel** 04 93 04 32 50. 🕐 daily (Oct–Jun: Wed–Mon). 🔴 public hols, 2 wks mid-Mar & mid-Nov. 🚻 📷

## Saorge 31

**Road map** F3. 🏠 400. 🚉 🛈 La Mairie (04 93 04 51 23).

Saorge is the prettiest spot in the Roya Valley. Set in a natural amphitheatre high over the river, its slate-roofed houses are tiered between narrow alleys, in the style of a typical stacked village or *village empilé*.

Olive-wood carvings are traditional, and carved lintels date many houses to the 15th century, when Saorge was a stronghold. It was taken by the French under Masséna in 1794.

Churches range from the dank 15th-century St-Sauveur with an Italian organ to the Baroque church of the Franciscan monastery and the octagonal tower and Renaissance frescoes of **La Madone-del-Poggio** (appointment only).

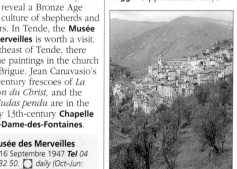

View of Saorge from the Franciscan monastery terrace

## Sospel ❷

**Road map** F3. 🚶 *2,600.* 🚉 🚌 🛈
*19 av Jean Medecin (04 93 04 15 80).*
🛒 *Thu.* **www**.sospel-tourisme.com

This charming resort has a
13th-century toll tower, which
was restored after Sospel was
badly damaged by bombs in
World War II, when the bravery
of the town's citizens earned
it the Croix de Guerre. Fort St-
Roch, built in 1932 as protection against a possible Italian
invasion, has a museum with
exhibits on the Maginot line.
The church of St-Michel contains one of François Bréa's
best works, and has a lovely
façade, as does the Palais Ricci.
The interior of the White
Penitent chapel is magnificent.

**🏛 Musée de la Ligne
Maginot des Alpes**
Fort St-Roch. **Tel** 04 93 04 00 70.
⏱ Jun–Sep: Tue–Sun pm; Apr, May,
Oct: Sat, Sun & public hols pm. 🖼

**Trompe l'oeil** houses in Sospel

## Gorbio ❸

**Road map** F3. 🚶 *1,160.* 🚉
🛈 La Mairie, 30 rue Garibaldi
(04 92 10 66 50).

More than a thousand species
of flowers have been
identified in the sunny Gorbio
valley, which produces
vegetables and fruit, wine and
oil. Until the last century the
area was entirely supported
by its olive production.
Often shrouded in mist in
the mornings, Gorbio itself
is a *village perché (see pp20–
21)*, with sea views. The old
Malaussène fountain stands
by the entrance to the narrow
cobbled lanes, and an elm tree

**Early morning Gorbio, surrounded by olive groves**

in the square was planted in
1713. The church has a conical
belfry, a typical feature of the
region. Each June a procession
marks the Penitents' ritual,
when the village lanes twinkle
with the lights from oil lamps
made from snail shells.
A good hour's walk from
Gorbio is Ste-Agnès, at 671 m
(2,200 ft) it is the highest
*village perché* on the coast.

## Roquebrune-Cap-Martin ❹

**Road map** F3. 🚶 *12,400.* 🚉 🚌
🛈 *218 av Aristide Briand (04 93 35
62 87).* 🛒 *Wed.* **www**.roquebrune-
cap-martin.com

Roquebrune is said to have
the earliest feudal **château** in
France, the sole example of
the Carolingian style. Built in
the 10th century by Conrad I,
Count of Ventimiglia, to ward
off Saracen attack, it was later
remodelled by the Grimaldis

**View of Château de Roquebrune,
overlooking Cap Martin**

*(see p91).* Wealthy Englishman
Sir William Ingram, one of the
first wave of tourist residents,
bought the château in 1911
and added a mock medieval
*tour anglaise.*
At the turn of the century,
Cap Martin was the smartest
resort on the Côte d'Azur,
attracting the era's glitterati.
Empératrice Eugénie, wife of
Napoléon III, and England's
Queen Victoria wintered here.
Winston Churchill, Coco
Chanel and Irish poet WB
Yeats also visited. Architect
Le Corbusier, who drowned
off the cape in 1965, has a
coastal path named after him.
A number of important prehistoric remains have been
found around Roquebrune,
some in caves such as the
**Grottes du Vallonet**. Just outside the village, on the Menton
road, is the *olivier millénaire,*
one of the oldest olive trees in
the world, which is believed
to be at least 1,000 years old.
Every August since 1467,
in gratitude for being spared
from the plague, Roquebrune's
inhabitants take part in scenes
from the Passion *(see p33).*

**⛪ Château de Roquebrune**
**Tel** 04 93 35 07 22. ⏱ daily. 🖼

## Menton ❺

**Road map** F3. 🚶 *30,000.* 🚉
🚌 🛈 Palais de l'Europe, 8 av Boyer
(04 92 41 76 76). 🛒 daily.
**www**.menton.fr

Just a mile from the border,
Menton is the most Italian of
the French resorts. Tucked in
by mountains, it is a sedate

town with a Baroque square and a promenade stretching towards Cap Martin.

Menton has several fine tropical gardens, and citrus fruits thrive in a climate mild enough for the lemon festival in February *(see p35)*. The **Palais de l'Europe** of the Belle Epoque (1909), once a casino, now a cultural centre, is beside the **Jardin Biovès**. The **Jardin Botanique Exotique** has tropical plants and is in the grounds of Villa Val Rahmeh. Above the town is the **Jardin des Colombières** designed by artist and writer Ferdinand Bac (1859–1952). This private garden reputedly has France's oldest carob tree.

The jetties offer good views of the old town, and steps lead to Parvis St-Michel, a fine square paved with the Grimaldi coat of arms, where summer concerts are held. To the left side are the twin towers of the Baroque **Basilica St-Michel**, its main altarpiece by Manchello (1565). Behind the new marina is the suburb of Garavan where the tubercular New Zealand writer Katherine Mansfield lived, in the Villa Isola Bella, from 1920–22.

### ⛫ Musée des Beaux-Arts

Palais Carnolès, 3 av de la Madone. ***Tel*** *04 93 35 49 71.* ☐ *Wed–Mon.* ⬤ *public hols.* ⬛
The 17th-century palace, now Menton's main art museum, was once summer residence of

### JEAN COCTEAU (1889–1963)

Born near Paris in 1889, Cocteau spent much of his very public life around the Côte d'Azur. A man of powerful intellect and great *élan*, he became a member of the Académie Française in 1955. Among other talents, Cocteau was a dramatist (*La Machine Infernale, 1934*); the writer of *Les Enfants Terribles* (1929), and a surrealist film director. *Orphée* (1950) was partly shot against the barren landscape at Les Baux *(see p142)*. He died before his museum opened in 1967.

**Mosaic at the entrance of the Musée Jean Cocteau in Menton**

the princes of Monaco. It has paintings by Graham Sutherland (1903–80), an honorary citizen, 13th- to 18th-century Italian, French and Flemish art, and works by Utrillo and Dufy.

### ♛ Salle des Mariages

17 rue de la République. ***Tel*** *04 92 10 50 29.* ☐ *Mon–Fri.* ⬤ *public hols.* ⬛
Jean Cocteau decorated this room in 1957 with colourful images of a fisherman and his bride, and the less happy story of Orpheus and Eurydice, and Provençal motifs such as using a fish for a fisherman's eye.

### ⛫ Musée Jean Cocteau

Vieux Port. ***Tel*** *04 93 57 72 30.* ☐ *Wed–Mon.* ⬤ *public hols.* ⬛
Cocteau supervised the conversion of this former 17th-

century fort into his museum. He designed the salamander mosaic on the ground floor, and donated his first tapestry, set designs and drawings.

### ⛫ Cimetière du Vieux-Château

Each terrace of this former castle site accommodates a separate faith. Webb Ellis, inventor of rugby, is buried here, as is Rasputin's assassin, Prince Youssoupov.

### ⛫ Musée de Préhistoire Régionale

Rue Loredan Larchey. ***Tel*** *04 93 35 84 64.* ☐ *Wed–Mon.* ⬤ *public hols.*
The museum's fine local history and archaeological pieces include the skull of 30,000-year-old "Grimaldi Man".

**View over Menton from Ferdinand Bac's Jardin des Colombières**

# THE VAR AND THE ILES D'HYÈRES

*T**he Var is a region of rolling lands, rocky hills, thick forests and swathes of vineyards. To the north, Provençal villages are thinly scattered by mountain streams, on hilltops and in valleys; to the south, a series of massifs slope down to the coast making this stretch of the Côte d'Azur the most varied and delightful shore in France.*

Through the centre of the Var, dividing it roughly into two sections, runs the A8 autoroute. To the south of this artery the influence of the sea is unmistakable. Toulon, the departmental capital, occupies a fine deep-water harbour that is home to the French Mediterranean fleet. Beyond it are the pleasant resorts of Bandol and Sanary, where Jacques Cousteau first put scuba-diving to the test. To the east are the sandy beaches beneath the great slab of the Massif des Maures. The Var's most famous resort, St-Tropez, facing north in the crook of a bay, lies in a glorious landscape of vineyards. Beyond it, just past Fréjus, the first Roman settlement in Gaul, the land turns blood red in the twinkling inlets and coves below the beautiful Corniche de l'Esterel, which heads east towards the Riviera. The more remote areas to the north of the autoroute have always provided a retreat from the bustling activity of the coast. This is where the Cistercians built their austere Abbaye du Thoronet. Today visitors escape inland from the summer traffic around St-Tropez to the sparsely populated Haut Var, where towns seem to grow from tufa rock.

Highlights include wines from the Côtes de Provence, and fresh tuna from quayside restaurants. Music enthusiasts should spare time to hear both the organ at St-Maximin-la-Ste-Baume, Provence's finest Gothic building, and the string quartets at the festival in the hill towns near Fayence. Visitors can also go walking, sailing and sunbathing, and enjoy a rich collection of museums and architecture.

Sunrise over the boats in St-Tropez harbour

◁ A traditional shop in the centre of Cotignac in the Haut Var

# Exploring the Var and the Iles d'Hyères

The Var Departement covers about 6,000 sq km (2,300 sq miles). It combines a stunning coastline sprinkled with red cliffs, delightful bays and the Iles d'Hyères, which spill out from its southernmost point, with dramatic chains of hills behind the coast and further inland. Although the hills have been partly depleted by forest fires, they are still home to a fascinating array of flora and fauna as well as to the many producers of Côtes-de-Provence wines.

### SEE ALSO
- **Where to Stay** pp197–9
- **Where to Eat** p213

**View of the Abbaye du Thoronet**

## SIGHTS AT A GLANCE

Abbaye du Thoronet ❿
Bandol ⓮
Bargemon ❻
Barjols ❶
Bormes-les-Mimosas ⓴
Brignoles ⓬
Comps-sur-Artuby ❸
Draguignan ❼
Fayence ❺
Fréjus ㉙
Grimaud ㉕
Haut Var ❷
Hyères ⓲
*Iles d'Hyères pp114–15* ⓱
Le Lavandou ⓳
Les Arcs ❽
Lorgues ❾
Massif de l'Esterel ㉘
Mons ❹
Port-Grimaud ㉔

Ramatuelle ㉒
Ste-Maxime ㉖
*St-Maximin-la-Ste-Baume pp110–11* ⓭
St-Raphaël ㉗
*St-Tropez pp118–22* ㉓
Sanary-sur-Mer ⓯
*Toulon pp112–13* ⓰

**Tours**
Côtes de Provence ⓫
Massif des Maures ㉑

## KEY

| | |
|---|---|
| ═══ | Motorway |
| ══ | Major road |
| ── | Secondary road |
| ┈┈ | Minor road |
| ── | Scenic route |
| ┄─ | Main railway |
| ── | Minor railway |
| ═══ | Regional border |
| △ | Summit |

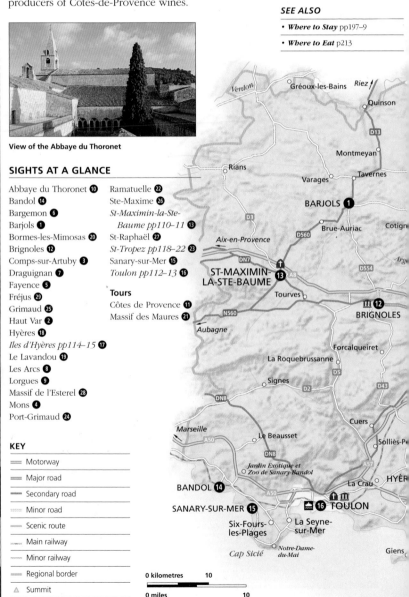

Verdon
Gréoux-les-Bains  Riez
Quinson
D13
Montmeyan
Rians
Varages  Tavernes
BARJOLS ❶
D3
Brue-Auriac  Cotign
D560
Aix-en-Provence
DN7  D554
ST-MAXIMIN-  A8  Arg
LA-STE-BAUME ⓭
Tourves
N560  ⓬
Aubagne  BRIGNOLES
Forcalqueiret
La Roquebrussanne
Signes  D5
D2  D43
DN8
Cuers
Marseille
A50  Le Beausset  Solliès-P
DN8
Jardin Exotique et  A57
Zoo de Sanary-Bandol
La Crau  HYÈR
BANDOL ⓮  A50
SANARY-SUR-MER ⓯  ⓰ TOULON
Six-Fours-  La Seyne-
les-Plages  sur-Mer
Notre-Dame-  Giens
Cap Sicié  du-Mai

0 kilometres   10

0 miles   10

Les Issambres beach, north of Ste-Maxime

## GETTING AROUND

The uplands of the Maures and Esterel force the A8 auto-route and DN7 national road inland, leaving the coast to the more scenic routes: the Corniche d'Or in the Massif de l'Esterel is thought to be France's loveliest. The combination of stunning views and tight bends means that you should allow plenty of time for your journey. The unspoiled Haut Var is easy to get to by car. Alternatively, the railway reaches as far as Draguignan, from where you can explore the region by bus. Comps-sur-Artuby is a good tour base for the Gorges du Verdon (see pp184–5).

A narrow street in St-Tropez old town

A traditional flute-maker at work in Barjols

# Barjols ❶

**Road map** D4. 👥 *2,150.* 🚌
ℹ️ *bd Grisolle (04 94 77 20 01).*
🅿️ *Sat.* **www.**ville-barjols.fr

Once renowned for its seething tanneries, Barjols lies peacefully among woods and fast-flowing streams. In 1983, after almost 400 years, the leather industry finally folded. The many abandoned factories have now become bustling artisans' studios.

Today, it is these local craftsmen who bring manufacturing acclaim to the area. Two traditional Provençal instruments, the three-holed flute (*galoubet*) and the narrow drums (*tambourins*), were still made in Barjols until recently.

The *Champignon* fountain in Barjols

These instruments resound each January at the annual *fête* of St-Marcel, the town's patron saint. About every four years the ceremony includes the slaughter and roasting of an ox in the square. This is followed by a colourful "tripe dance" inside and outside the 11th-century church of Notre-Dame-de-l'Assomption, where St-Marcel's relics can be seen. The ceremony commemorates the survival of the town after a siege in 1350. For roastings contact the tourist office.

Of the many stone fountains dotted around the town, the most famous is the mossy *Champignon* in place Capitaine Vincens. It stands under what is reputed to be the largest plane tree in Provence.

Between the church and the old tanneries are the restored buildings of the old quartier du Réal. Exotic porticoes, particularly on the Renaissance Hôtel de Pontevès, add spice to some otherwise drab streets.

# Haut Var ❷

✈️ *Toulon-Hyères, Nice.* 🚉 *Les Arcs.*
🚌 *Aups.* ℹ️ *Aups (04 94 84 00 69).*
**www.**aups-tourisme.com

The most remote and unspoiled lands of the Var are situated between Barjols and Comps-sur-Artuby, up towards the Gorges du Verdon (*see pp184–5*). Much of the land near here has been taken over by the military.

Aups, set among undulating hills on the plateau edge, is the region's centre. Epicureans may be drawn by the local honey and the truffle market each Thursday in winter. It is an attractive town with a grand old square and castle ruins. The 15th-century St-Pancrace church has a Renaissance doorway. Also worth a visit is the **Musée Simon Segal**, which is housed in a former Ursuline convent. The museum contains works by Segal and Paris painters, as well as local scenes.

About 5 km (3 miles) northwest on the D9 is the village of Moissac-Bellevue. Many of its buildings date from the 16th and 17th centuries and its church was mentioned in a papal edict of 1225.

South from Aups is Villecroze. The town is set against a natural backdrop of caves on two levels, which local lords in the 16th century turned into dwellings, known as the **Grottes Troglodytes**. The arcaded streets and the keep of the feudal castle give the town a medieval flavour. A short drive from Villecroze leads up to the hill village of Tourtour, a smaller, prettier and more popular place.

View of Entrecasteaux château near Cotignac, Haut Var

From Tourtour there are fine views of Montagne Ste-Victoire, which was one of Cézanne's favourite painting subjects.

The valley town of Salernes lies in the opposite direction, 10 km (6 miles) west on the D51. Smoke pumps from the kilns of its 15 ceramic factories.

Troglodyte dwellings in Villecroze

The 110 m (361 ft) Artuby bridge spanning the Canyon du Verdon

Salernes is one of the best-known Provençal tile-making centres, noted for *tomettes* – hexagonal terracotta floor-tiles.

Cotignac, west of Salernes, is an echo of Villecroze, with a cave-pocked cliff behind it. Behind the *mairie*, a river springs from the rocks and beyond is an open-air theatre.

The region's most intriguing château is **Entrecasteaux**, 15 km (8 miles) east of Cotignac. The 17th-century castle is filled with the present owner's 17th- to 18th-century collection of paintings, artifacts, tapestries and furniture. The garden, by Le Nôtre, is publicly owned.

🏛 **Musée Simon Segal**
Rue Albert Premier, Aups. *Tel* 04 94 70 01 95. ☐ Jul, Aug: Wed–Mon.

🏚 **Grottes Troglodytes**
Villecroze. *Tel* 04 94 70 63 06.
☐ Feb & Easter hols, May–Jun: Sat, Sun; Jul–mid-Sep: daily; mid-Sep–mid-Oct: Sat–Sun pm. ● Nov–Easter. 🗎

🏚 **Château d'Entrecasteaux**
83570 Entrecasteaux.
*Tel* 04 94 04 43 95. ☐ Sun–Fri.
● mid-Nov–Easter. 🗎 🗎

# Comps-sur-Artuby ❸

**Road map** D3. 🚶 *320.* 🚌
ℹ La Mairie (04 94 50 24 00).

The eastern approach to the Gorges du Verdon (*see pp184–5*) passes through Comps-sur-Artuby. The village nestles at the foot of a rock topped by the 13th-century chapel of **St-André**, which was restored recently. From the church there are grand views of the Artuby Gorges.

To the east lies Bargème, a village of steep streets and hollyhocks with a population of just 86. At 1,094 m (3,589 ft) it is the highest community in the Var. The village itself is closed to all traffic.

Dominating Bargème is a large, partially ruined but nevertheless remarkably well preserved 14th-century castle. Also worth a visit is the 13th-century Romanesque **Eglise St-Nicolas** which contains a carved, wooden altarpiece depicting Saint Sebastian.

# Mons ❹

**Road map** E3. 🚶 *720.* 🚌
ℹ pl St Sébastien (04 94 76 39 54).

Dramatically situated on a rock-spur, Mons, with its tiny lanes and overhanging arches, has an almost magical appeal. The place St-Sébastien looks out across the entire coast, from Italy to Toulon.

Originally a Celtic-Ligurian settlement, its Château-Vieux quarter dates from the 10th century, but it was mainly built by Genoese who repopulated the village after ravages by the plague in the 14th century. The first families came in 1461 from Figounia near Ventimiglia; their legacy is the local dialect, *figoun*, which still survives thanks to the unusually isolated position of the village. Nearby is the *roche taillée*, a Roman aqueduct carved from solid rock. There are also many dolmens in the surrounding area.

The Roman-built *roche taillée* aqueduct near Mons

---

## TRUFFLES

This richly flavoured and treasured fungal delicacy of the Var is traditionally sniffed out by trained pigs. The golfball-sized truffles are collected during the winter, when they are at their most fragrant, from underground near the roots of oak trees. Local markets specialize in truffles when they are in season, though their rarity means that they tend to be very expensive.

**A trained pig hunting for truffles**

**View over Bargemon's terracotta rooftops to the wooded hills beyond**

## Fayence ❺

**Road map** E3. 🏠 *4,300.* 🚗 ℹ️ *pl Léon Roux (04 94 76 20 08).* 🚌 *Tue, Thu & Sat.* **www**.*paysdefayence.com*

The hillside town of Fayence is the largest one between Draguignan and Grasse and is a centre for both local crafts and gliding. Dominated by a wrought-iron clock tower, it still has a few remains of its 14th-century defences including a Saracen-style gate.

The **Eglise St-Jean-Baptiste** was built in the 18th century with a baroque marble altar (1757) by a local mason, Dominique Fossatti. Its terrace offers a sweeping view over the town's glider airfield.

On the hillside opposite, in the community of Tourettes,

there is a striking château. Part modelled on the Cadet school in St Petersburg, it was constructed in 1824 for General Alexandre Fabre, who once worked as a military engineer for Tsar Alexander I of Russia. He originally intended to make the building a public museum, but failed to finish the task and so it remains private.

There are a number of attractive villages nearby. Among the best are Callian and Montauroux to the east and Seillans, 5 km (3 miles) to the west, where the German-born painter Max Ernst (1891–1976) chose to spend his last years. The prestigious Musique en Pays de Fayence festival in October brings string quartets who perform in some of the charming local churches.

## Bargemon ❻

**Road map** E3. 🏠 *1,500.* 🚉 *Les Arcs.* 🚗 ℹ️ *av Pasteur (04 94 47 81 73).* 🚌 *Thu.* **www**.*ot-bargemon.fr*

This medieval village, fortified in AD 950, has three 12th-century gates and a tower from the mid-16th-century. The village is laid out around a number of squares with fountains, shaded by plane trees.

The angels' heads on the high altar of the 15th-century church, **St-Etienne**, now the Musée-Galerie Honoré Camos, are attributed to the school of Pierre Puget, like those in the **Chapelle Notre-Dame-de-Montaigu** above the town. The chapel also contains an oak-wood carving of the Virgin brought here in 1635. The **Fossil and Mineral Museum** on place de la Mairie opened in 2004.

## Draguignan ❼

**Road map** D4. 🏠 *35,000.* 🚗 ℹ️ *2 ave Lazare Carnot (04 98 10 51 05).* 🚌 *Wed, Sat.* **www**.*dracenie.com*

During the day, the former capital of the Var *département* has the busy air of a small market town. At night, however, the only sign of life is groups of young people in the place des Herbes. Baron Haussmann, planner of modern

---

### TRADITIONAL POTTERY AND CRAFTS

Fayence, Cotignac, Aups and Salernes are at the centre of an exciting revitalization of Provençal crafts, which includes weaving, pottery, stone and wood carving. A regional speciality is hand-crafted domestic pottery made using traditional techniques and designs, as well as local clays in a wonderful variety of colours. Examples of all these crafts can be found in small shops and studios, or craft fairs and local markets. There are good buys to be had, but do shop around to avoid being unknowingly overcharged.

**A Provençal potter at work**

---

Paris, laid out Draguignan's 19th-century boulevards. At the end of his plane-tree-lined allées d'Azémar, there is a Rodin bust of the prime minister Georges Clemenceau (1841–1929) who represented Draguignan for 25 years.

The main interest lies in the pedestrianized old town. Its 24-m (79-ft) clockless clock tower, built in 1663, stands on the site of the original keep and there is a good view from its wrought-iron campanile. The **Eglise St-Michel**, in the place de la Paroisse, contains a statue of St Hermentaire, first bishop of Antibes. In the 5th century he slew a local dragon, hence giving the town its name.

Draguignan has two good local museums. The **Musée des Traditions Provençales** is concerned with the region's social and economic history. It occupies buildings that date back to the 17th century. Regional country life is illustrated using reconstructed kitchens and barns. Exhibits include beautiful hand-painted wooden horses.

**St Hermentaire slaying the dragon**

The **Musée Municipal** shows local and regional archaeology as well as eye-catching collections of both ceramics and furniture. The adjoining library houses a lavishly illuminated 14th-century manuscript of the *Roman de la Rose*, considered to be the most important book of courtly love *(see p142)* in France (by appointment only).

Northwest of the town on the D955 is the enormous prehistoric dolmen Pierre de la Fée, or Fairy Stone *(see p39)*.

🏛 **Musée des Traditions Provençales**
15 rue Joseph-Roumanille. *Tel* 04 94 47 05 72. ☐ Tue–Sat, Sun pm. ⬤ 1 May, 25 Dec. 🅿 🚻 ♿ ltd.

🏛 **Musée Municipal**
9 rue de la République. *Tel* 04 98 10 26 85. ☐ Mon–Sat. ⬤ public hols. ♿

**Pierre de la Fée, the giant dolmen outside Draguignan**

## Les Arcs ⑧

**Road map** D4. 🏘 *6,400.* 🚉 🚌
ℹ *place du Général de Gaulle (04 94 73 37 30).* 🛒 *Thu.*

Wine centre for the Côtes de Provence *(see p109)*, Les Arcs has a medieval quarter, Le Parage, based around the 13th-century Château de Villeneuve. The **Eglise St-Jean-Baptiste** (1850), in the rue de la République, contains a screen by Louis Bréa (1501) and a mechanical crib.

East of Les Arcs on the D91 is the 11th-century Abbaye de Ste-Roseline, which was named after Roseline de Ville-neuve, daughter of the hard-hearted Arnaud de Villeneuve, Baron of Arcs. Legend has it that when Roseline's father stopped her while taking food to the poor, her provisions turned miraculously into roses. She entered the abbey in 1300 and later became its abbess.

The Romanesque **Chapelle Ste-Roseline** contains the well-preserved body of the saint in a glass shrine. There is also an abundance of Renaissance and Baroque detail, and a famous Chagall mosaic *(see p27)*.

🔒 **Chapelle Ste-Roseline**
Les Arcs-sur-Argens. *Tel* 04 94 99 50 30. ☐ Tue–Sun pm. ⬤ public hols. ♿ **www**.sainte-roseline.com

**Mosaic by Marc Chagall (1887–1985) in the Chapelle Ste-Roseline**

## Lorgues 9

**Road map** D4. 🏠 10,000. 🚉 ℹ️
pl Trussy (04 94 73 92 37). 🅿️ Tue.

Nestling on a slope beneath oak and pine woodland, Lorgues is surrounded by vineyards and olive groves. Its old town was fortified in the 12th century. Today, two 14th-century gates and city wall remains can be seen. The town centre's handsome square is shaded by a large plane tree. Lorgues has a grand array of 18th-century municipal buildings and monuments and one of the longest plane-tree avenues in France.

In the centre of town is the stately **Collégiale St-Martin**, consecrated in 1788. Its organ, dating from 1857, is the finest example of the work of the Augustin Zeiger factory, Lyon. Also on display is a marble Virgin and Child (1694) which came from the Abbaye du Thoronet and is attributed to the school of Pierre Puget.

## Abbaye du Thoronet 10

**Road map** D4. 83340 Le Thoronet.
**Tel** 04 94 60 43 90. ◯ daily. ● 1 Jan, 1 May, 1 & 11 Nov, 25 Dec.
♿ ▦ ◻ ▯

Founded in 1146, Le Thoronet was the first Cistercian building in Provence. Lost in deep woodland, it occupies a

**Graceful cloisters on the north side of the Abbaye du Thoronet**

typically remote site. Along with the two Romanesque abbeys of Sénanque (see p164) and Silvacane (see p147), it is known as one of the three "Cistercian sisters" of Provence.

The cool geometry of the church, cloister, dormitory and chapter house reflects the austerity of Cistercian principles. Only the belltower breaks with the order's strict building regulations: instead of wood, it is made of stone, to enable it to withstand the strong Provençal winds.

Dilapidated by the 1400s, the abbey was finally abandoned in 1791. Its restoration, like that of many medieval Provençal buildings, was instigated by Prosper Mérimée, Romantic novelist and Napoleon III's Inspector of Historic Monuments, who visited in 1834.

Just beside the abbey is the modern Monastère de Bethléem, home to some 20 silent Cistercian nuns whose handicrafts are on sale in a shop.

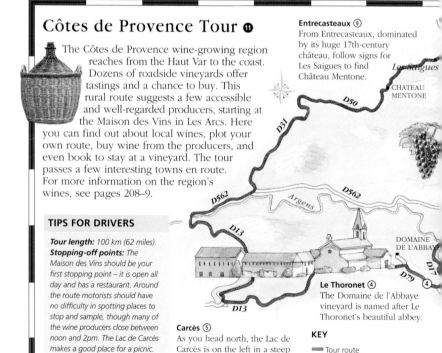

## Côtes de Provence Tour 11

The Côtes de Provence wine-growing region reaches from the Haut Var to the coast. Dozens of roadside vineyards offer tastings and a chance to buy. This rural route suggests a few accessible and well-regarded producers, starting at the Maison des Vins in Les Arcs. Here you can find out about local wines, plot your own route, buy wine from the producers, and even book to stay at a vineyard. The tour passes a few interesting towns en route. For more information on the region's wines, see pages 208–9.

### TIPS FOR DRIVERS

**Tour length:** 100 km (62 miles).
**Stopping-off points:** The Maison des Vins should be your first stopping point – it is open all day and has a restaurant. Around the route motorists should have no difficulty in spotting places to stop and sample, though many of the wine producers close between noon and 2pm. The Lac de Carcès makes a good place for a picnic. (See also pp250–51.)

**Entrecasteaux** ⑥
From Entrecasteaux, dominated by its huge 17th-century château, follow signs for Les Saigues to find Château Mentone.

Les Saigues

CHATEAU MENTONE

D50

D31

D562

Argens

D562

D13

DOMAINE DE L'ABBAY

D79

4

D17

**Le Thoronet** ④
The Domaine de l'Abbaye vineyard is named after Le Thoronet's beautiful abbey.

**Carcès** ⑤
As you head north, the Lac de Carcès is on the left in a steep valley. The town's castle remains and gardens are worth seeing.

D13

### KEY

▬▬ Tour route

— Other roads

La Gayole sarcophagus, dating from the 2nd or 3rd century, in the Musée du Pays Brignolais

# Brignoles ⑫

**Road map** D4. 15,000. Maison du Tourisme, Carrefour de l'Europe (04 94 72 04 21). Wed, Sat. www.provenceverte.fr

Bauxite mines have stained the Brignoles countryside red: vital to the region's economy, over a million tonnes of metal are mined here annually. The medieval town remains above it all, quiet and empty for most of the year. An unexpected delight is the **Musée du Pays Brignolais** in a 12th-century castle that was built as a summer retreat for the Counts of Provence. The eclectic collection includes La Gayole marble sarcophagus, which is carved with images in both the pagan and Christian traditions; a boat made of cement designed by J Lambot (1814–87), who gave the world reinforced concrete; and a collection of votive offerings. St Louis, bishop of Toulouse and patron of Brignoles, was born in a palace beside the Eglise St-Sauveur in 1274. The church has a 12th-century portico and a side entrance in the rue du Grand Escalier.

**Ⅲ Musée du Pays Brignolais**
2 place des Comtes de Provence. **Tel** 04 94 69 45 18. Wed–Sun. 1 Jan, Easter, 1 May, 1 Nov, 25 Dec.

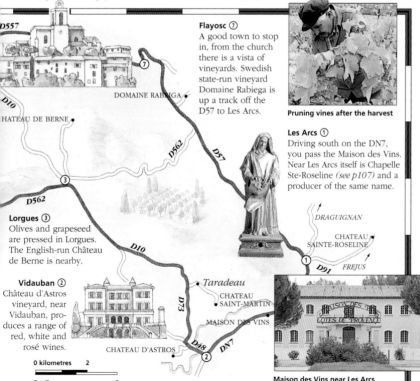

**Flayosc ⑦**
A good town to stop in, from the church there is a vista of vineyards. Swedish state-run vineyard Domaine Rabiega is up a track off the D57 to Les Arcs.

Pruning vines after the harvest

**Les Arcs ①**
Driving south on the DN7, you pass the Maison des Vins. Near Les Arcs itself is Chapelle Ste-Roseline (see p107) and a producer of the same name.

**Lorgues ③**
Olives and grapeseed are pressed in Lorgues. The English-run Château de Berne is nearby.

**Vidauban ②**
Château d'Astros vineyard, near Vidauban, produces a range of red, white and rosé wines.

D557

DOMAINE RABIEGA

HATEAU DE BERNE

DRAGUIGNAN

CHATEAU SAINTE-ROSELINE

FREJUS

Taradeau

CHATEAU SAINT-MARTIN

MAISON DES VINS

CHATEAU D'ASTROS

0 kilometres 2

0 miles 2

Maison des Vins near Les Arcs

# St-Maximin-la-Ste-Baume ⑬

Surrounded by hills and vineyards, St-Maximin-la-Ste-Baume is dominated by the basilica Ste-Marie-Madeleine and its attached monastery. According to legend, the basilica was built on the site of the tombs of St Mary Magdalene and of St Maximin, martyred first bishop of Aix *(see pp148–9)*. The saints' remains, hidden from the Saracens *(see pp42–3)*, were rediscovered in 1279. The building, started 16 years later by Charles II, Count of Provence, is the region's finest example of Gothic architecture.

**Sarcophagus of St Cedonius**
*This is one of four 4th-century saints' sarcophagi in the crypt, which was once the burial vault of a Roman villa.*

**★ Relics of St Mary Magdalene**
*This bronze gilt reliquary (1860) holds the skull of St Mary Magdalene. Pilgrim popes and princes took away other parts of her body.*

**Stairs to crypt**

**The apse**
was completed in the early 14th century; a staircase tower has become the belfry.

**★ Ronzen's Retable** *(1520)*
*François Ronzen's wood retable and surrounding panels include the first picture of the Papal Palace in Avignon (see pp44–5).*

**★ Organ**
*One of the finest in France, with some 3,000 pipes, the organ was made in 1773 by Jean-Esprit Isnard. Napoleon's brother Lucien saved it in the Revolution by having the Marseillaise played on it whenever a visiting official arrived.*

### Basilica Entrance

*The western side of the basilica has two matching wooden doors. They feature studied carving that contrasts sharply with the surrounding façade, which appears to have been crudely chopped off. When work stopped on the building in 1532, this part was left unfinished.*

### Hôtel de Ville

*The town hall is in the pilgrims' hostelry. It adjoins the refectory and chapel of the Royal Monastery.*

### Milestone

*Discovered along the Roman Aurelian Way (see p125), this 1st-century milestone is now on display at the entrance to the cloisters.*

**Former Refectory**

## STAR SIGHTS

- ★ Relics of St Mary Magdalene
- ★ Organ
- ★ Ronzen's Retable

### Cloisters

*The cloisters are at the centre of the Royal Monastery, so called because the French kings were its priors. The monks left in 1957 and it is now a hotel-restaurant.*

Boats in the colourful, palm-fringed harbour at Sanary-sur-Mer

## Bandol ⓮

**Road map** *C4.* *8,000.* *Service du Tourisme, allée Vivien (04 94 29 41 35).* *daily.* **www**.bandol.fr

Tucked away in a bay, this cheerful resort has a tree-lined promenade, casino and large yachting harbour. The shelter of encircling hills makes for excellent grape-growing conditions. Indeed, Bandol has produced superb wines since 600 BC. Outside town, the **Jardin Exotique et Zoo de Sanary-Bandol** contains wildlife and greenhouses of tropical plants.

Bandol wine label

**Jardin Exotique et Zoo de Sanary-Bandol**
Quartier Pont-d'Aran. ***Tel*** *04 94 29 40 38.* *Mon–Sat, Sun pm.* *public hols am.*

## Sanary-sur-Mer ⓯

**Road map** *C4.* *18,000.* *Ollioules-Sanary.* *Maison du Tourisme, 1 quai du Levant (04 94 74 01 04).* *Wed.* **www**.sanarysurmer.com

In the agreeable, clear blue waters of Sanary-sur-Mer, the diver Jacques Cousteau's experiments to develop the modern aqualung took place. Diving and fishing (mainly for tuna and swordfish) are still popular pursuits in this delightful resort, where rows of pink and white houses line the bay. Its name derives loosely from St-Nazaire; the lovely local 19th-century church took the saint's name in its entirety. Dating from about 1300, the landmark medieval tower in the town still contains the cannon that saw off an Anglo-Sardinian fleet in 1707. It is now part of a hotel. Sanary-sur-Mer has enticed visitors for many years. Once the home of the British writer Aldous Huxley (1894–1963), it was a haven between the wars for innumerable other authors. Bertolt Brecht (1898–1956) and Thomas Mann (1875–1955) fled here from Nazi Germany.

To the east of Sanary, the coast becomes dramatic and rocky. By the peninsula's extremity at the Cap Sicié is the **Notre-Dame-du-Mai** chapel, which was built in the 17th century. A pilgrimage destination full of votive offerings, its stepped approach offers a wonderful panorama over the coast and surrounding hills.

## Toulon ⓰

**Road map** D4. *172,000.* *334 rue de la République (04 94 18 53 00).* *Tue–Sun.* **www**.toulontourisme.com

Tucked into a fine natural harbour, Toulon is home to France's Mediterranean fleet. In the old town, or along the quays of the Darse Vieille, the *matelots* and the bars reinforce the maritime connection.

In Roman times, Toulon was renowned for its sea snails *(murex)* which, when boiled, produced an imperial-quality purple dye. During the reign of Louis XIV, Pierre Puget (1620–94) was in charge of the port's decoration. Two of his best-known works now

Ornate Baroque entrance to the Musée de la Marine

support the town-hall balcony. These are *Strength* and *Tiredness*, his 1657 carved marble figures of Atlantes.

The port was extensively damaged in World War II by the Allies and Nazis. Today, much of the town is under restoration. Toulon has a large opera house and several interesting museums, including the **Musée des Arts Asiatiques** located in the Villa Jules Verne, which has been entirely redesigned to house it.

### 🏛 Musée de la Marine

Place Monsenergue. *Tel 04 94 02 02 01.* ◯ *Wed–Mon.* ● *15 Dec–Jan.* 🖼 🔨 *restricted.* 📷
The museum's grand entrance is decorated with imposing statues of Mars and Bellona. It was once the gateway to the 17th-century city arsenal. This stretched for more than 240 ha (595 acres) behind it.

Inside, the museum boasts two vast model galleons, *La Sultane* (1765) and *Duquesne* (1790), used for training. Some figureheads and ships' prows are on show, as are two wooden figures that were carved by Pierre Puget, and various 18th-century naval instruments.

### 🏛 Musée d'Art de Toulon

113 bd du Maréchal Leclerc. *Tel 04 94 36 81 01.* ◯ *Tue–Sun pm only.* ● *public hols.* 🔨 *limited.*
A permanent collection of traditional and contemporary Provençal paintings makes up the core of this small but illuminating museum. Works by international artists are often included in the first-floor temporary exhibitions.

### 🏛 Musée du Vieux Toulon

69 cours Lafayette. *Tel 04 94 62 11 07.* ◯ *Tue–Sat pms.* ● *public hols.*
This quaint museum features the young Napoleon and his endeavours in the defence of Toulon, as well as old weapons and a number of historical sketches by Puget.

### 🔒 Cathédrale Ste-Marie-de-la-Seds

Place de la Cathédrale. *Tel 04 94 92 28 91.* ◯ *daily.*
Directly inland from the town hall, in the Darse Vieille, is the city's 11th-century cathedral. It was treated to a Classical facelift and extended in the 1600s.

Inside, there are works by Puget and Jean Baptiste Van Loo (1684–1745), as well as a spectacular Baroque altar.

Place Victor Hugo and the opera house in Toulon

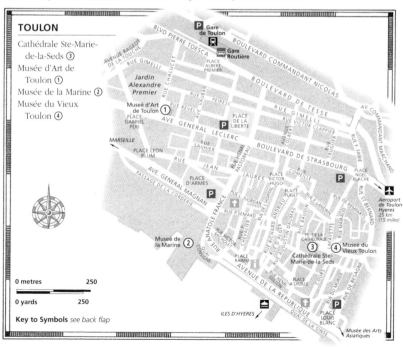

**TOULON**

0 metres        250
0 yards         250

Key to Symbols *see back flap*

# Iles d'Hyères ⓱

The Iles d'Hyères are three unspoilt islands, found 10 km (6 miles) off the Var coast – Porquerolles, Le Levant and Port-Cros. Their history has been chequered due to their important strategic position: occupiers have included Greeks, Romans and Saracens, as well as ruthless pirates. Today the French Navy uses much of Le Levant. Porquerolles, the largest island, is partly cultivated with vineyards, but also has expanses of pine forest and *maquis*. Port-Cros has been a national park since 1963, protected for its woodlands (including holm oak, strawberry tree and myrtle), rare birds and rich underwater habitats.

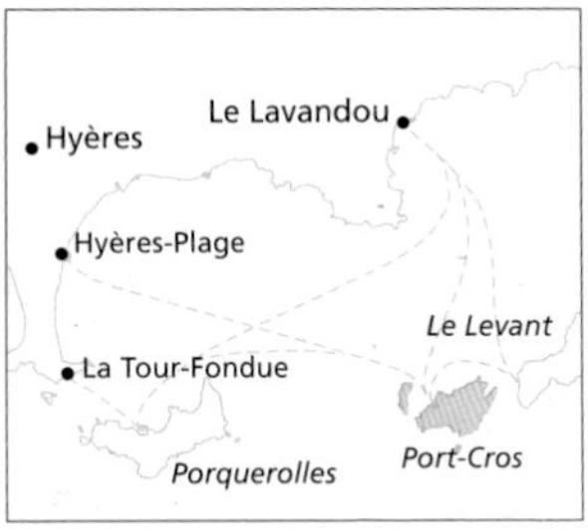

Bottle of the rare Côte des Iles wine

**LOCATOR MAP**

Le Lavandou
Hyères
Le Levant
Hyères-Plage
La Tour-Fondue
Porquerolles
Port-Cros

## PORT-CROS MARINE LIFE

The wooded slopes of the island shelve down into unpolluted sea, where colourful fish swim among beds of Neptune grass. A ready-planned swimming route makes exploration easy.

Fort du Moulin, over-looking Port-Cros harbour

Sponge alga
*Codium bursa*

Mermaid's cup
*Acetabularia mediterranea*

Bath sponge
*Spongia officinalis*

Neptune grass
*Posidonia oceanica*

Peacock's tail
*Padina pavonia*

Sea peacock
*Thalassoma pavo*

Saupe
*Sarpa salpa*

Moray eel
*Muraena helena*

Sea urchins, *Paracentrotous lividus*

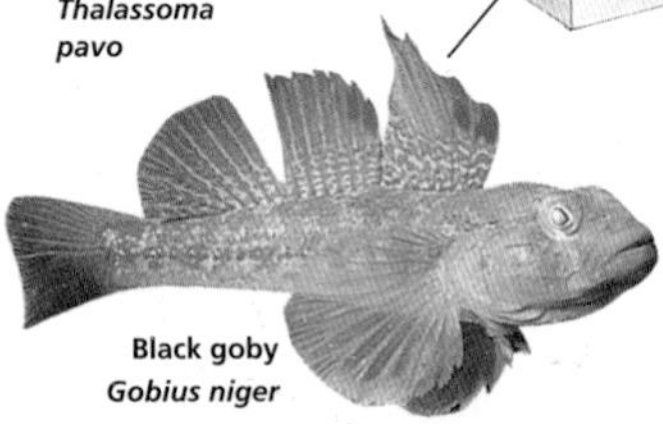

Black goby
*Gobius niger*

**Port-Cros Harbour**
*The tiny, palm-fringed harbour and village of Port-Cros nestle in a sheltered bay to the northwest of the island.*

**VISITORS' CHECKLIST**

**Road map** D5. 🚉 *Toulon-Hyères.* 🚌 *Hyères.* 🚤 *Hyères.* 🚢 *from Hyères (Tour Fondu) to Porquerolles daily (every 30 mins in summer); from Hyères and Le Lavandou to Port-Cros and Le Levant daily (Nov–Mar: 3–4 times a week).* ℹ *Porquerolles (04 94 58 33 76).*

**Scuba diving off the coast of Port-Cros**

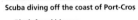

Black-faced blenny
*Trypterygion tripteronotus*

Cardinal fish
*Apogon imberbis*

Diplodus
*Diplodus sargus*

Grey mullet
*Chelon labrosus*

Octopus
*Octopus vulgaris*

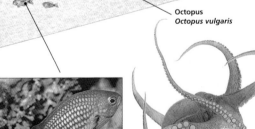
**Damsel fish, *Chromis chromis***

## Hyères ⑱

**Road map** D4. 🚶 *54,000.* 🚉 *Toulon-Hyères.* 🚌 🚌 🚤 ℹ *av A Thomas (04 94 01 84 50).* 📅 *Tue, Sat & 3rd Thu of month.* **www**.hyeres-tourisme.com

Hyères is one of the most agreeable towns on the Côte d'Azur, and the oldest of the south of France winter resorts. The town lies at the centre of well-cultivated land that provides fresh fruit and vegetables all year. It has three leisure ports, 35-km (22-miles) of sandy beach and a peninsula facing the Iles d'Hyères.

The new town was called Hyères-les-Palmiers. A palm-growing industry was established here in 1867, soon becoming the largest in Europe. The industry is still important and hundreds of palms line the new town boulevards.

Hyères' main church is **St-Louis** in place de la République. Romanesque and Provençal Gothic, it was completed in 1248. From place Massillon, rue St-Paul leads past the 11th-century **Eglise St-Paul**, full of 17th-century ex-votos. The road continues to the ruined 12th-century Château St-Bernard, which has good views. In the gardens is the Cubist-inspired **Villa de Noailles** (1924), built by Robert Mallet-Stevens for the Vicomte de Noailles (tours during exhibitions). **Jardins Olbius Riquier** has a zoo and exotic plants.

**✗ Jardins Olbius Riquier**
Av Ambroise Thomas.
**Tel** 04 94 00 78 65. ⏺ *daily.* ♿

**Moorish architecture inspired by the many palms in Hyères**

**Beach at Le Lavandou overlooked by hotels and exclusive villas**

## Le Lavandou ⑲

**Road map** D4. 🏠 5,500. 🚌 ⛴
🛈 quai Gabriel Péri (04 94 00 40 50).
🚋 Thu. **www**.lelavandou.com

An embarkation port for the nearby Iles d'Hyères, Le Lavandou is a fishing village now almost entirely given over to tourism. This is due to its twelve sandy beaches, each of a different colour sand. It is a centre for water sports and offers moorings for luxury yachts. Full of bars, nightclubs and restaurants, Le Lavandou is a favourite of younger, less well-heeled visitors.

It takes its name not from the lavender fields in the surrounding hills, but from a *lavoir* (wash-house) depicted in a painting of the town by Charles Ginoux dating from 1736. During the last century, when it was no more than a fishing village, Le Lavandou was popular with artists. The most famous, though not so well known outside France, was Ernest Reyer (1823–99), a composer and music critic after whom the main square is named. From this square there is a view over the Iles du Levant and Port-Cros.

Much of nearby Brégançon is in the hands of the military and the French president has a summer residence there.

## Bormes-les-Mimosas ⑳

**Road map** D4. 🏠 7,000. 🚌
🛈 1 place Gambetta (04 94 01 38 38). 🚋 Tue & Wed.
**www**.bormeslesmimosas.com

Bormes is a medieval hill village on the edge of the Dom Forest, bathed in the scent of oleander and

**Rue Rompi-Cuou, one of the steep, old streets in Bormes-les-Mimosas**

## Tour of the Massif des Maures ㉑

The ancient mountain range of Maures takes its name from the Provençal *maouro*, meaning dark or gloomy, for the Massif is carpeted in sweet chestnuts, cork trees, oaks and pines with a deeply shaded undergrowth of myrrh and briar, though forest fires have reduced some of it to scrubland. Lying between Hyères and Fréjus, the Massif is nearly 60-km (40-miles) long and 30-km (18-miles) wide. This tour is a simple route that takes you through the wild and often deserted heart of the Massif, through dramatic countryside ranging from flat valley floors covered in cork trees to deep valleys and lofty peaks. A few of the roads are steep and winding.

**Village des Tortues ③**
Keep bearing left on the D75 for the "Tortoise Village", which has saved France's only remaining species of wild tortoise.

**Notre-Dame-des-Anges ④**
Beside this priory and its chapel full of votive offerings, is the highest summit in the Massif at 780 m (2,559 ft).

*Gonfaron*

**Collobrières ⑤**
This riverside village with its hump-backed bridge is famed for its *marrons glacés*. Nearby forests supply bottle corks.

### TIPS FOR DRIVERS

*Tour length:* 75 km (47 miles).
*Stopping-off points: Collobrières is a pleasant lunchtime stop. Allow time to visit Chartreuse de la Verne (04 94 48 08 00 for opening times), which is reached up narrow, steep roads. (See also pp250–51.)*

**Farm workers at Collobrières**

eucalyptus and topped with a flower-lined walk around its castle. "Les Mimosas" was not added to its name until 1968, a century after the plant was first introduced to the south of France from Mexico. A pretty and popular village, Bormes serves a marina of more than 800 berths. Plummeting streets such as Rompi-Cuou lead to lively cafés and coastal views.

A statue of St Francis di Paola stands in front of the attractive 16th-century **Chapelle St-François**, commemorating the saint's timely arrival during a plague outbreak in 1481. The 18th-century church of **St-Trophyme** has newly restored 18th-century frescoes. The works of local painter Jean-Charles Cazin (1841–1901) are well represented in the **Musée d'Arts et Histoire**.

🏛 **Musée d'Arts et Histoire**
103 rue Carnot. **Tel** 04 94 71 56 60. ⬜ Tue–Sun (public hols & Sun: am only).

Ramatuelle village enclosed by wooded slopes and vineyards

## Ramatuelle ㉒

Road map E4. 🏘 2,000. 🚌 🛈 pl de l'Ormeau (04 98 12 64 00). 🛒 Thu & Sun. **www**.ramatuelle-tourisme.com

Surrounded by vineyards, this attractive hilltop village was called "God's Gift" (Rahmatu 'llah) by the Saracens who left a gate, now well-restored, in its fortifications, as well as a penchant for figs. It is one of three particularly quaint villages on the St-Tropez peninsula (with Grimaud and Gassin). Gérard Philipe (1922–59), the leading young French actor during the 1950s, is buried here. Theatre and jazz festivals take place here annually.

Nearby, Les Moulins de Paillas (322 m, 940 ft), offers a fine panorama, as does Cap Camarat, with its lighthouse, at the tip of the peninsula, 5 km (3 miles) east of Ramatuelle.

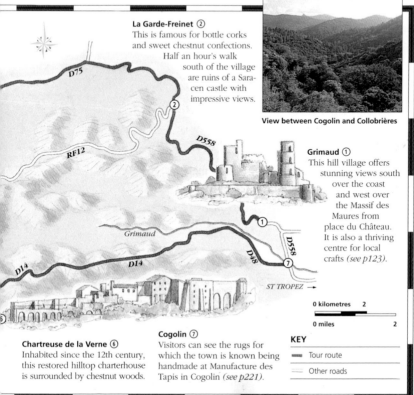

**La Garde-Freinet** ②
This is famous for bottle corks and sweet chestnut confections. Half an hour's walk south of the village are ruins of a Saracen castle with impressive views.

View between Cogolin and Collobrières

**Grimaud** ①
This hill village offers stunning views south over the coast and west over the Massif des Maures from place du Château. It is also a thriving centre for local crafts (see p123).

ST TROPEZ →

0 kilometres 2
0 miles 2

**KEY**

▬▬ Tour route
--- Other roads

**Chartreuse de la Verne** ⑥
Inhabited since the 12th century, this restored hilltop charterhouse is surrounded by chestnut woods.

**Cogolin** ⑦
Visitors can see the rugs for which the town is known being handmade at Manufacture des Tapis in Cogolin (see p221).

# Street-by-Street: St-Tropez ㉓

**St Torpès in his boat**

Clustered around the old port and nearby beaches, the centre of St-Tropez, partly rebuilt in its original style after World War II *(see p52)*, is full of fishermen's houses. In the port itself, traditional fishing boats are still to be seen moored side-by-side with sleek luxury cruisers of all shapes and sizes. Behind the port-side cafés of the quai Jean-Jaurès, the narrow, bustling streets are packed with boutiques and restaurants. The town is overlooked by the church's wrought-iron belltower in the centre and the citadel just outside.

**La Fontanette** beach leads to a coastal walk with views over Ste-Maxime.

**The Ponche quarter** is a comparatively quiet and unspoiled area of St-Tropez.

**Tour Vieille**

**The Port de Pêche**
*The Tour Vieille separates this port from La Glaye next door.*

**Place de la Ponche**

LA GLAYE

RUE DE LA PONCHE

**Tour du Portalet**

**St-Tropez Old Town**
*Fashionable motorcyclists pose along the narrow streets of central St-Tropez.*

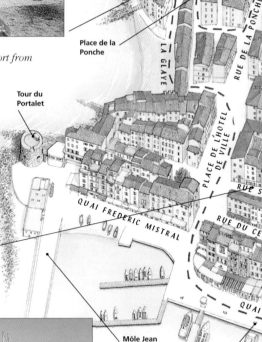

PLACE DE L'HÔTEL DE VILLE

RUE SIBI

QUAI FREDERIC MISTRAL

RUE DU CEPO

QUAI JE

**Môle Jean Réveille**

**★ Quai Jean-Jaurès**
*The attractively painted houses and packed cafés lining the quay have enticed visitors and inspired artists for over a century.*

**View from the Ramparts of the Citadel**
*The hilltop citadel, situated east of St-Tropez, offers spectacular views over the rooftops of the town and beyond.*

## VISITORS' CHECKLIST

**Road map** E4. 5,750.
Gare Routière (08 92 68 48 28). quai Jean-Jaurès (08 92 68 48 28). Tue & Sat.
Bravades: 16–18 May, 15 Jun.
www.ot-saint-tropez.com

To the citadel

**★ Eglise Notre-Dame de l'Assomption**
*Its bust of St Torpès features in the bravade (see p228).*

RUE FONTANETTE

RUE DES PECHEURS

REMPARTS

RUE D'AUMAVE

RUE DE LA CITADELLE

RUE DU CLOCHER

RUE DE L'EGLISE

ANMARTIN

RUE VICTOR LAUGIER

URES

QUAI SUFFREN

To place des Lices

**Open Window on the Harbour at St-Tropez** *(1925–6)*
*Charles Camoin's painting is now in the Annonciade.*

### KEY

– – –  Suggested route

0 metres          50
0 yards           50

### STAR SIGHTS

★ Quai Jean-Jaurès

★ Eglise Notre-Dame

Statue of Pierre André de Suffren

To Musée de l'Annonciade *(see pp120–21)*

# Musée de l'Annonciade

This innovative gallery opened in 1955 in the former Chapelle de l'Annonciade by the old port in St-Tropez. Built in 1568, the building was converted into a museum by architect Louis Süe (1875–1968), funded by art collector Georges Grammont. The collection began with the paintings of Paul Signac and the other artists who followed him to St-Tropez, and now contains many stunning Post-Impressionist works from the late 19th and early 20th centuries. In 1961, 65 valuable works were stolen from the museum, but were recovered and restored a year later.

**Le Rameur** *(1914)*
*This bold Cubist work is by Roger de la Fresnaye.*

★ **St-Tropez, la Place des Lices et le Café des Arts**
*This painting (1925) is one of several that Charles Camoin made of St-Tropez's famous square after he followed Paul Signac and settled in the town.*

★ **L'Orage** *(1895)*
*Paul Signac's atmospheric work vividly depicts the onset of a storm in St-Tropez harbour.*

Temporary exhibition room

## GALLERY GUIDE

*Exhibition space is too limited for all works to be permanently on view, so the display changes frequently. An exhibition room holds temporary displays linked with the permanent collection.*

### KEY TO FLOORPLAN

| | |
|---|---|
| ☐ | Ground floor |
| ☐ | Mezzanine |
| ▨ | First floor |
| ☐ | Non-exhibition space |

★ **Nu Devant la Cheminée** *(1919)*
*In this warm, intimate picture, characteristic of the artist, Pierre Bonnard uses delicate tones within a limited colour range to create an effect of light and shade.*

*For hotels and restaurants in this region see pp197–9 and p213*

**Le Temps d'Harmonie**
*In this study (1893–5)
for a larger work, Paul
Signac departs from his
more usual Pointillist
technique, using simple,
fluid lines.*

Balcony

**VISITORS' CHECKLIST**

Place Grammont, St-Tropez.
**Tel** 04 94 17 84 10.
☐ Jul–Oct: daily; Dec–Jun:
Wed–Mon.
● 1 Jan, Ascension, 1 May, 17
May, Nov, 25 Dec. 🖼 🚫 🚻
♿ ground floor only.

**La Nymphe** *(1930)*
*This Classically
influenced bronze
sculpture, one of several
excellent works by
Aristide Maillol in
the Annonciade, is a
graceful evocation
of ideal beauty.*

**Deauville, le Champ de Courses**
*Raoul Dufy's racecourse, painted
in 1928, is typical of his interest in
glamorous subjects.*

**STAR PAINTINGS**

★ Nu Devant la
Cheminée by Pierre
Bonnard

★ L'Orage by Paul
Signac

★ St-Tropez, la Place
des Lices et le Café
des Arts by Charles
Camoin

18th-century main
entrance

# Exploring St-Tropez

This exceptional resort has become a victim of its own charms – the August high season attracts about 80,000 hell-bent hedonists. Following their departure, however, the genuine, peaceful nature of the village still shines through. Surrounded by slopes covered with vineyards, looking out over the millpond bay of Golfe St-Tropez and protected by an imposing citadel, its situation remains inviolate. It does, however, face the northerly Mistral which thunders through the town for much of the winter, ensuring it remains a summer haunt.

Paintings by local artists for sale on the quai Jean-Jaurès

### A glimpse of the town

Activity is centred north of the Musée de l'Annonciade, beside the port. Here, local artists sell their wares and people pass the time of day in the Café de Paris, le Gorille or Senequier *(see p219)*.

The pretty, pastel-painted houses lining the quai Jean-Jaurès can be viewed at their best from the harbour breakwater, the Môle Jean Réveille. These buildings were among the town's sights that inspired Paul Signac (1863–1935) to start painting in St-Tropez. Many other artists followed, all well represented in the Annonciade *(see pp120–21)*.

The old town, just behind the waterfront, is flagged by the tower of the Eglise Notre-Dame de l'Assomption. To its north lies the Hôtel de Ville and the Tour Suffren, home of the former local lords. Admiral Pierre André de Suffren (1726–88), "terror of the English", is commemorated by a statue on the quay. Behind the quai Suffren is the place des Lices, a large square crowded with cafés.

Out to the east, beyond the old Ponche quarter and the unspoiled fishing port nearby, lies the 16th-century hexagonal citadel. With fine views from the ramparts, it contains the Musée Naval de St-Tropez. Further east, is La Madrague where Brigitte Bardot used to live. *And God Created Woman*, the 1959 film shot in St-Tropez starring Bardot, started the celebrity rush to the town.

**🏛 Musée de l'Annonciade**
See pp120–21.

Eglise Notre-Dame de l'Assomption

### 🔒 Eglise Notre-Dame de l'Assomption
Rue de l'Eglise. ☐ *Tue–Sun.*
This 19th-century Baroque church contains several busts of saints, including one of St Torpès after whom St-Tropez is named. Beheaded for his Christianity, his body was put in a boat with a dog and a cockerel and the boat landed here in AD 68. Every year, his bust is carried through the town in the 16 May *bravade.*

The hilltop citadel east of St-Tropez

### 🏛 Musée de la Citadelle
Forteresse. **Tel** 04 94 97 59 43.
🔴 for renovation until 2010. 🖼
Located in the dungeon of the citadel keep, to the east of the town, the Musée de la Citadelle houses temporary exhibitions on the history of St-Tropez and the navy.

### 🏛 Maison des Papillons
9 rue Etienne Berny. **Tel** 04 94 97 63 45. ☐ Mon–Sat pm. 🔴 1 Jan, 1 & 17 May, Ascension, 15 Aug, 1 Nov, 25 Dec. 🖼
Hidden in a narrow medieval lane is this amazingly complete collection of butterflies found in France, as well as rare specimens from the Amazon.

Fishing boats and luxury cruisers docked at quai Jean-Jaurès

*For hotels and restaurants in this region see pp197–9 and p213*

# Port-Grimaud

**Road map** E4. 🏠 *150.* 🚗
ℹ *chemin communal (04 94 56 02 01 in summer) or 1 bd des Aliziers, 83310 Grimaud (04 94 55 43 83).*
🚌 *Thu & Sun.* **www**.grimaud-provence.com

This newly created port was dreamed up entirely by the Alsace architect François Spoerry (1912–98). In 1962 he bought up the marshy delta lands of the River Giscle west of the Golfe St-Tropez. Four years began on a mini-Venice of 2,500 canalside houses with moorings covering 90 ha (222 acres). There are now three "zones", a marina and a beach. Its church, **St-François-d'Assise**, in the place d'Eglise, contains some stained glass by Victor Vasarély (1908–97) and offers a sweeping view of the port from the top of its tower.

The whole port is free of traffic and the *coche d'eau* offers a water-taxi service. A major tourist attraction, Port-Grimaud brings in about one million visitors a year.

**View of Port-Grimaud from the Eglise de St-François-d'Assise**

# Grimaud

**Road map** E4. 🏠 *3,300.* 🚗 ℹ *1 bd des Aliziers (04 94 55 43 83).* 🚌 *Thu.* **www**.grimaud-provence.com

The ancient, fortified, traffic-free *village perché (see pp20–21)* of Grimaud is yet another legacy of the ubiquitous Grimaldi family *(see p91),* after which the village is named. Gibelin de Grimaldi, a doughty Genoese knight, was rewarded with a fief here after helping William the Good of Provence drive the Saracens out of this part of France in AD 973, after 83 years of occupation. The castle dates from the 11th century and was reduced to ruins under the direction of Cardinal Richelieu as punishment for the town's Protestant leanings.

The view of the coast from its heights made it an ideal vantage point from which to watch for further invasion. This task was adopted in 1119 by the Knights Templar. These were a clandestine military and religious order of knights founded during the First Crusade.

Once called rue Droite, the rue des Templiers is the town's oldest street, lined with arcades designed to be battened down in case of attack. Legend has it that the Knights Templar stayed in Grimaud, but this fact has not been historically attested. In the same street is the pure Romanesque 12th-century church of St-Michel.

**Grimaud, dominated by the castle ruins**

# Ste-Maxime

**Road map** E4. 🏠 *12,000.* 🚗 *St-Raphaël, St Tropez.* ℹ *promenade Simon-Lorière (04 94 55 75 55).* 🚌 *Fri.*

**Beach at Ste-Maxime**

Facing St-Tropez across the neck of the Gulf, Ste-Maxime is protected by hills. Its year-round clientele reaches saturation point in summer. The attractions of this smart resort are its port, promenade, good sandy beaches, watersports, night-life, fairs and casino.

Ste-Maxime was once protected by the monks of Lérins, who named the port after their patron saint and put up the defensive Tour Carrée des Dames which now serves as the **Musée de la Tour Carrée**. The church opposite contains a 17th-century green marble altar that was brought from the former Carthusian monastery of La Verne in the Massif des Maures.

🏛 **Musée de la Tour Carrée**
Place des Aliziers.
**Tel** *04 94 96 70 30.*
◻ *Wed–Mon.* ● *1 Jan, 1 May, 25 Dec, 1 mth in winter.* 🖌

# St-Raphaël ㉗

**Road map** E4. 🏔 *40,000.* 🚉
📧 ℹ️ *quai Albert Premier (04 94 19
52 52).* 🛍 *daily.*
**www**.saint-raphael.com

This staid and sensible family
resort dates to Roman times
when rich families came to
stay at a spot near the modern
seafront casino. Napoleon put
the town on the map when
he landed here in 1799 on
his return from Egypt, and
15 years later when he left
St-Raphaël for exile on Elba.
 Popularity came when the
Parisian satirical novelist Jean-
Baptiste Karr (1808–90) pub-
licized the town's delights. In
the old part is the 12th-century
church of St-Raphaël and the
**Musée Archéologique**, which
contains Greek amphorae and
other underwater finds.

🏛 **Musée Archéologique**
Place de la Vieille Eglise. **Tel** *04 94
19 25 75.* 🕐 *Tue–Sat.* ⬤ *public hols.*

**Tourist poster of St-Raphaël from
the 19th century**

# Massif de l'Esterel ㉘

**Road map** E4. 🚂 *Nice.* 🚉 🚌
*Agay, St-Raphaël.* ℹ️ *quai Albert
Premier, St-Raphaël (04 94 19 52 52).*

The Esterel, a mountainous
volcanic mass, is a wilderness
compared to the popular coast.
Although it rises to no more
than 620 m (2,050 ft), and a
succession of fires have laid
waste its forests, its innate
ruggedness and the dramatic
colours of its porphyry rocks
remain intact. Until the mid-
1800s, it was a refuge for

**Château de la Napoule, now an art centre**

highwaymen and escaped
prisoners from Toulon. Here,
after being fêted on arrival in
St Raphaël, Napoleon and his
coach were robbed of all their
valuables while on their way
out of town heading to Paris.
 The north side of the massif
is bounded by the DN7 which
runs through the Esterel Gap,
following the Roman Aurelian
way from Cannes to Fréjus. At
the Testannier crossroads 11
km (7 miles) from Fréjus a
road leads to Mont Vinaigre;
the final 15 minutes of the
journey must be made on
foot. This is the highest point
on the massif, and there is a
fine panorama from the Alps
to the Massif des Maures.
 On the seaward side of the
massif the D1089 from St-
Raphaël twists along the top of
startlingly red cliffs to Agay.
This resort has the best anchor-
age on the coast. It is famous
for its red porphyry, from
which the Romans cut columns
for their Provençal monuments.
 Round the bay is Pointe de
Baumette where there is a
memorial to French writer and
World War II aviator, Antoine
de St-Exupéry *(see p29).* The
road continues to Anthéor and
the Pointe de l'Observatoire.
Just before here, a left turn
leads to the circuit of the Cap
Roux and Pic de l'Ours.
 The coast road continues
through a series of resorts to
the start of the Riviera, at La
Napoule. Here there is a 14th-
century château refurbished by
American sculptor Henry Clews
(1876–1937), who left work
scattered about the estate. The
château is now an art centre,
the **Fondation Henry Clews**.

The route leading inland to
the Col Belle-Barbe from the
coast passes on the right a
turn to the 452-m (1483-ft)
Pic du Cap Roux. An hour's
walk to the top is rewarded
by a sweeping coast view.
 From the car park at Col
Belle-Barbe, a path leads to
the Mal Infernet, a dramatic
ravine that concludes a 40-
minute walk away at the Lac
de l'Ecureuil. Continuing
inland from Col Belle-Barbe
over the Col du Mistral up
to the Col des Trois Termes,
the path then twists south to
Col Notre-Dame. A 45-minute
walk leads on to the dramatic
Pic de l'Ours, rising to 496 m
(1,627 ft). Between here and
the coast is the 323-m (1,060-
ft) Pic d'Aurelle, which also
provides an impressive vista.

🏛 **Fondation Henry Clews**
1 av Henry Clews, La Napoule.
**Tel** *04 93 49 95 05.* 🕐 *daily.*
⬤ *25 Dec.* 🎫 📷 📹 *Apr–Sep.*
🌐 **www**.chateau-lanapoule.com

**Remaining timber on the fire-
ravaged Massif de l'Esterel**

# Fréjus ㉙

**Road map** E4. 🚉 53,000. 🚃 St Raphaël. 🚌 🛈 249 rue Jean-Jaurès (04 94 51 83 83). 🚢 Tue, Wed, Fri, Sat & Sun. **www**.frejus.fr

Visibly, though not ostentatiously, wealthy in history, Fréjus is one of the highlights of the coast. The oldest Roman city in Gaul, it was founded by Julius Caesar in 49 BC and greatly expanded by Augustus. Lying on the Aurelian way – a huge road built in the reign of Augustus from Rome to Arles – it covered 40 ha (100 acres), had a population of 30–40,000 and, as a port, was second in importance only to Marseille.

Although substantial sections of the Roman city were decimated by the Saracens in the 10th century, a few parts of their walls remain, including a tower of the western Porte des Gaules. The opposite eastern entrance, the Porte de Rome, marks one end of a 40-km (25-mile) aqueduct, the ruins of which amble alongside the

**Mosaic in the Musée Archéologique in Fréjus**

DN7 towards the Siagnole river near Mons. Just to the north of here the remains of the semi-circular, 1st-century theatre can be viewed. In their midst, performances are still held. The praetorium or Plateforme – military headquarters that formed the eastern citadel – lie to the south. North of the Porte des Gaules, on the road to Brignoles, stands the large 1st–2nd-century **Arènes**, built to hold 6,000 spectators, now used for bullfights and music.

The spectacular **Cathédrale St-Léonce et Cloître** houses a Musée Archéologique with finds from all around Fréjus. The Chapelle Notre-Dame, decorated by Cocteau, and Musée d'Histoire Locale are also well worth a visit. South of the town is the Butte St-Antoine citadel, which once overlooked the harbour. The canal linking the harbour to the sea began silting up in the 10th century; by the 1700s it was entirely filled in, forming Fréjus-Plage.

**Well in the centre of the Cathedral cloisters at Fréjus**

A little over 2 km (1 mile) from the town's centre, this modern resort stretches along a sandy beach towards St-Raphaël. North of the Arènes is a Buddhist Pagoda commemorating Vietnamese soldiers who died serving in the French army.

🏛 **Arènes de Fréjus**
Rue Vadon. **Tel** 04 94 51 34 31.
🕐 Tue–Sun. 🔴 public hols.

🏛 **Cathédrale St-Léonce**
Place Formigé. **Tel** 04 94 51 26 30.
🕐 daily. Cloisters: daily (Oct–May: Tue–Sun). 🔴 public hols. 🔄 cloisters. 🔲 🔲

## CATHEDRALE ST-LÉONCE ET CLOÎTRE

The fortified cathedral and the marble-columned cloister date from the 12th century, while the 5th-century baptistry is one of the oldest in France.

**The choir stalls**, in two rows, date from the 15th century and are ornately carved.

**Musée Archéologique**

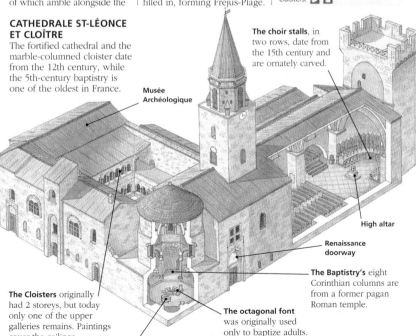

**High altar**

**Renaissance doorway**

**The Baptistry's** eight Corinthian columns are from a former pagan Roman temple.

**The octagonal font** was originally used only to baptize adults.

**The Cloisters** originally had 2 storeys, but today only one of the upper galleries remains. Paintings cover the ceilings.

**Earthenware basin**

# BOUCHES-DU-RHÔNE
# AND NÎMES

This southwestern corner of Provence has a feel that's unique in the region. It is the land of Van Gogh, brightly patterned materials and beaches of shifting sands. Its wildest point is the Camargue in the Rhône delta, a place of light and colour, lived in for centuries by gypsies and by cowboys who herd the wild horses and bulls.

Many inland towns reflect the region's Greek and Roman past. The Greeks first settled in France circa 600 BC and founded Marseille, now a cosmopolitan cultural centre and the country's second largest city. The Romans, who arrived after them, built the theatre at Arles and the amphitheatre at Nîmes, and left the remains of Classical houses at Glanum. The skeleton of a Roman aqueduct runs beween a spring at Uzès to a water tower at Nîmes, a great feat of engineering best seen at Pont du Gard.

"A race of eagles" is how Frédéric Mistral, the Provençal writer (see p28) described the Lords of Baux, bloodthirsty warriors who ruled in the Middle Ages from an extraordinary eyrie in Les Baux-de-Provence. This former fief was paradoxically famous as a Court of Love (see p142) during the 13th century. Louis IX (Saint Louis) built the fortified city of Aigues-Mortes for the Crusaders. In the 15th century, Good King René (see pp46-7), held his court in the castle of Tarascon and in Aix-en-Provence, the ancient capital of Provence. Aix's university, founded by René's father in 1409, is still the hub of this lively student town.

The area provides great walks and stunning scenery, particularly in the Alpilles and around Marseille. The films and books of Marcel Pagnol (see 153) and the stories of Daudet (see p143), which have influenced perceptions of Provençal people and life, are set in this region. The Camargue maintains a unique collection of flora and fauna, providing, in addition to fine vistas, superb horse riding and birdwatching.

**Produce on display in the colourful food market, Aix-en-Provence**

◁ Joseph Sec's statue of Saul in Aix-en-Provence, made in 1792 in honour of the French Revolution

# Exploring Bouches-du-Rhône and Nîmes

At the mouth of the Rhône lie the flat, wetland marshes and sand dunes of the Camargue wildlife reserve. Further inland, cities such as Aix-en-Provence, Arles and Nîmes are awash with ancient architecture. Northeast of Arles, the herb-covered chain of the Alpilles rises from the surrounding plains to the heady heights of Les Baux, and there are some stunning walks through the mountains. St-Rémy-de-Provence makes a good base for exploring the Alpilles. Popular coastal towns are Marseille and the scenic port of Cassis. A short car or boat away lie Les Calanques, deep, narrow inlets set between pine trees and white cliffs.

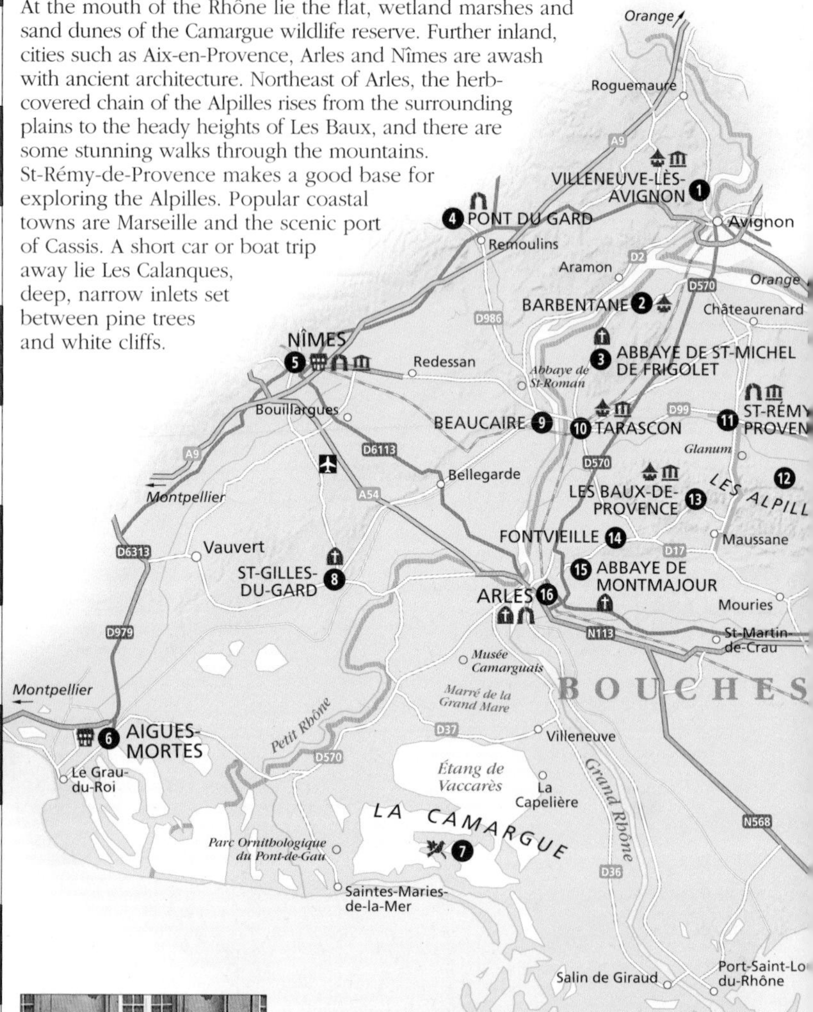

*Map locations:*

Orange
Roguemaure
VILLENEUVE-LÈS-AVIGNON **1**
Avignon
**4** PONT DU GARD
Remoulins
Aramon
Orange
Châteaurenard
BARBENTANE **2**
NÎMES **5**
Redessan
Abbaye de St-Roman
**3** ABBAYE DE ST-MICHEL DE FRIGOLET
ST-RÉMY PROVEN **11**
Bouillargues
BEAUCAIRE **9**  **10** TARASCON
Glanum
**12** LES ALPILL
Montpellier
Bellegarde
LES BAUX-DE-PROVENCE **13**
Maussane
FONTVIEILLE **14**
Vauvert
ST-GILLES-DU-GARD **8**
**15** ABBAYE DE MONTMAJOUR
ARLES **16**
Mouries
St-Martin-de-Crau
Montpellier
Musée Camarguais
Marré de la Grand Mare
B O U C H E S
AIGUES-MORTES **6**
Le Grau-du-Roi
Villeneuve
Étang de Vaccarès
La Capelière
L A   C A M A R G U E
Parc Ornithologique du Pont-de-Gau
**7**
Saintes-Maries-de-la-Mer
Salin de Giraud
Port-Saint-Lo du-Rhône

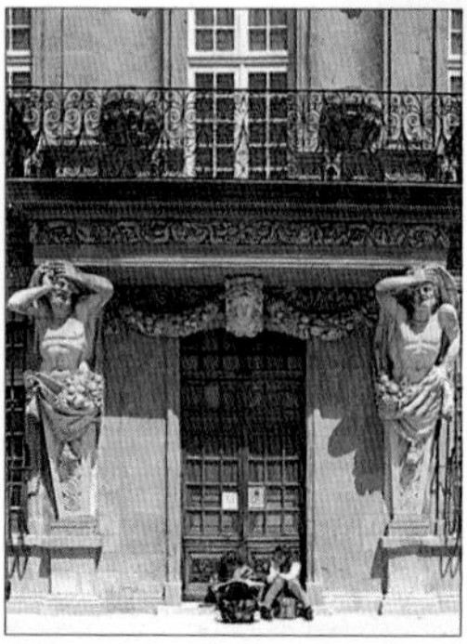

Atlantes grace the doorway of the Pavillon de Vendôme in Aix

## SIGHTS AT A GLANCE

**View across the harbour of Fort St-Jean, Marseille**

## GETTING AROUND

If you have a car, the auto-routes are fast and bypass slow traffic in the towns. The A8 autoroute which leads along the Riviera meets the Paris-Marseille A7 Autoroute du Soleil 17 km (11 miles) west of Aix, while the A9 Languedocienne heads west through Nîmes towards Spain.

The main towns are all linked by trains and buses, though bus services tend to be poor outside towns. Arles and Aix-en-Provence make particularly good bases for getting around. Boat trips are organized from Arles and Stes-Maries-de-la-Mer in the Camargue, where a good way to see the countryside is to hire the native horses.

## SEE ALSO

- *Where to Stay* pp199–202
- *Where to Eat* pp214–16

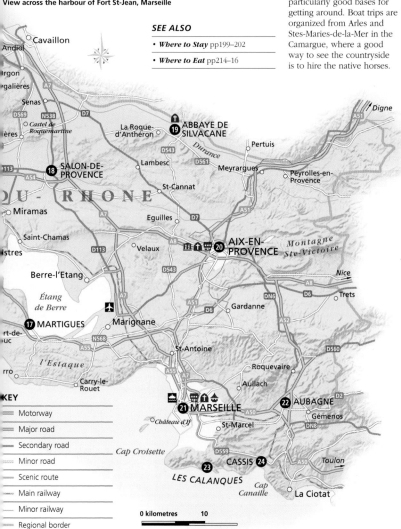

**KEY**

| | |
|---|---|
| ═══ | Motorway |
| ━━━ | Major road |
| ─── | Secondary road |
| ···· | Minor road |
| ─── | Scenic route |
| ┄┄┄ | Main railway |
| ┄┄┄ | Minor railway |
| ─── | Regional border |

0 kilometres 10

0 miles 10

**Part of the Chartreuse du Val-de-Bénédiction, Villeneuve**

# Villeneuve-lès-Avignon ❶

**Road map** B3. 🏛 *12,500.* 🚉
*Avignon.* 🚌 🛈 *1 pl Charles David
(04 90 25 61 33).* 🛒 *Thu & Sat.*
**www**.villeneuvelesavignon.fr

This town arose beside the
Rhône, opposite Avignon *(see
pp166–7),* and the connecting
bridge, Pont St-Bénézet, was
guarded by the **Tour de
Philippe le Bel**, built in 1307.
Its rooftop terrace, 176 steps
up, gives a fine panorama of
the papal city. Even better is
the view from the two giant
40-m (130-ft) round towers at
the entrance to the impressive
14th-century **Fort St-André**,
which enclosed a small town,
monastery and church.

Between these two bastions
lies the 14th-century Eglise-
Collégiale Notre-Dame. In the
**Musée Pierre de Luxembourg**
is *The Coronation of the Virgin*
(1453) by Enguerrand
Quarton, regarded as the best

work of the Avignon School.
This work was painted for the
abbot of the **Chartreuse du
Val-de-Bénédiction**, which was
founded by Innocent VI in
1356. There are three cloisters
and a chapel dedicated to
St John the Baptist decorated
with frescoes by Giovanetti
da Viterbo. The building is
now used as a cultural centre.

⚓ **Fort St-André**
***Tel*** *04 90 25 45 35.* ⭘ *daily.* ⬤ *1
Jan, 1 May, 1 & 11 Nov, 25 Dec.* 🏛

🏛 **Musée Municipal Pierre
de Luxembourg**
*Rue de la République.* ***Tel*** *04 90 27
49 66.* ⭘ *Tue–Sun.* ⬤ *Feb, 1 Jan,
1 & 11 Nov, 25 Dec.* 🏛 ♿

⛪ **Chartreuse du Val-de-
Bénédiction**
*Rue de la République.* ***Tel*** *04 90 15
24 24.* ⭘ *daily.* ⬤ *1 Jan, 1 May,
1 & 11 Nov, 25 Dec.* 🏛 📷 *in
summer.* 🍴 *in summer.* 📷 *in
winter.* 🛈 **www**.chartreuse.org

# Barbentane ❷

**Road map** B3. 🏛 *3,600.*
🚉 *Avignon, Tarascon.* 🚌
🛈 *Le Cours (04 90 90 85 86).*

Members of Avignon's Papal
court liked to build summer
houses in Barbentane, on the
slopes beside the Rhône 10
km (6 miles) south of the city.
One such was the handsome
Renaissance Maison des
Chevaliers with an arcaded
gallery, opposite the 13th- to
15th-century Notre-Dame-de-
Grace. Only the 40-m (130-ft)
Tour Anglica remains of the
town's 14th-century castle.

Just outside the medieval
quarter is the **Château de**

Barbentane, a finely decorated Italianate mansion, built
in 1674 by the Barbentane
aristocracy who still own it.

In the town is the 12th-
to 13th-century **Moulin de
Mogador**, which was used
as an oil and flour mill.

⚓ **Château de Barbentane**
***Tel*** *04 90 95 51 07.* ⭘ *Easter–Jun,
Oct: Thu–Tue; Jul–Sep: daily; Nov &
Mar: Sun.* ⬤ *Dec–Feb.* 🏛

**Provençal doll and doll's carriage,
Château de Barbentane**

# Abbaye de
St-Michel de
Frigolet ❸

**Road map** B3. ***Tel*** *04 90 95 70 07.*
⭘ *from 4:30pm daily. Phone to
reserve for groups.* 🏛 📷

The abbey is situated south of
St-Michel de Frigolet, in the
unspoiled La Montagnette
countryside. A cloister and
small abbey church date from
the 12th century, but in 1858 a
Premonstratensian abbey was
founded and one of the most
richly decorated and, indeed,
flamboyant churches of that
period was built. The whole
interior is colourfully painted,
with stars and saints on the
pillars and ceiling. After a brief
period of exile in Belgium
early this century, the monks
returned to Frigolet, and there
are now 15 of them. There is
a restaurant, accommodation
in 40 rooms and the monks
sell their deceptively potent
traditional liqueur based on
local herbs here. *Frigolet* is
Provençal for thyme.

**The ceiling of the abbey church of St-Michel de Frigolet**

# Pont du Gard ❹

**Road map** A3. 🚌 *Nîmes.*
🛈 *Route du Pont du Gard,
30210 Vers (04 66 37 50 99).*
**www**.pontdugard.fr

Begun around 19 BC, this
bridge is part of an aqueduct
which transported water from
a spring near Uzès to Roman
Nâmes *(see pp132–3).* An
underground channel, bridges
and tunnels were engineered
to carry the 20 million litre
(4.4 million gallon) daily water
supply 50 km (31 miles). The
three-tiered structure of the
Pont du Gard spans the
Gardon valley and was the
tallest aqueduct in the Roman

The Pont du Gard, the tallest of all Roman aqueducts at 48 m (158 ft)

**Trademark graffiti left by 18th-
century masons on the stones**

empire. Its huge limestone
blocks, some as heavy as 6
tonnes, were erected without
mortar. The water channel,
covered by stone slabs, was
in the top tier of the three.
Skilfully designed cutwaters
ensured that the bridge has
resisted many violent floods.

It is not known for certain
how long the aqueduct
continued in use but it may
still have been functioning as
late as the 9th century AD.
The adjacent road bridge was
erected in the 1700s. The **Site
du Pont du Gard** has a museum
(open daily in summer)
tracing the aqueduct's history.

**Protruding stones for supporting
scaffolding during construction**

## THE REMAINS OF THE AQUEDUCT

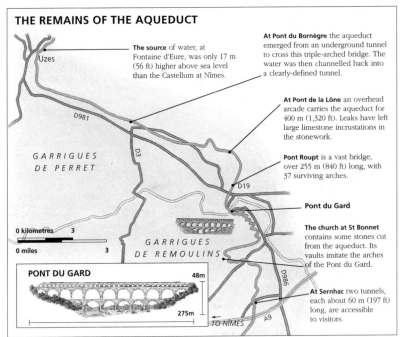

**The source** of water, at
Fontaine d'Eure, was only 17 m
(56 ft) higher above sea level
than the Castellum at Nîmes.

**At Pont du Bornègre** the aqueduct
emerged from an underground tunnel
to cross this triple-arched bridge. The
water was then channelled back into
a clearly-defined tunnel.

**At Pont de la Lône** an overhead
arcade carries the aqueduct for
400 m (1,320 ft). Leaks have left
large limestone incrustations in
the stonework.

**Pont Roupt** is a vast bridge,
over 255 m (840 ft) long, with
37 surviving arches.

**Pont du Gard**

**The church at St Bonnet**
contains some stones cut
from the aqueduct. Its
vaults imitate the arches
of the Pont du Gard.

**At Sernhac** two tunnels,
each about 60 m (197 ft)
long, are accessible
to visitors.

Uzes

D981

GARRIGUES
DE PERRET

D3

D19

GARRIGUES
DE REMOULINS

D986

A9

TO NÎMES

0 kilometres  3
0 miles  3

**PONT DU GARD**

48m

275m

# Nîmes ❺

**Publicity poster for a Nîmes festival**

A magnificent carved black bull at the end of the avenue Jean-Jaurès highlights Nîmes' passion for bullfighting. Crowds fill Les Arènes, the Roman amphitheatre, for bullfights during the three annual *ferias (see pp32–3)*. Year round, the city's biggest draw is its fine Roman architecture, and it is a great city of the arts. The city's textile industry is famous for creating denim *(de Nîmes)*, the tough material used for blue jeans and worn by the Camargue cowboys. Most shops stock Provençal fabrics *(see p221)*.

## Exploring Nîmes

Roman veterans from Emperor Augustus's 31 BC Egyptian campaign introduced the city's coat of arms: a crocodile chained to a palm tree. Today, the logo is splashed on everything from bollards to road signs.

Nîmes' generous boulevards give it a wide-open feel. A renaissance of modern building, art and design, including the fine Carré d'Art, lends a touch of class. Some of the newer monuments, such as the Fontaine du Crocodile in place du Marché, are becoming as well known as Nîmes' most familiar landmark, the Castellum.

**The city's coat of arms: a crocodile and palm tree**

## 🏛 Les Arènes

Bd des Arènes. 📞 04 66 21 82 56. ⭕ daily. ● Feria des Vendanges & performance days. 🎫 ♿ restricted. 🌐 www.arenesdenimes.com

The most dramatic of the city's Roman ruins is the 1st-century amphitheatre. At 130 m (427 ft) by 100 m (328 ft) and with seating for 22,000, it is slightly smaller than Arles' amphitheatre *(see p146)*. It was built as a venue for gladiatorial combat, and you can see a demonstration of their fighting technique. After Rome's collapse in AD 476, it became a fortress and knights' headquarters. Until its 19th-century restoration, it was used as home to 2,000 people in slum conditions. Today it is thought to be one of the best preserved of all Roman amphitheatres.

## 🏛 Porte d'Auguste

Bd Amiral Courbet.

With a central arch 6 m (20 ft) high and 4 m (13 ft) wide, this gate was built to take horsemen and carriages, since the main road from Rome to Spain, the Domitian Way, passed through the middle of Nîmes.

An ancient inscription tells visitors that the city walls were built in 15 BC.

## 🏛 Musée du Vieux Nîmes

Pl aux Herbes. *Tel* 04 66 76 73 70. ⭕ Tue–Sun. ● 1 Jan, 1 May, 1 Nov, 25 Dec. 🅿

The 17th-century Bishop's Palace just east of the cathedral houses this museum. The old-fashioned interior has been beautifully restored: the summer room has Directoire and Empire-style furnishings and Old Town views.

## 🏛 Carré d'Art

Pl de la Maison Carrée. 📞 04 66 76 35 70. ⭕ Tue–Sun. 🎫 🅿 ♿ 🅿

On the opposite side of the square from the Maison Carrée is the Carré d'Art. This modern, light-flooded art complex opened in 1993 and was designed by Norman Foster.

**Norman Foster's Carré d'Art**

## 🏛 Maison Carrée

Pl de la Maison Carrée. *Tel* 04 66 21 82 56. ⭕ daily. ● 1 Jan, 1 May, 25 Dec. 🎫

The Maison Carrée ("square house") is the world's best-preserved Roman temple. Built by Marcus Agrippa, it is Hellenic with Corinthian columns around the main hall. Louis XIV's chief minister, Colbert, wanted it taken brick by brick to Versailles. A 3D film of the history of Nîmes is shown inside the temple.

## 🏛 Musée Archéologique et Musée d'Histoire Naturelle

13 bis bd Amiral Courbet. *Tel* 04 66 76 74 80. ⭕ Tue–Sun. ● 1 Jan, 1 May, 1 Nov, 25 Dec. 🅿

The ground-floor gallery of this museum has a number of pre-Roman carvings, including busts of Gallic warriors, friezes and also contemporary objects. Upstairs, Gallo-Roman tools

**The Roman amphitheatre, today used for bullfights at festival times**

and household utensils give a good idea of life at the time. There is also a range of glassware and bronze objects. The pottery collection includes the pre-Roman Warrior of Grézan. The atmospheric chapel in this one-time Jesuits' College is used for temporary displays.

### 🏛 Musée des Beaux-Arts

Rue Cité Foulc. *Tel 04 66 67 38 21.* ☐ *Tue–Sun.* ☐ *1 Jan, 1 May, 1 Nov, 25 Dec.* 🗷 ᴛ
A diverse collection in the Fine Art Museum includes paintings by Boucher, Rubens and Watteau. The ground floor displays a large Roman mosaic, *The Marriage of Admetus,* found in 1883 in Nîmes' former covered market.

### 🔓 Cathédrale Notre-Dame et St-Castor

Pl aux Herbes. *Tel 04 66 67 27 72.* ☐ *daily during services.*
Nîmes' cathedral, in the centre of the Old Town, dates from the 11th century but was extensively rebuilt in the 19th century. The west front has a partly Romanesque frieze with scenes from the Old Testament.

### 🔮 Castellum

Rue de la Lampèze.
Between the Porte d'Auguste and the Tour Magne, set in the Roman wall, is the Castellum, a tower used for storing the water brought in from Uzès via the aqueduct at Pont du Gard *(see p131).* The water was distributed in the town by means of a canal duct system.

**Archaeological museum statue**

### 🌿 Jardin de la Fontaine

Quai de la Fontaine. *Tel 04 66 21 82 56 (Tour Magne).*
The city's main park lies at the end of the wide avenue Jean-Jaurès. It was named after an underground spring harnessed in the 18th century. The park's 2nd-century Temple of Diana, part of a complex of baths, is today in ruins. Benedictine nuns lived there during the Middle Ages and converted it into a church, which was sacked in the Wars of Religion *(see pp46-7).*

At the summit of the 114-m (374-ft) Mont Cavalier stands the 34-m (112-ft) octagonal Tour Magne. Of all the towers originally set in Nîmes' Roman wall, this is the most remarkable. Dating from 15 BC, it is the earliest surviving Roman building in France. There are 140 steps, worth climbing for a fine view of Mont Ventoux.

**VISITORS' CHECKLIST**

**Road map** A3. 🏙 *130,000.*
✈ *Nîmes-Arles-Camargue.*
🚆 🚌 *bd Talabot.* 🛈 *6 rue Auguste (04 66 58 38 00).*
🗓 *daily.* 🎭 *Feria d'Hiver (Feb); Feria de Pentecôte (May/Jun); Feria des Vendanges (late Sep).*
**www**.ot-nimes.fr

***L'Obéissance Récompensée* by Boucher, Musée des Beaux-Arts**

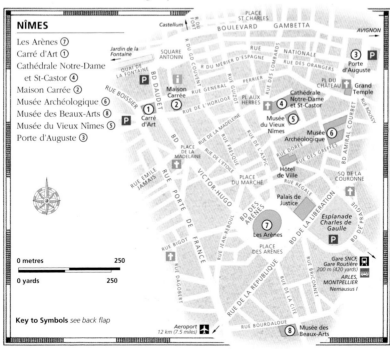

# NÎMES

Les Arènes ⑦
Carré d'Art ①
Cathédrale Notre-Dame et St-Castor ④
Maison Carrée ②
Musée Archéologique ⑥
Musée des Beaux-Arts ⑧
Musée du Vieux Nîmes ⑤
Porte d'Auguste ③

0 metres          250
0 yards           250

**Key to Symbols** *see back flap*

# Aigues-Mortes ⑥

A lone, sturdy sentinel set among the salt marshes of the Camargue, Aigues-Mortes ("dead waters" in Provençal) looks today much as it must have done when it was completed, around 1300. Then, however, the Rhône had not deposited the silt which now landlocks the town. Canals brought the vast stone blocks to make its walls from the quarries of Beaucaire, and the town's founder, Louis IX set sail from under the shadow of Tour de Constance on his crusade of 1248 (see pp42–3). Only the Hundred Years' War saw its ramparts breached: now its gates are always open to the besieging armies of admiring visitors.

**Tour de la Poudrière**
was the arsenal, where weapons and gunpowder were stored.

**Porte de l'Arsenal**

**King Louis IX**
Saint Louis, as he was to become, built Aigues-Mortes as his only Mediterranean sea port. People had to be bribed to come and settle in this inhospitable spot.

**Porte de la Reine**
was named for Anne of Austria, who visited the town in 1622.

**★ The Ramparts**
The 1,634-m (1-mile) long walls are punctuated by ten gates, six towers, arrow slits and overhanging latrines.

**Tour de la Mèche**
or "wick tower" held a constant flame used to light cannon fuses.

**Chapelle des Pénitents Blancs**

**Tour des Sels**

**Chapelle des Pénitents Gris**
Built from 1676–99, this chapel is still used by an order founded in 1400. Named for their grey cowls, they walk with their white-cowled former rivals in the Palm Sunday procession.

## STAR SIGHTS

★ Tour de Constance

★ The Ramparts

**Porte de la Marine**
*This was the main portside gate. Ships were moored by the Porte des Galions, anchored to a vast metal ring known as an* organeau.

**VISITORS' CHECKLIST**

**Road map** A4. 🏛 *6,150.* 🚉 *25 km (15 miles) W Montpellier.* 🚌 *av de la Liberté.* 🚕 *rte de Nîmes.* ℹ *Pl St-Louis (04 66 53 73 00).* 🛒 *Wed, Sun.* 🎵 *Nuits d'Encens (Mediterranean music; Jun); Festival St-Louis (Aug).*

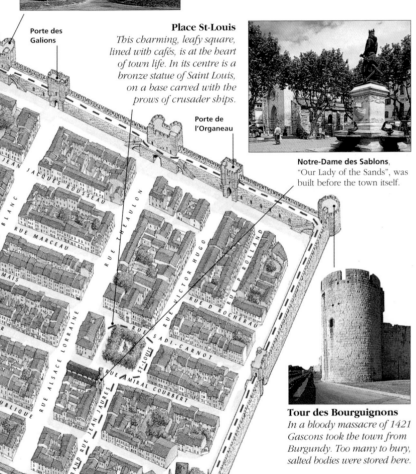

**Place St-Louis**
*This charming, leafy square, lined with cafés, is at the heart of town life. In its centre is a bronze statue of Saint Louis, on a base carved with the prows of crusader ships.*

Porte des Galions

Porte de l'Organeau

**Notre-Dame des Sablons**, "Our Lady of the Sands", was built before the town itself.

**Tour des Bourguignons**
*In a bloody massacre of 1421 Gascons took the town from Burgundy. Too many to bury, salted bodies were stored here.*

Porte de la Gardette

**KEY**

– – – Suggested route

0 metres       100

0 yards        100

★ **Tour de Constance**
*This tower often held religious prisoners: first Catholic, then Calvinist, and then Huguenot women like Marie Durand, freed in 1768 after 38 years.*

# The Camargue ❼

**Gardians** look after the horses and bulls

This flat, scarcely habited land is one of Europe's major wetland regions and natural history sites. Extensive areas of salt marsh, lakes, pastures and sand dunes, covering a vast 140,000 ha (346,000 acres), provide a romantic and haunting environment for the wildlife. Native horses roam the green pastures and are ridden by the traditional cowboys of the region, the *gardians, (see p22)* who herd the black bulls. Numerous sea birds and wildfowl also occupy the region, among them flocks of greater flamingoes. North of the reserve, rice is cultivated in paddy fields. Many of the thousands of visitors confine their exploration to the road between Arles and Saintes-Maries-de-la-Mer, and miss the best of the wild flora and fauna.

**Camargue Bulls**
*Periodically, the herds of black bulls are rounded up by the* gardians *to perform in local bullfights. The larger bulls are sold to Spain.*

**Camargue Horses**
*These hardy animals are direct descendants of pre-historic horses. The foal's coat turns white between the age of four and seven.*

**Parc Ornithologique du Pont-de-Gau** bird reserve *(see p138)* is where most birds in the Camargue live and where, twice a year, over 350 species of migrating birds stop off on their journey north or south.

Méjanes

PLAINE DE LA CAMARGUE

Le Petit Rhône

PETITE CAMARGUE

Centre de Ginès

Stes-Maries-de-la-Mer

---

## CAMARGUE BIRDS

This region is a haven for bird spotters, particularly during the spring when migrant birds visit on their journey north. Resident birds include little egrets and marsh harriers. This is the only French breeding site of the slender-billed gull, and the red-crested pochard, rarely seen in Europe, also breeds here.

**Little egret**
*(Egretta garzetta)*

**Slender-billed gull**
*(Larus genei)*

**Marsh harrier** *(Circus aeruginosus)*

**Collared pratincole**
*(Glareola pratincola)*

**Black-winged stilt**
*(Himantopus himantopus)*

**Red-crested pochard**
*(Netta rufina)*

### European Beavers
*European beavers came close to extinction at the start of the 20th century, when they were hunted for their fur. These nocturnal animals were protected in 1905 and began to colonize the region in the 1970s.*

**VISITORS' CHECKLIST**

**Road map** B4. ✈ 90 km (56 miles) E Montpellier-Méditerranée. 🚌 🚉 av Paulin Talbot, Arles. ℹ 5 av Van Gogh, Stes-Maries-de-la-Mer (04 90 97 82 55). 🎭 Pèlerinage des Gitans (24–25 May, end Oct). **www**.parc-camargue.fr

Musée Camarguais *(P139)*

Information Centre for Nature Reserve

Villeneuve

La Capelière

PLAINE DE LA CAMARGUE

Salin de Giraud

### Greater Flamingoes
*Some 10,000 pairs of these exotic, bright pink birds breed in the Camargue. They are often seen feeding on the marshes of the Etang de Vaccarès, although their main breeding ground is on the saltier lagoons towards the south.*

### The Salt Industry
*Flat, shallow lagoons fill with sea water which then evaporates in the sun, leaving behind huge salt deposits. These expanses provide a rich feeding ground for waders such as avocets.*

### Dune Vegetation
*The sand dunes form a line between the lagoons and salt marshes and the sea. Among the many wild flowers that grow here is sea chamomile.*

**KEY**

— Nature reserve boundary

- - Walking routes

- - Walking and cycling routes

0 kilometres    5

0 miles    5

# Exploring the Camargue

**Entrance to Méjanes bullring**

The unique character of the Camargue has given rise to unusual traditions. The native white horses and black bulls are ranched by *manadiers* and herded, branded and tended by the region's cowboys, or *gardians*, whose small, low, whitewashed houses dot the landscape. Local bullfights are advertised in Saintes-Maries-de-la-Mer, the main tourist centre of the region and chief place to stay, also renowned for its gypsy population. It has a sandy beach and offers watersports and boat trips. Tourist offices throughout the area provide information on walks, but the best views are from the 7-km (5-mile) footway and cycle path along the Digues-de-la-Mer (sea dyke) from the town. Several sights within the Camargue have been turned into museums and exhibitions of local life and natural history. Several ranches and activity centres organize rides and riding holidays.

**A bloodless Camargue bullfight in Méjanes**

## A place of pilgrimage

The three Marys who gave Saintes-Maries-de-la-Mer its name are Mary Magdalene, Mary Jacobea (the Virgin Mary's sister) and Mary Salome, mother of the apostles James and John. Set adrift after the Crucifixion with, among others, their servant Sara, Saint Martha and her brother Lazarus, they landed here in their boat. They built a shrine to the virgin, and while the others went to spread the word of the gospel, Mary Jacobea, Mary Salome and Sara stayed behind.

In winter, the town is an unpretentious, whitewashed, low-rise resort. It overflows during the May and October festivals, when Mary Salome and Mary Jacobea are celebrated, their statues marched to the sea to be blessed. The larger festival is in May, when gypsies from all over the world come to pay homage to their patron saint, Sara, the richly dressed black Madonna who lies in the crypt of the 9th-century Eglise de Notre-Dame-de-la-Mer. An effigy is also paraded through the streets to the sea. Afterwards there are bullfights, horse races and flamenco dances *(see pp228–9)*.

Throughout the centre of the town are cheery restaurants with checked tablecloths, and shops selling patterned skirts, shirts and scarves, lucky charms and Romany souvenirs. The prominent church is also worth visiting for the view from the rooftop walkway of its simple, fortified exterior. Just 40 m (44 yards) away from the church, the **Musée Baroncelli** in the old town hall is devoted to zoology and archaeology.

Still in the Saintes-Maries area, 4.5 km (3 miles) north of the centre on the banks of the Etang de Ginès, lies the **Parc Ornithologique du Pont-de-Gau**, with a vast range of Camargue birdlife *(see p136)*.

### 🏛 Musée Baroncelli
Ancien Hôtel de Ville, rue Victor Hugo. **Tel** 04 90 97 87 60. ⭘ Apr–11 Nov: Wed–Mon. 🈺
The documents and artifacts relating to bull rearing and local life on display here were amassed by Marquis Folco de Baroncelli-Javon (1869–1943), a *manadier* who promoted the *gardian* life and the region's customs and traditions.

### 🏛 Ginès Information Centre
Pont-de-Gau. **Tel** 04 90 97 86 32. ⭘ daily. ⬤ 1 Jan, 1 May, 25 Dec. www.parc-camargue.fr
This information centre offers wonderful views over the flat lagoon. Photographs and documents chronicle the history of the Camargue and its diverse flora and fauna.

### 🦅 Parc Ornithologique du Pont-de-Gau
Pont-de-Gau **Tel** 04 90 97 82 62. ⭘ daily. ⬤ 25 Dec. 🈺 ♿ 🚻
www.parcornithologique.com
Most of the birds that live in or migrate through the region are represented in this reserve. Huge aviaries house birds that might otherwise be hard to spot. Try to keep to the sign-posted paths to avoid damage or disturbance *(see p136)*.

**Honey buzzard enclosure at the Pont-de-Gau bird sanctuary**

### 🏛 Musée Camarguais

Parc Naturel Régional de Camargue, Mas du Pont de Rousty. (On the D570, 10 km south-west of Arles). *Tel 04 90 97 10 82*. ☐ *daily (Oct–Mar: Wed–Mon)*. ● *Jan, 1 May, 25 Dec*. 🎫 ♿ 🖳 *www.parc-camargue.fr*

A traditional Provençal *mas* or farmhouse *(see pp22–3)*, that only a short time ago was part of a farm raising cattle and sheep, has been converted to accommodate a fascinating museum of the Camargue. The main part of the museum is housed in a huge sheep barn, built in 1812 and skilfully restored. Displays, including video footage and slide shows, provide an excellent introduction to traditional life in the Camargue and to the unique plant and animal life of the Camargue delta. Among the many subjects covered are

**Eglise de Notre-Dame-de-la-Mer, in Saintes-Maries-de-la-Mer**

the lives of the Camargue cowboys, and the *grand* and *petit* Rhône rivers which once flowed far to the east past Nîmes. Many of the displays are focused on traditional life at the time of poet and champion of the Provençal language, Frédéric Mistral, *(see p28)*, a local man who won the Nobel Prize for literature in 1904.

A signposted 3.5-km (2-mile) nature trail leads out from the museum to the Marré de la Grand Mare and back again by a pleasant circular route. Examples of traditional *mas* husbandry are marked on the way. An observation tower at the end of the walk gives great views over the surrounding countryside.

**The fine Romanesque façade of the abbey church at St-Gilles-du-Gard**

## St-Gilles-du-Gard ❽

**Road map** A3. 🚹 *12,200*. 🚉 ℹ️ *1 place F Mistral (04 66 87 33 75)*. 🗓 *Thu & Sun*. **www**.ville-saint-gilles.fr

Called the "Gateway to the Camargue", St-Gilles is famous for its **Abbaye de St-Gilles.** In medieval times the abbey was vast. The building was damaged in 1562 during the Wars of Religion and all that remains are the west façade, chancel and crypt. The carved façade is the most beautiful in all Provence. It includes the first sculpture of the Passion in Christendom, from the late 12th century. Founded by Raymond VI of Toulouse, the abbey church was the Knights of St John's first priory in Europe. It soon became a key place on the pilgrimage route to Santiago de Compostela in Spain and a port of embarkation for the Crusades *(see pp42–3)*. The crypt houses the tomb of Saint Gilles, a hermit who arrived by raft from Greece.

The belltower of the original abbey contains *La Vis*, a spiral staircase which is a masterpiece of stonemasonry.

## Beaucaire ❾

**Road map** B3. 🚹 *14,000*. 🚉 *Tarascon*. 🚌 ℹ️ *24 cours Gambetta (04 66 59 26 57)*. 🗓 *Thu & Sun*. **www**.ot-beaucaire.fr

The bullring in Beaucaire occupies the site of one of the largest fairs in Europe. Held every July for the past seven

centuries, it attracted up to a quarter of a million people. A smaller version of the fair takes place today, with a procession through the town on 21 July. It was inaugurated by Raymond VI in 1217, who enlarged the **Château de Beaucaire**.

This was later used by the French kings to look down on their Provençal neighbours across the river. It was partly dismantled on the orders of Cardinal Richelieu but the triangular keep and enough of the walls remain to indicate its impressive scale. There is a Romanesque chapel within the walls, and medieval spectacles, including frequent displays of falconry.

The **Abbaye de St-Roman** is situated 5 km (3 miles) to the northwest of Beaucaire. Dating from the 5th century, it is the only troglodyte monastery in Europe.

### ⛪ Château de Beaucaire

Place Raymond VII. *Tel 04 66 59 47 90*. ☐ *Wed–Mon*. 🎫 🖳

**The unique troglodyte Abbaye de Saint-Roman near Beaucaire**

The legendary Tarasque, the terror of Tarascon

# Tarascon ⑩

**Road map** B3. 🚶 13,000. 🚗 🚉
🛈 pl Général de Gaulle (04 90 91 03
52). 🗓 Tue & Fri. www.tarascon.org

The gleaming white vision
of the **Château de Tarascon**
is one of the landmarks of
the Rhône. Little is left of the
glittering court of Good King
René who finished the building
his father, Louis II of Anjou, began early in the 15th century
(see pp46–7). Following René's
death in 1480, Provence fell to
France, and the castle became
a prison until 1926. A draw-
bridge leads to the poultry yard
and garrison quarters. Beside
it rises the impressive main
castle, centred on a courtyard
from where two spiral staircases lead to royal apartments
and other rooms in its sturdy
towers. Prisoners' graffiti and
some painted ceiling panels
remain, but the only adorn-
ment is a handful of borrowed
17th-century tapestries which
depict the deeds of Roman
general Scipio (237–183 BC).

The **Collégiale Ste-Marthe,**
nearby has a tomb in the crypt
to the monster-taming saint.
According to legend, St Martha
(see p42) rescued the inhabitants from the Tarasque, a
man-eating monster, half lion,
half armadillo, which gave the
town its name. The event is
celebrated each June in the
Fête de la Tarasque (see p33).

In the old town is the 16th-
century Cloître des Cordeliers
where exhibitions are held.
On the arcaded Rue des
Halles is the 17th-century
town hall, with an attractively
carved façade and balcony.

The traditional life of the area
and its hand-printed fabrics is
seen in the **Musée Souleïado**.
The ancient textile industry
was revived in 1938, under
the name Souleïado, meaning
"the sun passing through the
clouds" in Provençal. In the
museum are 40,000 18th-
century woodblocks, many
of them still used for the
company's colourful prints.

The **Maison de Tartarin** is
a museum devoted to the tall-
story telling Provençal "hero"
of three comic novels by
Alphonse Daudet (see p28).

⛵ **Château de Tarascon**
Bd du Roi René. **Tel** 04 90 91 01
93. ⏰ daily (Oct–May: Tue–Sun).
⬛ 1 Jan, 1 May, 1 & 11 Nov, 25
Dec. 🖼 🅿

🏛 **Musée Souleïado**
39 rue Proudhon. **Tel** 04 90 91 50
11. ⏰ Tue–Sat. ⬛ 1 Jan, 1 & 11
Nov, 25 Dec. 🖼

🏛 **Maison de Tartarin**
55 bis bd Itam. **Tel** 04 90 91 05 08.
⏰ Apr–Nov: Thu–Tue.
⬛ 1 May, 1 & 11 Nov. 🖼

The fairy tale Château de Tarascon,
stronghold of Good King René

# St-Rémy-de-Provence ⑪

**Road map** B3. 🚶 10,000.
🚗 Avignon. 🛈 pl Jean-Jaurès
(04 90 92 05 22). 🗓 Wed & Sat.
www.stremy-de-provence.com

St-Rémy is ideal for exploring
the Alpilles countryside which
supplies the plants for its
traditional herboristeries,
or herb shops. The **Musée
des Arômes** displays implements of their craft and
properties of the local flora.

St-Rémy's **Eglise St-Martin**
contains an exceptional organ
which can be heard during
the summer festival "Organa",
or on Saturday recitals.

One of the town's most
attractive 15th–16th-century
mansions is now a museum.
The **Musée des Alpilles** has a
fine ethnographic collection.
The well-known 16th-century
physician and astrologer,

**Herbs and spices on sale in St-Rémy
market, place de la République**

Nostradamus, was born in a
house in the outer wall of
the avenue Hoche, in the
old quarter of St-Rémy.

The **Musée Estrine Centre
d'Interpretation Van Gogh**, in
the 18th-century Hôtel Estrine,
is a reminder of the great
artist's association with St-
Rémy. In May 1889, after he
had mutilated his ear, he
arrived at the **Clinique St-Paul**,
which is situated between the
town and the Roman remains
at Glanum. The grounds and
the 12th-century cloisters of
the clinic can be visited, and
the tourist office gives a map
of some of the views Van Gogh
painted while he stayed here.

Just behind the clinic is Le
Mas de la Pyramide, a farm-
stead half-built into the rock,
which has remained in the
same family for generations.
It was formerly a Roman

*For hotels and restaurants in this region see pp199–202 and pp214–16*

The triumphal arch at Glanum, built in the reign of Augustus, a 15-minute walk from the centre of St-Rémy

quarry, but now houses an agricultural museum. The remains of the earliest Greek houses in Provence, from the 4th-century BC, are in **Glanum** (see p40), a Greco-Roman town set against magnificent scenery at the head of a valley in the Alpilles. Dramatic memorials, known as Les Antiques, still stand along the roadside and are well worth visiting – a triumphal arch from 10 BC, celebrating Caesar's conquest of the Greeks and Gaul, and a mausoleum dating from about 30 BC.

🏛 **Musée des Arômes**
34 bd Mirabeau.
*Tel* 04 90 92 48 70. ⬤ Mon–Sat.
⬤ public hols. ♿ 🚻

🏛 **Musée des Alpilles**
Place Favier. *Tel* 04 90 92 68 24.
⬤ Tue–Sat. ⬤ 1 Jan, 1 May,
25 Dec. 🚻

🏛 **Musée Estrine Centre d'Interpretation Van Gogh**
8 rue Estrine. *Tel* 04 90 92 34 72.
⬤ Tue–Sun. ⬤ Jan & Feb. 🚻
restricted.

🏛 **Clinique St-Paul**
Chemin St-Paul. *Tel* 04 90 92 77 00. ⬤ daily. ⬤ 1 Jan, 1 Nov,
25 Dec. 🚻 ♿

⛪ **Glanum**
Rte des Baux. *Tel* 04 90 92 23 79.
⬤ Apr–Aug: daily; Sep–Mar: Tue–Sun. ⬤ 1 Jan, 1 May, 1 & 11 Nov,
25 Dec. 🚻 ♿ 🚻
www.monuments-nationaux.fr

## Les Alpilles ⓬

**Road map** B3. 🚉 Arles, Tarascon,
Salon-de-Provence. 🚌 Les Baux-de-Provence, St-Rémy-de-Provence,
Eyguières, Eygalières. ℹ St-Rémy-de-Provence (04 90 92 05 22).

St-Rémy-de-Provence is on the western side of the limestone massif of Les Alpilles, a 24-km (15-mile) chain between the Rhône and Durance rivers. A high point is **La Caume**, at 387 m (1,270 ft), reached from St-Rémy, just beyond Glanum.

East of St-Rémy, the road to Cavaillon runs along the north side of the massif, with a right turn to Eygalières. The painter Mario Prassinos (1916–85), whose work is displayed in

Notre-Dame-de-Pitié in St-Rémy, lived here. Just beyond the village is the 12th-century Chapelle St-Sixte.

The road continues towards Orgon where there are views across the Durance Valley and the Luberon. Orgon skirts the massif on the eastern side. A right turn leads past the ruins of Castelas de Roquemartine and Eyguières, a pleasant village with a Romanesque church. It is a two-hour walk to Les Opiés, a 493-m (1,617-ft) hill crowned by a tower. This forms part of the GR6 which crosses the chain to Les Baux, one of the best walking routes in Provence. From Castelas de Roquemartine the road heads back west towards Les Baux.

The chalky massif of Les Alpilles, "Little Alps", in the heart of Provence

A late 18th-century fresco showing the Baux warriors in battle against the Saracens in 1266

# Les Baux-de-Provence ⓭

**Road map** B3. 🏠 460. 🚗 ℹ️
*La Maison du Roy (04 90 54 34 39).*
**www**.lesbauxdeprovence.com

Les Baux sits on a spur of the Alpilles (*bau* in Provençal means escarpment), with views across to the Camargue *(see pp136–9)*. The most dramatic fortress site in Provence, it has nearly two million visitors a year, so avoid midsummer, or go early in the morning. The pedestrianized town has a car park beside the Porte Mage gate.

When the Lords of Baux built their fine citadel here in the 10th century, they claimed one of the three wise men, King Balthazar, as ancestor and took the star of Bethlehem as their emblem. These fierce warriors originated the troubadour Courts of Love and wooed noble ladies with poetry and songs. This became the medieval convention known as courtly love and paved the way for a literary tradition.

The citadel ruins lie on the heights of the escarpment. Their entrance is via the 14th-century Tour-du-Brau, which houses the **Musée d'Histoire des Baux-de-Provence**. A plateau extends to the end of the escarpment, where there is a monument to the poet Charloun Rieu (1846–1924). In the town centre, two other museums of local interest are

the **Fondation Louis Jou** and the **Musée des Santons**. Next door to the 12th-century Eglise St-Vincent is the Chapelle des Pénitents Blancs, decorated in 1974 by the local artist Yves Brayer. Just north of Les Baux lies the **Cathédrale d'Images**.

## 🏛 Musée d'Histoire des Baux-de-Provence

Hôtel de la Tour-du-Brau, Rue du Trenca. **Tel** *04 90 54 55 56.*
🕐 *daily.* 🎫 ♿ *restricted.* 📷
This small archaeological museum contains objects from Les Baux and its environs.

**Monument to poet Charloun Rieu**

## 🏛 Fondation Louis Jou

Hôtel Brion, Grande Rue. **Tel** *04 90 54 34 17.*
🕐 *by appt.* 🎫
Medieval books are housed here, along with a collection of prints and drawings by Dürer, Goya and Jou, the local engraver after whom the museum is named.

## 🏛 Musée des Santons

Place Louis Jou. **Tel** *04 90 54 34 39.*
🕐 *daily.*
In the 16th-century old town hall, a Provençal crib scene has been created, representing the nativity at Les Baux. Handmade clay *santons* or figurines *(see p48)*, representing saints and local figures, show the evolution of Provençal costume.

## 🏛 Cathédrale d'Images

Route de Maillane. **Tel** *04 90 54 38 65.* 🕐 *Mar–Dec: daily.* 🎫 ♿
**www**.cathedrale-images.com
Located on the D27 road to the north of Les Baux and within walking distance of the main car park in Les Baux is the Val d'Enfer or the Valley of Hell. This jagged gorge, said to be inhabited by witches and spirits, may have inspired some of Dante's poetry. It is also the site where bauxite was discovered in 1822 by the mineralogist Berthier, who named it after the town. It was in this big quarry that the

View of the citadel and village of Les Baux

Cathédrale d'Images or Picture Palace was established. The imaginative slide show is projected not only onto the white limestone walls of the natural theatre, but also the floor and ceiling, creating a three dimensional effect. The 30-minute show is renewed each year. Accompanied by captivating music, it is an extraordinary audio-visual experience.

**Les Baux's Chapelle des Pénitents, next to the Eglise St-Vincent**

## Fontvieille ⓮

**Road map** B3. *3,500.* 
*av des Moulins (04 90 54 67 49).*
*Mon & Fri.* **www**.fontvieille-provence.com

Fontvieille is an agreeable country town in the flat fruit and vegetable lands of the irrigated Baux Valley. Half-way between Arles and Les Alpilles, the town makes an excellent centre from which to explore. Until the French Revolution in 1789, the town's history was bound up with the Abbaye de Montmajour. The oratories that stand at the four corners of the small town were erected in 1721 to celebrate the end of the plague *(see pp48–9)*.

To the south on the D33, set on a stony hill is the Moulin de Daudet and further on at Barbegal are the remarkable remains of a Roman aqueduct.

## Abbaye de Montmajour ⓯

**Road map** B3. *Route de Fontvieille.* ***Tel*** *04 90 54 64 17.* *Apr–Sep: daily; Oct–Mar: Tue–Sun.* *1 Jan, 1 May, 1 & 11 Nov, 25 Dec.*

Standing out like Noah's ark on Mount Ararat, 5 km (3 miles) northwest of Arles, this Benedictine abbey was built in the 10th century. At the time, the site was an island refuge in marshland. The handful of monks in residence spent all their spare time draining this area of marshland between the Alpilles chain and the Rhône.

The abbey is an imposing place, though all the Baroque buildings were destroyed by fire in 1726 and never restored. The original church is said to have been founded by Saint Trophime as a sanctuary from the Romans. It grew rich in the Middle Ages when thousands of pilgrims arrived at Easter to purchase pardons. After 1791, the abbey was broken up by two successive owners who

**The cloisters and keep of the Abbaye de Montmajour**

bought it from the state. The abbey was largely restored in the 19th century.

The **Eglise Notre-Dame** is one of the largest Romanesque buildings in Provence. Below, the 12th-century crypt has been built into the sloping hill. The cloister has double pillars ornamented with beasts and lies in the shadows of the 26-m (85-ft) tower, built in the 1360s. It is worth climbing the 124 steps to the tower platform to see the stunning view across to the sea. Also carved into the hillside is the atmospheric **Chapelle de St-Pierre**. It was established at the same time as the abbey and is a primitive place of worship. There are a number of tombs in the abbey grounds, but the principal burial area is the 12th-century **Chapelle Ste-Croix**. It lies not far to the east and is built in the shape of a Greek cross.

### DAUDET'S WINDMILL

The Moulin de Daudet is one of the most famous literary landmarks in France. Alphonse Daudet was born in Nîmes in 1840 and made his name in Paris. The windmill is the setting of Daudet's Letters from my Windmill, stories about Provençal life, first published in 1860 and popular ever since. He observed the local characters and wrote about their lives with irony and pathos. He never actually lived in the mill, but made imaginative use of some of the resident miller's tales. When he stayed in Fontvieille he was a guest in the 19th-century Château de Montauban. He came to find respite from the capital, but returned there in order to write his stories. The restored mill can be visited, and there is a small museum dedicated to Daudet.

# Street-by-Street: Arles ⑯

Many of the tourist sites in Arles bear the stamp of their Roman past, and all are within comfortable walking distance of the central place de la République. On its north side is the Hôtel de Ville, behind which is the place du Forum. This square is the heart of modern life in Arles. Another place to sit at a café and observe the Arlésiens is the boulevard des Lices, where the lively twice-weekly market is held. Some of the shops here and in nearby rue Jean-Jaurès sell bright Provençal fabrics. For museum-buffs, an inclusive ticket gives access to all the museums except the Espace Van Gogh.

**Les Thermes de Constantin** are all that remain of Constantine's Palace, built in the 4th century AD.

**Musée Réattu**
*This museum on the banks of the Rhône houses 18th–19th-century and modern art, including this figure of* Le Griffu *(1952) by Germaine Richier.*

**Hôtel de Ville**

**Museon Arlaten**
*The Hôtel de Laval-Castellane contains the largest folklore collection in Provence, a treasure house of local history.*

**★ Eglise St-Trophime**
*This fine Romanesque church has a 12th-century portal of the* Last Judgment, *including saints and apostles.*

**L'Espace Van Gogh**, a cultural centre

## STAR SIGHTS

- ★ Les Arènes
- ★ Théâtre Antique
- ★ Eglise St-Trophime

**Egyptian Obelisk**
*An ancient obelisk with fountains at its base (one of which is shown here) stands in the place de la République. It came from the Roman circus across the Rhône.*

## ★ Les Arènes

*This is one of the largest, best-preserved Roman monuments in Provence. The top tier provides an excellent panoramic view of Arles.*

### VISITORS' CHECKLIST

**Road map** B3. 🏛 *53,000.*
✈ Nîmes-Garons. 🚊 🚌 av P
Talabot. 🛈 esp C de Gaulle (04
90 18 41 20). 🚍 Wed, Sat. 🎭
Feria Pascale (Easter); Fête des
Gardians (1 May); Fêtes d'Arles
(Jul); Feria des Prémices du Riz
(Sep). www.arlestourisme.com

## ★ Théâtre Antique

*Once a fortress, its stones were later used for other buildings. These last remaining columns are called the "two widows".*

**Notre-Dame-de-la-Major** is dedicated to Saint George, patron saint of the Camargue *gardians* (cowboys).

### Cloisters of St-Trophime

*This sculpted capital is a fine example of the Romanesque beauty of the cloisters.*

**KEY**

- - - Suggested route

| | |
|---|---|
| 0 metres | 100 |
| 0 yards | 100 |

### VAN GOGH IN ARLES

Vincent Van Gogh painted over 300 canvases in the 15 months he lived in Arles, but the town has none of his work. In belated appreciation of this lonely artist, the Hôtel-Dieu has been turned into L'Espace Van Gogh, with a library and exhibition space. Several sites are evocative of him, however; the Café Van Gogh in the place du Forum has been renovated to look as it did in his *Café du Soir*.

*L'Arlésienne* by Van Gogh (1888)

# Exploring Arles

The city of Arles was a Greek site expanded by the Romans into a "little Rome". Here, on the most southerly crossing point on the Rhône, they built shipyards, baths, a racetrack and an arena. Then the capital of the three Gauls – France, Spain and Britain – Arles remains one of the most distinctive towns in Provence with fine relics from its Gallo-Roman past. Cars should be parked outside the narrow lanes of the old town.

Sarcophagi on Les Alyscamps

## ⋔ Les Arènes

Rond-point des Arènes. **Tel** 04 90 49 59 05. ☐ daily. ● 1 Jan, 1 May, 1 Nov, 25 Dec & for bullfights. ▨ ☑

The most impressive of the surviving Roman monuments, the amphitheatre is on the east side of the old town. It was the largest of the Roman buildings in Gaul. Slightly oval, it measures 136 m (446 ft) by 107 m (351 ft) and could seat 20,000. The floors of some of the internal rooms were decorated with mosaics, the better to wash down after bloody affrays. Today both Provençal and Spanish bullfights are held regularly in the arena.

View of Arles from the opposite bank of the Rhône

Just to the southwest of the amphitheatre is the elegant Roman **Théâtre Antique**, which has 2,000 tiered seats arranged in a hemisphere.

## 🏛 Musée de l'Arles Antique

Presqu'île du Cirque Romain. **Tel** 04 90 18 88 88. ☐ daily. ● 1 Jan, 1 May, 1 Nov, 25 Dec. ▨ ☒ ☐ www.arlesantique.org

Arles became Christian after Constantine's conversion in AD 312. This museum displays fine examples of Romano-Christian sculpture, as well as local ancient artifacts and pagan art, including a copy of the Venus of Arles and Roman mosaics.

## ⋔ Cryptoporticus

Rue Balze. **Tel** 04 90 49 59 05. ☐ daily. ● 1 Jan, 1 May, 1 Nov, 25 Dec. ▨

These huge subterranean galleries (see p41), ventilated by air shafts, were part of the forum's structure.

## ⋔ Les Alyscamps

Av des Alyscamps. ☐ daily. ● 1 Jan, 1 May, 1 Nov, 25 Dec. ▨ ☒

From Roman to late Medieval times, Les Alyscamps was one of the largest and most famous cemeteries in the Western world. Romans

Roman mosaic of *Europa and the Bull*, in the Musée de l'Arles Antique

avoided it at night, making it an ideal meeting place for early Christians, led by St Trophime. Christians were often buried by the tomb of Genesius, a Roman servant and beheaded Christian martyr.

## ♙ Eglise St-Trophime

Place de la République. **Tel** 04 90 96 07 38. ☐ daily. ● 1 Jan, 1 May, 1 Nov, 25 Dec. ▨ cloisters. ☑ ☒

This is one of the most beautiful Romanesque churches in Provence. The portal and cloisters are exquisitely decorated with biblical scenes. St Trophime, thought to be the first bishop of Arles in the early 3rd century, appears with St Peter and St John on the carved northeast pillar.

## 🏛 Museon Arlaten

Hôtel Laval-Castellane, 29 rue de la République. **Tel** 04 90 93 58 11. ☐ Jul–Sep: daily; Oct–Jun: Tue–Sun. ● 1 Jan, 1 May, 1 Nov, 25 Dec. ▨

With costumes, tableaux and artifacts, this folklore museum is a treasure trove of information about local customs, superstitions and traditions. It was founded in 1896 by the poet Mistral (see p28), who refurbished the 16th-century Hôtel Laval-Castellane using his Nobel prize money.

## 🏛 Musée Réattu

10 rue du Grand-Prieuré. **Tel** 04 90 49 37 58. ☐ daily. ● 1 Jan, 1 May, 1 & 11 Nov, 25 Dec. ▨

The local artist Jacques Réattu (1760–1833) and his contemporaries form the basis of this collection. A Picasso donation and a photographic display are among 20th-century works.

*For hotels and restaurants in this region see pp199–202 and pp214–16*

## Martigues ⑰

**Road map** B4. 🏛 *45,000.* 🚉 🚌
🛈 *Rond-Point de l'Hôtel de Ville
(04 42 42 31 10).* 🛒 *Thu & Sun.*
www.martigues-tourisme.com

The Etang de Berre, situated
between Marseille and the
Camargue, has the largest
petroleum refinery industry
in France, which dominates
the landscape. However, on
the inland side of the Canal
de Caronte is the former
fishing port and artists' colony
of Martigues, which still
attracts a holiday crowd.
   Martigues lies on both banks
of the canal and on the island
of Brescon, where the Pont San
Sébastien is a popular place for
artists to set up their easels.
Félix Ziem (1821–1911) was
the most ardent admirer of
this "little Venice" *(see p26);*
his paintings and works by
contemporary artists can be
viewed in the **Musée Ziem.**

**🏛 Musée Ziem**
Bd du 14 Juillet. *Tel 04 42 41 39
60.* ◯ *Wed–Sun pm.* ◉ *public
hols.*

**Canal San Sébastien in Martigues,
known as the Birds' Looking-Glass**

## Salon-de-Provence ⑱

**Road map** B3. 🏛 *40,000.*
🚉 🚌 🛈 *56 cours Gimon
(04 90 56 27 60).* 🛒 *Wed & Sun.*
www.salondeprovence.fr

Known for its olives (the olive
oil industry was established in
the 1400s) and soap, Salon-de-
Provence is dominated by the
castellated **Château de l'Empéri.**
Once home of the archbishops

**The 12th-century Cistercian Abbaye de Silvacane**

of Arles, this now contains the
Musée de l'Empéri, which has
a large collection of militaria
from Louis XIV to World War I.
   The military tradition in the
town is upheld by the French
Air Force officers' college, La
Patrouille Aérienne de France.
   Near the château is the 13th-
century **Eglise de St-Michel**
and in the north of the old
town is the Gothic **St-Laurent**,
where the French physician
and astrologer Nostradamus is
buried. Nostradamus is Salon's
most famous citizen. Here, in
his adopted home, he wrote
*Les Centuries*, his book
of predictions,
published in 1555.
It was banned by
the Vatican, as it
foretold the dimin-
ishing power of
the papacy. But
his renown was
widespread and
in 1560 he was
made Charles
IX's physician.
   Salon's four-day
Gospel music festival
in July echoes throughout the
town, with concerts in the
château, free street performances and song workshops.

**Nostradamus, astrologer
and citizen of Salon**

**⛪ Château de l'Empéri**
Montée du Puech. *Tel 04 90 56 22
36.* ◯ *Wed–Mon.* ◉ *1 Jan, 1
May, 1 Nov, 24–25 Dec, 31 Dec.* 📷

## Abbaye de Silvacane ⑲

**Road map** C3. *Tel 04 42 50 41 69.*
◯ *Apr–Sep: daily; Oct–Mar: Wed–
Mon.* ◉ *1 Jan, 1 May, 25 Dec.* 📷
🖥 www.ville-laroquedantheron.fr

Like her two Cistercian sisters,
Silvacane is a harmonious
12th-century monastery tucked
away in the countryside. A bus
from Aix-en-Provence runs
regularly to Roque-d'Anthéron,
the nearest village. The abbey
was founded on the site of a
Benedictine monastery,
in a clearing of a
"forest of reeds"
*(silva canorum).*
It adheres to the
austere Cistercian
style, with no
decoration. The
church, with nave,
two aisles and a
high, vaulted tran-
sept, is solid, bare
and echoing. The
cloisters, arcaded
like a pigeon loft, are
13th century and the refectory 14th century. Shortly after
the refectory was built, all the
monks left and the church
served the parish. After the
Revolution, it was sold as
state property and became
a farm until transformed
back into an abbey.

# Aix-en-Provence ❷⓪

Provence's former capital is an international students' town, with one of the region's most cosmopolitan streets of restaurants and bars, rue de la Verrerie. The university was founded by Louis II of Anjou in 1409 and flourished under his son, Good King René *(see p46–7)*.

Another wave of prosperity transformed the city in the 17th century, when ramparts, first raised by the Romans in their town of Aquae Sextiae, were pulled down, and the mansion-lined cours Mirabeau was built. Aix's renowned fountains were added in the 18th century.

The cours Mirabeau, grandest of Aix's boulevards

### Exploring Aix

North of the cours Mirabeau, sandwiched between the Cathédrale St-Sauveur and the place d'Albertas, lies the town's old quarter. Sights include the Musée des Tapisseries, housed in the former Bishop's palace, and the splendid 17th-century Hôtel de Ville. Built around a courtyard by Pierre Pavillon from 1655–1670, it stands in a square now used as a flower market. Nearby is the 16th-century clock tower.

Just outside the old town are the ancient Roman baths, the **Thermes Sextius**, and nearby is the 18th-century spa complex.

Aix's finest street, the cours Mirabeau, is named after the orator and revolutionary Comte de Mirabeau. At its western end is the Fontaine de la Rotonde, a cast-iron fountain built in 1860. The north side is lined with shops, pâtisseries and cafés, the most illustrious being the 18th-century Les Deux Garçons *(see p219)*. The south side is lined with

**Pavillon de Vendôme detail**

elegant hôtels: No. 4, Hôtel de Villars (1710); No. 10, the Hôtel d'Isoard de Vauvenargues, (1710), former residence of the Marquis of Entrecasteau who murdered his wife here; No. 19, Hôtel d'Arbaud Jouques (1730); No. 20, Hôtel de Forbin (1658); and Hôtel d'Espagnet at No. 38, once home to the Duchess of Montpensier, known as "La Grande Mademoiselle", niece of Louis XIII. South of the cours Mirabeau is the Quartier Mazarin built during the time of Archbishop Michel Mazarin. Aix's first Gothic church, St-Jean-de-Malte, now houses the Musée Granet.

### 🅐 Cathédrale St-Sauveur

34 pl des Martyrs-de-la-Résistance. **Tel** 04 42 23 45 65. ⬜ daily. 🔲 for cloisters.

The cathedral at the top of the old town creaks with history. The main door has solid walnut panels sculpted by Jean Guiramand of Toulon (1504). On the right there is a fine 4th–5th-century baptistry, with a Renaissance cupola standing on 2nd-century Corinthian columns. These are from a basilica which stood here beside the Roman forum. The jewel of the church is the triptych of *The Burning Bush* (1476, *see pp46–7)* by Nicolas Froment (restored in 2008). South of the cathedral are the tiled Romanesque cloisters.

### 🏛 Musée des Tapisseries

28 place des Martyrs-de-la-Résistance. **Tel** 04 42 23 09 91. ⬜ Wed–Mon. 🔴 31 Dec–1 Jan, 1 May, 24–25 Dec. 🖼

Apart from magnificent 17th- and 18th-century Beauvais tapestries, the museum has opera costumes and stage designs from 1948 onwards, used in the annual Festival International d'Aix *(see p33)*.

### 🏛 Musée du Vieil Aix

17 rue Gaston-de-Saporta. **Tel** 04 42 21 43 55. 🔵 until further notice. 🖼

This eclectic collection of local memorabilia includes furniture, marionettes, a 19th-century *crèche parlante* and figures from the Corpus Christi parade commissioned by King René.

The 17th-century Hôtel de Ville, with the flower market in front

### 🏛 Muséum d'Histoire Naturelle

6 rue Espariat. **Tel** 04 42 27 91 27. ⬜ daily. 🖼 🔲 🎫 www.museum-aix-en-provence.org

Located in the Hôtel Boyer d'Eguilles, designed by Pierre Puget and built in 1675, the museum has some fascinating collections of mineralogy and palaeontology. Dinosaur eggs which were found locally are a high point of the exhibits.

Cézanne's studio, filled with his furniture and personal belongings

## VISITORS' CHECKLIST

**Road map** C4. ⚑ 140,000. 🚉
av Victor Hugo. 🚌 Av de l'Europe.
🛈 2 pl du Gén de Gaulle (04 42
16 11 61). 🛒 daily. 🎭 Fest
d'Art Lyrique (Jun–Jul). **www**.
aixenprovencetourism.com

### 🏛 Musée Granet

pl St-Jean de Malte. **Tel** 04 42 52
88 32. 🕐 Tue–Sun pm. ● 1 Jan,
1 May, 25 Dec. 📷 🎟 🛈

The city's main museum is in an impressive 17th-century former priory of the Knights of Malta. François Granet (1775–1849) was a local painter, and bequeathed his collection of French, Italian and Flemish paintings to Aix. These include Ingres' *Portrait of Granet* and *Jupiter and Thetis*. There are also works by Granet himself and other Provençal painters, with eight canvases by Paul Cézanne, plus archaeological material from Roman Aix.

### 🏛 Fondation Vasarely

1 av Marcel Pagnol. **Tel** 04 42 20 01
09. 🕐 Tue–Sat. ● public hols. 📷
🚻 ground floor only. 🎟 🛈 📷

One of Aix's most distinctive landmarks, this series of black-and-white metal hexagons was designed by the king of Op Art Victor Vasarely in the mid-1970s to house his foundation. Alongside his monumental works, its exhibitions promote art in the city at a national and international level.

### ⚑ Atelier Paul Cézanne

9 av Paul Cézanne. **Tel** 04 42 21
06 53. 🕐 daily. ● 1 Jan, 1 May,
25 Dec. 📷 🎟 🛈 Apr–Sep. 🛈
**www**.atelier-cezanne.com

Ten minutes' walk uphill from the cathedral is the modest house of artist Paul Cézanne (*see p26*). The studio, designed by Cézanne himself, is much as he left it when he died in 1906. Not far from here you can see the Montagne Ste-Victoire, a favourite subject.

### 🏛 Pavillon de Vendôme

13 rue de la Molle. **Tel** 04 42 21 05
78. 🕐 Wed–Mon. ● Jan, 1 May,
25 & 26 Dec. 📷

One of Aix's grandest houses, built for Cardinal de Vendôme in 1667 and later enlarged, the main entrance is supported by two figures of Atlantes (*see p48*), and the rooms are filled with Provençal furniture.

### AIX-EN-PROVENCE

Cathédrale St-Sauveur ③
Fontaine de
  la Rotonde ⑧
Hôtel de Ville ⑥
Musée Granet ⑨
Muséum d'Histoire
  Naturelle ⑦
Musée des Tapisseries ④
Musée du Vieil Aix ⑤
Pavillon de Vendôme ①
Thermes Sextius ②

0 metres          500
0 yards           500

**Key to Symbols** see back flap

Gare Routière
500m (550 yards)
Gare TGV
8 km (5 miles)

Fondation
Vasarely
Gare SNCF

Atelier
Cézanne
BOULEVARD A. BRIAND
Cathédrale
St-Sauveur ③
Muséé des Tapisseries ④
Thermes
Sextius ②
Musée du
Vieil Aix ⑤
Hôtel de Ville ⑥
Pavillon de
Vendôme ①
Ancienne Halle
aux Grains
Eglise de la
Madeleine
Palais de
Justice
Muséum
d'Histoire
Naturelle ⑦
COURS MIRABEAU
Fontaine de
la Rotonde ⑧
Musée
Arbaud
St-Jean-de-Malte
Musée
Granet ⑨
BOULEVARD DU ROI RENE
Parc Jourdan
Mont
Ste Victoire
TOULON

# Marseille ㉑

France's premier port and oldest major city is in a surprisingly attractive setting, centred on the Vieux Port, which fishing boats enter between the guardian forts of St-Jean and St-Nicolas. On the north side are the commercial docks and the old town, rebuilt after World War II. People have lived here for 26 centuries, its mixture of cultures being so varied that Alexandre Dumas called it "the meeting place of the entire world".

The Vieux Port looking south, with Notre-Dame-de-la-Garde on high

## Exploring Marseille

Inland, running from the end of the port, is La Canebière – cannabis walk – a big, bustling boulevard which stretches from former hemp fields down to the port where the hemp was made into rope.

At the top of La Canebière is the Neo-Gothic Eglise des Réformés. A left and a right turn lead to boulevard Longchamp, and a walk along its length brings you to the Palais Longchamp. This is not really a palace, but more an impressive folly in the form of a colonnade that fans out around a fountain and ends in two large wings. These wings support a natural history and a fine arts museum.

Behind the palace is the city's zoo. Beyond the grid of shopping streets to the south, the town rises towards the basilica of Notre-Dame-de-la-Garde, which provides an unparalleled view of the city.

If you visit the morning fish market on the quai des Belges, you can delight in Marseille's famed *bouillabaisse (see p207)* at one of the countless nearby fish restaurants. Just behind the quai des Belges, at the back of St-Ferréol, is the Jardin des Vestiges, where remains of the ancient Greek settlement from the 4th century BC have been recently discovered.

## ♿ Vieille Charité

2 rue de la Vieille Charité. *Tel* 04 91 14 58 80. ⬜ Tue–Sun. ⬤ public hols. 🅿 🏠 🏠 🏠 ♿

The old town's finest building is the Vieille Charité, a large, well-restored hospice designed by Pierre Puget (1620–94), architect to Louis XIV. Begun in 1671, its original purpose was to house rural migrants. It is centred on a beautifully proportioned chapel with an oval dome, now used as an exhibition centre. The first floor has a small but rich collection of ancient Egyptian artifacts in the Musée d'Archéologie Méditerranéenne and the second floor displays African and Oceanic art.

## ♉ Cathédrale de la Major

Place de la Major. *Tel* 04 91 90 53 57. ⬜ daily.

The old town descends on the west side to the Cathédrale de la Major, a Neo-Byzantine confection completed in 1893. Its crypt contains the tombs of the bishops of Marseille. Beside it, small and beautiful, is the 11th-century Ancienne Cathédrale de la Major, part of which was sacrificed in the building of the new cathedral. Inside are a reliquary altar of 1073 and a 15th-century altar.

## ☗ Musée des Docks Romains

28 place Vivaux. *Tel* 04 91 91 24 62. ⬜ Tue–Sun. ⬤ public hols. 🅿

During post-war rebuilding the Roman docks were uncovered. A small museum, mainly displaying large storage urns once used for wine, grain and oil, occupies the site of the docks, now buried in the foundations of a residential block.

The Palais Longchamps, a 19th-century folly set around a fountain

Stall at the daily fish market, on the old port's quai des Belges

## VISITORS' CHECKLIST

**Road map** C4. 🏠 900,000. ✈
25 km (15 miles) NW Marseille. 🚉
🚌 pl Victor Hugo. ⛴ SNCM, 61
bd des Dames; Chateau d'If ferry,
Quai des Belges. 🛈 4 la Canebière
(04 91 13 89 00). 🏛 Mon–Sat.
📅 Fête de la Chandeleur (2 Feb).

### 🏛 Musée du Vieux Marseille

Maison Diamantée, 2 rue de la
Prison. **Tel** 04 91 55 28 68. 🕐 Tue–
Sun. 🔵 public hols. 🎫 ☑
The quai du Port follows the
north side of the port past the
17th-century Hôtel de Ville.
Behind it lies the most interesting museum of the town's
history: the recently renovated Musée du Vieux Marseille,
in the 16th-century Maison
Diamantée. The building
takes its name from the
diamond-shaped stones in its
façade. It houses 18th-century
Provençal furniture, domestic
objects and *santons*.

### 🏛 Musée d'Histoire de Marseille

Centre Bourse, square Belsunce.
**Tel** 04 91 90 42 22. 🕐 Mon–Sat.
🔵 public hols. 🎫 ♿ ☑
In the Centre Bourse shopping
centre is the Musée d'Histoire
de Marseille. Reconstructions
of the city at the height of the
Greek period make this a good
starting point for a tour. From
here there is access to the
Jardin des Vestiges, with
remains of Greek fortifications
and ancient docks dating
from the 1st century AD.

### 🏛 Musée Cantini

19 rue Grignan. **Tel** 04 91 54 77 75.
🕐 Tue–Sun. 🔵 public hols. 🎫 ☑
The Musée Cantini is housed
in the 17th-century Hôtel de
Montgrand. Its collection of 20th-
century art, given by the sculp-
tor Jules Cantini, includes Fauve,
Cubist and Surrealist paintings.

### 🏛 Musée de la Faïence

157 av Montredon. **Tel** 04 91 72 43 47.
🕐 Tue–Sun. 🔵 pub hols. 🎫 ♿ 📷

Marseille's fine new ceramic
museum, in the 19th-century
Château Pastré, has over
1,200 items of local, national
and European ceramics from
Neolilithic times to today.

The imposing, heavily fortified
walls of the Abbaye de St-Victor

### 🔒 Abbaye de St-Victor

Place St-Victor. **Tel** 04 96 11 22 60.
🕐 daily. 🎫 for crypt.
Marseille's finest piece of religious architecture is St Victor's
basilica, between Notre-Dame
and the port. This religious
fortress belonged to one of
the most powerful abbeys in
Provence. It was founded in
the 5th century by a monk, St
Cassian, in honour of St Victor,
martyred two centuries earlier,
and was enlarged from the
11th to the 14th centuries.
There are crypts containing
catacombs, sarcophagi and
the cave of St Victor.
On 2 February each year St-
Victor becomes a place of pilgrimage. Boat-shaped cakes
are sold to commemorate the
legendary arrival in Provence
of the Stes-Maries *(see p41)*.

### 🔒 Basilique de Notre-Dame-de-la-Garde

Rue Fort du Sanctuaire.
**Tel** 04 91 13 40 80. 🕐 daily. 📷
The basilica of Notre-Dame-
de-la-Garde, which dominates
the south of the town at 155 m
(500 ft), is a 19th-century Neo-
Byzantine extravaganza. It is
presided over by a golden
Madonna on a 46-m (150-ft)
bell tower. Much of the interior
decoration is by the Düsseldorf
School. Many come for the
incomparable view over the
city, while others come here
to leave votive offerings.

### 🏛 Musée Grobet-Labadié

140 bd Longchamp. **Tel** 04 91 62 21
82. 🕐 Tue–Sun. 🔵 pub hols. 🎫 📷
To the north of the city, at the
top of boulevard Longchamp,
is the finest house in Marseille,
with one of the most unusual
interiors in the region. It was
built in 1873 for a Marseille
merchant, Alexandre Labadié.
The house and its collection
were given to the city in 1919
by his daughter, Marie-Louise.
The Musée Grobet-Labadié
has a fine furniture collection,
tapestries, 17th–19th century
paintings, and many objects
of interest, including unusual
musical instruments, among
them silk and ivory bagpipes.

Detail of *The Flagellation of Christ*,
in the Musée Grobet-Labadié

## 🏛 Palais Longchamp

*42 bd Longchamp.* **Musée des Beaux-Arts** ● *until 2012.* **Musée d'Histoire Naturelle** *Tel 04 91 14 59 50.* ○ *Tue–Sun.* ● *public hols.* ▨

This 19th-century palace is home to both the Musée des Beaux-Arts and the Musée d'Histoire Naturelle, with its collection of stuffed animals. The Musée des Beaux-Arts contains important works by local artists Pierre Puget (1620–94) and Daumier (1808–79), as well as paintings by French, Italian and Flemish old masters.

The Château d'If in the bay of Marseille, a prison in reality and fiction

*Le Sacrifice de Noé* by Pierre Puget in the Musée des Beaux Arts

## ⚓ Château d'If

*Tel 04 91 59 02 30.* ○ *daily (Sep–Mar: Tue–Sun).* ▨ **⊓** *Feb–Nov.*

Fact, fiction and legend mingle in this island castle in the bay of Marseille. Until the 16th century it was a barren island, only visited by local fishermen. On a trip to Marseille in 1516, François I decided to make it a fortress. It was built in 1529, and turned into a prison from 1540 till World War I. Famous inmates have included Alexander Dumas' fictional Count of Monte Cristo, the legendary Man in the Iron Mask *(see p71)* and the real Comte de Mirabeau. In 1516, the first rhinoceros ever to set foot in Europe was brought ashore here, and drawn by Albrecht Dürer *(see p47)*.

## 🏛 Cité Radieuse

*280 bd Michelet.* *Tel 04 91 16 78 00 (for guided tour information).*

A landmark in modern architecture, the Cité Radieuse or Radiant City was opened in 1952. This vertical, concrete construction by Le Corbusier includes shops, social clubs schools and crèches *(see p25)*.

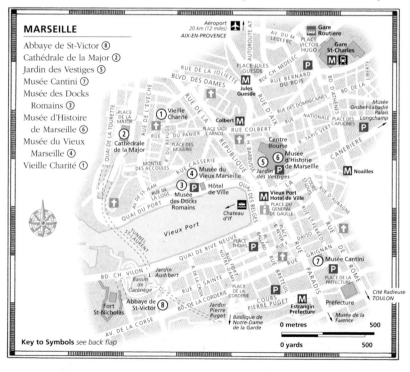

**MARSEILLE**

**Key to Symbols** *see back flap*

# Aubagne ⚁

**Road map** C4. 👥 45,000. 🚉 🚌
🛈 8 cours Barthélemy (04 42 03 49
98). 🛍 Tue, Thu, Sat & Sun.
www.agglo-paysdaubagne.com

Marcel Pagnol's life and
work is the main attraction of
this unprepossessing market
town. It has a tradition of
making ceramics and *santons*
*(see p48)*. The tableaux can
be seen in the Petit Monde
de Marcel Pagnol display
opposite the tourist office.

Just outside the town is the
headquarters of the French
Foreign Legion, moved here
from Algeria in 1962. The
headquarters has a **Musée
de la Légion Etrangère** with
memorabilia on display from
a variety of campaigns ranging from Mexico to Indochina.

🏛 **Musée de la Légion
Etrangère**
Chemin de la Thuilière. *Tel 04 42
18 12 41.* 🕐 Tue, Wed, Fri–Sun
(Oct–May: Wed, Sat, Sun). 🔥 restr.
www.legion-etrangere.com

# Les Calanques ⚂

**Road map** C4. 🚠 Marseille. 🚉
Marseille, Cassis. 🚌 Cassis. ⚓ Cassis,
Marseille. 🛈 Cassis (08 92 25 98 92).

Between Marseille and Cassis
the coast is broken up by
*calanques* – enticing fjord-like
inlets lying between vertical
white cliffs. Continuing deep
under the blue waters, they
offer safe natural harbours and

**Poster for Pagnol's film *Angèle***

fascinating aquatic life, with
glorious views from the high
clifftops *(see also pp30–31)*.
Their precipitous faces provide
a challenge to climbers.

Access to some inlets is by
boat. From Cassis, it is possible
to walk to the nearest
*calanque*, Port-Miou. Beyond
it lies Port-Pin, with occasional
pine trees and a shady beach,
but the most scenic is En-Vau,
which has a sandy beach and
needle-like rocks rising from
the sea. On the western side,
the Sormiou and Morgiou inlets
can be approached by road.

In 1991, a cave was found
with its entrance 100 m (350 ft)
beneath the sea at Sormiou. It
is decorated with pictures of
prehistoric animals resembling
the ancient cave paintings at
Lascaux in the Dordogne.

Bear in mind when visiting
the area that the main car parks
serving Les Calanques beaches
are notorious for theft.

# Cassis ⚃

**Road map** C4. 👥 8,000. 🚉 🚌
🛈 Le Port (08 92 25 98 92).
🛍 Wed & Fri. www.ot-cassis.fr

A favourite summer resort of
artists such as Derain, Dufy and
Matisse, Cassis is a lovely port,
tucked into limestone hills. The
Romans liked it, too, and built
villas here, and when Marseille
prospered in the 17th century
a number of mansions were
erected. It was also a busy
fishing centre in the 19th
century, and is still known for
its excellent seafood. The local
delicacy is fresh sea urchins,
enjoyed with a glass of Cassis'
reputed AOC white wine.

There is a charming **Musée
Municipal Méditerranéen**,
with items dating back to the
Greeks, some rescued from the
seabed. It also shows Cassis to
have been a substantial trading
port up till World War II, when
the Germans effectively dem-
olished its fleet. There are
paintings by Félix Ziem *(see
p26)* and by other early 20th-
century artists who were
equally drawn to Cassis, like
Winston Churchill, who learnt
to paint here.

Apart from Les Calanques,
there are three good beaches,
notably the Plage de la Grande
Mer. Between Cassis and La
Ciotat are the red cliffs of Cap
Canaille, with a 4-hour walk
along the Route des Crêtes.

🏛 **Musée Municipal
Méditerranéen**
Rue X-d'Authier. *Tel 04 42 01 88
66.* 🕐 Wed–Sat. 🌑 public hols.
🚫 🔥 restricted.

**En-Vau, the most beautiful of Les Calanques, along the coast from Cassis**

# VAUCLUSE

*Vaucluse is a land of vines and lavender, truffles and melons, which many know about through the books of the English expatriate Peter Mayle, depicting village life in the Luberon, an idyllic countryside where Picasso spent his last years. Roussillon, set among ochre quarries, also became the topic of a book, when American sociologist LaurenceWylie experienced village life there in the 1950s.*

The jewel of Vaucluse is the fortified riverside city of Avignon, home to the popes during their "Babylonian exile" from 1309–77, and now host to one of the great music and theatre festivals of France. The popes' castle at Châteauneuf-du-Pape is now a ruin, but the village still produces stupendous wines. The Rhône valley wine region is justly renowned, and its vineyards spread as far northeast as the slopes of the towering giant of Provence, Mont Ventoux.

The Roman legacy in Vaucluse is also remarkable. It is glimpsed in the great theatre and triumphal arch in Orange, and in the ruins of Vaison-la-Romaine which were not built over by successive civilizations. Carpentras was also a Roman town, but its claim to fame is its possession of France's oldest synagogue. The story of the Jews, who were given papal protection in Vaucluse, is one of many religious histories which can be traced through the region. Another is the Baron of Oppède's brutal crusade against the Vaudois heretics in 1545, when many villages were destroyed.

Near Oppède, at Lacoste, a path leads to the château of France's notorious libertine Marquis de Sade. Perhaps a more elevated writer was Petrarch, who lived in Fontaine-de-Vaucluse, where the Sorgue river emerges from a mysterious source.

Façade of vine-covered house at Le Bastidon, near the Luberon

◁ Lavender fields in glorious bloom near Valreas

# Exploring Vaucluse

Vaucluse, which takes its name from the Latin *vallis clausa* (closed valley), covers 3,540 sq km (2,200 sq miles). It is bordered by the Rhône on the west, the Durance in the south, and the foothills of the Alps to the east, and has a series of highland chains, dominated by the serene Mont Ventoux *(see p160)*. The extraordinary Dentelles pinnacles are in the west and to the south is the Vaucluse Plateau, where the river Sorgue flows in the beautiful and dramatic setting of Fontaine-de-Vaucluse.

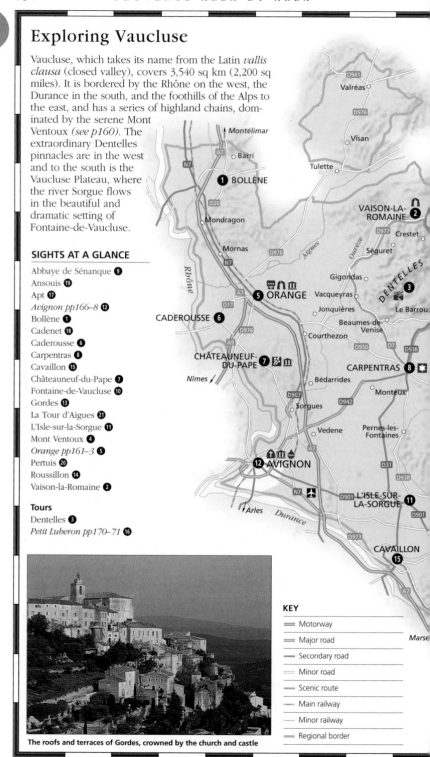

## SIGHTS AT A GLANCE

Abbaye de Sénanque **9**
Ansouis **19**
Apt **17**
*Avignon pp166–8* **12**
Bollène **1**
Cadenet **18**
Caderousse **6**
Carpentras **8**
Cavaillon **15**
Châteauneuf-du-Pape **7**
Fontaine-de-Vaucluse **10**
Gordes **13**
La Tour d'Aigues **21**
L'Isle-sur-la-Sorgue **11**
Mont Ventoux **4**
*Orange pp161–3* **5**
Pertuis **20**
Roussillon **14**
Vaison-la-Romaine **2**

## Tours

Dentelles **3**
*Petit Luberon pp170–71* **16**

**The roofs and terraces of Gordes, crowned by the church and castle**

### KEY

Motorway
Major road
Secondary road
Minor road
Scenic route
Main railway
Minor railway
Regional border

**For additional map symbols** *see back flap*

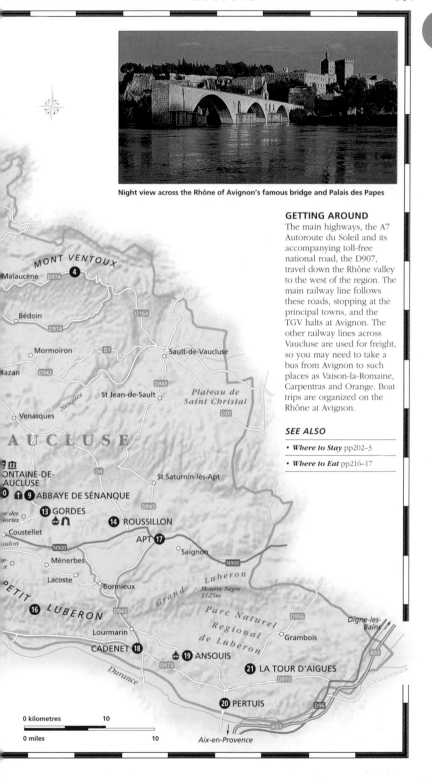

**Night view across the Rhône of Avignon's famous bridge and Palais des Papes**

## GETTING AROUND

The main highways, the A7 Autoroute du Soleil and its accompanying toll-free national road, the D907, travel down the Rhône valley to the west of the region. The main railway line follows these roads, stopping at the principal towns, and the TGV halts at Avignon. The other railway lines across Vaucluse are used for freight, so you may need to take a bus from Avignon to such places as Vaison-la-Romaine, Carpentras and Orange. Boat trips are organized on the Rhône at Avignon.

### SEE ALSO

- **Where to Stay** pp202–3
- **Where to Eat** pp216–17

MONT VENTOUX

Malaucène  D974  **4**

Bédoin  D974

D164

Mormoiron  D1

azan  D942

St Jean-de-Sault  Sault-de-Vaucluse

D943

Nesques  Plateau de Saint Christal

Venasques  D30

**AUCLUSE**

ONTAINE-DE-AUCLUSE  D4  St Saturnin-lès-Apt

**9** ABBAYE DE SÉNANQUE

e des  ories  **13** GORDES  D943

Coustellet  **14** ROUSSILLON

oulon  N900  APT **17**

e-x  Ménerbes  Saignon

Lacoste  Bonnieux  N900

Grand  Luberon

**PETIT**  Mourre Nègre  1125m

**16** LUBERON  D943  Parc Naturel

Lourmarin  Régional  D956

CADENET **18**  de Luberon  Grambois  Digne-les-Bains

Durance  **19** ANSOUIS  A51

D973  **21** LA TOUR D'AIGUES

D973

**20** PERTUIS  D96

0 kilometres  10  A51

0 miles  10  Aix-en-Provence

The Belvédère Pasteur garden in Bollène

## Bollène 1

**Road map** B2. *14,500.* *pl Reynaud de la Gardette (04 90 40 51 44).* *Mon.* **www**.bollene.fr

Despite being spread along the A7 autoroute, Bollène is pleasant, with airy boulevards and walks beside the river Lez, where there is a camping site. The narrow streets of the old quarter lead to the 11th-century **Collégiale St-Martin**, with its timber saddleback roof and Renaissance doorway. Bollène became famous in 1882, when Louis Pasteur stayed here and developed innoculation against swine fever. The **Belvédère Pasteur** garden above the town has views over the Rhône valley to the Cévennes, the Bollène hydroelectric power station and Tricastin nuclear power plant. The town hosts a world music festival during the last two weeks of July.

Just north of Bollène is the ghost village of Barri. Its trogolodyte houses, some still in use at the end of the last century, proved handy hiding places in World War II.

## Vaison-la-Romaine 2

**Road map** B2. *6,100.* *pl du Chanoine Sautel (04 90 36 02 11).* *Tue.* **www**.vaison-la-romaine.com

The pavement cafés in this attractive stone-and-red-roof town on the river Ouvèze are among Provence's most chic. The modern town sits beside the Roman town, opposite the hilltop Haute-Ville on the other side of the river. Vaison is a smart address for Parisians' second homes and, judging by the opulent remains left by the Romans, it has long been sought after. The Romans lived with the native Celtic Vocontii and the population was around 10,000. Two sites have been excavated, divided by the avenue Général-de-Gaulle. The upper site, known as the Puymin Quarter, has a Roman theatre, still used for Vaison's summer festival in July, centred on dance. Its stage is cut out of rock, and the theatre seats up to 6,000. Many Roman remains come from the villa of a wealthy family, the House of the Messii, and an elegant, colonnaded public building, Pompey's Portico. The site is dotted with copies of original statues that are now kept in the **Musée Théo Desplans**, and include a powerful nude of Hadrian and his well-draped empress, Sabina. Many statues were designed to have their heads replaced whenever there was a change of local officials. Other remains include a communal six-seater latrine and a 3rd-century silver bust which once stood in the hall of a patrician's house in La Villasse, the district on the other side of the avenue Général-de-Gaulle.

Mosaic in the museum at Vaison-la-Romaine

The Haute-Ville, which artists and craftspeople helped to repopulate, is reached by means of a Roman bridge, a single 56-ft (17-m) span used for more than 2,000 years until recent devastating floods necessitated huge repairs. Entrance is via a 14th-century fortified gate. The Romanesque church, built as a **cathedral**, has 7th-century columns in the apse, and a 12th-century cloister. A walk to the summit will reveal the ruined castle the victorious Counts of Toulouse built here in 1160.

**Roman City**
Fouilles de Puymin and Musée Théo Desplans, pl du Chanoine Sautel.
***Tel*** *04 90 36 50 48.* *daily.*
*1 Jan, 25 Dec.*

Grounds of Roman house with 3rd-century silver bust, Vaison-la-Romaine

*For hotels and restaurants in this region see pp202–3 and pp216–17*

# A Tour of the Dentelles ❸

Dentelle means "lace", and the Dentelles de Montmirail is the name of the 15-km (9-mile) range of hills which form a lacework of delicate peaks. Not as high or rugged as they initially seem, the Dentelles have good paths and offer some of the most accessible, enjoyable mountain walks in Provence. The paths are bright with broom and flanked by pines, oaks and wild almond trees. When you have had your fill of the stunning scenery, enjoy fine Côtes-du-Rhône wines and delicious goat's cheese produced in the picturesque villages tucked into the folds of the Dentelles.

Muscat grapes outside Beaumes-de-Venise

**Vaison-la-Romaine** ①
A chic town, favoured by wealthy Parisians, Vaison is built on separate Roman and medieval sites. Among its many attractions are the cathedral with its 6th-century sarcophagus of healer St Quenin, and a Romanesque chapel.

*Crestet*

*VALREAS*

*D977*

*D88*

*D938*

*Séguret*

*D23*

**Gigondas vineyard**

**Gigondas** ⑥
The local red wine is highly regarded and its producers include the master-chef Roux brothers. The Counts of Orange built the 14th-century château.

**D80** ⑥

*DENTELLES DE MONTMIRAIL*

**D90** ②

**Malaucène** ②
This former Huguenot strong-hold has a clock tower, originally built as a watchtower during the Wars of Religion *(see pp46–7).*

*D90*

*Lafare*

**Le Barroux** ③
Surrounded by olive and apricot trees, this tiny village is overlooked by a 12th-century château, once a stronghold of the lords of Baux. It has fine views.

*Montmirail* ⑤ ③

*ORANGE* ← *AVIGNON*
*D7* ④ *D21*

**Vacqueyras** ⑤
The home of the famous troubadour, Raimbaud, who died on a Crusade, this village has a church with a 6th-century baptistry.

**KEY**

| | |
|---|---|
| ▬▬▬ | Tour route |
| ═══ | Other roads |

**Beaumes-de-Venise** ④
This is a town of many restaurants, and the home of Muscat, the town's famous fortified sweet white dessert wine, which can be enjoyed with lunch or dinner.

0 kilometres    2
0 miles              2

## TIPS FOR DRIVERS

**Tour length:** 50 km (30 miles).
**Stopping off points:** The hilltop village of Crestet; Lafare, a hamlet leading to the 627-m (2057-ft) Rocher du Turc; and Montmirail, a 19th-century spa resort visited by Mistral. (See also pp250–51.)

For additional map symbols *see back flap*

# Mont Ventoux ❹

✈ Avignon. 👥 2,600. 🚌 Orange, Bedoin. ❗ Av de la Promenade, Sault-en-Provence (04 90 64 01 21). www.ventoux-en-provence.com

The "Giant of Provence" is the dominant feature west of the Alps, a limestone massif which reaches 1,912m (6,242 ft). It is easy to reach the car park at the top, unless there is deep snow, which can last until April. The snowline starts at 1,300 m (4,265 ft), but the limestone scree of its summit forms a year-round white cap.

Until 1973 there was a motor race on the south side of Mont Ventoux, to the top: speeds reached up to 145 km/h (90 mph). A car rally takes place in Bedoin in June. The roads have gradually improved and the worst hairpins are now ironed out, but the mountain roads are often included as a gruelling stage on the Tour de France. Britain's cyclist Tommy Simpson suffered a fatal heart attack here in 1967.

It takes around five hours to walk to the summit of Mont Ventoux. Petrarch (see p45) made the first recorded journey from Malaucène on one May dawn in 1336. As there were no roads then, it took him a great deal longer.

The mountain is often windy and its name comes from the

Summit of Mont Ventoux during the Mistral season

French word (vent) for wind. When the northerly Mistral blows, it can almost lift you out of your boots. But the winds dry the moisture in the sky, painting it a deep blue colour and leaving behind clear vistas.

There are three starting points for a walking tour of the mountain: Malaucène, on the north slopes, Bedoin to the south and Sault to the east. Another direct route for hikers is from Brantes on the northeast side, up the Toulourenc valley. The first two towns both have tourist offices which organize guided hikes to see the sun rise at the summit. The 21-km

**Monument to cycling hero Tommy Simpson**

(13-mile) road from Malaucène passes the 12th-century Chapelle Notre-Dame-du-Groseau and the Source Vauclusienne, a deep pool tapped for an aqueduct by the Romans. The ski centre at Mt Serein is based 5 km (3 miles) from the summit. A viewing table at the peak helps to discern the Cévennes, the Luberon and Ste-Victoire. Descending, the road passes the Col des Tempêtes, known for its stormy weather. The ski centre of Le Chalet-Reynard is at the junction to Sault and les Gorges de la Nesque, and St-Estève has fine views over the Vaucluse.

**Engraving of motor rally car ascending Mont Ventoux (1904)**

## PROVENCAL FLOWERS

Because the temperature on Mont Ventoux drops between the foot and the summit by around 11° C (20° F), the vegetation alters from the lavender and peach orchards of the plain via the oak, beech and conifer woodlands to the arctic flowers towards the summit. June is the best month for flowers.

**Early purple orchid**
*Orchis mascula*

**Alpine poppy**
*Papaver rhaeticum*

Trumpet gentian
*Gentiana clusii*

# Orange ⑤

Road map 2B. 🚶 30,000. 🚆 🚌
ℹ 5 cours Aristide Briand (04 90 34
70 88). 🛍 Thu. www.otorange.fr

This historical town contains
two of the finest Roman
mon-uments in Europe. The
Théâtre Antique d'Orange is
known for its world-famous
concerts (see pp162–3),
while the Arc de Triomphe
celebrates Julius Caesar's
conquest of the Gauls and
victory over the Greek fleet.
Orange is also the centre for
the Côtes-du-Rhône vineyards
and produce such as olives,
honey and truffles. Around
the 17th-century Hôtel de
Ville, streets open on to
peaceful, shady squares
with café terraces.

**Side-chapel altar in the Ancienne
Cathédrale Notre-Dame, Orange**

## Roman Orange

When the first Roman army
attempted to conquer Gaul, it
was defeated near Orange with
a loss of 100,000 men in 105
BC. When it came back three
years later and triumphed, one
of the first monuments built to
show supremacy was the 22-m
(72-ft) Arc de Triomphe on the
via Agrippa between Arles and
Lyons, today cast to one side.

## The Old Town

Old Orange is centred around
the 17th-century town hall and
**Ancienne Cathédrale Notre-
Dame**, with its crumbling
Romanesque portal, damaged
in the Wars of Religion (see
pp46–7). The theatre's wall
dominates the place des
Frères-Mounet. Louis XIV
described it as "the greatest
wall in my kingdom". There

is an excellent view of the
theatre, the city of Orange
and the Rhône plain from
**Colline St-Eutrope**. This is
the site of the remains of the
castle of the princes of Orange,
who gave the Dutch royal
family its title, the House of
Orange, through marriage.
The family also lent their
name to states and cities
around the world.

### 🏛 Arc de Triomphe

Av de l'Arc de Triomphe.
The monument has excellent
decorations devoted to war
and maritime themes. There is
a modernistic quality, particularly visible in the trophies
above the side arches. On the
east face, Gallic prisoners,
naked and in chains, broad-
cast to the world who was in
charge. Anchors and ropes
showed maritime superiority.
When Maurice of Nassau
fortified the town in 1622 by
using Roman buildings as
quarries, the arch escaped this
fate by being incorporated into
the defensive walls as a keep.

### 🏛 Musée d'Orange

Rue Madeleine Roch. Tel 04 90 51
17 60. ⏲ daily. 📷
The exhibits found in the
courtyard and ground floor
reflect the history of Orange.
They include more than 400
marble fragments which, when
assembled, proved to be plans
of the area, based on three

**Stone carving of a centaur in the
Musée d'Orange**

surveys dating from AD 77,
and extending from Bollène
to Auzon. Also in the museum
are portraits of members of the
Royal House of Orange and
paintings by the British artist,
Sir Frank Brangwyn (1867–
1956). One room demonstrates
how printed fabrics were made
in 18th-century Orange.

### 🏛 L'Harmas de Fabre

Harmas de J-H Fabre. Tel 04 90 30
57 62. ⏲ Apr–Oct. ⏲ Wed, Sat
am, Sun am. 📷 🚫
At Sérignan-du-Comtat, 8 km
(5 miles) northeast of Orange
is L'Harmas, the estate of the
entomologist and poet Jean-
Henri Fabre (1823–1915). His
superb collection of insects
and fungi, and the glorious
surrounding botanical garden,
attract visitors from all over
the world.

**Arc de Triomphe monument, representing Julius Caesar's conquests**

# Théâtre Antique d'Orange

Orange's Roman theatre is one of the best preserved in Europe. It was built at the start of the Christian era against the natural height of the Colline-St-Eutrope. Its stage doors were hollow so that actors could stand in front and amplify their voices; today other acoustic touches make it ideal for concerts. The *cavea*, or tiered semicircle, held up to 7,000 spectators. From the 16th to 19th centuries, the theatre was filled with squalid housing, traces of which can still be seen. A new roof, held up by a 60-m (195-ft) beam, has been built above the stage. A multimedia presentation of great moments in the theatre's history takes place in four grottoes behind the tiers of the amphitheatre.

**Awning Supports**
*Still visible on the exterior walls are corbels which held the huge* velum-*bearing masts.*

**Main entrance**

## ROMAN THEATRE

This reconstruction shows the theatre as it would have looked in Roman times. Today it owes its reputation to its exceptional stage wall, the only Roman stage wall to remain intact.

**A canvas awning**, known as a *velum*, protected the theatregoers from sun or rain.

**Night Concerts**
*Cultural events such as* Les Chorégies d'Orange, *a festival of opera, drama and ballet, once frequented by Sarah Bernhardt, have been held here since 1869 (see p33). The theatre is also a popular rock concert venue.*

**The stage curtain** (*aulaeum*) was lowered to reveal the stage, rather than raised. It was operated by machinery concealed beneath the floor of the stage.

**The Great Wall**
*Built of red limestone, this massive construction is 103 m (338 ft) long, 36 m (117 ft) high and over 1.8 m (5 ft) thick.*

### Emperor Augustus

*This 3.5-m (11-ft) statue, with a hand raised in greeting, dominates the stage at the third level. At its base kneels a figure in breeches, possibly a defeated enemy. Other statues have been destroyed, but this copy was returned to the niche in 1951.*

### VISITORS' CHECKLIST

Rue Madeleine Roch. **Tel** 04 90 51 17 60. ☐ daily. Apr–Sep: 9am–6pm (to 7pm Jun–Aug); Oct–Mar: 9:30am–4:30pm (to 6:30pm Mar, Oct). ● 1 Jan, 25 Dec. also valid for Musée d'Orange (see p161). 🖪🖩🖂🛗🛈🎵
www.theatre-antique.com

**Side rooms,** or *parascaenia,* were where actors could rest, and props be stored, when not required on stage.

### Stage Wall

*The inner face of the stage wall (Frons Scaenae) still bears fragments of marble friezes and mosaics. A frieze of centaurs framed the royal doorway in the centre.*

**Each strip** of *velum* awning could be rolled individually to suit the direction of the sunlight.

### Marble Columns

*The stage wall had three levels, the two upper levels with 76 marble columns, of which only two remain. The wall's many surfaces broke up sound waves, so that the actors could speak without their voices having an echo.*

**Winched capstans** held and tightened the ropes supporting the *velum.*

### The Great Roman Temple

*From 1925–37, excavations took place to the west of the theatre, where 22 houses had been pulled down. They unearthed a vast semi-circle and ruins of a temple. Together with the theatre, they would have formed an* Augusteum, *an architectural unit devoted to the worship of Roman emperors.*

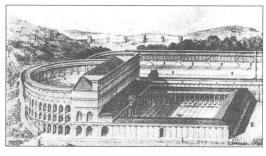

Romanesque church at Caderousse

## Caderousse **6**

**Road map** B2. 🏔 *2,500*. ℹ️ *La Mairie (04 90 51 90 69)*. 🚌 *Tue.*

This bankside village lies at a point where Hannibal is said to have crossed the river Rhône with his elephants on his way to Rome in 218 BC. For centuries, Caderousse has stoically endured the floods of the River Rhône, and plaques on the town hall record the high levels of floodwater. By 1856, the villagers had had enough, and erected a dyke which is still in place today. Its four entry points can close if floods should threaten again.

Caderousse has a Romanesque church, **St-Michel**, to which the Flamboyant Gothic chapel of St-Claude was added during the 16th century.

## Châteauneuf-du-Pape **7**

**Road map** B3. 🏔 *2,100*. 🚌 🚆 *Sorgues, then taxi*. ℹ️ *place du Portail (04 90 83 71 08)*. 🚌 *Fri.*

The best-known of the Côtes-du-Rhône wine labels takes its name from an unassuming yellowstone village on a small hill, given over to cellars and restaurants selling the products of the local growers entitled to the *appellation contrôlée*. The **Musée du Vin** traces the history and current state of the local viniculture.

At the top of the village are the ruins of the **Château des Papes**, mostly burned down in the 16th-century Wars of Religion. From the remaining walls there is a superb view of Avignon and the vineyard-lined clay fields where smooth stones deposited by the Rhône reflect the sun's heat onto 13 varieties of grapes. The château

was built in 1317 by John XXII, an Avignon pope who planted the first vineyards, but it took some 400 years for the wine's reputation to spread. Today, there are 350 Châteauneuf-du-Pape domaines. The nearby town of Pernes-les-Fontaines is known for its 40 fountains, in particular the 18th-century Fontaine du Cormoran. Until 1914, each of the fountains had an individual keeper.

**🏛 Musée du Vin**
Rte d'Avignon, Châteauneuf-du-Pape. **Tel** *04 90 83 70 07*. 🕐 *daily.* ⬤ *1 Jan, 1 May, 25 Dec.* ♿ *restricted.* 📷

## Carpentras **8**

**Road map** B3. 🏔 *29,000*. 🚌 ℹ️ *97 place 25 Août 1944 (04 90 63 00 78)*. 🚌 *Fri.*

As the capital of the Comtat Venaissin, this market town is in the centre of the Côtes-du-Ventoux wine region.

Boulevards encircle the old town, but the Porte d'Orange is the only surviving part of the medieval ramparts. In the Middle Ages, the town had a large Jewish community, and their 14th-century **synagogue** is the oldest in France, now used by some 100 families. While not openly persecuted under papal rule, many Jews changed faith and entered the **Cathédrale-St-Siffrein** by its 15th-century south door, the *Porte Juive*. The cathedral is in the centre of the old town, near a smaller version of Orange's Arc de Triomphe. In it are Provençal paintings

and statues by local sculptor Jacques Bernus (1650–1728). The *Hôtel-Dieu* has a fine 18th-century pharmacy, and there are regional costumes in the **Musée Comtadin-Duplessis**.

**✡ Synagogue**
Pl Maurice Charretier. **Tel** *04 90 63 39 97*. 🕐 *Mon–Fri.* ⬤ *Jewish feast days.*

**⛪ Cathédral St-Siffrein**
Pl de Gaulle. **Tel** *04 90 63 08 33.* ♿ ⬤ *Mon, Sun pm.*

**🏛 Musée Comtadin-Duplessis**
234 bd Albin-Durand. **Tel** *04 90 63 04 92.* 🕐 *Wed–Mon.* ⬤ *pub hols.* 📷

Pharmacy in the 18th-century *Hôtel-Dieu* at Carpentras

## Abbaye de Sénanque **9**

**Road map** C3. **Tel** *04 90 72 05 72.* 🕐 *Feb–mid-Nov: Mon–Sat & Sun pm; mid-Nov–Jan: pms only, by guided tour.* 📷 ℹ️ **www**.senanque.fr

The beautifully sited Abbaye de Sénanque, surrounded by a tranquil sea of lavender, is best approached from Gordes *(see p169)*. Its monks are often to be seen in the fields.

Like the other abbeys that make up the Cistercian triumvirate in Provence *(see p43)*, Sénanque is harmonious and

Châteauneuf-du-Pape vineyards

unadorned. It was founded in 1148 by an abbott and 12 monks, and the building of the serene north-facing abbey church started 12 years later.

Some roofs of the building are still tiled with limestone slates called *lauzes*, also used for making traditional stone dwellings known as bories *(see p169)*. The abbey's simply designed interior has stone walls, plain windows and a barrel-vaulted ceiling.

Sénanque reached its zenith in the early 13th century, when the abbey owned several local farms. But new riches brought corruption in the 14th century, and by the 17th century, only two monks remained. In 1854 it was restored and housed Cistercian monks, some of whom remained there from 1926 to 1969. Then a wealthy industrialist formed the *Association des Amis de Sénanque* to restore the abbey. The monks have been living there since 1988, and some of their home produce is for sale.

Fontaine-de-Vaucluse, where the Sorgue river begins

Abbaye de Sénanque with lavender

# Fontaine-de-Vaucluse ⑩

**Road map** B3. 🏘 *580.* 🚍 *Avignon.* ⓘ *residence du Pont (04 90 20 32 22).* **www**.*oti-delasorgue.fr*

The source of the Sorgue river is one of the natural wonders of Provence. It begins underground, with tributaries that drain the Vaucluse plateau, an area of around 2,000 sq km (800 sq miles). In the closed valley above the town, water erupts from an unfathomable depth to develop into a fully fledged river. Beside the river is the **Moulin à Papier Vallis Clausa**, which produces handmade paper using the same method as in the 15th century. It now sells maps, prints and lampshades.

The underground museum, the **Eco-Musée du Gouffre**, features a speleologist's findings over 30 years of exploring Sorgue's dams, caves and waterfalls. The **Musée d'Histoire 1939–1945**, traces the fate of the Resistance during WWII and daily life under Occupation. The **Musée Pétrarque** was the house where the poet lived for 16 years, and wrote of his unrequited love for Laura of Avignon.

**🪧 Moulin à Papier Vallis Clausa**
Chemin du Gouffre. **Tel** *04 90 20 34 14.* ◯ *daily.* ⬤ *1 Jan, 25 Dec.* ♿ 🄿

**🏛 Eco-Musée du Gouffre (Musée de Spéléologie)**
Chemin du Gouffre. **Tel** *04 90 20 34 13.* ◯ *Feb–15 Nov: daily.* 📷♿📷🄿

**🏛 Musée d'Histoire 1939–45**
Chemin du Gouffre. **Tel** *04 90 20 24 02.* ◯ *Apr–Oct: Wed–Mon; Nov–Dec & Mar: Sat–Sun.* ⬤ *Jan, Feb, 1 May, 25 Dec.* 📷📷

**🏛 Musée Pétrarque**
Rive gauche de la Sorgue. **Tel** *04 90 20 37 20.* ◯ *Apr–Oct: Wed–Mon.* 📷

# L'Isle-sur-la-Sorgue ⑪

**Road map** B3. 🏘 *20,000.* 🚍 🚍 ⓘ *pl de la Liberté (04 90 38 04 78).* 🛒 *Thu & Sun (antiques and flea).*

This attractive town is a major haunt for antique hunters at weekends. It lies on the river Sorgue which once powered 70 watermills that pressed grain and oil. Today, nine idle wheels remain. The town's 17th-century **Notre-Dame-des-Anges** is ornate inside. The tourist office is in an 18th-century granary, and the Hôpital, also 18th century, has a collection of Moustiers pottery jars in its pharmacy.

Water wheel near place Gambetta, l'Isle-sur-la-Sorgue

# Street-by-Street: Avignon ⑫

**St Jerome, Petit Palais**

Bordered to the north and west by the Rhône, the medieval city of Avignon is the chief city of Vaucluse and gateway to Provence. Its walls cover nearly 4.5 km (3 miles) and are punctuated by 39 towers and seven gates. Within the walls thrives a culturally rich city with its own opera house, university, several foreign language schools and numerous theatre companies. The streets and squares are often filled with buskers, and the Avignon festival in July, which includes theatre, mime and cabaret, has now become a major international event.

**Chapelle St-Nicolas**, named after the patron saint of bargemen, is a 16th-century building on a 13th-century base. Entrance is via Tour du Châtelet.

**Porte du Rhône**

RUE FERRU
RUE DE LIMAS
RUE GRANDE FUSTERIE
RUE DES GROTTES
RUE DE LA BALANCE
RUE ST-ETIENNE
RUE PETITE FUSTERIE
RUE RACINE
PLACE DE L'HORLOGE
PLACE DE LA BALANCE

**★ Pont St-Bénézet**
*Begun in 1177 by shepherd boy Bénézet, this bridge is the subject of the famous rhyme* Sur le Pont d'Avignon.

**Conservatoire de Musique**
*The façade of this former mint, the Hôtel des Monnaies (1619), bears the arms of Cardinal Borghese.*

**Place de l'Horloge**
*The main square was laid out in the 15th century and is named after the Gothic clock tower above the town hall. Many of today's buildings date from the 19th century.*

**KEY**

– – –   Suggested route

| 0 metres | | 100 |
| 0 yards | | 100 |

**Musée du Petit Palais**
*The former episcopal offices house a museum of medieval and Renaissance Italian paintings and French works by the Avignon School, including this 1457* Vierge de Pitié.

## VISITORS' CHECKLIST

**Road map** B3. 88,300.
8 km (5 miles) Avignon-Caumont. bvd St-Roch.
41 cours Jean-Jaurès (04 32 74 32 74). Tue–Sun. Le Festival d'Avignon (see p33).
**www**.avignon-tourisme.com

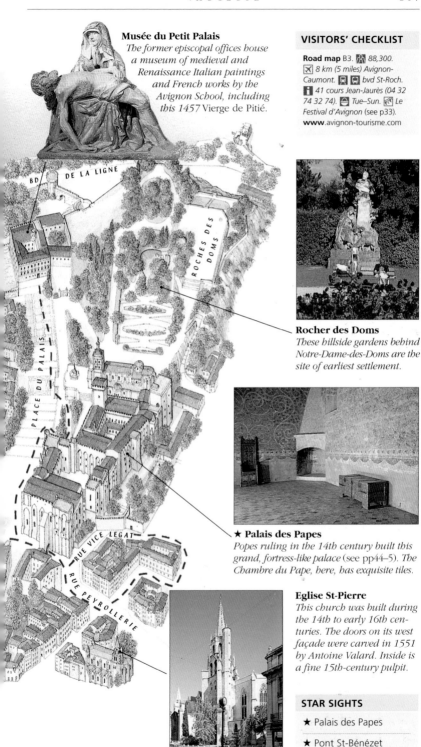

**Rocher des Doms**
*These hillside gardens behind Notre-Dame-des-Doms are the site of earliest settlement.*

**★ Palais des Papes**
*Popes ruling in the 14th century built this grand, fortress-like palace (see pp44–5). The Chambre du Pape, here, has exquisite tiles.*

**Eglise St-Pierre**
*This church was built during the 14th to early 16th centuries. The doors on its west façade were carved in 1551 by Antoine Valard. Inside is a fine 15th-century pulpit.*

## STAR SIGHTS

★ Palais des Papes

★ Pont St-Bénézet

# Exploring Avignon

Massive ramparts enclose one of the most fascinating towns in southern France. A quick stroll reveals *trompe l'oeil* windows and mansions such as King René's house in the rue du Roi-René. This street leads to the rue des Teinturiers, named after local dyers and textile-makers, where a bridge for pedestrians crosses the river Sorgue to the 16th-century Chapelle des Pénitents Gris.

Palais des Papes in Avignon glimpsed across the river Rhône

### ♣ Palais des Papes

Pl du Palais. *Tel* 04 90 27 50 00.
◯ daily (times vary). 📷 🎫 🅿 🍴
📷 www.palais-des-papes.com
These buildings (see pp44–5) give an idea of the grand life under the seven French popes who built a miniature Vatican during their rule here, lasting from 1309–77. They owned their own mint, baked a vast number of loaves every day, and fortified themselves against the French.

Entrance is by means of the Porte des Champeaux, beneath the twin pencil-shaped turrets of the flamboyant Palais Neuf (1342–52), built by Clement VI, which extends south from the solid Palais Vieux (1334–42) of Benoit XII. In the new palace, the main courtyard, La Cour d'Honneur, is the grand central setting for the summer festival (see p229). La Chambre du Pape in the Tour des Anges opposite the entrance has exquisite tiles, and there are fine 14th-century deer-hunting scenes painted by Matteo Giovanetti and others in the adjoining Chambre du Cerf.

**Bird tile in the Chambre du Pape**

The larger rooms around the Palais Vieux include the 45-m (148-ft) banqueting hall, Le Grand Tinel, and La Salle du Consistoire, where pictures of all the popes are displayed. The chapel beside it has exquisite frescoes painted by Giovanetti between 1346 and 1348.

### ♠ Cathédrale Notre-Dame-des-Doms

Pl du Palais. *Tel* 04 90 86 81 01. ◯ Apr–Nov: daily.
This building beside the Palais des Papes was begun in the 12th century. Since then it has been damaged and rebuilt several times. A gilded Madonna was added on to the tower as recently as the 19th century, and the original 6th-century altar is now located in the Chapelle St-Roch, where two popes are entombed.

### 🏛 Musée du Petit Palais

Pl du Palais. *Tel* 04 90 86 44 58.
◯ Wed–Mon. ● 1 Jan, 1 May, 14 Jul, 1 Nov, 25 Dec. 📷 🎫 🅿
Set around an arcaded court-yard, the "little palace", built in 1318, was modified in 1474 to suit Michelangelo's patron and nemesis, Cardinal Rovere,

later Pope Julius II. It became a museum in 1958, and houses Avignon's medieval collection, which includes works by Simone Martini and Botticelli, as well as frescoes and sculptures from the Avignon School, and many French and Italian religious paintings.

### 🏛 Musée Lapidaire

27 rue de la République.
*Tel* 04 90 85 75 38. ◯ Wed–Mon.
● 1 Jan, 1 May, 25 Dec. 📷
Once a 17th-century Baroque Jesuit college, the museum has Celtic-Ligurian, Egyptian, Gallic and Roman artifacts, including masks from Vaison-la-Romaine and a 2nd-century Tarasque monster (see p158).

### 🏛 Musée Calvet

65 rue Joseph Vernet. *Tel* 04 90 86 33 84. ◯ Wed–Mon. ● 1 Jan, 1 May, 25 Dec. 📷 ♿ restricted.
This evocative museum was visited by the French writer Stendhal, who left his inscription behind. Renovated in 2003 to permit the display of many of the treasures previously stored in their vaults, the highlight is undoubtedly the 19th–20th-century collection, with works by Soutine, Manet, Dufy, Gleizes and Marie Laurencin.

### 🏛 Fondation Angladon-Dubrujeaud

5 rue Laboureur. *Tel* 04 90 82 29 03. ◯ pm only Wed–Sun; also Tue in high season. 📷 🎫
This museum cleverly combines modern technology with the intimacy of a private home for displaying this outstanding private collection of 18th–20th-century works of art.

### 🏛 Collection Lambert

Musée d'Art Contemporain, 5 rue Violette. *Tel* 04 90 16 56 20. ◯ Tue–Sun. ● 1 May. 📷 🎫 ♿ 🅿
🍴 www.collectionlambert.com
Opened in 2000, the Collection Lambert is located in an elegant 18th-century mansion, next to the new School of Art. The museum houses the out-standing collection of con-temporary art on loan to the city for 20 years from gallery-owner Yvon Lambert. The paintings date from the 1960s, and represents all the major art movements since then.

# Gordes ⓲

**Road map** C3. 🏘 *2,000.*
🛈 *pl de Château (04 90 72 02 75).*
🗓 *Tue.* **www**.gordes-village.com

Expensive restaurants and
hotels provide a clue to
the popularity of this hilltop
village, which spills down in
terraces from a Renaissance
château and the church of St-
Firmin. Its impressive position
is the main attraction, although
its vaulted, arcaded medieval
lanes are also alluring. The
village has been popular with
artists ever since the academic
Cubist painter André Lhote
began visiting in 1938.

The **Château de Gordes** was
built in the 16th century on
the site of a 12th-century
fortress. One of the château's
best features is an ornate 16th-
century fireplace in the great
hall on the first floor, decorated
with shells, flowers and pilas-
ters. In the entrance there is
an attractive Renaissance door.
The building was rented and
restored by the Hungarian-
born Op Art painter Victor
Vasarely (1908–97), and once
housed a museum of his

abstract works. The 17th-
century Caves du Palais St-
Firmin have an impressive
old stone olive press.

Just outside Gordes is the
**Village des Bories** (*see box*),
now a museum of rural life.

⛪ **Château de Gordes**
*Tel* 04 90 72 02 75. 🔲 *daily.*
⬤ *1 Jan, 25 Dec.* 🏷

🏠 **Village des Bories**
Rte de Cavaillon.
*Tel* 04 90 72 03 48. 🔲 *daily.*
⬤ *1 Jan, 25 Dec.* 🏷

## BORIES

The ancient dwellings known
as *bories* were domed dry-
stone buildings made from
*lauzes* (limestone slabs), with
walls up to 1.5 m (4 ft) thick.
They dated from 2,000 BC and
were regularly rebuilt, using
ancient methods, until the
last century when they were
abandoned. Around 3,000
bories are still standing, many
in fields where they were
used for shelter or storing
implements. Twenty have
been restored in the Village
des Bories, outside Gordes.

# Roussillon ⓳

**Road map** C3. 🏘 *1,200.* 🛈 *pl de
la Poste (04 90 05 60 25).* 🗓 *Thu.*
**www**.roussillon-provence.com

The deep ochres used in the
construction of this hilltop
community are stunning. No
other village looks so warm
and rich, so harmonious and
inviting. Its hues come from
at least 17 shades of ochre
discovered in and around the
village, notably in the dramatic
former quarries along the
Sentier des Ochres. The
quarries are to the east of the
village, a 45-minute round
trip from the information
office. The Conservatoire des
Ochres et Pigment Appliqués
in the old factory (*open daily
in summer*), is worth visiting.
It displays a huge collection
of natural pigments, and runs
day courses on the subject.

A superb panorama to the
north can be seen from the
Castrum, the viewing table
beside the church, above the
tables with umbrellas in the
main square.

Before its recent housing
boom, Roussillon was a typical
Provençal backwater. In the
1950s, American sociologist
Laurence Wylie spent a year in
Roussillon with his family and
wrote a book about village life,
*Un Village du Vaucluse*. He
concluded that Roussillon was
a "hard-working, productive
community" for all its feuds
and tensions. Playwright
Samuel Beckett lived here
in WWII, but his impression
was much less generous.

The hilltop village of Gordes, spilling down in terraces

Triumphal arch behind Cavaillon

## Cavaillon **⑮**

**Road map** B3. 🏛 *25,000.* 🚌 🚉
ℹ *pl François Tourel (04 90 71 32 01).*
🗓 *Mon.* **www**.cavaillon-luberon.fr

Perhaps the best place to get
your bearings is the viewing
table outside the **Chapelle St-
Jacques** at the top of the town,
which renders the Luberon
range in perspective against
Mont Ventoux and the Alpilles
chain. In closer proximity are
the acres of fruit and vegetable
plots, for Cavaillon is France's
largest market garden, synonymous especially with melons.
Its local market competes with
the one in Apt for renown as
the most important in Vaucluse.

Colline St-Jacques was the
site of the pre-Roman settlement that, under Rome, was
moved down from its heights
and prospered. There is a
1st-century Roman arch in
place Duclos nearby. Roman
finds have been collected in
the **Musée Archéologique**
in the Grand Rue, which leads
north from the church, a former cathedral dedicated to
its 6th-century bishop, Saint
Véran. The synagogue in rue
Hébraïque dates from 1772,
although there has been one
on this site ever since the 14th
century. A small museum,
the **Musée Juif Comtadin**,
commemorates its history.

🏛 **Musée Archéologique**
Hôtel Dieu, Porte d'Avignon.
**Tel** 04 90 76 00 34. 🕐 May–Oct:
Wed–Mon. 🖼

🏛 **Musée Juif Comtadin**
Rue Hébraïque. **Tel** 04 90 76 00 34.
🕐 Oct–Mar: Mon, Wed–Fri; Apr–
Sep: Wed–Mon. 🔴 1 Jan, 1 May,
25 Dec. 🖼

# A Tour of the Petit Luberon **⑯**

The Parc Naturel Régional covers 1,200 sq km (463 sq
miles) of a limestone mountain range running east
from Cavaillon towards Manosque in the Alpes-de-
Haute–Provence. It embraces about 50 communities
and a past peppered with such infamous figures as
the Baron of Oppède and the Marquis de Sade. An unspoiled area, it is ideal for walking. Its two main centres
are Apt and Lourmarin. The D943 in the Lourmarin
Coomb valley divides the park: the Grand Luberon
*(see p172)* is to the east; and to the west is the Petit
Luberon, a land of limestone cliffs, hidden corries and
cedar woods, with most
towns and villages to the
north side of the range.

**Oppède-le-Vieux** ①
The dominating ruined castle belonged to Jean Maynier, Baron of
Oppède, whose bloody crusade
against the Luberon Vaudois in
1545 destroyed 11 villages.

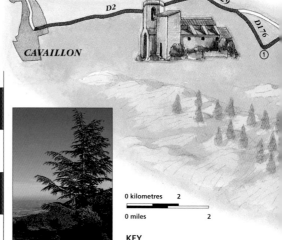

*AVIGNON*

**CAVAILLON**

D2

D943

D29

D176

①

0 kilometres      2

0 miles                    2

**KEY**

━━━ Tour route

═══ Other roads

Cedar Forest Botanical Trail,
**Bonnieux**

## LUBERON WILDLIFE

The Parc Naturel Régional is rich
in flora and fauna. The central
massif is wild and exposed on
the north side, sheltered and
more cultivated in the south. A
wide range of habitats exist in
a landscape of white chalk and
red ochre cliffs, cedar forests,
moorlands and river-hewn
gorges. Information is available
from La Maison du Parc in Apt
*(see p172)* which publishes
suggested walks and tours.

**Monkey orchid** (Orcis
simia) *is found on the
sunny, chalky grasslands.*

For hotels and restaurants in this region see pp202–3 and pp216–17

The rugged peaks of the Petit Luberon

### TIPS FOR DRIVERS

**Tour length:** 40 km (25 miles).
**Stopping-off points:** *Ménerbes has several cafés, Bonnieux is good for lunch and the Cedar Forest has attractive picnic spots. Lourmarin, where Albert Camus lived and was buried, is handy for the Petit and Grand Luberon. All these villages are small, and quickly fill with cars, so you may have to walk some distance, and even climb to castle heights.*
**www.parcduluberon.com**

### Ménerbes ②

At the foot of this stronghold of 16th-century Calvinists is the Musée du Tire-Bouchon, a fascinating collection of corkscrews, dating from the 17th century.

### Bonnieux ④

The Musée de la Boulangerie gives a history of bread making. From here the two-hour Cedar Forest Botanical Trail is a pleasant, scenic walk.

### Lacoste ③

Little remains of the Marquis de Sade's château. Arrested for corrupt practices in 1778, he spent 12 years in prison writing up his experiences.

Abbaye St-Hilaire

MONTAGNE DU LUBERON

### Lourmarin ⑤

The Countess of Agoult, whose family owned the village château, bore the composer Franz Liszt (1811-86) three children: one married Richard Wagner.

*AIX-EN-PROVENCE*

**Wild boar** (Sus scrofa, *known as* sanglier *in French) is a hunter's prize and a chef's delight.*

**Eagle owl** (Bubo bubo, *known as* dugas *in Provençal) is judged Europe's largest owl.*

**Beaver** (Castor fiber, *known as* castor *in French) builds dams on the Calavon and Durance.*

For additional map symbols *see back flap*

## GRAND LUBERON

This spectacular range of mountains to the east of the Lourmarin Coomb rises as high as 1,125 m (3,690 ft) at Mourre Nègre. The fine view at the summit must be appreciated on foot, and takes several hours from where you leave the car at Auribeau. The area is outstandingly beautiful and ideal to escape from the crowds. The panorama from the top takes in Digne, the Lure mountain and Durance valley, the Apt basin, l'Etang de Berre and Mont Ventoux.

## Apt ⑰

**Road map** C3. 👥 11,500. 🚌
🚆 Avignon. 🚏 20 av Philippe de Girard (04 90 74 03 18). 🗓 Tue & Sat. **www**.ot-apt.fr

Apt is the northern entry to the Parc Naturel Régional du Luberon (see pp170–71). The Maison du Parc, a restored 17th-century mansion, provides a full introduction to the area, with details of walks, gîtes d'étapes and flora and fauna.

The busy old town of Apt has a square for playing boules, fountains and plane trees. Surrounded by cherry orchards, it claims to be the world capital of crystallized fruit. The **Musée de l'Aventure Industrielle** explains how the production of crystallized fruits and earthenware pottery combined with the extraction of ochre to bring prosperity to Apt in the 18th and 19th centuries. The town is also famous for truffles and lavender essence.

The Saturday market offers a wide range of Provençal delicacies as well as entertainment, including jazz, barrel organ music and some stand-up comedy. Excursions can be made to the *Colorado de Rustrel*, the best ochre quarry site by the River Dôa, to the northeast.

The medieval **Cathédrale Ste-Anne** lies at the heart of Apt's old town. Legend has it that the veil of St Anne was brought back from Palestine and hidden in the cathedral by Auspice, who is thought to have been Apt's first bishop. Each July her festival is celebrated with a procession through the town. The Royal Chapel commemorates Anne of Austria. She paid a pilgrimage to Apt to pray for fertility and contributed the funds to finish the chapel, which was finally

**14th-century priest's embroidery**

completed around 1669–70. The treasury inside the sacristy contains the saint's shroud and an 11th-century Arabic standard from the First Crusade (1096–9). In the apse is a 15th–16th-century window that depicts the tree of Jesse. Nearby is the 17th-century Hôtel d'Albertas. The items on display in the **Musée Archéologique** consist of prehistoric flints, stone implements, Gallo-Roman carvings, jewellery and mosaics from that period; phone to book. The second floor shows local ceramics.

Just a few miles from Apt, **L'Observatoire Sirene** has an idyllic location and state-of-the-art technology, ideal for star-gazing.

🔔 **Cathédrale Ste-Anne**
Rue Ste-Anne. **Tel** 04 90 04 85 44.
⬜ daily. **www**.apt-cathedrale.com

🏛 **Musée de l'Aventure Industrielle**
Pl du Postel. **Tel** 04 90 74 95 30.
⬜ Oct–Apr: Wed–Sat; May–Sep: Wed–Sun. ⬤ public hols. 📷 ♿

🏛 **Musée Archéologique**
27 rue de l'Amphithéâtre.
**Tel** 04 90 74 95 30. ⬜ by appointment for groups only. 📷

🏛 **L'Observatoire Sirene**
D34 Lagarde d'Apt. **Tel** 04 90 75 04 17. ⬜ Mon–Sat. ⬤ pub lic hols.
📷 ♿ **www**.obs-sirene.com

**Jam label illustrating traditional produce of Apt**

*For hotels and restaurants in this region see pp202–3 and pp216–17*

# Cadenet ⑱

**Road map** C3. 👥 4,000. 🚌
Avignon. 🚉 🛈 11 pl du Tambour
d'Arcole (04 90 68 38 21). 🛒 Mon
& Sat (marché paysan, May–Oct).

Tucked underneath the
hills in the Durance
valley, Cadenet has 11th-
century castle ruins and
a 14th-century church
with a fine square bell
tower. Its font is made
from a Roman sarco-
phagus. In the main
square, which is used
as the *marché paysan*
(farmers' market), is a
statue of the town's
heroic drummer
boy, André Estienne,
who beat such a
raucous tattoo in the battle for
Arcole Bridge in 1796 that the
enemy thought they could
hear gunfire, and retreated.

**Drummer boy in
Cadenet town square**

# Ansouis ⑲

**Road map** C3. 👥 3,000. 🛈 pl du
Château (04 90 09 86 98). 🛒 Thu,
Sun. www.tourisme-ansouis.com

One of the most remarkable
things about the Renaissance
**Château d'Ansouis** is that it
was owned by the Sabran
family from 1160 until 2008,
when it was sold to a new
owner. The Sabrans have a
proven pedigree: in the 13th
century, Gersende de Sabran
and Raymond Bérenger IV's
four daughters became queens
of France, England, Romania
and Naples respectively. In
1298, Elzéar de Sabran married

Delphine de Puy, a descendant
of the Viscount of Marseille.
But she had already resolved
to become a nun, so
agreed to the marriage,
but not to its consum-
mation. Both
were canonized
in 1369. The
castle's original
keep and two of its
four towers are still
visible. Its gardens
include the Renais-
sance Garden of
Eden, built on the
former cemetery. The
**Musée Extraordinaire de
Georges Mazoyer**,
located south of the
village, has an
individual mix of
the artist's work,
Provençal furniture and a
recreated underwater cave,
all in 15th-century cellars.

⛪ **Château d'Ansouis**
**Tel** 04 90 09 82 70. ⏰ call for
opening times. 🔵 Nov–Mar. 📷
www.chateau-ansouis.com

🏛 **Musée Extraordinaire de
Georges Mazoyer**
Rue du Vieux Moulin.
**Tel** 04 90 09 82 64.
⏰ daily pm only. 📷 🔲

# Pertuis ⑳

**Road map** C3. 👥 18,000. 🚉 🚌
🛈 Le Donjon, pl Mirabeau (04 90
79 15 56). 🛒 Wed & Sat (marché
paysan), Fri.

Once the capital of the Pays
d'Aigues, present-day Pertuis
is a quiet town, whose rich
and fertile surrounding area
was gradually taken over by

**Duchess's bedroom in the Château d'Ansouis**

Aix-en-Provence. Pertuis was
the birthplace of the
philandering Count of
Mirabeau's father, and the
13th-century clock tower is
located in place Mirabeau.

The **Eglise St-Nicolas**, rebuilt in Gothic style in the
16th century, has a 16th-
century triptych and two 17th-
century marble statues. To the
southwest is the battlemented
14th-century **Tour St-Jacques**.

**Triumphal arch entrance to La
Tour d'Aigues' Renaissance château**

# La Tour d'Aigues ㉑

**Road map** C3. 👥 4,600. 🚌 to
Pertuis. 🛈 Château de la Tour
d'Aigues (04 90 07 50 29). 🛒 Tue.

Nestling beside the Luberon,
and surrounded by vineyards
and orchards, this town takes
its name from a 10th-century
tower. The 16th-century castle
completes the triumvirate of
Renaissance châteaux in the
Luberon (the others are
Lourmarin and Ansouis). Built
on the foundations of a medieval castle by Baron de Cental,
its massive portal is based on
the Roman arch at Orange *(see
p161)*. The castle was damaged
in the French Revolution (1789
–94), but has been partially
restored. Its cellars house two
museums, one on ceramics,
the other on local architecture
– both tell the region's story.

🏛 **Salle de l'Habitat Rural en
Pays d'Aigues et Musée des
Faïences et des Céramiques**
Caves du Château, La Tour
d'Aigues. **Tel** 04 90 07 50 33. ⏰
daily. 🔵 Sep–Jul: Mon am, Tue pm
& Sun am; 1 Jan, 25 Dec. 📷

# ALPES-DE-HAUTE-PROVENCE

*I*n this, the most undiscovered region of Provence, the air is clearer than anywhere else in France, which is why it was the chosen site for France's most important observatory. But the terrain and the weather conditions can be severe. Inaccessibility to areas has restricted development and the traditional, rural way of life is still followed.

Irrigation has helped to improve some corners of this mountainous land. The Valensole plain is now the most important lavender producing area of France. Peaches, apples and pears have been planted in orchards only recently irrigated by the Durance, the region's main river, which has been tamed by dams and a hydro-electric power scheme. These advances have created employment and helped bring prosperity to the region. Another modern development is the Cadarache nuclear research centre, situated just outside Manosque. The town's population has grown rapidly to 20,300 inhabitants, overtaking the region's capital, Digne-les-Bains. Famous for its lavender and healthy living, Digne is a handsome spa town that has attracted visitors for more than a century and now hopes to enhance its appeal through its devotion to sculpture, which fills the streets. The region's history and architecture have also been greatly influenced by the terrain and climate. Strategically positioned citadels crown mountain towns such as Sisteron, which was won over by Napoleon in 1815, and the frontier town of Entrevaux. The design of towns and buildings has remained practical, in keeping with the harsh winter and strong Mistral winds. Undoubtedly, the beauty of the region is seen in the high lakes and mountains, the glacial valleys and the colourful fields of Alpine flowers.

Bundles of cut lavender drying in fields near the Gorges du Verdon

◁ Olive groves on the hills outside the fortified town of Entrevaux

# Exploring Alpes-de-Haute-Provence

This remote and rugged area in the north of Provence covers 6,944 sq km (2,697 sq miles) of mountainous landscape. Its main artery is the Durance river which is dotted with dams, gorges and lakes – a haven for mountaineers and canoeists. One tributary is the Verdon, which runs through the stunning Gorges du Verdon, Europe's answer to the Grand Canyon. The scenery becomes wilder and more rugged in the northeast, with Mont Pelat at the heart of the Parc National du Mercantour. Further south lie the plains of Valensole, which colour the landscape in July when the abundant lavender blossoms.

**Fields of lavender on the Valensole plains**

## SIGHTS AT A GLANCE

Annot **18**
Barcelonnette **3**
Castellane **16**
Colmars **5**
Digne-les-Bains **6**
Entrevaux **19**
Forcalquier **9**
Gréoux-les-Bains **11**
Les Pénitents des Mées **7**
Lurs **8**
Manosque **10**
Mont Pelat **4**
Moustiers-Ste-Marie **15**
Riez **13**
St-André-les-Alpes **17**
Seyne **2**
Sisteron **1**
Valensole **12**

**Tour**
*Gorges du Verdon (see pp184–5)* **14**

## KEY

━━ Motorway
━━ Major road
═══ Minor road
━━ Scenic route
── Minor railway
▬▬ International border
▬▬ Regional border
△ Summit

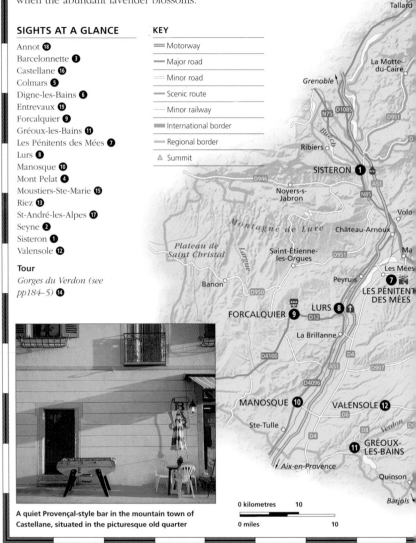

**A quiet Provençal-style bar in the mountain town of Castellane, situated in the picturesque old quarter**

0 kilometres 10

0 miles 10

## GETTING AROUND

The Durance river provides the point of entry into the region. The A51 autoroute from Aix-en-Provence follows the river to Sisteron and on to La Saulce, just short of Gap. National roads continue to follow the Durance, to Lac de Serre-Ponçon in the north, then east along the Ubaye to Barcelonnette. The region's capital, Digne-les-Bains, is well connected by national roads, but otherwise there are only minor roads. The region's railway line also follows the Durance, connecting Sisteron and Manosque with Aix.

Coitian Alps

Saint-Paul

Lac de Serre Ponçon

Le Lauzet-Ubaye

D900

Jausiers

Ubaye

D900

Col della Maddalena

J51

Turriers

D900

D900

D64

**3** BARCELONNETTE

Pra-Loup

Parc National du Mercantour

**2** SEYNE

D908

D902

MONT PELAT

Col d'Allos

**4**

La Foux d'Allos

Mont Pelat 3050m

Col de Cayolle

ALPES-DE-

Allos

HAUTE

La Javie

**5** COLMARS

PROVENCE

D900

D908

**6** DIGNE-LES-BAINS

D3

N85

D20

Montagne de Coupe

D955

Meailles

Var

Chaudon-Noraate

N85

SAINT-ANDRÉ-LES-ALPES

D908

Puget-Théniers

Mézel

Barrême

N202

**17**

ANNOT **18**

ENTREVAUX **19** D4202

Nice

D907

Lac de Castillon

Jaussiers

Sénez

Saint-Auban

953

**15** MOUSTIERS-SAINTE-MARIE

D952

CASTELLANE **16**

D952

RIEZ

Rougon

D4085

Le Logis-du-Pin

Aiguines

D952

D71

**14** La Palud

GORGES DU VERDON

Lac de Ste-Croix

The dramatic Rocher de la Baume, just outside the town of Sisteron

### SEE ALSO

• *Where to Stay* p203

• *Where to Eat* p217

# Sisteron ❶

**Road map** D2. 👥 *7,500.* 🚉 🚌
ℹ️ *Hôtel de Ville, pl de la République
(04 92 61 12 03).* 🛒 *Wed & Sat.*
**www**.sisteron.fr

Approaching Sisteron from
the north or south, it is easy
to see its strategic importance.
The town calls itself the "gateway to Provence", sitting in a
narrow valley on the left bank
of the Durance river, surrounded by olive groves. It is a
lively town, protected by the
most impressive fortifications
in Provence. However, it has
suffered for its ideal military
position, most recently in heavy
Allied bombardment in 1944.

The **citadelle**, originally built
in the 12th century, dominates
the town and gives superb
views down over the Durance.
These defences, though incom-
plete, are a solid assembly of
keep, dungeon, chapel, towers
and ramparts, and offer a fine
setting for the Nuits de la
Citadelle, the summer festival
of music, theatre and dance.
The cathedral in the main
square, **Notre-Dame des
Pommiers**, is an example of

the Provençal Romanesque
school, dating from 1160. At
its east end, the 17th-century
Chapelle des Visitandines
houses the new **Musée Terre
et Temps**. In the Old Town,
small boutiques, cafés and
bars line the narrow alley-
ways called *andrônes*.

**Rocher de la Baume** on the
opposite bank is a popular
practice spot for mountaineers.

🏰 **La Citadelle**
04200 Sisteron. **Tel** *04 92 61 06
00.* ⬜ *Apr–11 Nov: daily.*

**A traditional Provençal farmhouse just outside the village of Seyne**

# Seyne ❷

**Road map** D2. 👥 *1,400.* 🚌
ℹ️ *place d'Armes (04 92 35 11 00).*
🛒 *Tue & Fri.*

The small mountain village of
Seyne dominates the Vallée de
la Blanche, sitting 1,210 m
(3,970 ft) above sea level.
Horses and mules graze in the
nearby fields, and there is a
celebrated annual horse and
mule fair. Beside the main road
is **Notre-Dame de Nazareth**, a
13th-century Romanesque
church with Gothic portals,
sundial and large rose window.
The path by the church leads
up to the **citadelle**, built by
Vauban in 1693, which encloses
the still-standing 12th-century
watchtower. The town is also
a centre for winter sports, with
facilities nearby at St-Jean, Le
Grand Puy and Chabanon.

# Barcelonnette ❸

**Road map** E2. 👥 *3,500.* 🚌 ℹ️ *pl
Frédéric Mistral (04 92 81 04 71).* 🛒
*Wed & Sat.* **www**.barcelonnette.net

In the remote Ubaye Valley,
surrounded by a demi-halo of
snowy peaks, lies Provence's
northernmost town. It is a flat,
open town of cobbled streets,
smart cafés and restaurants and
quaint gift shops, selling specialities such as raspberry and
juniper liqueurs. The town was
named in 1231 by its founder
Raymond-Bérenger V, Count
of Barcelona and Provence,
whose great-grandfather of the
same name married into the
House of Provence in 1112.

**Sisteron citadel, strategically positioned high above the Durance valley**

## NAPOLEON IN PROVENCE

In his bid to regain power after his exile on Elba, Napoleon knew his only chance of success was to win over Sisteron. On 1 March, 1815, he secretly sailed from the island of Elba, landing at Golfe-Juan with 1,026 soldiers.

He hastily started his journey to Paris via Grenoble, making his first stop at Grasse, where the people shut their doors against him. Abandoning carriages, cannon and horses, Napoleon and his troops scrambled along mule-tracks and across difficult terrain, surmounting summits of more than 3,000 ft (1,000 m). At Digne, he lunched at the Hôtel du Petit Paris before spending the night at Malijai château where he waited for news of the royalist stronghold of Sisteron. He was in luck. The arsenal was empty and he entered the town on 5 March – a plaque on the Jeu-de-Paume honours the event. The people were, at last, beginning to warm to him.

The dramatic *Napoleon Crossing the Alps*, painted by Jacques Louis David in 1800

**One of the distinctive residential villas in Barcelonnette**

The town's Alpine setting gives it a Swiss flavour; it also has Mexican spice. The Arnaud brothers, whose business in Barcelonnette was failing, emigrated to Mexico and made their fortune. Others followed, and on their return in the early 20th century, they built grand villas which encircle the town.

Housed in one of the villas is the **Musée de la Vallée**, where the Mexican connection is explained through illustrations and costumes. There are four other branches of this museum in the Ubaye valley, at St-Paul, Jauziers, Pontis and Le Lauzet.

In summer there is an information point here for the Parc National du Mercantour. The park stretches along the Italian border and straddles the Alpes Maritimes region in the south (*see p97*). It is a haven for birds, wildlife and fauna, with two major archaeological sites.

🏛 **Musée de la Vallée**
10 av de la Libération. *Tel* 04 92 81 27 15. ⬜ Wed, Thu, Fri & Sat pm (Jul & Aug: daily). ● mid–Nov–mid-Dec. 🎫 📷 in summer.

## Mont Pelat ❹

🚉 Digne-les-Bains, Thorame-Verdon. 🚌 Colmars, Allos. 🛈 place du Presbytère, Allos (04 92 83 02 81).

This is the loftiest peak in the Provençal Alps, rising to a height of 3,050 m (10,017 ft) and all around are mountains and breathtaking passes, some of them closed by snow until June. Among them are the Col de Cayolle (2,327 m/7,717 ft) on the D2202 to the east, and the hair-raising Col d'Allos (2,250 m /7,380 ft) on the D908 to the west. South of Mont Pelat, in the heart of the Parc National du Mercantour, is the beautiful 50-ha (124-acre) Lac d'Allos. It is the largest natural lake in Europe at this altitude. The setting is idyllic, ringed by snowy mountains, its crystal-clear waters swimming with trout and char. Another record-breaker is Cime de la Bonette, on the D64 northeast of Mont Pelat, at 2,862 m (9,390 ft) the highest pass in Europe. It has what is perhaps the most magnificent view in all this abundant mountain scenery.

**Cime de la Bonette, the highest mountain pass in Europe**

# Colmars **⑤**

**Road map** 2E. 🎿 *400*. 🚌
ℹ️ *Ancienne Auberge Fleurie (04 92 83 41 92).* 🚌 *Tue & Fri (Jun–Sep).*

Colmars is an unusually complete fortified town, nestling between two medieval forts. You can walk along the 12-m (40-ft) ramparts, which look across oak-planked roofs, patched in places with sheet steel. The town is named after the hill on which it is built, *collis Martis*, where the Romans built a temple to the god Mars. Vauban, the military engineer, designed its lasting look. On the north side, an alley leads to the 17th-century **Fort de Savoie**, a fine example of military architecture. From the Porte de France a path leads to the Fort de France.

Situated among wooded hills Colmars is popular in summer, when time is spent relaxing on wooden balconies (*soleillades, lit,* sun-traps), or strolling along alpine paths, soaking up the beautiful views. Signposts lead from the town to the Cascade de la Lance, a waterfall half-an-hour's walk away.

The fortified town of Colmars, flanked by two compact forts

**⚜ Fort de Savoie**
04370 Colmars. **Tel** *04 92 83 41 92.* ⭕ *Sep–Jul by appointment only; Jul–Aug: daily.* 🎫 📷 *obligatory.*

# Digne-les-Bains **⑥**

**Road map** 2D. 🎿 *17,700.* 🚆 🚌
ℹ️ *Rond point du 11 Novembre (04 92 36 62 62).* 🚌 *Wed & Sat.* **www.ot-dignelesbains.fr**

The capital of the region has been a spa town since Roman times, primed by seven hot springs. It still attracts those seeking various cures, who visit the Etablissement Thermal, a short drive southeast of the town. Health seems to radiate from Digne's airy streets, particularly from the boulevard Gassendi, named after the local mathematician and astronomer Pierre Gassendi (1592–1655). This is where the town's four-day lavender carnival rolls out in August *(see p229),* for Digne styles itself the *"capitale de la Lavande".* In recent years, the town has promoted itself as an important centre for modern sculpture, which liberally furnishes the town.

Renovated in 2003, the **Musée Gassendi** is found in the old town hospice and houses 16th–19th-century French, Italian and Dutch paintings, a collection of contemporary art and 19th-century scientific instruments. Among portraits of Digne's famous is Alexandra David-Néel, one of Europe's most intrepid travellers, who died in 1969 aged 101. Her house, *Samten-Dzong* (fortress of meditation) is now the **Musée Alexandra David-Néel** and includes a Tibetan centre and a museum.

Street sculpture in Digne

At the north end of boulevard Gassendi is the 19th-century **Grande Fontaine** and just beyond this lies the oldest part of Digne-les-Bains, now a residential suburb. The most impressive architectural site is the cathedral of **Notre-Dame-du-Bourg**. It is the largest Romanesque church in Haute Provence, built 1200–1330.

The **Jardin Botanique des Cordeliers**, an enchanting walled garden in a converted convent, houses a large collection of medicinal plants.

**🏛 Musée Gassendi**
64 bd Gassendi. **Tel** *04 92 31 45 29.* ⭕ *Wed–Mon.* ⬤ *public hols, 25 Dec–2 Jan.* 🎫 ♿ 📷

**🏛 Musée Alexandra David-Néel**
27 av Maréchal Juin. **Tel** *04 92 31 32 38.* ⭕ *daily.* 🎫 *4 per day (3 from Oct–Jun).* 📷

**🌿 Jardin Botanique des Cordeliers**
Couvent des Cordeliers, av Paul Martin. **Tel** *04 92 31 59 59.* ⭕ *Mar–Nov: Mon–Fri.* ⬤ *public hols.* ♿ 📷

# Les Pénitents des Mées ❼

**Road map** 3D. 🛫 *Marseille*. 🚉 *St-Auban*. 🚌 *Les Mées*. 🛈 *21 bd de la République (04 92 34 36 38) pms.*

One of the most spectacular geological features in the region is Les Pénitents des Mées, a serried rank of columnar rocks more than 100 m (300 ft) high and over a mile (2 km) long. The strange rock formation is said to be a cowled procession of banished monks. In local mythology, monks from the mountain of Lure took a fancy to some Moorish beauties, captured by a lord during the time of the Saracen invasion in the 6th century. Saint Donat, a hermit who inhabited a nearby cave, punished their effrontery by turning them into stone.

The small village of Les Mées is tucked away at the north end. Walk up to the chapel of St-Roch for a clear view of the rocks' strange formation of millions of pebbles and stones.

The curiously-shaped Pénitents des Mées, dominating the area

# Lurs ❽

**Road map** 3D. 🏘 *350*. 🚉 *La Brillane*. 🛈 *Apr–Sep: 04700 Lurs (04 92 79 10 20); Oct–Mar: Mairie (04 92 79 95 24).*

The Bishops of Sisteron and the Princes of Lurs were given ownership of the fortified town of Lurs in the 9th century,

under the command of Charlemagne. In the early 20th century the small town was virtually abandoned, and was only repopulated after World War II, mainly by printers and graphic artists, who keep their trade in the forefront of events with an annual competition.

The narrow streets of the old town, entered through the Porte d'Horloge, are held in by the medieval ramparts. North of the restored Château of the Bishop-Princes is the beginning of the 300-m (900-ft) **Promenade des Evêques** (Bishops' walk), lined with 15 oratories leading to the chapel of Notre-Dame-de-Vie and stupendous views over the sea of poppy fields and olive groves of the Durance valley.

Head north out of Lurs on the N96, to the 12th-century **Prieuré de Ganagobie**. The church contains beautifully restored red-, black- and white-tiled mosaics, inspired by

oriental and Byzantine design and imagery. Offices are held several times a day by the monks – visitors may attend.

**🏠 Prieuré de Ganagobie**
N96, 04310. **Tel** *04 92 68 00 04.*
⬜ *Tue–Sat pms, & Sun.* 🏠

Floor mosaic of the church of the 12th-century Prieuré de Ganagobie

---

## LE TRAIN DES PIGNES

An enjoyable day out is to be found on the Chemin de Fer de Provence, a short railway line that runs from Digne-les-Bains to Nice. It is the remaining part of a network that was designed to link the Côte d'Azur with the Alps, built between 1891 and 1911. Today the Train des Pignes, a diesel train, usually with two carriages, runs four times a day throughout the year. It is an active and popular service, used by locals going about their daily business as much as by tourists. It rattles along the single track at a fair pace, rolling by the white waters of

the Asse de Moriez and thundering over 16 viaducts, 15 bridges and through 25 tunnels.

The train journey is a great way of seeing the surrounding countryside, although the ride can be bumpy at times. The most scenic parts are in uninhabited countryside, such as between St-André-les-Alps and Annot, where the *grès d'Annot* can be seen clearly *(see p187)*. The journey takes about 3 hours each way and can be broken en route. Entrevaux *(see p187)* is a good place to stop. For tickets, call 04 92 31 01 58 or visit www.trainprovence.com.

The vaulted scriptorium of the Couvent des Cordeliers in Forcalquier

## Forcalquier **❾**

Road map C3. 🚶 4,500. 🚌 ℹ️
13 pl du Bourguet (04 92 75 10 02).
🛒 Mon. **www**.forcalquier.com

Crowned by a ruined castle and domed chapel of the 19th-century Notre-Dame-de-Provence, this town – once an independent state and the capital of the region – is now a shadow of its former self. Streets that once rang with trade and troubadours are now silent, although the weekly market is a lively affair drawing local artists and artisans.

There are some fine façades in the old town, but only one remaining gate, the Porte des Cordeliers. The Couvent des Cordeliers (closed to visitors) nearby dates from 1236, and is where the local lords have been entombed.

The **Musée Départemental Ethnologique** in nearby Mane preserves the history of the people and culture of Haute-Provence. The **Observatoire de Haute Provence** to the south of the town was sited here after a study in the 1930s to find the town with the cleanest air. The Centre d'Astronomie nearby is a must for star-gazers.

### 🏛 Musée Départemental Ethnologique
N100, Mane. **Tel** 04 92 75 70 50.
🕐 daily (Nov: Sun only). ● Jan, 24, 25 & 31 Dec. 🎫 🎥 for groups. 📷

### ♨ Observatoire de Haute Provence
St-Michel l'Observatoire.
**Tel** 04 92 70 64 00. 🕐 Easter–1 Nov: Wed pm. 🎫 🎥 only.

## Manosque **❿**

Road map C3. 🚶 20,300. 🚌 🚌
ℹ️ pl du Docteur Joubert (04 92 72 16 00). 🛒 Sat. **www**.manosque-tourisme.fr

France's national nuclear research centre, Cadarache, has brought prosperity to Manosque, an industrial town which has sprawled beyond its original hill site above the Durance. The centre has 13th- and 14th-century gates, Porte Soubeyrand and Porte Saunerie. The perfume shop in rue Grande was once the atelier of writer Jean Giono's father *(see p28)*. The **Centre Jean Giono** tells the story of his life. The town's adoptive son is the painter Jean Carzou, who decorated the interior of the **Couvent de la Présentation** with apocalyptic allegories of modern life.

### ♨ Centre Jean Giono
3 bd E Bourges. **Tel** 04 92 70 54 54. 🕐 Tue–Sat (Jul–Sep: Tue–Sun). ● public hols, 25 Dec–2 Jan. 🎫 📷

### ♨ Couvent de la Présentation
9 bd Elémir Bourges. **Tel** 04 92 87 40 49. 🕐 Jun–Sep: Tue–Sat (Jul, Aug: Tue–Sun); Oct–May: Wed–Sat pm. ● 23 Dec–3 Jan. 🎫

## Gréoux-les-Bains **⓫**

Road map D3. 🚶 2,000. 🚌
ℹ️ 5 av des Marronniers (04 92 78 01 08). 🛒 Tue & Thu.

The thermal waters of this spa town have been enjoyed since antiquity, when baths were built by the Romans in the 1st century AD. Gréoux flourished in the 19th century, and the waters can still be enjoyed at the Etablissement Thermal, on the east side of the village, on Avenue du Verdon, where bubbling, sulphurous water arrives at the rate of 100,000 litres (22,000 gallons) an hour.

A restored castle ruin of the Templars is on a high spot and

---

### LAVENDER AND LAVENDIN

The famous flower of Provence colours the Plateau de Valensole every July. Lavender began to be cultivated in the region in the 19th century and provides the world with around 80 per cent of its needs. Harvesting continues until September and is mostly mechanized although, in some areas, it is still collected in cloth sacks slung over the back. After two or three days' drying it is sent to a distillery.

These days the cultivation of a hybrid called lavendin has overtaken traditional lavender. Lavender is now used mainly for perfumes and cosmetics, lavendin for soaps.

Harvesting the abundant lavender in Haute Provence

The sweeping fields of the Plateau de Valensole, one of the largest lavender-growing areas of Provence

an open-air theatre is in the grounds. **Le Petit Monde d'Emilie** is a museum with 148 miniatures from 1832 to the present, including dolls, costumes and toy trains.

**⚏ Le Petit Monde d'Emilie**
16 av des Alpes. *Tel 04 92 78 16 52.* ◯ mid-Mar–Nov: Mon–Fri pm (daily for groups by appt). ⬤ public hols. 📷 ♿ 📷 📷 for groups.

Corinthian columns front the Gallo-Roman baths in Gréoux-les-Bains

## Valensole ⑫

Road map D3. 👥 2,500. 🅿 pl des Héros de la Résistance (04 92 74 90 02). 📅 Sat. **www**.valensole.fr

This is the centre of France's most important lavender-growing area. It sits on the edge of the Valensole plains with a sturdy-towered Gothic church at its height. Admiral Villeneuve was born here in 1763, the unsuccessful adversary of Admiral Nelson at the Battle of Trafalgar. Signs for locally made lavender honey are everywhere and just outside the town is the **Musée**

**Vivant de l'Abeille**. This is an interactive museum explaining the intriguing life of the honey bee, with informative demonstrations, photographs and videos. In the summer, you can visit the beehives and see the beekeepers at work.

**🏛 Musée Vivant de l'Abeille**
Rte de Manosque. *Tel 04 92 74 82 35.* ◯ Tue–Sat. ⬤ public hols. ♿ 📷

## Riez ⑬

Road map D3. 👥 1,700. 🚌
🅸 pl de la Mairie (04 92 77 99 09).
📅 Wed & Sat. **www**.ville-riez.fr

At the edge of the sweeping Valensole plateau is this unspoiled village, filled with small shops selling ceramics and traditional *santons*, honey and lavender. Its grander past is reflected in the Renaissance façades of the houses and mansions in the old town. This is entered through the late-13th-century Porte Aiguyère, which leads on to the peaceful, tree-

lined Grand'Rue, with the finest examples of Renaissance architecture at numbers 27 and 29.

The most unusual site is the remains of the 1st-century AD Roman temple dedicated to Apollo. It stands out of time and place, in the middle of a field by the river Colostre; this was the original site of the town where the Roman colony, *Reia Apollinaris*, lived. On the other side of the river is a rare example of Merovingian architecture, a small baptistry dating from the 5th century.

The village has a number of fountains: Fontaine Benoîte, opposite Porte Sanson, dates to 1819, although a fountain has existed on this spot since the 15th century; the 17th-century Fontaine de Blanchon is fed by an underground spring – its use was reserved for washing the clothes of the infirm in the days before antibiotics and vaccines; and the soft waters of the spring-fed Fontaine de Saint-Maxime were believed to possess healing qualities for the eyes.

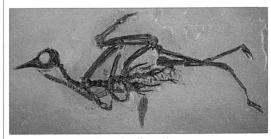

Fossil of a wader bird in the tourist office at Riez

# Tour of the Gorges du Verdon ⓮

The breathtaking chasm of the Gorges du Verdon is
one of the most spectacular natural phenomena in
France. The Verdon river, a tributary of the Durance,
cuts into the rock up to 700 m (2,300 ft) deep. A tour
of the gorges takes at least a day and this circular route
encompasses its most striking features. At its east and
west points are the historic towns of Castellane, the
natural entry point to the gorges, and Moustiers-Ste-
Marie. Parts of the tour are particularly mountainous,
so drivers must be aware of hairpin bends and narrow
roads with sheer drops. Weather conditions can also
be hazardous and roads can be icy until late spring.

Hikers in one of the deep gorges

**Moustiers-Ste-Marie** ④
Set on craggy heights, the town
is famed for its *faïence (p186)*.

Flowered-façade in Moustiers

**KEY**

| | |
|---|---|
| ▬ | Tour route |
| ═ | Other roads |
| ☀ | Viewpoint |

**Aiguines** ③
The beautifully restored 17th-
century château crowns the
small village, with fine views
down to the Lac de Ste-Croix.

0 kilometres     2

0 miles           2

## TIPS FOR DRIVERS

*Tour length:* 113 km (72 miles).
*Stopping-off points:* La Palud-
sur-Verdon has several cafés and
Moustiers-Ste-Marie is a good
place to stop for lunch. For an
overnight stop, there are hotels
and camp sites in the town of
Castellane. (See also pp250–51.)

**The azure-blue waters of the enormous Lac de Ste-Croix**

## OUTDOOR ACTIVITIES

The Verdon gorges have offered fantastic opportunities for the adventurous since Isadore Blanc (1875–1932) made the first complete exploration in 1905. Today's activities include hiking, climbing, canoeing and white-water rafting *(see pp226–7)*. Boating needs to be supervised as the river is not always navigable and the powerful water flow can change dramatically.

White-water rafting down the fast-flowing Verdon river

**Gorge explorer Isadore Blanc**

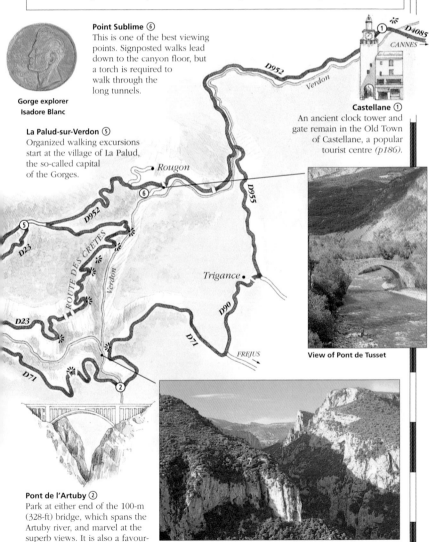

**Point Sublime** ⑥
This is one of the best viewing points. Signposted walks lead down to the canyon floor, but a torch is required to walk through the long tunnels.

**Castellane** ①
An ancient clock tower and gate remain in the Old Town of Castellane, a popular tourist centre *(p186)*.

**La Palud-sur-Verdon** ⑤
Organized walking excursions start at the village of La Palud, the so-called capital of the Gorges.

*Rougon*

*Trigance*

View of Pont de Tusset

**Pont de l'Artuby** ②
Park at either end of the 100-m (328-ft) bridge, which spans the Artuby river, and marvel at the superb views. It is also a favourite spot for bungee jumping.

Stunning view across the meandering river Verdon

# Moustiers-Ste-Marie ⑮

**Road map** 3D. 🏃 630. 📷
ℹ️ Pl de l'Eglise (04 92 74 67 84).
🚍 Fri am; craft market (Jul/Aug).
**www**.moustiers.fr

The setting of the town of Moustiers is stunning, high on the edge of a ravine, beneath craggy rocks. Situated in the town centre is the parish church, with a three-storey Romanesque belfry. Above it, a path meanders up to the 12th-century chapel of Notre-Dame-de-Beauvoir. The view across to the Gorges du Verdon (*see pp184–85*) is magnificent.

A heavy iron chain, 227 m (745 ft) in length, is suspended above the ravine. Hanging from the centre is a five-pointed, golden star. Although it was renewed in 1957, it is said to date back to the 13th century, when the chevalier Blacas hoisted it up in thanks for his release from captivity during the Seventh Crusade of St Louis (*see p42*).

Moustiers is a popular tourist town, the streets crowded in summer. This is due to its setting and its ceramics. The original Moustiers ware is housed in the **Musée de la Faïence**. Modern reproductions can be bought in the town. The new **Musée de la Préhistoire** in Quinson, 40 km (25 miles) south, is a must.

## 🏛️ Musée de la Faïence
Moustiers-Ste-Marie. **Tel** 04 92 74 61 64. ☐ Apr–Oct: Wed–Mon (Jul, Aug: daily); Nov–Mar: Sat–Sun pm only. 🔴 Jan. 🖼️ 🎞️

Notre-Dame-du-Roc chapel, perched high above the town of Castellane

# Castellane ⑯

**Road map** 3D. 🏃 1,500. 📷
ℹ️ rue Nationale (04 92 83 61 14).
🚍 Wed & Sat. **www**.castellane.org

This is one of the main centres for the Gorges du Verdon, surrounded by camp-sites and caravans. Tourists squeeze into the town centre in summer and, in the evenings, fill the cafés after a day's hiking, climbing, canoeing and white-water rafting. It is a well-sited town, beneath an impressive 180-m (600-ft) slab of grey rock. On top of this, dominating the skyline, is the chapel of **Notre-Dame-du-Roc**, built in 1703. A strenuous, 30-minute walk from behind the parish church to the top is rewarded with superb views.

Castellane was once a sturdy fortress and repelled invasion several times. The lifting of the siege by the Huguenots in 1586 is commemorated every year with firecrackers at the Fête des Pétardiers (last Sat in Jan).

The town's fortifications were completely rebuilt in the 14th century after most of the town, dating from Roman times, crumbled and slipped into the Verdon valley. Most social activity takes place in the main square, place Marcel-Sauvaire, which is lined with small hotels that have catered for generations of visitors.

All that remains of the ramparts is the Tour Pentagonal and a small section of the old wall, which lie just beyond the 12th-century St-Victor church, on the way up to the chapel.

## MOUSTIERS WARE

The most important period of Moustiers faïence was from its inception in 1679 until the late 18th century, when a dozen factories were producing this highly-glazed ware. Decline followed and production came to a standstill in 1874, until it was revived in 1925 by Marcel Provence. He chose to follow traditional methods, and output has continued ever since.

The distinctive glaze of Moustiers faïence was first established in the late 17th century by Antoine Clérissy, a monk from Faenza in Italy. The first pieces to be fired had a luminous blue glaze and were decorated with figurative scenes, often copied from engravings of hunting or mythological subjects. In 1738, Spanish glazes were introduced and brightly coloured floral and fauna designs were used.

A number of potters continue the tradition, with varying degrees of quality, and can be seen at work in their *ateliers*.

A tureen in Moustiers' highly glazed faïence ware

The narrow streets of Moustiers

# St-André-les-Alpes ⑰

**Road map** 3D. 🚂 *950.* 🚌 🚗
ℹ️ *place Marcel Pastorelli (04 92 89 02 39).* 🛒 *Wed & Sat.*

Lying at the north end of the Lac de Castillon, where the river Isolde meets the river Verdon, is St-André. It is a popular summer holiday and leisure centre, scattered around the sandy flats on the lakeside. The lake is man-made, formed by damming the river by the 90-m (295-ft) Barrage de Castillon and is a haven for rafting, canoeing and kayaking as well as swimming and fishing.

Inland, lavender fields and orchards make for picturesque walks and hang-gliding is so popular here that one of the local producers advertises its wine as "the wine of eagles".

# Annot ⑱

**Road map** 3E. 🚂 *1,000.* 🚗
ℹ️ *place du Germe (04 92 83 23 03).* 🛒 *Tue.* **www**.annot.fr

The town of Annot, on the Train des Pignes railway line *(see p181)*, has a distinct Alpine feel. Annot lies in the the Vaïre valley, crisscrossed by icy waters streaming down from the mountains. The surrounding scenery however, is a more unfamiliar pattern of jagged rocks and deep caves.

Vast sandstone boulders, known as the *grès d'Annot*, are strewn around the town, and local builders have con-

The steep path of zigzag ramps leading to the citadel of Entrevaux

structed houses against these haphazard rocks, using their sheer faces as outside walls. The *vieille ville* lies behind the main road, where there is a Romanesque church. The tall buildings that line the narrow streets have retained some of their original 15th- to 18th-century carved stone lintels.

Most Sundays in summer, a 1909 Belle Epoque steam train chugs its way from Puget-Théniers to Annot, a pleasant way for visitors to enjoy the unspoiled countryside.

# Entrevaux ⑲

**Road map** 3E. 🚂 *875.* 🚌 🚗
ℹ️ *Porte Royale (04 93 05 46 73).*
🛒 *Fri.* **www**.entrevaux.info

It is clear why Entrevaux is called a "fairytale town", as you cross the draw-bridge and enter through the Porte Royale. The dramatic entrance is flanked by twin towers, the Porte de France and the Porte d'Italie, and from here you enter the Ville Forte. A good time to visit is early August, when the town holds its biennial music festival *(see p33)*.

Fortified in 1690 by the military engineer Vauban (1633–1707), Entrevaux became one of the strongest military sites on the Franco-Savoy border. Even the 17th-century cathedral was skilfully incorporated into the turreted ramparts.

Unlike most military strongholds, the citadel was not built on top of a hill, but strategically placed on a rocky outcrop. A steep, zigzag track leads to the citadel, 135 m (440 ft) above the village. The 20-minute climb to the top, past basking lizards, should not be made in the midday heat.

**Houses in the town of Annot built against huge sandstone rocks**

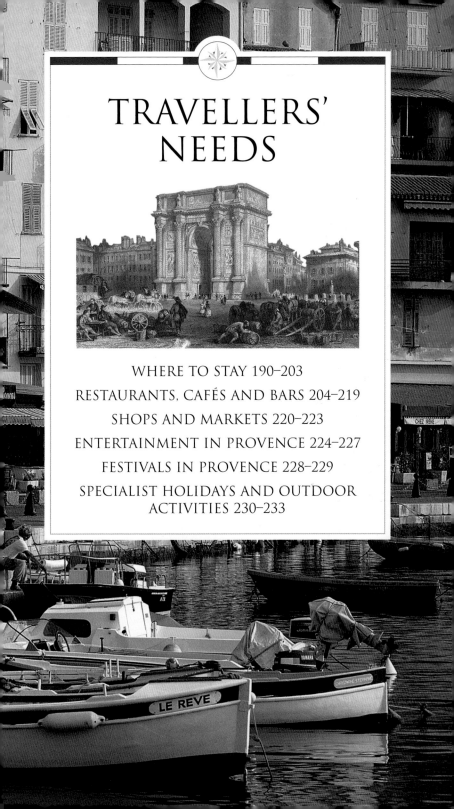

# TRAVELLERS' NEEDS

# WHERE TO STAY

The diversity of Provence is reflected in the wide range of hotels it has to offer. Accommodation varies from luxurious palaces like the Carlton in Cannes to simple country cottages where a warm welcome, peaceful setting and often excellent cuisine are more customary than mod cons.

A broad range of hotels from all price categories has been selected across the length and breadth

**Négresco doorman**

of Provence. The hotel listings on pages 194–203 are arranged by *département* and town according to price. They have been selected for offering interesting accommodation and good value for money. Self-catering holidays are a popular and inexpensive option and on pages 192–3 information is given on renting a rural home or *gîte*, and camping, as well as how to find B&Bs and youth hostels in the area.

## WHERE TO LOOK

There is no shortage of hotels in Provence and the Côte d'Azur. Ever since the crusades of the Middle Ages, the medieval villages and ports have accommodated travellers, to varying degrees of luxury.

Some of the most attractive and best value coastal accommodation is found along the shores of the Var between Toulon and St-Tropez. The glamour and glitz come further east – the coast from Fréjus to Menton is predictably extravagant, but you can find accommodation to suit all budgets and tastes, from the exclusive Eden Roc, favourite of film-stars on Cap d'Antibes, to the 15th-century town house of the Hôtel des Arcades in Biot.

Inland, the major towns and cities of Provence offer a good variety of hotels, from the luxurious mansions of Aix-en-Provence and Arles to the more simple hostelries of the Luberon and the Var. Most villages offer at least one small hotel. Pleasant surprises are to be found – the dreamy ideal of a converted farmhouse or medieval priory lost in the midst of vibrant lavender fields is very much a reality if you know where to look.

If you are seeking tranquillity, travel north to the wilds of Haute Provence where several châteaux and *relais de poste* (post-houses and coaching inns) provide excellent accommodation and regional cuisine in rustic surroundings.

Those seeking a country idyll should head to the hills and valleys of the Central Var, the Luberon National Park or the foothills of Mont Ventoux. More refined bases include the university town of Aix, the papal capital of Avignon or the Roman town of Arles. Much-maligned Marseille does in fact make an exciting, cosmopolitan base, offering excellent hotels and restaurants.

## HOTEL PRICES

Single occupancy rates are usually the same as two sharing – prices are normally per room, not per person. Tax and service are included in the price, with the exception of full board *(pension)* and half board *(demi-pension)*, and rates posted are exclusive of breakfast. You are not required to take breakfast and should stipulate if you want it.

Rooms with a shower tend to be 20 per cent cheaper than those with a bath. In more remote areas, half board may

The palatial Hôtel Carlton in Cannes *(see p195)*

be obligatory and is often necessary in places where the hotel has the only restaurant. In high season, popular coastal hotels may give preference to visitors who want half board.

Prices drop considerably in Provence in low season (Oct–Mar). Many hotels close for five months of the year, reopening for Easter. During festivals *(see pp32–5 & pp228–9)*, prices can rival high-season tariffs. In low season, discount packages are common along the coast. It is worth checking with travel agents or contacting the hotels directly as many of the biggest and most famous hotels offer dramatic discounts – even the palaces of the Riviera need to fill their rooms in winter.

Hôtel de Paris entrance *(see p196)*

## HOTEL GRADINGS

French hotels are classified by the tourist authorities into five categories: one to four stars, plus a four-star deluxe rating. A few very basic places are unclassified. These ratings give an indication of the level of facilities you can expect but offer little idea of cleanliness, ambience or friendliness of the owners. Some of the most charming hotels are blessed with few stars, while the higher ratings often turn out to be impersonal business hotels.

## FACILITIES AND MEALS

Facilities will vary greatly depending on the location and rating of each hotel. In remoter areas most hotels have adjoining restaurants, and nearly all feature a breakfast

The elegant reception area of the Grand Hôtel du Cap-Ferrat *(see p196)*

room or terrace. Many three-star hotels have swimming pools which can be a godsend in the summer. Parking is readily available at country hotels. Some city hotels have underground or guarded parking – in the larger cities like Marseille and Nice this is becoming a necessity as car crime is an increasing problem. Most hotels will have telephones in the bedrooms. Televisions are rarer, especially outside towns. Double beds *(grands lits)* are common, but it is advisable to specify you want one.

Many Provençal hotels are converted buildings and, while this adds a definite charm, it can mean enduring eccentric plumbing, erratic electricity and ceilings that go bump in the night. Some hotels are near a main road or town square – choosing a room at the back is usually all that is required for a peaceful night.

Many hotels use the time-honoured French bolster – a long cushion which many find uncomfortable – if you desire a pillow, ask for *un oreiller*. You have to ask specifically for a room with a bath or toilet – a *cabinet de toilette* simply has a basin and bidet.

Traditional French breakfasts are common in Provence and in summer are often enjoyed outside. Evening meals are served daily until about 9pm, except Sunday when dining rooms are often closed – check before you arrive. Check-out time is about noon – if you stay any longer you will have to pay for an extra day.

## BOOKING

In high season it is imperative to book well in advance, especially for any popular coastal hotels. During peak season, proprietors may ask for a deposit. Tourist offices *(see p237)* are useful if you want personal descriptions and recommendations of places. Tourist offices will also book for you. Outside peak season (Jun–Sep) you may be able to turn up on the day, but it is always wise to phone ahead to make sure the establishment is open.

The exclusive Eden Roc *(see p195)*

## CHILDREN

Families with young children can often share a room at no extra cost, since prices are per room and not per person. Few hotels will refuse children although some insist they must be well behaved. Numerous country hotels boast modern annexes with bungalow apartments specifically designed for visiting families, often only a few steps away from the swimming pool.

One of the many typical Provence château-hotels

## THE MODERN CHAIN HOTEL

Outside the main motorway routes there are few chain hotels in Provence. For those wishing to break their journey or seeking inexpensive accommodation on the outskirts of towns, the chains **Campanile**, **Formule 1** and **Ibis** offer modern and comfortable rooms. They are a safe and practical bet if nothing else is available, and can be booked directly over the phone by credit card. However, they do lack the charm and intimacy of an authentic Provençal hotel. Often you can find accommodation in the town itself or the surrounding countryside for an equivalent price, albeit with a less sanitized decor.

Other modern chains are geared to the business traveller and are found in most major towns. **Sofitel**, **Novotel** and **Mercure** all have hotels in Aix, Nice, Marseille and Avignon. For more information, phone the French Government Tourist Office.

## THE CLASSIC FAMILY HOTEL

If you are travelling on a budget, the friendly, family-run hotel is ideal. These establishments are found in virtually every village and the atmosphere is extremely informal, with children, cats and dogs running in and out. It is likely to be the focal point of the village, with the dining room and bar open to non-residents.

The annual *Logis de France* guide, available from the **French Government Tourist Office**, lists these one- and two-star restaurants-with-rooms *(auberges)*, often specializing in regional cuisine. Most are basic roadside inns, with only a few listed in the main towns and cities, but off the beaten track you can find charming converted farmhouses and inexpensive seaside hotels.

---

# DIRECTORY

### CHAIN HOTELS

**Campanile**
France **Tel** 01 42 91 46 00.
www.campanile.com

**Formule 1**
UK (for brochure) **Tel** (020) 8507 0789. France
**Tel** 0892 685 685.
www.hotelformule1.com

**Ibis, Novotel, Sofitel, Mercure**
UK **Tel** (020) 8283 4500.
France **Tel** 08 25 01 20 11.
www.accorhotels.com

### SELF-CATERING/ BED AND BREAKFAST

**Brittany Ferries**
*For brochure with gîtes.*
UK **Tel** (08712) 441 408.
www.brittany-ferries.co.uk

**Maison des Gîtes de France**
59 rue St Lazare, 75009 Paris. **Tel** 01 49 70 75 75.
**Fax** 01 42 81 28 53.
www.gitesdefrance.com

### HOSTELS

**American Youth Hostel Association**
USA **Tel** (301) 495 1240.
www.hiusa.org

**BIJ Aix-en-Provence**
37 bis bd Aristide-Briand.
**Tel** 04 42 91 98 01.

**CRIJ Marseille**
96 La Canebière.
**Tel** 04 91 24 33 50.
www.crijpa.com

**CRIJ Nice**
19 Rue Gioffredo.
**Tel** 04 93 80 93 93.
www.crijca.fr

**CROUS**
France **Tel** 01 40 51 36 00.
www.crous-paris.fr

**FUAJ (Fédération Unie des Auberges de Jeunesse)**
France **Tel** 01 44 89 87 27.
www.fuaj.org

**Youth Hostel Association**
UK **Tel** (01629) 592 600.
www.yha.org.uk

### CAMPING

**Camping and Caravanning Club**
UK **Tel** (08451) 307 631.
www.campingand caravanningclub.co.uk

**Eurocamp UK**
UK **Tel** (08444) 060 402.
UK **Fax** (01606) 787 036.
www.eurocamp.co.uk

**Family Campers and RVers (US)**
US **Tel** (800) 245 9755.
www.fcrv.org

**Fédération Française de Camping-Caravaning**
78 rue de Rivoli, 75004 Paris. **Tel** 01 42 72 84 08.
www.ffcc.fr

### DISABLED TRAVELLERS

**APF**
17 bd Auguste Blanqui, 75013 Paris. **Tel** 01 40 78 69 90. www.apf.asso.fr

### GIHP

32 rue de Paradis, 75010 Paris.
**Tel** 01 45 23 83 50.
**Fax** 01 45 23 16 11.

**Holiday Care**
The Hawkins Suite, Enham Place, Enham Alamein, Andover SP11 6JS.
**Tel** (0845) 124 9971.
www.holidaycare.org.uk

**Mobility International USA**
132 E Broadway, Eugene, Oregon 97401.
**Tel** (541) 343 1284.
www.miusa.org

### FURTHER INFORMATION

**French Government Tourist Office**
UK: Lincoln House, 300 High Holborn, London WC1V 7JH.
**Tel** (09068) 244 123.
US: 29th Floor, 825 Third Ave, New York, NY 10022.
**Tel** (514) 288 1904.
www.franceguide.com

## BED AND BREAKFAST

In rural areas, some cottages, farms and private houses offer bed-and-breakfast accommodation. These *chambres d'hôtes* come in all shapes and sizes and may provide dinner on request. They are listed separately in tourist office brochures, and many are inspected and registered by the **Gîtes de France** organization; look out for their distinctive green and yellow *chambres d'hôtes* road signs. Departmental brochures are available from the Paris office, and the website has a useful online research and reservation facility.

**Gîtes de France road sign**

## HOSTELS

For the single traveller this is the cheapest, and often the most convivial, accommodation option. A membership card from your national **Youth Hostel Association** is required, or an *Ajiste* card, which you can obtain from French hostels.

During the summer months, it is also possible to stay in vacated university residences; contact **CROUS**, the Centre Régional des Oeuvres Universitaires, for more details. The region's main university is Aix-en-Provence/Marseille; the campuses are shared between the two cities. Other large universities are located in Avignon and Nice. In each university town, both the **Bureau Information Jeunesse (BIJ)** and the **Centre Régional Information Jeunesse (CRIJ)** can provide a great deal of information about student life and a list of inexpensive accommodation options.

## SELF-CATERING

Provence is a popular self-catering destination, and many companies specialize in renting anything from rural farm cottages to beach apartments. One of the best organizations is **Gîtes de France**, with its headquarters **Maison des Gîtes de France** in Paris, which provides detailed lists of accommodation to rent by the week in each *département*.

The owners are obliged to live nearby and are always welcoming, but rarely speak much English. Don't expect luxury from your *gîte* as facilities are basic, but it is a great way to get a better insight into real Provençal life.

## CAMPING

Long a popular pastime in Provence, camping remains an invitingly cheap and atmospheric way of seeing the area. Facilities vary, from a basic one-star farm or vineyard site to the camping metropolises of the Riviera, complete with water fun parks and satellite TV. **Eurocamp** specializes in family holidays. Luxury tents are pre-assembled at the campsite of your choice, and everything is ready on arrival. Organized children's entertainment and baby-sitting are available on site. Some campsites will not accept visitors unless they have a special *camping carnet*, available from the AA, RAC and clubs such as the **Fédération Française de Camping-Caravaning**.

## DISABLED TRAVELLERS

Due to the venerable design of most Provençal hotels, few are able to offer unrestricted wheelchair access. Larger hotels have lifts, and hotel staff will go out of their way to aid disabled guests. The **Association des Paralysés de France (APF)** publishes a guide to accessible accommodation.

Other useful sources of information are the **Groupement pour l'Insertion des Personnes Handicappés Physiques (GIHP)** and **Holidaycare**, who publish a guide to France listing specialized tour operators for disabled travellers.

## FURTHER INFORMATION

A selection of brochures is available from Maison de la France (www.franceguide.com) including *Riviera: Hotels*. There is also the special booking agency, *Loisirs Accueil*, which deals with queries for hotels, campsites, *gîtes* and B&Bs. Visit www.loisirs-accueil.fr for more details about their offers in Provence.

**Camping in Provence, a popular accommodation alternative**

# Choosing a Hotel

These hotels have been selected across a wide price
range for their good value, excellent facilities, and
location. This chart lists the hotels by area in the same
order as the rest of the guide. Within each area, entries
are listed alphabetically within each price category,
from the least expensive to the most expensive.

**PRICE CATEGORIES**
For a standard double room (not per
person) with shower for one night,
including tax and service, but not
breakfast:
€ Under €90
€€ €90–€140
€€€ €140–€180
€€€€ €180–€260
€€€€€ over €260

## THE RIVIERA AND THE ALPES MARITIMES

### ANTIBES L'Auberge Provençale    €€
*61 pl Nationale, 06600* **Tel** *04 93 34 13 24* **Fax** *04 93 34 89 88* **Rooms** *6*    **Road map** *E3*

A large town house under the spreading plane trees of the town's bustling main square. Despite its location in one
of the Riviera's trendiest spots, this *auberge* creates the atmosphere of an old-fashioned inn. Has spacious and clean
rooms furnished with rustic furniture and canopied beds. Excellent value for money. **www.aubergeprovencale.com**

### ANTIBES Mas Djoliba    €€
*29 av Provence, 06600* **Tel** *04 93 34 02 48* **Fax** *04 93 34 05 81* **Rooms** *13*    **Road map** *E3*

Mas Djoliba is an old-fashioned farmhouse set among lots of greenery, in a location that is a convenient distance
from old Antibes and the beaches. A low-rise property with palm trees around its pool-terrace. It is surprisingly good
value for money. Closed end Oct–beg Feb. **www.hotel-djoliba.com**

### BEAULIEU SUR MER La Reserve de Beaulieu    €€€€€
*5 boulevard du Général Leclerc, 06310* **Tel** *04 93 01 00 01* **Fax** *04 93 01 28 99* **Rooms** *37*    **Road map** *E3*

Situated on the seafront in the heart of Beaulieu, near the sailing harbour, this elegant hotel has extremely
comfortable rooms decorated in warm but light pastel tones. Each room has a king-size bed, Internet connection and
a safe. The magnificent pool is next to the sea and overflows with heated salt water. **www.reservebeaulieu.com**

### BIOT Hôtel des Arcades    €
*16 pl des Arcades, 06410* **Tel** *04 93 65 01 04* **Fax** *04 93 65 01 05* **Rooms** *12*    **Road map** *E3*

This 15th-century inn is a haven of tranquillity in the quiet place des Arcades. The bedrooms are small (some might
say poky), but atmospheric. Top-floor rooms have terraces with views over the hills to the sea. The hotel bar also
serves as a breakfast room and restaurant.

### BIOT Domaine du Jas    €€€
*625 route de la Mer, 06410* **Tel** *04 93 65 50 50* **Fax** *04 93 65 02 01* **Rooms** *19*    **Road map** *E3*

Just outside Biot, this hotel seems much more luxurious than its three-star rating would lead the visitor to expect.
A terrace pool (heated all summer) is shaded by palms and oleanders. The rooms are well equipped with WiFi
access, and there's a free private garage. **www.domainedujas.com**

### CANNES Blue Riva    €
*35 rue Hoche, 06400* **Tel** *04 93 38 33 67* **Fax** *04 93 38 65 22* **Rooms** *15*    **Road map** *E4*

When you walk the red carpet, no one has to know where you are staying, and it's hard to beat the prices at this
budget hotel near the Palais des Festivals and the beach. The owners have made an effort with the rooms, which
have bright colour schemes, cheerful bedspreads and free WiFi. **www.hotel-blueriva.com**

### CANNES Eden Hôtel    €€€
*133 rue d'Antibes, 06400* **Tel** *04 93 68 78 00* **Fax** *04 93 68 78 01* **Rooms** *116*    **Road map** *E4*

This hotel is bright and furnished in the trendiest possible style, with a hint of 1960s retro complementing modern
touches. It is located close to the town's fashionable shopping streets, and its facilities include an outdoor and indoor
heated pool, whirlpool, massage room and fitness centre. **www.eden-hotel-cannes.com**

### CANNES Hôtel Molière    €€€
*5–7 rue Molière, 06400* **Tel** *04 93 38 16 16* **Fax** *04 93 68 29 57* **Rooms** *24*    **Road map** *E4*

This 19th-century building is just minutes away from la Croisette, Cannes' sea-front esplanade. Bright and
comfortable rooms and balconies overlook an attractive garden, which compensates for the absence of a
swimming pool. Very good value and much in demand, so book well in advance. **www.hotel-moliere.com**

### CANNES Hôtel Splendid    €€€
*4–6 rue Felix Faure, 06400* **Tel** *04 97 06 22 22* **Fax** *04 93 99 55 02* **Rooms** *62*    **Road map** *E4*

For those whose budget will not stretch to the magnificent Carlton, this white wedding cake of a hotel with its Belle
Epoque frontage is a superb alternative. Fantastic views of the yacht harbour from the rooftop restaurant. Some sea-
facing rooms have great balconies. Good service and a warm, friendly atmosphere. **www.splendid-hotel-cannes.fr**

**Key to Symbols** *see back cover flap*

### CANNES Hotel 3.14

*5 rue François Einesy, 06400* **Tel** *04 92 99 72 09* **Fax** *04 92 99 72 12* **Rooms** *96*    **Road map** *E4*

The Hotel 3.14 is a bit wacky – each of the five floors is dedicated to a different continent – and the restaurant could be better, but it does provide an alternative to other, more predictable palace hotels. The beach, which is a short walk from the hotel, is one of the liveliest in Cannes. **www.3-14hotel.com**

### CANNES Carlton Inter-Continental

*58 la Croisette, 06400* **Tel** *04 93 06 40 06* **Fax** *04 93 06 40 25* **Rooms** *338*    **Road map** *E4*

The grandest of the grand hotels, this is where the stars come to stay. There is a long waiting list for reservations during the Cannes Film Festival. It is worth paying a premium for rooms amid Art Deco surroundings that offer a view of the sea and the private beach with its loungers and parasols. **www.international.com/cannes**

### CAP D'ANTIBES La Jabotte

*13 avenue Max Maurey, 06160* **Tel** *04 93 61 45 89* **Fax** *04 93 61 07 04* **Rooms** *10*    **Road map** *E3*

A small hotel with a comfortable bed-and-breakfast feel, La Jabotte is fully booked weeks ahead in the summer thanks to its tastefully decorated rooms, warm welcome, proximity to the beach and incredible value. A house apéritif is served every evening in the courtyard, and the beach is just a few steps away. **www.jabotte.com**

### CAP D'ANTIBES La Gardiole et La Garoupe

*60–74 chemin de la Garoupe, 06160* **Tel** *04 92 93 33 33* **Fax** *04 93 67 61 87* **Rooms** *40*    **Road map** *E3*

Pines and cypresses surround the 1920s buildings of this affordable hotel, at least by Cap d'Antibes standards. Beamed ceilings and whitewashed walls perpetuate the rural image. Light and airy bedrooms vary in price according to size. There's a shady terrace, and the restaurant serves Provençal cuisine. **www.hotel-lagaroupe-gardiole.com**

### CAP D'ANTIBES Hôtel du Cap – Eden-Roc

*Boulevard Kennedy, 06601* **Tel** *04 93 61 39 01* **Fax** *04 93 67 76 04* **Rooms** *120*    **Road map** *E3*

Built in 1870, this ultimate Antibes palace is a hideaway for the rich and famous, who arrive by private yacht at the hotel's own jetty. Features luxury suites or apartments and seaside cabanas. Also offers a huge heated sea-water pool, superb food, obsequious service and cutting edge facilities. **www.hotel-du-cap-eden-roc.com**

### EZE Hermitage du Col d'Eze

*Grande Corniche, 06360* **Tel** *04 93 41 00 68* **Fax** *04 93 41 24 05* **Rooms** *32*    **Road map** *F3*

Probably the best value for money in expensive Eze, although the price includes compulsory half board in July and August. The location, a short distance from Eze, is hard to beat, with its fine views of the mountains. This is a good choice for an overnight halt or a longer stay. **www.ezehermitage.fr**

### EZE La Chèvre d'Or

*Rue du Barri, 06360* **Tel** *04 92 10 66 66* **Fax** *04 93 41 06 72* **Rooms** *34*    **Road map** *F3*

The "golden goat" has gradually taken over half the perched village of Eze, and each luxurious room is decorated in its own individual style. There are private gardens dotted with sculptures, a pool and three restaurants, one of which serves exquisite haute cuisine. **www.chevredor.com**

### EZE Château Eza

*Rue de la Pise, 06360* **Tel** *04 93 41 12 24* **Fax** *04 93 41 16 64* **Rooms** *10*    **Road map** *F3*

This building is a collection of medieval houses perched high at the summit of Eze's "eagle's nest". Once home to Sweden's Prince William, it has been converted into a luxury hotel, with elegant rooms and breathtaking views from its terraces. The hotel also boasts an award-winning restaurant and a private beach. **www.chateaueza.com**

### JUAN-LES-PINS Eden Hotel

*16 av Louis Gallet, 06160* **Tel** *04 93 61 05 20* **Fax** *04 93 92 05 31* **Rooms** *17*    **Road map** *E3*

It's hard to find a better budget option than the Eden in Juan-les-Pins. This 1930s building has a certain slightly faded charm, with unpretentious rooms and a location close to the beach, that makes up for its lack of a pool. Although there is no full-service restaurant, breakfast is served on a pleasant terrace.

### JUAN-LES-PINS Hôtel des Mimosas

*Rue Pauline, 06160* **Tel** *04 93 61 04 16* **Fax** *04 93 92 06 46* **Rooms** *40*    **Road map** *E3*

Palm trees surround this gracious hotel, built at the turn-of-the-19th-century, offering character and style at a reasonable rate. The cool, comfortable rooms are simply furnished. Request a room with a balcony overlooking the swimming pool, or on the ground floor; the ones facing outward can be a little noisy. **www.hotelmimosas.com**

### MENTON Hôtel Aiglon

*7 av de la Madone, 06500* **Tel** *04 93 57 55 55* **Fax** *04 93 35 92 39* **Rooms** *28*    **Road map** *F3*

Not far from the seafront, the comfortable Aiglon has a heated swimming pool and a luxuriant garden. Housed in a charming 19th-century town house, it has a well-regarded restaurant with tables on a terrace shaded by palms. Although not the cheapest place to stay in Menton, it offers a lot for the price. **www.hotelaiglon.net**

### MENTON Hôtel Napoléon

*29 porte de France, 06500* **Tel** *04 93 35 89 50* **Fax** *04 93 35 49 22* **Rooms** *47*    **Road map** *F3*

This modern hotel offers simple rooms and suites overlooking the sea and the mountains, with balconies in some. Don't miss its ice-cream parlour on the private beach, where sundaes are sold by the weight. The beach restaurant is also very good, and is open all year round. **www.napoleon-menton.com**

## MONACO Hôtel Alexandra

*35 boulevard Princesse Charlotte, 98000* **Tel** *00 377 93 50 63 13* **Fax** **Rooms** *56*          **Road map** *F3*

Proving that not all hotels in Monaco have to be costly, Hôtel Alexandra conceals comfortable bedrooms behind its grandiose Belle Epoque façade. Perhaps not ideal for a long stay, but good for a weekend break. To make up for the lack of a restaurant, breakfast is delivered to your room each morning.

## MONACO Columbus

*23 av des Papalins, 98000* **Tel** *00 377 92 05 90 00* **Fax** *00 377 92 05 91 67* **Rooms** *153*          **Road map** *F3*

This newish arrival on the Monegasque hotel scene is in the trendy Fontvielle quarter. The look is modern, with dark stone and polished metal. Cutting-edge rooms with facilities such as broadband access. The swimming pool, state-of-the-art fitness centre and an excellent restaurant and cigar bar are sure to impress. **www.columbushotels.com**

## MONACO Hôtel de Paris

*Pl du Casino, 98000* **Tel** *00 377 98 06 25 25* **Fax** *00 377 92 16 38 50* **Rooms** *191*          **Road map** *F3*

The opulent Hôtel de Paris has been the flagship of Monaco's grand hotels for more than a century. Features magnificent facilities, flawless service, fine dining and a location next to the casino. The celebrity guest list includes Queen Victoria and other crowned heads of Europe, to film stars and other bigwigs. **www.sbm.mc**

## MONACO L'Hermitage

*Square Beaumarchais, 98000* **Tel** *00 377 98 06 25 25* **Fax** *00 377 98 06 59 78* **Rooms** *280*          **Road map** *F3*

This cream-coloured Belle Epoque palace is one of the grandest hotels in Europe and a Monaco landmark, with its glass-domed Winter Garden foyer, lavish restaurant and marble terrace. Huge, opulent rooms have lots of luxury trimmings. This is the place to stay if you have just made a fortune at the Monte Carlo casino. **www.sbm.mc**

## NICE Nice Garden Hotel

*11 rue du Congrès, 06000* **Tel** *04 93 87 35 62* **Fax** *04 93 82 15 80* **Rooms** *9*          **Road map** *F3*

Green spaces are not easy to come by in Nice, so this nine-room hotel with its own private garden is understandably popular with visitors. Rooms are bright and tastefully decorated, some in a very romantic style, and each one looks on to the garden. You can eat breakfast under the shade of the orange tree. **www.nicegardenhotel.com**

## NICE Hôtel Le Grimaldi

*15 rue Grimaldi, 06000* **Tel** *04 93 16 00 24* **Fax** *04 93 87 00 24* **Rooms** *46*          **Road map** *F3*

Combining Provençal charm and affordability, the Grimaldi is located a short walk from the pedestrianized shopping streets and the beach. Small but comfortable rooms are decorated in bright Provençal tones. There is a friendly bar downstairs and several good restaurants nearby. **www.le-grimaldi.com**

## NICE Hôtel Windsor

*11 rue Dalpozzo, 06000* **Tel** *04 93 88 59 35* **Fax** *04 93 88 94 57* **Rooms** *57*          **Road map** *F3*

The Hôtel Windsor provides a wide array of services and facilities, including a pool in an exotic palm garden, a children's play area and a health and beauty centre offering massage and a sauna. Some rooms are individually decorated by local artists. Snack bar and restaurant. **www.hotelwindsornice.com**

## NICE Le Négresco

*37 promenade des Anglais, 06000* **Tel** *04 93 16 64 00* **Fax** *04 93 88 35 68* **Rooms** *121*          **Road map** *F3*

The Négresco is the grande dame of Riviera hotels and has been a landmark on the Promenade des Anglais since it opened in 1913. Hosts a seemingly endless list of rich and famous guests. Superb decoration featuring works of art, flawless service and modern facilities make this one of the world's greatest hotels. **www.hotel-negresco-nice.com/**

## ST-JEAN-CAP-FERRAT La Fregate

*11 ave Denis Séméria, 06230* **Tel** *04 93 76 04 51* **Fax** *04 93 76 14 93* **Rooms** *10*          **Road map** *F3*

This is a family-run hotel with simply decorated rooms on a small street near the harbour. There is no restaurant (apart from a small breakfast room) but there are lots of places to eat and drink nearby. Definitely the best place to stay in if you are exploring Provence on a tight budget or just passing through.

## ST-JEAN-CAP-FERRAT Clair Logis

*12 av Prince Rainier de Monaco, 06230* **Tel** *04 93 76 51 81* **Fax** *04 93 76 11 85* **Rooms** *16*          **Road map** *F3*

This villa, set in a large garden, is very good value and has, over the years, attracted a list of famous guests, including former French president Général de Gaulle. The rooms are comfortable in a slightly old-fashioned way, with smaller, more modern rooms in the annexe. There is no pool, but the beach is not far away. **www.hotel-clair-logis.fr**

## ST-JEAN CAP FERRAT Royal Riviera

*3 av Jean Monnet, 06230* **Tel** *04 93 76 31 00* **Fax** *04 93 01 23 07* **Rooms** *96*          **Road map** *F3*

This luxury hotel inspired by the nearby Villa Kerylos *(see p88)* has an enviable position in this glitzy resort, with easy access to a private beach. Some of the rooms seem on the small side for the price, but service aims to satisfy every whim. A new building facing the swimming pool, L'Orangerie, houses 16 pleasant rooms. **www.royal-riviera.com**

## ST-JEAN-CAP-FERRAT Grand Hôtel du Cap Ferrat

*Boulevard du Général de Gaulle, 06230* **Tel** *04 93 76 50 50* **Fax** *04 93 76 04 52* **Rooms** *53*          **Road map** *F3*

Located at the southern tip of Cap Ferrat, this is one of the world's most expensive hotels. Its Mediterranean-style rooms are set in tropical garden surroundings. A funicular railway transports guests to and from the Olympic-sized, landscaped sea-water pool, where Charlie Chaplin taught his children how to swim. **www.grand-hotel-cap-ferrat.com**

**Key to Price Guide** *see p194* **Key to Symbols** *see back cover flap*

### ST-PAUL-DE-VENCE Hostellerie des Remparts

*72 rue Grande, 06570* **Tel** *04 93 32 09 88* **Fax** *04 93 32 06 91* **Rooms** *9*        **Road map** *E3*

In the heart of this picturesque *village perché*, the Hostellerie des Remparts offers modern comforts within a medieval setting. The bedrooms are furnished with antiques, and all of them have marvellous views. The village is car-free and the car park is some distance away, so this is not a good place for those with mobility difficulties.

### ST-PAUL-DE-VENCE Le Saint Paul

*86 rue Grande, 06570* **Tel** *04 93 32 65 25* **Fax** *04 93 32 52 94* **Rooms** *16*        **Road map** *E3*

The only luxury hotel within the walls of St-Paul, Le Saint Paul serves as a hushed haven for well-heeled travellers. Rooms are lavishly furnished and the walled-in restaurant terrace looks on to the surrounding hills. The hotel is not accessible by car, though you can drop your bags nearby. **www.lesaintpaul.com**

### VENCE Villa La Roseraie

*128 av Henri Giraud, 06140* **Tel** *04 93 58 02 20* **Fax** *04 93 58 99 31* **Rooms** *14*        **Road map** *E3*

Colourful Provençal fabrics and furniture adorn the lovingly decorated bedrooms of this smart Belle Epoque town house, Vence's most sought-after boutique hotel by far. It requires reservations months or even years in advance. Palm trees and magnolias shade the enticing garden, where breakfast is served. **www.villaroseraie.com**

### VILLEFRANCHE Hôtel Versailles

*7 boulevard Princesse Grace, 06230* **Tel** *04 93 76 52 52* **Fax** *04 93 01 97 48* **Rooms** *46*        **Road map** *F3*

This modern hotel has enough facilities for a longer stay, including a swimming pool, a restaurant specializing in Provençal cuisine and bedrooms with great views. Perhaps the only drawback is its location on a busy thoroughfare. However, this makes the hotel easy to find. It also offers secure parking. **www.hotelversailles.com**

### VILLEFRANCHE Hôtel Welcome

*1 quai Amiral Courbet, 06230* **Tel** *04 93 76 27 62* **Fax** *04 93 76 27 66* **Rooms** *36*        **Road map** *F3*

This ochre-painted hotel has a certain period charm and great views of the sea and the port of Villefranche. Most rooms have balconies or terraces. Ask for a room overlooking the bay, as the view from those facing the town is less attractive. Artist Jean Cocteau stayed here in the 1920s. **www.welcomehotel.com**

## THE VAR AND THE ILES D'HYERES

### BORMES-LES-MIMOSAS Le Grand Hôtel

*167 route de Baguier, 83230* **Tel** *04 94 71 23 72* **Fax** *04 94 71 51 20* **Rooms** *46*        **Road map** *D4*

This hotel is aptly named, with its grand location in the Massif des Maures, high above the Mediterranean. Its decor is a slightly faded Belle Epoque style of the 1900s. The beautiful rooms (some with balconies), spectacular setting, sun-soaked terrace and friendly service go a long way in making it a memorable stay. **www.augrandhotel.com**

### BORMES-LES-MIMOSAS Domaine du Mirage

*38 rue de la Vue des Iles, 83230* **Tel** *04 94 05 32 60* **Fax** *04 94 64 93 03* **Rooms** *33*        **Road map** *D4*

Perched above the Lavandou bay and a 10-minute drive from one of the Riviera's best beaches, this Victorian-style hotel has spectacular views from its balconies, attentive staff and a beautiful pool. Light dishes are served by the pool at lunch, while in the evening you can choose from a short seasonal menu. **www.domainedumirage.com**

### COGOLIN La Maison du Monde

*63 rue Carnot, 83310* **Tel** *04 94 54 77 54* **Fax** *04 94 54 77 55* **Rooms** *12*        **Road map** *E4*

Located on the town's busy main street, this 12-room hotel has a peaceful interior garden and pool. The rooms are simply decorated but charming, and there are bicycles available to visit the surrounding area. A substantial breakfast is served either in your room, on the terrace or by the fire in winter. **www.lamaisondumonde.fr**

### COLLOBRIERES Hôtel des Maures

*19 boulevard Lazare-Carnot, 83310* **Tel** *04 94 48 07 10* **Fax** *04 94 48 02 73* **Rooms** *10*        **Road map** *D4*

This small and simple family-run affair is great value for money. The hotel has a highly popular restaurant, which serves traditional Provençal food. Although the rooms are not en suite, there are bathrooms on each floor. A good option for budget travellers.

### FAYENCE Moulin de la Camandoule

*Chemin de Notre-Dame, 83440* **Tel** *04 94 76 00 84* **Fax** *04 94 76 10 40* **Rooms** *11*        **Road map** *E3*

A converted 15th-century olive mill is the setting for this peaceful hotel in a valley beneath the village of Fayence. The machinery that was originally used to press the olives can still be seen here. The restaurant serves delicious traditional Provençal dishes, and there's a terraced garden to soak up the sun. **www.camandoule.com**

### FOX-AMPHOUX Auberge du Vieux Fox

*Pl de l'Eglise, 83670* **Tel** *04 94 80 71 69* **Fax** *04 94 80 78 38* **Rooms** *8*        **Road map** *D4*

A former staging post for the Knights Templar in the Middle Ages, this hotel has retained many of its medieval features, which more than compensate for the small rooms. The restaurant's excellent food, served in a rustic dining room, draws locals from miles around. There's also a terrace with parasols to enjoy the views.

### FREJUS Hôtel Arena
€€

*145 rue Général de Gaulle, 83600* **Tel** *04 94 17 09 40* **Fax** *04 94 52 01 52* **Rooms** *36*　　　**Road map** *E4*

A real taste of Provence can be found here in both the decor – warm bright colours evoking the sea, wooden furniture and mosaic tiles – and in the fine restaurant. The rooms look out over lovely patios, and the garden is landscaped with palm trees, oleander and geraniums. The restaurant serves top-class Provençal cuisine. **www.arena-hotel.com**

### GRIMAUD VILLAGE Côteau Fleuri
€€

*Pl des Pénitents, 83310* **Tel** *04 94 43 20 17* **Fax** *04 94 43 33 42* **Rooms** *14*　　　**Road map** *E4*

Panoramic views of the Massif des Maures are among the many attractions of this grey-stone inn on the side of a hill. The restaurant boasts a huge fireplace and in summer, food is served on the lovely flower-filled terrace. The speciality is fish and other local seasonal ingredients. **www.coteaufleuri.fr**

### HYERES Hôtel du Soleil
€

*Rue du Rempart, 83400* **Tel** *04 94 65 16 26* **Fax** *04 94 35 46 00* **Rooms** *22*　　　**Road map** *D4*

A charming ivy-clad old house, perched on a hill high above this pretty medieval town. Some rooms have panoramic sea views; others are set in the eaves of the house, but all are traditionally furnished. There's also a sunny terrace with parasoled tables. **www.hotel-du-soleil.fr**

### ILE DE PORQUEROLLES Auberge des Glycines
€€€

*Pl d'Armes, 83400* **Tel** *04 94 58 30 36* **Fax** *04 94 58 35 22* **Rooms** *11*　　　**Road map** *D5*

Situated in the heart of the village, near the pier and the church, this is a wonderful island getaway. The rooms are decorated with sweeping curtains and antique furniture, as is the dining room, which also has a large open fire. Enjoy breakfast and dinner on the shaded patio. Half board accommodation is obligatory. **www.auberge-glycines.com**

### ILE DE PORT-CROS Le Manoir d'Hélène
€€€€

*Port-Cros, 83400* **Tel** *04 94 05 90 52* **Fax** *04 94 05 90 89* **Rooms** *22*　　　**Road map** *D5*

A hotel situated on this island paradise is a rarity. Le Manoir d'Hélène is a simple, yet seductive 19th-century manor house, offering a warm welcome and delicious food, served among groves of eucalyptus trees. Offers only half-board accommodation, but with food this good, that's certainly not a problem.

### LA CADIERE D'AZUR Hostellerie Bérard
€€€

*Rue Gabriel-Péri, 83740* **Tel** *04 94 90 11 43* **Fax** *04 94 90 01 94* **Rooms** *38*　　　**Road map** *C4*

This 11th-century convent is now an attractive inn, with a heated outdoor pool, a shady terrace, lovely gardens and a well-respected restaurant. The rooms, cells of former nuns, are comfortable and spacious, despite their austere look. The hotel also offers courses in cooking, wine-tasting and watercolour painting. **www.hotel-berard.com**

### LA CELLE Abbaye de la Celle
€€€€

*Place du Général de Gaulle, 83170* **Tel** *04 98 05 14 14* **Fax** *04 98 05 14 15* **Rooms** *10*　　　**Road map** *D4*

This former Benedictine abbey is now in the hands of Alain Ducasse, who has delegated kitchen duties to Benoît Witz. Staff dressed in floaty white cottons ensure that every moment here is relaxing. It can hardly fail to be given the beauty of the pool and grounds. For extra tranquillity choose a room with a private garden. **www.abbaye-celle.com**

### LE LAVANDOU Hôtel le Rabelais
€

*Rue Rabelais, 83980* **Tel** *04 94 71 00 56* **Fax** *04 94 71 82 55* **Rooms** *20*　　　**Road map** *D4*

This seafront hotel has brightly-decorated, sun-drenched rooms, even if some of them are a bit on the small side. There's also a pretty flower-filled terrace from which you can watch all the bustling portside activity. Breakfast is served on the terrace in summer. The beach is nearby. **www.le-rabelais.fr**

### LES ARCS SUR ARGENS Logis du Guetteur
€€€

*Pl du Château, 83460* **Tel** *04 94 99 51 10* **Fax** *04 94 99 51 29* **Rooms** *13*　　　**Road map** *D4*

The hotel forms part of an 11th-century castle overlooking this small village. The medieval atmosphere is sustained in the sturdy stonework and wooden doors. The rooms, however, have all modern amenities and comforts. The dining room is evocatively set in the basement. The ramparts provide superb views. **www.logisduguetteur.com**

### PORT GRIMAUD Hôtel le Suffren
€€€

*16 place du Marché, 83310* **Tel** *04 94 55 15 05* **Fax** *04 94 55 15 06* **Rooms** *19*　　　**Road map** *E4*

Brightly decorated rooms overlook the port or the market square in this pleasant hotel. The Suffren provides very good value for money in a low-key village just a boat ride away from St-Tropez. Six studio apartments and three one-bedroom flats are also available. A good choice for families. **www.hotelleriedusoleil.com**

### SEILLANS Hôtel des Deux Rocs
€

*Pl Font d'Amont, 83440* **Tel** *04 94 76 87 32* **Fax** *04 94 76 88 68* **Rooms** *14*　　　**Road map** *E3*

This 18th-century Provençal mansion on the peaceful village square has both a strong family atmosphere and good Mediterranean cuisine. Some bedrooms are smaller and darker than others – those at the front of the building are the biggest, brightest and best. In summer, meals are served beside the square's fountain. **www.hoteldeuxrocs.com**

### ST-TROPEZ Lou Cagnard
€

*Av Paul Roussel, 83990* **Tel** *04 94 97 04 24* **Fax** *04 94 97 09 44* **Rooms** *19*　　　**Road map** *E4*

The bedrooms in this hotel, in an old town house, have been smartened up. There is no air conditioning, and the rooms facing the street are noisy. Make advance reservations for a room overlooking the small garden with mulberry trees. The hotel is only a minute's walk away from the lively place des Lices. **www.hotel-lou-cagnard.com**

**Key to Price Guide** *see p194* **Key to Symbols** *see back cover flap*

### ST-TROPEZ Château de la Messardière

🏨 ♨ 📺 🅿 🅿  €€€€

*Route de Tahiti, 83990* **Tel** *04 94 56 76 00* **Fax** *04 94 56 76 01* **Rooms** *80*     **Road map** *E4*

The biggest luxury hotel in St-Tropez, the Messardière feels almost like a private château, surrounded by its own substantial grounds. It can be hard to find the first time, but it is worth the extra effort. The food is exceptional, the service is generally superb and there is a free shuttle to the centre of town. **www.messardiere.com**

### ST-TROPEZ Pastis Hôtel St Tropez

♨ 📺 🅿 🅟  €€€€

*6 avenue du Général Leclerc, 83990* **Tel** *04 98 12 56 50* **Fax** *04 94 96 99 82* **Rooms** *9*     **Road map** *E4*

St-Tropez attracts more than its share of show-offs, but this nine-room inn decorated with contemporary art and a judicious mix of modern and antique furniture is for those who prefer a more discreet charm. The heated pool is surrounded by centuries-old palm trees. There is a strict "no dress code" policy. **www.pastis-st-tropez.com**

### ST-TROPEZ Le Byblos

🏨 ♨ 🏃 📺 🅿 🅿  €€€€€

*Av Paul Signac, 83990* **Tel** *04 94 56 68 00* **Fax** *04 94 56 68 01* **Rooms** *97*     **Road map** *E4*

This is the height of glamour for those with an unlimited budget. A luxurious complex of brightly coloured houses sets the tone at the Mediterranean's most famous resort. The sumptuous bedrooms will make you feel like a Hollywood star. In addition, there is a beauty salon and spa treatments. **www.byblos.com**

### TOULON Hôtel Mercure

📺 🏨 🖼 🅿  €€

*Pl Besagne, 83000* **Tel** *04 98 00 81 00* **Fax** *04 94 41 57 51* **Rooms** *139*     **Road map** *D4*

Next door to the Palais des Congrès and close to the harbour, this chain hotel has been brightly decorated to reflect the warm colours of the Mediterranean. Palm trees and stained-glass windows add to the uniqueness of the spacious restaurant, which serves traditional Mediterranean fare. **www.accorhotels.com**

### TOURTOUR L'Auberge St-Pierre

🏨 ♨ 🏃 📺 🅿  €

*St-Pierre, 83690* **Tel** *04 94 50 00 50* **Fax** *04 94 70 59 04* **Rooms** *16*     **Road map** *D4*

Situated in a converted 16th-century farmhouse, this hotel makes for a tranquil stay. A trickling fountain graces the dining room, while the terrace offers wonderful views across the Haut Var. A fully-functioning farm still surrounds the hotel. Rooms have balconies looking out over the countryside. **www.guideprovence.com/hotel/saint-pierre**

### TOURTOUR La Bastide de Tourtour

🏨 ♨ 🏃 📺 🖼  €€€

*Montée St Denis, 83690* **Tel** *04 98 10 54 20* **Fax** *04 94 70 54 90* **Rooms** *25*     **Road map** *D4*

Located just outside the village, this ancient converted complex has panoramic views of the pine forests of the Haut Var. Some of the rooms have balconies that also offer sweeping views. The restaurant is set in a vaulted room and serves classical French cuisine. Along with the pool, the hotel also has tennis courts. **www.verdon.net**

## BOUCHES-DU-RHONE AND NIMES

### AIX-EN-PROVENCE Hôtel des Augustins

🛏 🖼  €€

*3 rue Masse, 13100* **Tel** *04 42 27 28 59* **Fax** *04 42 26 74 87* **Rooms** *29*     **Road map** *C4*

A converted 12th-century convent, with the reception housed in a chapel. Large, comfortable rooms in traditional Provençal style make the Hôtel des Augustins a haven of peace in the heart of Aix. The surprising absence of a restaurant is no real handicap with so many places to eat nearby. **www.hotel-augustins.com**

### AIX-EN-PROVENCE Saint Christophe

🛏 🏨 🏃 🖼 🅿 🅿  €€

*2 av Victor-Hugo, 13100* **Tel** *04 42 26 01 24* **Fax** *04 42 38 53 17* **Rooms** *60*     **Road map** *C4*

Fantastic value for money, this superb town house hotel has bedrooms with all modern facilities. Book in advance to secure a room with a balcony. The hotel is decorated in Art Deco style, and has a bustling old-fashioned brasserie on the ground floor. **www.hotel-saintchristophe.com**

### AIX-EN-PROVENCE Hotel Cézanne

🛏 🖼 🅿  €€€

*40 avenue Victor Hugo, 13100* **Tel** *04 42 91 11 11* **Fax** *04 42 91 11 10* **Rooms** *56*     **Road map** *C4*

Modern boutique hotels are rare in Provence, but designer Charles Montemarco has added a local touch by reinterpreting Cezanne's work with a bold colour scheme and arty objects in this establishment. Everything is designed for the utmost comfort, from the king-sized beds to the generous breakfast served until noon. **http://cezanne.hotelaix.com**

### ARLES Hotel de l'Amphithéâtre

🖼 🅿  €

*5–7 rue Diderot, 13200* **Tel** *04 90 96 10 30* **Fax** *04 90 93 98 69* **Rooms** *28*     **Road map** *B3*

This bargain hotel has plenty of character and a perfect location next to Arles' amphitheatre. Some of the rooms are on the small side, but the decor is charmingly Provençal. The public areas are pleasant, the service is helpful and there is discounted parking available nearby. A good choice for families. **www.hotelamphitheatre.fr**

### ARLES Hôtel Calendal

🏨 🏃 🖼 🅿  €€

*5 rue Porte de Laure, 13200* **Tel** *04 90 96 11 89* **Fax** *04 90 96 05 84* **Rooms** *38*     **Road map** *B3*

This good-value hotel in the historic centre of Arles, close to the Roman arena, has a mix of small rooms and large bedrooms – all charmingly decorated. A few have balconies with views of the arena or the Roman theatre. Breakfast is served in a garden shaded by palm trees. Original photographs grace the public areas. **www.lecalendal.com**

### ARLES Hôtel d'Arlatan
*26 rue du Sauvage, 13200* **Tel** *04 90 93 56 66* **Fax** *04 90 49 68 45* **Rooms** *47*    **Road map** *B3*

This 16th-century town residence of the Comtes d'Arlatan is one of the most beautiful hotels in the region. Glass panels in the salon floor offer glimpses of 4th-century Roman foundations. There's a walled garden and a stone terrace for breakfast in summer. Antiques and curios furnish individually-decorated bedrooms. **www.hotel-arlatan.fr**

### ARLES L'Hôtel Particulier à Arles
*Rue de la Monnaie, 13200* **Tel** *04 90 52 51 40* **Fax** *04 90 96 16 70* **Rooms** *13*    **Road map** *B3*

Once you've found this hidden gem of a hotel, you may never want to leave: just as the name suggests, it feels like an aristocratic private residence, complete with its own garden and swimming pool. Rooms are elegantly decorated with antique funiture, and the service is impeccable. **www.hotel-particulier.com**

### CASSIS Le Clos des Arômes
*10 rue Abbé Paul Mouton, 13260* **Tel** *04 42 01 71 84* **Fax** *04 42 01 31 76* **Rooms** *14*    **Road map** *C4*

This peaceful hotel in a sensitively-refurbished Cassis house stands amid a garden overflowing with flowers and greenery. Le Clos des Aromes is extremely good value for money, and is much in demand. Book well in advance. **www.le-clos-des-aromes.com**

### CASSIS Les Jardins de Cassis
*Rue A Favier, 13260* **Tel** *04 42 01 84 85* **Fax** *04 42 01 32 38* **Rooms** *36*    **Road map** *C4*

The most pleasant place to stay in the picturesque port of Cassis. The bedrooms, housed in a cluster of small pastel-coloured buildings, are well thought-out. The pool is found in a garden of lemon trees and bougainvillea. The restaurant (open from June to September) serves a Mediterranean lunch around the pool. **www.hotel-lesjardinsde-cassis.com**

### FONTVIEILLE La Régalido
*Av F Mistral, 13990* **Tel** *04 90 54 60 22* **Fax** *04 90 54 64 29* **Rooms** *15*    **Road map** *B3*

Housed in a converted olive oil mill, in the centre of sleepy Fontvieille, La Régalido is a luxurious and welcoming hotel, with tastefully decorated and inviting rooms and a delightful flower garden with palm and fig trees. The restaurant has a pretty terrace for al fresco dining, and the menu features delicious Provençal cuisine. **www.laregalido.com**

### LES-BAUX-DE-PROVENCE L'Hostellerie de la Reine Jeanne
*Grande rue, 13520* **Tel** *04 90 54 32 06* **Fax** *04 90 54 32 33* **Rooms** *10*    **Road map** *B3*

This old house is set in the centre of one of Provence's most charming and popular villages. Offers attractive, individually decorated and simply furnished rooms. Extremely well priced, the hotel provides a panoramic view of the village and the valley. Not ideal for small children. Parking is always a challenge here. **www.la-reinejeanne.com**

### LES-BAUX-DE-PROVENCE Auberge de la Benvengudo
*Vallon de l'Arcoule, 13520* **Tel** *04 90 54 32 54* **Fax** *04 90 54 42 58* **Rooms** *23*    **Road map** *B3*

This attractive former country house, with its ivy-clad walls, is one of the most charming places to stay on the fringes of the Bouches-du-Rhône. Has comfortable, lavishly decorated bedrooms, a large garden, swimming pool and tennis court. A good base for exploring the region by car. The restaurant serves regional cuisine. **www.benvengudo.com**

### MARSEILLE Hôtel Saint-Ferreol
*19 rue Pisancon, 13000* **Tel** *04 91 33 12 21* **Fax** *04 91 54 29 97* **Rooms** *18*    **Road map** *C4*

Located near the Vieux Port, this small, modern hotel has an air of glamour. The rooms are on the smaller side, but well equipped and thoughtfully designed. Most have double glazing (essential in noisy Marseille) and some have whirlpool baths. **www.hotel-stferreol.com**

### MARSEILLE Sofitel Marseille Vieux Port
*36 boulevard Charles Livon, 13007* **Tel** *04 91 15 59 00* **Fax** *04 91 15 59 50* **Rooms** *134*    **Road map** *C4*

Decorated in minimalist style, with dark wood and streamlined furniture, this luxury hotel is most remarkable for its spectacular views of the Vieux Port – if possible, try to book one of the 28 rooms with a terrace. The major sights are all nearby, and the top-floor restaurant offers good panoramic views. **www.accorhotels.com**

### MARSEILLE Villa Massalia
*17 place Louis Bonnefon, 13008* **Tel** *04 91 72 90 00* **Fax** *04 91 72 90 01* **Rooms** *140*    **Road map** *C4*

Loosely based on the architecture of the 18th-century Château Borély in Marseille, the Villa Massalia is decorated with contemporary furniture and soothing tones, with a Chinese-inspired dining room and bar. It's located in a chic residential area, near the Borély park and the beach. **http://marseille.concorde-hotels.com**

### MAUSSANE-LES-ALPILLES L'Oustaloun
*Pl de l'Eglise, 13520* **Tel** *04 90 54 32 19* **Fax** *04 90 54 45 57* **Rooms** *8*    **Road map** *B3*

This small town is less crowded with visitors in summer than tourist hotspots such as Les Baux. L'Oustaloun is a tiny hostelry on its main square, located within a restored 16th-century town house. Meals are served in a cool, vaulted dining room, which is a welcome escape from the summer heat. **www.loustaloun.com**

### NIMES Hôtel Kyriad Nîmes Centre
*10 rue Roussy, 30000* **Tel** *04 66 76 16 20* **Fax** *04 66 67 65 99* **Rooms** *28*    **Road map** *A3*

Located on a quiet street in the centre of the city, this hotel is near the Cathédrale Notre-Dame et St-Castor (*see p133*). Set in an old converted house, the colourful public spaces have a unique bullfighting theme. The rooms are individually decorated and the top-floor rooms have patios and views over the city's rooftops. **www.hotel-kyriad-nimes.com**

**Key to Price Guide** *see p194* **Key to Symbols** *see back cover flap*

## NIMES L'Orangerie
*755 rue Tour de l'Evèque, 30000* **Tel** *04 66 84 50 57* **Fax** *04 66 29 44 55* **Rooms** *37*   **Road map** *A3*

A modern, but appealing hotel, with the advantage of its own swimming pool. Decorated with the bright colours of the Mediterranean, some of the rooms have balconies, while others have whirlpool baths. The restaurant is highly rated, serving local produce prepared with flair, but is non-smoking only. **www.orangerie.fr**

## NIMES New Hotel de la Baume
*21 rue Nationale, 30000* **Tel** *04 66 76 28 42* **Fax** *04 66 76 28 45* **Rooms** *34*   **Road map** *A3*

Located in the heart of Nîmes' Old Town, boasts a spectacular central staircase and open courtyard, preserved from the 17th century, when this was a private home. The rooms are spacious, decorated in a mixture of traditional features and modern style. **www.new-hotel.com**

## NIMES Imperator Concorde
*Quai de la Fontaine, 30900* **Tel** *04 66 21 90 30* **Fax** *04 66 67 70 25* **Rooms** *60*   **Road map** *A3*

This charming hotel dates back to the 1930s, when its guests included such celebrities as Ernest Hemingway and Ava Gardner. It has all the facilities one would expect from a four-star member of the prestigious Concorde group, including an outstanding restaurant and a pretty courtyard. **www.concorde-hotels.com**

## SAINTES-MARIES-DE-LA-MER Hôtel de Cacharel
*Route de Cacharel, 13460* **Tel** *04 90 97 95 44* **Fax** *04 90 97 87 97* **Rooms** *16*   **Road map** *B4*

This historic ranch in the heart of the Camargue marshland, was once home to *gardians*, the cowboys that worked the land of this region. Today, this hotel is particularly popular with equestrians for its riding facilities. Although there's no restaurant, the hotel provides meat and cheese platters on request. **www.hotel-cacharel.com**

## SAINTES-MARIES-DE-LA-MER Mas de la Fouque
*Route du Petit Rhône, 13460* **Tel** *04 90 97 81 02* **Fax** *04 90 97 96 84* **Rooms** *19*   **Road map** *B4*

You get what you pay for at the Camargue's most luxurious hotel. The bedrooms have terraces overlooking the lagoon, while the dining room looks out over the park. Tennis courts, mini-golf facilities and a stable of the region's famous white horses are also available. There's even a heliport if you really want to arrive in style. **www.masdelafouque.com**

## SALON-DE-PROVENCE L'Abbaye de Ste-Croix
*Route de Val de Cuech, 13300* **Tel** *04 90 56 24 55* **Fax** *04 90 56 31 12* **Rooms** *21*   **Road map** *B3*

This picturesque hotel is housed in a converted 12th-century abbey. The rooms, which were originally monks' cells, are decorated in a rustic style. The breathtaking views can be enjoyed from a shaded terrace around the pool. The restaurant prides itself on its local cuisine. Closed Nov–Apr. **www.relaischateaux.com/saintecroix**

## ST-REMY-DE-PROVENCE Hôtel l'Amandiere
*Av Théodore–Aubanel, 13210* **Tel** *04 90 92 41 00* **Fax** *04 90 92 48 38* **Rooms** *26*   **Road map** *B3*

A peaceful retreat outside the main town, this hotel has a lovely rustic feel, from the decor of the rooms to the traditional masonry of the building and the gardens surrounding the pool. Nearby is the Alpilles canal, where you can take leisurely strolls and enjoy summer picnics. **http://Perso.wanadoo.fr/hotel.amandiere**

## SAINT-REMY-DE-PROVENCE Hôtel Sous Les Figuiers
*3 avenue Taillandier, 13210* **Tel** *04 32 60 15 40* **Fax** *04 32 60 15 39* **Rooms** *13*   **Road map** *B3*

A two-minute walk from the centre of town, this hotel gets its name from the centuries-old fig trees that shade the garden. All 13 rooms overlook the garden, and ten of them have terraces. You'll find figs in some form or other on the breakfast table all year round. Painting workshops are available. **www.hotel-charme-provence.com**

## ST-REMY-DE-PROVENCE Le Mas des Carassins
*1 chemin Gaulois, 13210* **Tel** *04 90 92 15 48* **Fax** *04 90 92 63 47* **Rooms** *14*   **Road map** *B3*

This typical Provençal farmhouse is outside the main town, picturesquely set amid lavender fields and olive groves. The building has been renovated with great care and retains its traditional feel. The open-air swimming pool is a welcome feature in the summer months. The restaurant is open only to hotel guests. **www.masdescarassins.com**

## ST-REMY-DE-PROVENCE L'Hôtel des Ateliers de l'Image
*36 boulevard Victor Hugo, 13210* **Tel** *04 90 92 51 50* **Fax** *04 90 92 43 52* **Rooms** *32*   **Road map** *B3*

Set in a former music hall, this contemporary hotel has a photography theme. The rooms and hallways are decorated with exhibitions of photos, and a developing lab allows eager guests to print their own images. The restaurant menu combines French classics with Japanese cuisine. **www.hotelphoto.com**

## ST-REMY-DE-PROVENCE Domaine de Valmouriane
*Petite route des Baux, 13210* **Tel** *04 90 92 44 62* **Fax** *04 90 92 37 32* **Rooms** *11*   **Road map** *B3*

A beautiful and luxurious converted 18th-century farmhouse, surrounded by pine forests and vineyards. The rooms are decorated with Provençal furniture and colourful fabrics. The restaurant serves local cuisine beneath a vaulted ceiling. There's an open fire in the bar, and a shaded terrace beside the pool. **www.valmouriane.com**

## VILLENEUVE-LES-AVIGNON Hôtel de l'Atelier
*5 rue de la Foire, 30400* **Tel** *04 90 25 01 84* **Fax** *04 90 25 80 06* **Rooms** *23*   **Road map** *B3*

A 16th-century house is the setting for this quiet, peaceful hotel. The public and guest rooms are dominated by antique furniture, art works and original wooden beams. There's a beautiful stone fireplace in the hotel lounge. The roof terrace has both sunny and shaded areas, filled with the fragrance of its blooming flower pots. **www.hoteldelatelier.com**

### VILLENEUVE-LES-AVIGNON La Magnaneraie    🍴🏊🎿📋P♿    €€€€

*37 rue Camp de Bataille, 30400* **Tel** *04 90 25 11 11* **Fax** *04 90 25 46 37* **Rooms** *29*     **Road map** *B3*

Used to breed silkworms in the 15th-century, this hotel is now a refined, tranquil place to stay. Some of the rooms have patios reached through sun-drenched French doors. The restaurant is decorated with frescoes and there are options for outdoor eating in the lovely gardens. **www.hostellerie-la-magnaneraie.com**

# VAUCLUSE

### AVIGNON Hôtel Bristol    📺📋P♿    €€

*44 cours Jean Jaurès, 84000* **Tel** *04 90 16 48 48* **Fax** *04 90 86 22 72* **Rooms** *67*     **Road map** *B3*

At first glance, this hotel might not seem at all remarkable, but its location a mere five-minute walk from the train station, on one of the town's prettiest and most convenient streets, is a big part of its appeal. Rooms are a little plain and some are bigger than others, but staff bend over backwards to please. **www.bristol-hotel-avignon.com**

### AVIGNON Hôtel de l'Horloge    📋♿    €€

*1–3 rue Félicien David, 84000* **Tel** *04 90 16 42 00* **Fax** *04 90 82 17 32* **Rooms** *66*     **Road map** *B3*

With a perfect location overlooking the place de l'Horloge, this hotel in a 19th-century building is very good value. All rooms are decorated in contemporary style, and five of them have terraces. There is free WiFi in the public areas and staff are particularly helpful. **www.hotels-ocre-azur.com**

### AVIGNON Hôtel d'Europe    🍴🎿📋P    €€€€

*14 pl Crillon, 84000* **Tel** *04 90 14 76 76* **Fax** *04 90 14 76 71* **Rooms** *44*     **Road map** *B3*

One of Avignon's finest hotels, dating back to the 16th century – Napolean is said to have stayed here. The top-floor rooms offer views of the Palais des Papes, which is beautifully floodlit at night. The restaurant serves top-class cuisine and wines. Sounds of a trickling fountain in the garden enhance the peaceful atmosphere. **www.heurope.com**

### AVIGNON La Mirande    🍴📋♿    €€€€€

*4 pl de la Mirande, 84000* **Tel** *04 90 14 20 20* **Fax** *04 90 86 26 85* **Rooms** *19*     **Road map** *B3*

Set in the shadow of the grand Palais des Papes, this is without doubt the best place to stay in town. What was once a cardinal's mansion, has now been renovated in 18th-century style. The restaurant is one of the finest in the region, with a beautiful Baroque interior and an outside area surrounded by trees and aromatic plants. **www.la-mirande.fr**

### GORDES Le Mas de Romarins    🏊🎿📋♿    €€

*Route de Sénanque, 84220* **Tel** *04 90 72 12 13* **Fax** *04 90 72 13 13* **Rooms** *13*     **Road map** *C3*

An 18th-century country house has been renovated to create this comfortable and peaceful three-star hotel. Traditional features include stone fires and bathrooms decorated with ceramic Provençal tiles. There's a pretty terrace where guests can enjoy breakfast. The pool is bordered by flower beds. **www.masromarins.com**

### LE BARROUX Hôtel les Géraniums    🍴🎿P    €

*Pl de la Croix, 84330* **Tel** *04 90 62 41 08* **Fax** *04 90 62 56 48* **Rooms** *22*     **Road map** *B2*

Set in an ancient house in one of the region's famous "perched villages", the rooms at this hotel are expectedly rustic, but comfortable. There is also a modern annexe, with slightly larger rooms. The restaurant, with original woodwork decor and a pleasant terrace, serves traditional Provençal dishes. **www.hotel-lesgeraniums.com**

### LE BARROUX Hostellerie Francois Joseph    🏊🎿P♿    €€

*Chemin de Rabassièrres, 84330* **Tel** *04 90 62 52 78* **Fax** *04 90 62 33 54* **Rooms** *18*     **Road map** *B2*

Two traditional farmhouses, tucked away in a garden with spectacular views of the countryside, have been converted into rooms and apartments with their own cooking facilities. There are also two cottages in the grounds with private gardens. Breakfast is served on the veranda or the patio. Closed Nov–Mar. **www.hotel-francois-joseph.com**

### LOURMARIN Le Mas des Guilles    🍴🏊📋    €€

*Route de Vaugines, 84160* **Tel** *04 90 68 30 55* **Fax** *04 90 68 37 41* **Rooms** *28*     **Road map** *C3*

Surrounded by a 20-hectare park, this Provençal *mas* with rooms decorated in classic style is something of a well-kept secret. It's not a luxury hotel, but a charming inn where guests are made to feel at home. There are tennis courts and a swimming pool, and the rooms have spectacular views. **www.guilles.com**

### LOURMARIN Auberge de la Fenière    🍴🏊🎿📋P♿    €€€

*Route de Cadenet, 84160* **Tel** *04 90 68 11 79* **Fax** *04 90 68 18 60* **Rooms** *9*     **Road map** *C3*

A haven in the heart of the Grand Luberon region, known for its abundant wildlife and superb views. The rooms are newly decorated and modern, one filled with canvases and the Basketweaver's Room decorated with wickerwork. The grounds have two gypsy caravans as well. **www.reinesammut.com**

### LOURMARIN Le Moulin de Lourmarin    📺🍴🎿📋P    €€€€€

*Rue Temple, 84160* **Tel** *04 90 68 06 69* **Fax** *04 90 68 31 76* **Rooms** *19*     **Road map** *C3*

This hotel preserves the original millstones from its days as an olive oil mill, and boasts regional cooking with four luscious menus (*see p217*). The rooms are located within the stone walls of the 300-year old mill. Not, perhaps, an ideal place for a long holiday, but good for savouring a meal and staying overnight. **www.moulindelourmarin.com**

**Key to Price Guide** *see p194* **Key to Symbols** *see back cover flap*

### PERNES-LES-FONTAINES Mas de la Bonoty

*Chemin de la Bonoty, 84210* **Tel** *04 90 61 61 09* **Fax** *04 90 61 35 14* **Rooms** *8*     **Road map** *B3*

This renovated 17th-century farmhouse is surrounded by fragrant lavender fields and olive groves. The rooms are decorated in a rustic way, although they are equipped with modern features. The dining room beautifully preserves its original stonework and wooden beams. Also offers striking views of Mont Ventoux. **www.bonoty.com**

### ROUSSILLON Le Mas de Garrigon

*Route de St-Saturnin d'Apt, 84220* **Tel** *04 90 05 63 22* **Fax** *04 90 05 70 01* **Rooms** *9*     **Road map** *C3*

A peaceful farmhouse located amid pine forests. Everything here is designed for refined tastes, including the classical music, which plays in the public lounges in the evenings. The brightly coloured rooms follow themes of artists or writers who contributed to Provence. **www.masdegarrigon-provence.com**

### SEGURET Domaine de Cabasse

*Route de Sablet, 84110* **Tel** *04 90 46 91 12* **Fax** *04 90 46 94 01* **Rooms** *13*     **Road map** *B2*

This hotel is part of a working vineyard, and wine tastings for guests are part of the appeal. The rooms are comfortable and clean, if a little sparse, and the swimming pool adds to the relaxing atmosphere. The restaurant is highly rated with lots of local produce and the wine list is, of course, excellent. **www.domaine-de-cabasse.fr**

### SEGURET La Table du Comtat

*Le Village, 84110* **Tel** *04 90 46 91 49* **Fax** *04 90 46 94 27* **Rooms** *8*     **Road map** *B2*

A stone house dating back to the 14th century, situated at the top of the medieval village. Offers wide-reaching views of the plains, particularly from the dining terrace. The staff are friendly and helpful, advising on activities within the area such as hiking or bike rides. The restaurant has a first-class reputation.

### VAISON LA ROMAINE (LE CRESTET) Le Mas d'Hélène

*Quartier Chante Coucou, 84110* **Tel** *04 90 36 39 91* **Fax** *04 90 28 73 40* **Rooms** *12*     **Road map** *B2*

Surrounded by a 3-ha (7-acre) park with a view of the Mont Ventoux, Le Mas d'Hélène successfully combines Provençal style and modern comforts. The garden has many quiet spots where guests can relax. It's worth opting for full-board accommodation as the creative cuisine is top-notch. **www.lemasdhelene.com**

## ALPES-DE-HAUTE-PROVENCE

### CASTELLANE Nouvel Hôtel du Commerce

*Pl de l'église, 04120* **Tel** *04 92 83 61 00* **Fax** *04 92 83 72 82* **Rooms** *35*     **Road map** *D3*

A good place to stay for a night or two in a picturesque town, that makes a good base for exploring. Rooms look out over the market square or the crag that surmounts Castellane. The bedrooms are prettily decorated, well equipped and immaculately clean. The dining room veranda is a lovely, airy spot in the heat of summer. **www.hotel-fradet.com**

### CHATEAU-ARNOUX La Bonne Etape

*Chemin du Lac, 04160* **Tel** *04 92 64 00 09* **Fax** *04 92 64 37 36* **Rooms** *18*     **Road map** *D2*

This renovated 18th-century building is run by a family that takes great pride in its service. The rooms are stunningly decorated with antiques, but each has its own individual feel. The restaurant has a well-deserved reputation for excellence in serving classic French cuisine amid elegant surroundings. **www.bonneetape.com**

### FORCALQUIER Hostellerie des Deux Lions

*11 pl du Bourguet, 04300* **Tel** *04 92 75 25 30* **Fax** *04 92 75 06 41* **Rooms** *12*     **Road map** *C3*

Right on the corner of the town's main square, the Deux Lions' central position has secured its role as a staging post since the 17th century. The rooms are spacious and nicely decorated; those at the front are protected from street noise with double glazing. **www.lesdeuxlions.com**

### MOUSTIERS-STE-MARIE La Bonne Auberge

*Rue Principale "Le Village", 04360* **Tel** *04 92 74 66 18* **Fax** *04 92 74 65 11* **Rooms** *19*     **Road map** *D3*

Refurbished recently, this hotel offers great value for money in terms of scenery and facilities. Within walking distance of Moustiers' restaurants and cafés, it is also a short drive from the breathtaking Verdon canyon. Bedrooms are light and simple, the cooking is tasty and the swimming pool is a bonus. **www.bonne-auberge-moustiers.com**

### MOUSTIERS-STE-MARIE La Bastide de Moustiers

*Chemin de Quinson, 04360* **Tel** *04 92 70 47 47* **Fax** *04 92 70 47 48* **Rooms** *12*     **Road map** *D3*

Housed in a 17th-century building, this hotel offers the latest facilities within its venerable exteriors. The Provençal buildings are surrounded by a gorgeous garden and the hotel has sweeping views of the surrounding mountains. The restaurant has a good wine list. **www.bastide-moustiers.com**

### REILLANNE Auberge de Reillanne

*D214 Le Pigonnier, 04110* **Tel** *04 92 76 45 95* **Fax** *04 92 76 45 95* **Rooms** *6*     **Road map** *C3*

This large and charming mansion (a converted fortified manor) in the Luberon region is surrounded by a vast garden. The living rooms and other public areas are lined with bookshelves, while the comfortable rooms are rustic with a mishmash of country furniture. The restaurant offers good French country cooking. **www.auberge-de-reillanne.com**

# RESTAURANTS, CAFÉS AND BARS

One of the joys of this sunny region is the abundance of fresh, enticing food on offer. The coast of Provence is famous for its seafood restaurants – these are best in the coastal towns of Marseille and Nice, but generally do not come cheap. For traditional Provençal fare, it is advisable to head inland to the villages of the Var and northern Vaucluse. In the valleys of Haute Provence, the cuisine is more simple, but delicious – local game and the much-loved truffle are

**Delicious seafood platter**

common menu features. Life in the south revolves around mealtimes and villages and towns come to a standstill during the main midday meal and dinner. Lunch is served from noon until 2pm with dinner from 7:30pm until about 10pm, while cafés and bars in towns tend to stay open later, especially in high season *(see pp218–19)*. The restaurants on pages 210–17 have been carefully selected for their excellence of food, decor and ambience, covering all price ranges.

## TYPES OF RESTAURANT

In the country, you may eat at a *ferme auberge*, a small, basic inn attached to a farm or wine estate. Here you will enjoy good, inexpensive meals, often made with fresh farm produce, eaten with the host's family as part of your room and board. Many country restaurants are attached to hotels but serve a predominantly non-residential clientele. These establishments are good value for money and are often the focus of local social activity.

In towns, there is the usual mixture of Americanized fast food joints and more traditional French restaurants. The larger towns such as Aix, Nice and Avignon provide a wide range of restaurants, including some of the best establishments outside Paris.

For those on the move, look out for the distinctive red and blue Les Routiers sign – this is a long

established organization that recommends anything from large family restaurants to smaller brasseries, serving good quality, inexpensive food in a friendly, relaxed atmosphere.

In Provence, as in the rest of France, the decor of a restaurant is very much secondary to the quality of the food. This said, there are many places that offer charming medieval interiors or superb views.

## HOW MUCH TO PAY

Prices in Provence are generally lower than those in urban France. Most restaurants offer fixed-price menus which are invariably better value than à la carte. Lunch is always good value – you can enjoy a large repast with wine for under €15 Inland you can dine very well for under €30 a head while, on the coast, the profusion of restaurants

**Les Deux Garçons in Aix** *(see p219)*

means that prices are kept competitively lower. In the deluxe dining rooms of the Côte d'Azur and the Riviera, you can expect to spend at least €70 a head, although the food will usually be of outstanding quality.

Restaurants are obliged by law to post menu prices outside. These generally include service, but a tip is often expected for good service – up to five per cent of the bill. The most widely accepted credit cards are Visa and Mastercard. American Express is slowly becoming more popular, as is the case with Diners Club. Travellers' cheques are virtually unheard of for settling bills.

## MAKING RESERVATIONS

For the up-market palaces of the Côte d'Azur and Riviera, reservations are often mandatory. In season, it may be necessary to reserve a table in

**Relaxing in the popular Café de Paris in St-Tropez** *(p218–19)*

the smallest restaurants. In rural areas it is normally possible to find a table – the owner will simply add one to the terrace or extend his or her establishment further into the street.

## DRESS CODE

The French are generally well-turned out, even when dressed casually, and visitors should aim for the same level of presentable comfort when eating out. Beach clothes are not acceptable, except in cafés and bars. The listings on pages 210–15 indicate which restaurants require formal dress.

## READING THE MENU

Menus usually comprise three courses. The waiter will take your choice of *entrée* (first course) and main course. Dessert is ordered afterwards. More expensive menus are often four courses, with cheese eaten before the dessert, while some country restaurants serve six course extravaganzas, which can take several hours to eat.

The *entrée* usually includes salads, pâté, Provençal soups and often shellfish. Main dishes are predominantly a choice of lamb, chicken or fish – game is widely available in season.

Coffee is always served after, not with, dessert – you will need to specify whether you want it *au lait* (with milk).

**Breakfast for two in a local café**

## CHOICE OF WINE

Wine is so much a part of everyday life in Provence that you will find a good range at even the smallest establishments *(see pp208–9)*. The price may be off-putting as all restaurants put a large mark-up on wine (up to 300 per cent).

**The elegant Colombe d'Or restaurant in St-Paul-de-Vence** *(see p212)*

Most wine is produced locally and usually served in carafes. Ordering a *demi* (50 cl) or *quart* (25 cl) is an inexpensive way of sampling the region's wines. French law divides the country's wines into four classes, in ascending order of quality: Vin de Table, Vin de Pays, Vin Délimité de Qualité Supérieure (VDQS) and Appellation d'Origine Contrôlée (AOC). If in doubt, order the house wine *(la réserve)* – few owners will risk their reputation on an inferior quality wine as this is their personal choice.

## VEGETARIAN FOOD

Uniquely vegetarian restaurants are hard to find, as this concept has largely yet to filter down to the carnivorous South. Most establishments will offer salads, omelettes or soup, or dishes from the *entrée* menu. Some can rustle up a concoction of Provençal vegetables if given warning.

## CHILDREN

Meals in Provence are very much a family affair and children are welcome in most places. However, special facilities like high chairs or baby seats are rarely provided. More and more establishments have a children's menu and many will be happy to provide smaller dishes at reduced rates.

## SERVICE

As eating is a leisurely pastime in France, service can be slow. In small restaurants do not expect rapid attention: there may be only one waiter and dishes are cooked to order.

## WHEELCHAIR ACCESS

Wheelchair access to many restaurants is restricted. In summer, this will be less of a problem at establishments with outside terraces; even so, when booking ahead, ask for a conveniently situated table.

## SMOKING

Despite their attempts to circumvent the no-smoking laws, the French have had to bow to the inevitable. Smoking is now banned in all public places in France, with restaurant and bar owners facing heavy fines if they do not adhere to the rules.

## PICNICS

Picnicking is the best way to enjoy the wonderful fresh produce, bread, cheeses and *charcuterie* from Provence's enticing markets and shops. Picnicking areas along major roads are well marked and furnished with tables and chairs; those along country lanes are better still.

# The Flavours of Provence

The cooking of Provence is known as *cuisine du soleil* ("the cuisine of the sun") with good reason. Famous for its abundance of glorious, sun-ripe fruit and vegetables, it is also healthy with plenty of fresh fish and seafood and fine-quality, lean meat from mountain pastures. Cheeses tend to be made with goats' milk. Good produce is enhanced by key ingredients: olive oil, garlic and aromatic herbs. Local markets are a colourful feast of seasonal produce: tomatoes, aubergines (eggplants), peppers and courgettes (zucchini), and freshly picked cherries, melons, lemons and figs. Most of all, though, Provence is the land of olives and of rich green olive oil.

Olives and olive oil

Scented, sun-ripened Cavaillon melons in a Provençal market

## VEGETABLES

In Provençal cooking, vegetables play a leading role. They may be served raw as crudités with *aioli* (garlic mayonnaise) or *tapenade* (puréed anchovies, olives and capers). Tomatoes and courgettes (zucchini) are often stuffed in the Niçois style, with minced meat, rice and herbs. Small violet arti-chokes come with a sauce of lemon and butter, or sautéed with bacon. A favourite soup is the robust *pistou*, beans and vegetables laced with a pungent sauce of basil, pine nuts and garlic. *Ratatouille* is a fragrant stew of vegetables cooked with olive oil, garlic and herbs. Popular salads include *salade niçoise* and *mesclun*, a regional mixture of leaves, including rocket, lamb's lettuce, dandelion leaves and chervil.

## MEDITERRANEAN FISH

The fish of the Mediterranean is highly prized, culminating in the famous *bouillabaisse*. A wide range of fish is caught, including rockfish, *rascasse* (scorpion fish), red mullet, sea bream, john dory, monkfish and squid. Around Nice, the main catch is sardines and anchovies. Most are best enjoyed simply grilled with herbs, like the classic *loup* (sea bass) with

Mussels · Lobster · Prawns (shrimp) · Sea bass · Monkfish · Squid · Clams

Selection of Mediterranean seafood available in Provence

## PROVENCAL DISHES AND SPECIALITIES

**Bouillabaisse** *Fish often found in this Provençal classic includes monkfish, snapper and conger eel.*

Provence has produced several renowned dishes, of which *Bouillabaisse* is the most famous. The ingredients of this fish stew vary from place to place, though Marseille claims the original recipe. A variety of local seafood (always including *rascasse,* or scorpion fish) is cooked in stock with tomatoes and saffron. The fish liquor is traditionally served first, with croûtons spread with *rouille*, a spicy mayonnaise, and the fish served afterwards. Once a fishermen's supper, it is now a luxury item you may need to order 24 hours in advance. A simpler version is *bourride*, a garlicky fish soup. Rich red wine stews, known as *daubes,* are another speciality, usually made with beef, but sometimes tuna or calamari. Other classics include *ratatouille* and *salade niçoise.*

Fresh figs

**Dried spices and herbs on sale at the market in Nice**

fennel. Seafood includes mussels *(moules)*, tiny crabs, giant prawns *(gambas)* and sea urchins *(oursins)*. Look out for trout from the Alpine streams north of Nice and freshwater eels in the Camargue. Popular fish dishes include *soupe de poissons* (fish soup), octopus cooked provençal style with white wine, tomatoes and herbs, and the famous *brandade de morue*, a speciality of Nîmes, a purée of salt cod, cream, potatoes and olive oil.

## MEAT AND GAME

Lamb is the most popular meat, especially that of Sisteron, where it is grazed on high mountain pastures, resulting in delicately herb-flavoured flesh. Beef is most often served as a *daube*, named after the pot-bellied

terracotta dish *(daubière)* in which it is gently cooked for hours. Another speciality is *boeuf gardien*, the bull's-meat stew of the Camargue, served with nutty local red rice. Game from the mountains and woods includes wild rabbit, hare and wild

**Display of the famous and delicious *saussicons d'Arles***

boar. Regional *charcuterie* features *caillettes* (cakes of chopped pork and liver with spinach and juniper berries) and the *saucisson* of Arles, once made from donkey but now usually pork.

## FRUIT AND HONEY

Elaborate desserts are rare, since there is so much sweet ripe fruit for the picking. Cavaillon melons are among the best in France, and the famous lemons of Menton are celebrated in an annual festival. Candied fruit has been produced in Apt since the Middle Ages. Local honeys are scented with chestnut, lavender or rosemary.

## ON THE MENU

**Beignets des fleurs de courgette** Courgette (zucchini) flower fritters.

**Fougasse** Flat olive oil bread often studded with olives.

**Ratatouille** Stew of aubergine (eggplant), tomatoes, courgettes (zucchini) and peppers.

**Salade Niçoise** Lettuce with hard-boiled egg, olives, green beans, tomatoes and anchovies.

**Socca** Chickpea (garbanzo) pancakes, a speciality of Nice.

**Tarte Tropezienne**, St-Tropez's indulgent sponge cake stuffed with *crème patissière*.

**Tourte des blettes** Pie of chard, raisins and pine kernels.

**Artichauts à la barigoule** *Small violet artichokes are stuffed with bacon and vegetables, cooked in wine.*

**Loup au fenouil** *A sea bass is stuffed with fennel twigs and baked with white wine or grilled over more twigs.*

**Boeuf en daube** *Beef is marinated in red wine, onions and garlic, then stewed with orange peel and tomato.*

# What to Drink in Provence

The region covered by this book could not encompass a more varied and enticing range of wines. To the north, the stony, heat-baked soil of the southern Rhône nurtures intense, spicy red wines, the best of which is Châteauneuf-du-Pape. In the south, the Mediterranean coast produces a range of lighter, fresh and fruity whites and rosés, as well as some delicious red wines. Especially good are the dry white wines of seaside Cassis and reds or rosés from the tiny fine wine pocket of Bandol. In the past, some Provençal wines had a reputation for not "travelling" well, but the introduction of modern wine-making techniques and more suitable grape varieties are fast improving quality. Here, we suggest a selection of wines to look out for on local menus.

**Two bottle styles distinctive of the region's wines**

## WHITE WINES

Grenache blanc grapes are often blended with other grape varieties to give a rich, bright flavour and crisp acidity to Provençal white wine. Those listed below are perfect with the region's delicious seafood.

**A fine white Châteauneuf-du-Pape**

### RECOMMENDED WHITES

- **Clos Ste-Magdeleine**
  Cassis
- **Châteaux Val Joanis**
  Côtes du Luberon
- **Domaine St-André-de-Figuière**
  Côtes de Provence
- **Domaines Gavoty**
  Côtes de Provence

**White Côtes-du-Rhône**

## ROSÉ WINES

Provençal rosé is no longer just a sweetish aperitif wine in a skittle-shaped bottle. Grape varieties like Syrah give a full flavour and more body. Tavel is a typical example – dry and weighty enough to accompany Provençal flavourings such as garlic and herbs. Bandol's *vin gris* is also highly regarded.

### RECOMMENDED ROSÉS

- **Château Romassan**
  Bandol
- **Commanderie de Bargemone**
  Côtes de Provence
- **Commanderie de Peyrassol**
  Côtes de Provence
- **Domaine la Forcadière**
  Tavel
- **Domaines Gavoty**
  Côtes de Provence

**Pale rosé (gris) from Bandol**

## WINE AREAS OF PROVENCE

Wine-producing areas are concentrated in the southwest of the region, where vineyards cluster on the rocky hillsides (*côtes*). Les Arcs is a good base for a Côtes de Provence wine tour (*see pp108–9*).

ORANGE · Gigondas
· Beaumes-de-Venise
Lirac
Tavel · Châteauneuf-du-Pape
· AVIGNON
· NIMES
· Les Baux-de-Provence
· ARLES
Rhône
AIX-EN-PROVENCE
Palette
MARSEILLE
Cassis
Bandol

**Terraced vineyards on the coast above Cassis**

## RED WINES

At its best, Châteauneuf-du-Pape produces heady, intense wines to accompany the most robust meat dishes. Bandol also makes superb, long-lived red wines. For a lighter alternative, choose a Provençal or Côtes-du-Rhône red. Wines from one of the named Rhône villages should be of superior quality – or seek out reds from reliable producers in, for example, Les Baux-de-Provence, or the Côtes du Luberon.

Fine red wine from Les Baux

A jewel in Côtes du Luberon's crown

A spicy Châteauneuf-du-Pape

### RECOMMENDED REDS

- *Château de Beaucastel*
  Châteauneuf-du-Pape
- *Château du Trignon*
  Sablet, Côtes-du-Rhône
- *Château Val Joanis*
  Côtes du Luberon
- *Domaine de Pibarnon*
  Bandol
- *Domaine des Alysses*
  Coteaux Varois
- *Domaine Font de Michelle*
  Châteauneuf-du-Pape
- *Domaine Tempier*
  Bandol

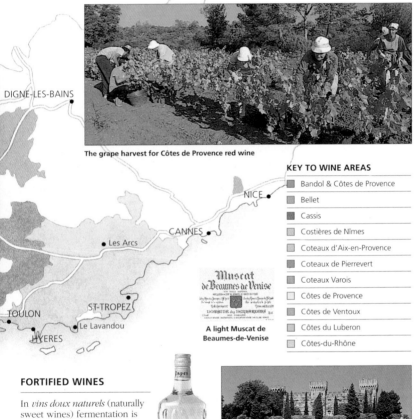

DIGNE-LES-BAINS

The grape harvest for Côtes de Provence red wine

NICE

CANNES

Les Arcs

ST-TROPEZ

TOULON

Le Lavandou

HYÈRES

**Muscat de Beaumes-de-Venise**

A light Muscat de Beaumes-de-Venise

### KEY TO WINE AREAS

- Bandol & Côtes de Provence
- Bellet
- Cassis
- Costières de Nîmes
- Coteaux d'Aix-en-Provence
- Coteaux de Pierrevert
- Coteaux Varois
- Côtes de Provence
- Côtes de Ventoux
- Côtes du Luberon
- Côtes-du-Rhône

## FORTIFIED WINES

In *vins doux naturels* (naturally sweet wines) fermentation is stopped before all the sugar has turned to alcohol, and the wine is then lightly fortified with spirit. Delicious as a chilled apéritif, with desserts or instead of a liqueur, most are based on the exotically scented Muscat grape and range from cloyingly sweet to lusciously fragrant. Others are based on the red Grenache grape.

Typical Muscat bottle shape

The stony, sun-reflecting soil of the Rhône valley

# Choosing a Restaurant

The restaurants in this section have been selected for their excellent food, decor and ambience. Within each area, entries are listed alphabetically within each price category, from the least to the most expensive. For *Flavours of Provence* see pages 206–7 and details of *Cafés, Bars and Casual Eating* are on pages 218–9.

**PRICE CATEGORIES**
For a three-course evening meal for one, including a half bottle of house wine, cover charge, tax and service:
€ under €30
€€ €30–€45
€€€ €45–€60
€€€€ €60–€90
€€€€€ over €90

## THE RIVIERA AND THE ALPES MARITIMES

### ANTIBES L'Auberge Provençale   €€€€
*61 pl Nationale, 06600* **Tel** *04 93 34 13 24* **Fax** *04 93 34 89 88*   **Road map** *E3*

Traditional Provençal dishes are served in two atmospheric dining rooms in this restaurant. In summer there are also tables in the pretty, flower-filled courtyard. Regulars of this hidden gem include a local Michelin-starred chef. Try the monkfish with chorizo or opt for the set lunch menu (€19), but call in advance if you would like a vegetarian option.

### BAR-SUR-LOUP L'Ecole des Filles   €
*380 av Amirale de Grasse, 06620* **Tel** *04 93 09 40 20* **Fax** *04 93 42 43 97*   **Road map** *E3*

Situated in a former village school, this restaurant is perennially popular with locals. The food and decor are Provençal in flavour and style. There's a delightful sunny terrace for the summer months. The restaurant offers à la carte and fixed-price menus. Closed Sun dinner, Mon.

### BIOT Les Terraillers   €€€€€
*11 route Chemin Neuf, 06410* **Tel** *04 93 65 01 59* **Fax** *04 93 65 13 78*   **Road map** *E3*

This sophisticated restaurant serves rich dishes, flavoured with truffles and the herbs of surrounding hills. The *foie gras* escalope is not to be missed, and the lamb is a culinary triumph. The wine list highlights some of the better *vins de pays* of the Provençal vineyards. Closed Wed, Thu.

### CAGNES-SUR-MER Fleur de Sel   €
*85 Montée de la Bourgade, 06800* **Tel** *04 93 20 33 33* **Fax** *04 93 20 33 33*   **Road map** *E3*

A delightful restaurant serving unpretentious cooking at affordable prices (especially when you choose from the set menus). The surroundings are rustic and the restaurant is in the heart of the village of Haut de Cagnes. There is an adequate choice of wines. Closed Wed.

### CAGNES-SUR-MER Le Cagnard   €€€€€
*45 rue Sous-Barri, Haut de Cagnes, 06800* **Tel** *04 93 20 73 21* **Fax** *04 93 22 06 39*   **Road map** *E3*

The outstanding Cagnard has an epicurean menu with truffles, pigeon langoustine and more, all perfectly prepared and immaculately presented in the surroundings of a 14th-century mansion. Some of the best Provence and Gard wines accompany the menu. Part of the Relais et Châteaux group. Closed Mon, Tue, Thu lunch.

### CANNES Le Pastis   €€
*28 rue du Commandant André, 06400* **Tel** *04 92 98 95 40*   **Road map** *E4*

With a decor that feels like a cross between an American diner and a French bistro, Pastis is the perfect place for a casual meal at any time of day. The menu is mostly Mediterranean, with dishes such as *daube à la niçoise* (beef stew), but you'll also find Caesar salad and steak tartare. Located near the main shopping street and the beach.

### CANNES La Cave   €€€
*9 boulevard de la République, 06400* **Tel** *04 93 99 79 87*   **Road map** *E4*

La Cave has been running for many years and is popular with both locals and visitors. Its large choice of traditional Provençal dishes are made from fresh, locally sourced ingredients. The wine list has over 350 references, including an excellent selection from local producers. Closed Sat lunch, Sun.

### CANNES Ondine   €€€
*15 la Croisette, 06400* **Tel** *04 93 94 23 15*   **Road map** *E4*

Beach restaurants usually have modest gastronomic aspirations, but Ondine is an exception to that rule. Chef Jean-Pierre Silva visits the market every day to hand-select the freshest ingredients, and the focus is firmly on fish, with dishes such as crab salad and turbot with spring vegetables. There is an excellent wine list too.

### CANNES 38, The Restaurant   €€€
*38 rue des Serbes, 06400* **Tel** *04 92 99 79 60* **Fax** *04 923 99 26 10*   **Road map** *E4*

It's difficult to eat more lavishly than in the surroundings of 38, The Restaurant, where diners can expect some of the finest cooking in Cannes at a surprisingly affordable price and with courteous service. The accent is on Provençal flavours and Mediterranean seafood, accompanied by an extensive wine list. Closed Sun, Mon.

**Key to Symbols** *see back cover flap*

### CANNES La Palme d'Or
*73 la Croisette, 06400* **Tel** *04 92 98 74 14* **Fax** *04 93 39 03 38* — **Road map** *E4*

Children are not barred from this restaurant of the stars, nor is it essential to wear a tie, but diners who are not dressed to impress may feel self-conscious here. The food is superb, with fresh seafood and a costly and impressive wine list. La Palme d'Or is the restaurant of the Hôtel Martinez. Booking is essential. Closed Sun, Mon.

### EZE Troubadour
*4 rue du Brec, 06360* **Tel** *04 93 41 19 03* — **Road map** *F3*

This restaurant, serving lunch and dinner can only be reached on foot. Its three small dining rooms, tucked away inside medieval walls, offer a respite from the summer sun. The set menus and à la carte options are inspired by classic Provençal cooking. Closed Sun, Mon; end-Jun–mid-Jul; mid-Nov–mid-Dec.

### GRASSE Bastide St Antoine
*48 av H. Dunant,* **Tel** *04 93 70 94 94* **Fax** *04 93 70 94 95* — **Road map** *E3*

Jacques Chibois's restaurant is attached to his delightful boutique-hotel in Grasse's quartier St-Antoine, close to the town centre. The menu will excite lovers of inventive French cuisine, with duckling, truffles, and an inventive approach to vegetables. The excellent wine list is mainly Provençal.

### JUAN-LES-PINS Les Pêcheurs
*10 boulevard Maréchal Juin Cap d'Antibes, 06160* **Tel** *04 92 93 13 30* **Fax** *04 92 93 15 04* — **Road map** *E4*

This wonderful place, fondly referred to as the "gastronomic cruise ship", overlooks the Cap d'Antibes. Indulge in the Grilled Royal Sea Bass with preserved lemons, marinated Provençal vegetables and basil. Open for lunch and dinner Thursday to Monday, and for dinner daily from May to October. Closed Jul, Aug lunch.

### LA TURBIE Café de la Fontaine
*4 avenue Gén de Gaulle, 06320* **Tel** *04 93 28 52 79* — **Road map** *F3*

Run by renowned chef Bruno Cirino, this unpretentious village café is where the coast's best chefs eat on their day off. Fresh ingredients simply prepared is the winning principle here, as witnessed in dishes such as asparagus-filled ravioli, garlic-roasted lamb and a terrific *tarte aux fraises* (strawberry tart) in summer.

### MENTON Auberge Pierrot-Pierrette
*Pl de l'Eglise, 06500* **Tel** *04 93 35 79 76* **Fax** *04 93 35 79 76* — **Road map** *F3*

Located on a hill 5 km (3 miles) from the town of Menton, this restaurant has a true rural feel and a friendly atmosphere. It also has wonderful views from its outside terrace. The food is uncompromisingly fresh and the bill of fare changes with the seasons. Dishes may include *écrevisses* (shrimps) and duck a l'orange. Closed Mon.

### MENTON Le Mirazur
*30 avenue Aristide Briand, 06500* **Tel** *04 92 41 86 86* — **Road map** *F3*

Born in Argentina but with strong Italian roots, promising young chef Mauro Colagreco has settled in Menton, where his contemporary restaurant has its own tropical garden. Like a painter, he decorates his plates with dabs and flourishes, often using wild herbs and flowers that he picks in the mountains. There is a €35 lunch menu.

### MONACO Maya Bay
*24 avenue Princesse Grace, 98000* **Tel** *00 377 97 70 74 67* — **Road map** *F3*

Chef Olivier Streiff's punk haircut and black eyeliner are tributes to the band The Doors, and his cooking also has a certain rock 'n' roll style: a typical dish is duckling with banana, dried fruits, confit apple and roasted juniper berries. The dining room has a lush, tropical feel, and the restaurant has a separate sushi bar. Popular with local royalty.

### MONACO Bar et Boeuf
*Av Princesse Grace, 98000* **Tel** *00 377 98 06 71 71* **Fax** *00 377 98 06 57 85* — **Road map** *F3*

Another Alain Ducasse masterpiece, the cutting-edge interior of this restaurant has been designed by Philippe Starck. The restaurant's theme is surf and turf as seen in its name – *bar* is a kind of sea bass; *boeuf* is beef. Some dishes are also influenced by Far Eastern flavours. Open mid-May–Sep for dinner.

### MONACO Le Louis XV
*Pl du Casino, 98000* **Tel** *00 377 98 06 88 64* **Fax** *00 377 98 06 59 07* — **Road map** *F3*

The kitchen is run by the renowned masterchef Alain Ducasse. Edward VII was a regular in his day and it was during his visit that the classic *crêpe suzette* (pancake flambéed with orange liqueur) was created, named after his mistress. Divine food and exceptional wine list. Closed Tue, Wed; end Feb–mid-Mar, Dec.

### MOUGINS Resto des Arts
*Rue du Maréchal-Foch, 06250* **Tel** *04 93 75 60 03* — **Road map** *E3*

A simple restaurant with a family feel, and serving equally simple but excellent local cuisine. Fixed-price menus are great value for money, particularly at lunch time and there is an à la carte menu. Specialities include *daube provençale* (beef stew) and *petits farcis* (tomatoes stuffed with minced meat, vegetable and garlic). Closed Mon, Tue.

### MOUGINS Le Moulin de Mougins
*Notre-Dame-de-Vie, route départementale 3, 06250* **Tel** *04 93 75 78 24* **Fax** *04 93 90 18 55* — **Road map** *E3*

Alain Llorca's two-star restaurant is 2.5 km (1.5 miles) from Mougins. Booking is essential, especially in high season. A great venue for a special treat, with its cuisine leaning towards innovative seafood. The wines include some of the best of Provence. Modern sculptures adorn the garden terrace. Closed Mon; also Tue & Wed in low season.

### NICE L'Acchiardo €

*38 rue Droite, 06000* **Tel** *04 93 85 51 16*     **Road map** *F3*

Set in the heart of Nice's Old Town, this is probably the most authentic bar and restaurant in the city, always buzzing with locals. Many people consider the fish soup to be the best there is, but all the cooking is delicious. The wines are served directly from the barrel. The restaurant only accepts cash payments. Closed Sun, Sat dinner; Aug.

### NICE Bistrot d'Antoine €€

*27 rue de la Préfecture, 06300* **Tel** *04 93 85 29 57*     **Road map** *F3*

Armand Crespo, formerly of Lou Cigalon in Valbonne, is behind the revival of this bistro. He can often be seen buying fresh produce at the nearby market, and meat off the grill is the main event here: try the duck *magret* or the veal kidneys, which could make an offal-lover out of anyone. The wines are well chosen and affordable.

### NICE Le Chantecler €€€

*37 promenade des Anglais, 06000* **Tel** *04 93 16 64 00* **Fax** *04 93 88 35 68*     **Road map** *F3*

A thriving 19th-century establishment that still retains its high standards and reputation. Decorated with artworks and tapestries, it has a Regency feel to it. Although there are a variety of fixed-price menus, the menu Chantecler is highly recommended for its four exceptional courses. The restaurant holds a Michelin star. Closed Mon, Tue; Jan.

### PEILLON Auberge de la Madone €€€

*Peillon village, 06440* **Tel** *04 93 79 91 17* **Fax** *04 93 79 99 36*     **Road map** *F3*

A restaurant specializing in vegetarian cuisine is an unusual find in France, but this is one that's continually popular. Try the *tourton des pénitents* (vegetable pie with almonds). The terrace is surrounded by olive trees and offers great views out over the valley. Closed Wed.

### ROQUEBRUNE-CAP-MARTIN Les Deux Frères €€€

*Pl des Deux Frères, 06190* **Tel** *04 93 28 99 00* **Fax** *04 93 28 99 10*     **Road map** *F3*

Provençal cooking, with an emphasis on lamb and duck can be savoured here. The restaurant is housed in a former school, and on warmer days, tables are placed on the square so diners can watch the world go by and enjoy the views down to Monaco and the Mediterranean. Closed Mon, Tue lunch, Sun dinner; mid-Nov–mid-Dec.

### ST-JEAN-CAP-FERRAT Le Pirate €

*Nouveau Port, 06230* **Tel** *04 93 76 12 97*     **Road map** *F3*

Overlooking the picturesque port, this family-run restaurant specializes in fish and seafood. Choose from dishes such as monkfish and lobster with garlic mayonnaise or *bouillabaisse*, a rich fish and seafood stew. The fixed-price menus are excellent value for money. Open for lunch all year, for dinner Apr–Oct. Closed Mon; Thu lunch Jul–Oct.

### ST-MARTIN-VESUBIE La Bonne Auberge €

*Allee de Verdun, 06450* **Tel** *04 93 03 20 49* **Fax** *04 93 03 20 69*     **Road map** *E2*

The restaurant of this old stone-built inn, set among a spectacular landscape, has tables on a leafy outdoor terrace. The menu is well-priced and offers an array of well-made local dishes and regional wines. It's a popular spot for lunch, so booking is advisable. The two-star hotel rooms are simple, clean and medium priced.

### ST-PAUL-DE-VENCE La Colombe d'Or €€€

*Pl du Général de Gaulle, 06570* **Tel** *04 93 32 80 02* **Fax** *04 93 32 77 78*     **Road map** *E3*

This is one of the most famous and atmospheric restaurants in Provence and is still frequented by the rich and famous as it was at the time when Impressionist painters paid for meals with their artworks. The walls are lined with original Picassos and Matisses. The cooking is traditional yet inventive. Closed Nov–mid-Dec.

### TOUET-SUR-VAR Restaurant Chez Paul €€

*Av Général de Gaulle, 06710* **Tel** *04 93 05 71 03* **Fax** *04 93 05 71 11*     **Road map** *E3*

The cosy interior of this family inn, located in the scenic valley of the Var, is warmed by a big open fire in winter and on cooler evenings, while in warmer months, there are tables outside amid shade and greenery. The menu is traditional home-made fare and the adequate wine list is modestly priced. Closing times vary throughout the year.

### VENCE Auberge des Seigneurs €€€

*Pl du Frène, 06140* **Tel** *04 93 58 04 24* **Fax** *04 93 24 08 01*     **Road map** *E3*

This inn, housed in a wing of a castle, has hosted artists, aristocrats and crowned heads. Works of local painters adorn the dining room. The menu is mainly Provençal, with dishes such as spit-roasted lamb and grilled fresh fish. The wide wine list is moderately priced. Closed Mon, Sun lunch.

### VILLEFRANCHE Le Carpaccio €€€

*Promenade des Marinières, 06230* **Tel** *04 93 01 72 97* **Fax** *04 93 01 97 34*     **Road map** *F3*

Book ahead in summer for a table on the terrace of this restaurant with its spectacular views across the bay to St-Jean-Cap-Ferrat. The view is on show in winter too, thanks to the big-picture windows. Seafood, pizzas from the wood-fired oven and other dishes complement the signature dish, carpaccio (thinly sliced raw beef).

### VILLEFRANCHE L'Oursin Bleu €€€

*11 quai Courbet, 06230* **Tel** *04 93 01 90 12* **Fax** *04 93 01 80 45*     **Road map** *F3*

A bubbling aquarium in the foyer hints that the accent is on fresh fish here. The location is delightful – the quayside of a lively yacht and fishing harbour, with tables under umbrellas on the terrace. The dining room is decorated with maritime memorabilia. Ideal for a long, lazy summer lunch. Closed Tue; Jan.

**Key to Price Guide** *see p210* **Key to Symbols** *see back cover flap*

# THE VAR AND THE ILES D'HYERES

### COGOLIN Grain de Sel                                                                     📖           €€
*6 rue du 11 Novembre, 83110* **Tel** *04 94 54 46 86*                                       **Road map** *E4*

Chef Philippe Audibert (formerly of the Byblos in St-Tropez) owns this cheerful bistro with a wooden terrace behind the town hall. Working in the open kitchen, he takes pride in the fresh ingredients that go into classic Provençal dishes such as octopus stew or roast guinea hen. Alongside the seasonal menu there is a frequently changing list of daily specials.

### COLLOBRIERES La Petite Fontaine                                                          📖 🚶 🌐        €€€
*1 pl de la République, 83610* **Tel** *04 94 48 00 12* **Fax** *04 94 48 03 03*             **Road map** *D4*

This restaurant is in the centre of Collobrières, a scenic hill village. The menu includes chicken and garlic fricassée, rabbit with fresh herbs, duck with wild mushrooms. The wines come from the local wine cooperative, by the glass or by the carafe. Closed Mon, Sun dinner; Feb; second week Sep.

### FAYENCE Le Castellaras                                                                   🚶 ♿ 🌐 🍷      €€€
*Route de Seillans, 83440* **Tel** *04 94 76 13 80* **Fax** *04 94 84 17 50*                 **Road map** *E3*

Only 4 km (2.5 miles) from the centre of Fayence, Le Castellaras merits a special journey for a range of dishes: lamb fillet with tarragon sauce, scampi marinated in olive oil, lemon and tarragon, polenta in truffle oil. The wine list is drawn from the Côtes de Provence vineyards. Closed Mon, Tue (except Jul, Aug); Jan.

### FAYENCE Le Moulin de la Camandoule                                                       🚶 📖 🌐        €€€€
*Chemin de Notre Dame des Cyprès, 83440* **Tel** *04 94 76 00 84* **Fax** *04 94 76 10 40*   **Road map** *E3*

In an ancient olive mill, this hotel-restaurant benefits from a peaceful and idyllic setting. Chef Phillipe Choisy offers several set menus and à la carte dishes of high quality. The flavours are Provençal and the ingredients all fresh and seasonal. Lunch is often served on the terrace. Closed Wed, Thu.

### ILE DE PORQUEROLLES Mas du Langoustier                                                   🚶 📖 ♿ 🌐 🍷   €€€€€
*Ile de Porquerolles Ouest, 83400* **Tel** *04 94 58 30 09* **Fax** *04 94 58 36 02*         **Road map** *D5*

An appropriately fishy menu at this restaurant includes John Dory roasted with sea urchin roe, grilled red mullet, and other dishes such as wild mushrooms and *foie gras*, complemented by Provençal wines. Diners are driven from the port to this hotel-restaurant, close to the western tip of the pictueresque island. Closed Oct–Apr.

### LA CADIERE D'AZUR Hostellerie Bérard                                                     🚶 📖 🌐 🍷      €€€
*Rue Gabriel-Péri, 83740* **Tel** *04 94 90 11 43* **Fax** *04 94 90 01 94*                  **Road map** *D4*

This hotel-restaurant in the converted buildings of an 11th-century convent has a fine view over the Bandol vineyards. Owner and chef René Bérard does marvellous things with fish and shellfish, including a sublime saffron-flavoured mussel soup. Bandol wines complement his excellent cooking. Closed Mon lunch, Sat lunch.

### LA GARDE-FREINET Longo Maï                                                               📖 🌐          €€
*Route Nationale 98, 83680* **Tel** *04 94 55 59 60* **Fax** *04 94 55 58 18*                **Road map** *E4*

This attractively located restaurant has a fire roaring on cooler evenings and prettily-arranged flowers adorning its tables outside in summer. Everything is home-made, with a good variety of meat and fish dishes. The home-made paté is exceptional. Closed Mon.

### ST-TROPEZ Le Bistrot Saint Tropez                                                        📖 🌐 ♿ 🍷     €€€
*3 pl des Lices, 83990* **Tel** *04 94 97 11 33*                                             **Road map** *E4*

This trendy brasserie's interior has low lighting and cleverly-placed gold mirrors, while the terrace looks over the pretty place des Lices. The cuisine has a "world food" influence, but French favourites such as scrambled eggs and truffles and lamb chops with *câpres* (mushrooms) can still be savoured.

### SAINT-TROPEZ Le Caprice des Deux                                                         🚶 📖 ♿ 🌐 🍷   €€€
*40 rue du Portail Neuf, 83990* **Tel** *04 94 97 76 78*                                     **Road map** *E4*

It's hard to find a more reliable restaurant than this one, hidden in one of the narrow pedestrian streets of St-Tropez. The €57 set menu is not cheap, but it will bring you dishes such as *foie gras* terrine with onion jam, and scallop *brochette* with truffle risotto. The three dining rooms are cheerful and unpretentious, with vintage ads on the walls.

### SAINT-TROPEZ La Pinède                                                                   📖 ♿ 🌐 P 🍴 🍷 🍷  €€€€€
*Plage de la Bouillabaisse, 83990* **Tel** *04 94 55 91 00*                                  **Road map** *E4*

Luxurious without being glitzy, this hotel-restaurant with a private beach is popular with a glamorous set that doesn't need to show off. Young chef Arnaud Donckele uses the finest seasonal products to turn out elegant food. Visit in the early autumn, before the restaurant closes for winter, to taste his game dishes. Closed Oct–mid-Apr.

### TOULON L'Arbre Rouge                                                                     📖 ♿ 🌐        €
*25 rue de la Comédie, 83000* **Tel** *04 94 92 28 58*                                       **Road map** *D4*

Tucked away in the back streets of Toulon, this lovely restaurant is easy to miss. The traditional Provençal cooking includes fresh pistou-stuffed sardines and king prawns with *persillade*. The service is attentive and friendly, and the atmosphere ideal for a romantic meal. Closed Thu, Fri & Sat dinner, Sat & Sun lunch.

## BOUCHES-DU-RHONE AND NIMES

### AIGUES-MORTES Les Enganettes                                    ⓔ
*12 rue Marceau, 30220* **Tel** *04 66 53 69 11*                    **Road map** *A4*

With tables on the pavement and in a more secluded inner courtyard, Les Enganettes serves an array of Mediterranean, Camarguais, Spanish, Italian and Moroccan-influenced dishes. The set menus and à la carte dishes are good value. There are musical evenings with live piano.

### AIGUES-MORTES La Salicorne                                      ⓔⓔⓔ
*9 rue Alsace-Lorraine, 30220* **Tel** *04 66 53 62 67*             **Road map** *A4*

Jean-Claude Achard and his wife Lydie travel the world in search of new flavours, which he then incorporates into the adventurous menu at this stone-walled restaurant. Typical of his style are spiced rack of lamb and monkfish *blanquette* with sorrel and smoked bacon; the wine list is equally well thought out.

### AIX-EN-PROVENCE Brasserie Leopold                               ⓔⓔ
*2 av Victor-Hugo, 13090* **Tel** *04 42 26 01 24* **Fax** *04 42 38 53 17*   **Road map** *C4*

A classic brasserie with dozens of tables on the ground floor of the comfortable Hotel Saint-Christophe. A great place for a full-scale meal, a snack or just a drink, with tables on the pavement as well as inside. Strong on regional cuisine and traditional brasserie fare, with few concessions to trendy modern cooking.

### AIX-EN-PROVENCE Mas d'Entremont                                ⓔⓔⓔⓔ
*Route Nationale 7, 13090* **Tel** *04 42 17 42 42* **Fax** *04 42 21 15 83*   **Road map** *C4*

The food here is typically Provençal, with lots of meat and fish, while the list of Provençal wines is good, if not outstanding. In summer, eat outdoors on a terrace overlooking the gardens, while in cooler weather, sit in the indoor dining room, where huge picture windows open onto the surrounding park. Closed Sun dinner, Mon lunch.

### AIX-EN-PROVENCE Le Clos de la Violette                         ⓔⓔⓔⓔⓔ
*10 av de la Violette, 13100* **Tel** *04 42 23 30 71* **Fax** *04 42 21 93 03*   **Road map** *C4*

An elegant address in a chic mansion, standing in its own gardens makes this an ideal place for a romantic evening. Though perhaps not for small children. People do dress up a little here. The extensive wine list is strong on local and Provençal wines. The à la carte is Provençal with a modern edge. Closed Sun, Mon.

### ARLES La Gueule du Loup                                         ⓔ
*39 rue des Arènes, 13200* **Tel** *04 90 96 96 69* **Fax** *04 90 96 96 69*   **Road map** *B3*

La Gueule du Loup ("the Wolf's Maw") is a lot more welcoming than its ferocious name implies. The menu is well-priced and changes almost everyday. Prompt service and a good choice of wines. Not for gourmets looking for cutting-edge cuisine, but brilliant at what it does – exquisite Provençal fare. Closed Sun, Mon lunch.

### ARLES Cilantro                                                  ⓔⓔⓔ
*31 rue Porte de Laure, 13200* **Tel** *04 90 18 25 05*            **Road map** *B3*

Jérôme Laurent resolutely avoids Provençal clichés in this stylish restaurant with exotic wooden floors, yellow walls and a conservatory. Among his signature dishes is farm-raised pigeon from Provence with a crust of cocoa beans and tonka, which tastes of vanilla and almond. Desserts are equally inspired.

### ARLES L'Atelier de Jean-Luc Rabanel                            ⓔⓔⓔⓔ
*7 rue des Carmes, 13200* **Tel** *04 90 91 07 69*                 **Road map** *B3*

Visit this small restaurant in the centre of Arles when you have an appetite, since there is a minimum of seven courses at lunch and 13 at dinner. Chef Jean-Luc Rabanel works almost solely with organic produce from his own vegetable garden, and each dish is a work of art. Reserve well ahead, or drop into his more casual bistro next door.

### ARLES Lou Marques                                               ⓔⓔⓔⓔ
*9 Boulevard Lices, 13200* **Tel** *04 90 52 52 52* **Fax** *04 90 52 52 53*   **Road map** *B3*

Lou Marques – the restaurant of the venerable Hôtel Jules César – is one of the best places to eat in Arles, with a central location, a nice terrace and a bill of fare that concentrates on classic Provençal dishes. The surroundings are dignified, as the hotel and restaurant are housed in a former convent. Closed Sat & Sun Nov–Apr.

### DIGNE LES BAINS Le Grand Paris                                  ⓔⓔⓔⓔ
*19 boulevard Thiers, 04000* **Tel** *04 92 31 11 15* **Fax** *04 92 32 32 82*   **Road map** *D2*

In the dignified surroundings of Digne's best hotel, this is also the town's best restaurant, with a menu that leans towards traditional dishes such as fillet of lamb and roasted duck breast with shallots. Adventurous gourmets may find the menu a little unimaginative, but the quality and quantity are unchallengeable and the wine list is great.

### LES BAUX DE PROVENCE La Riboto de Taven                         ⓔⓔⓔ
*Chemin du Val d'Enfer, 13520* **Tel** *04 90 54 34 23*            **Road map** *B3*

This country inn boasts a spectacular setting, tucked into the rocks of the Vallon de la Fontaine. The restaurant is mainly aimed at guests of the hotel, but it is open to the general public by reservation. Run by the same family for several generations, it serves traditional Provençal recipes handed down through the years.

**Key to Price Guide** *see p210* **Key to Symbols** *see back cover flap*

### LES-BAUX-DE-PROVENCE L'Oustau de Baumanière

*Route Départementale 27, Le Val d'Enfer, 13520* **Tel** *04 90 54 33 07* **Fax** *04 90 54 40 46*     **Road map** *B3*

This superb restaurant rates two Michelin stars and has a dazzling menu and a stellar wine list, along with lovely surroundings and magnificent views of the valley. Jean-André Charial's cuisine mixes traditional Provençal influences with the best of nouvelle cuisine to create a memorable dining experience. Closed Jan–Feb.

### MARSEILLE Le Boucher

*10 rue de Village, 13006* **Tel** *04 91 48 79 65*     **Road map** *C4*

What looks like an ordinary butcher shop from the outside houses a secret restaurant for meat-lovers, where you might tuck into a 1.2-kg rib of beef for two people or sample the typical Marseillais speciality *pieds et paquets* (little "packets" of meat-filled sheep's tripe cooked with sheep's trotters).

### MARSEILLE Les Arcenaulx

*25 cours d'Estienne d'Orves, 13000* **Tel** *04 91 59 80 30*     **Road map** *C4*

In the former warehouse district north of the Vieux Port, now the hub of the city's nightlife, Les Arcenaulx occupies the premises of a 17th-century bookseller-publisher. A great place to start or end an evening's bar-hopping. Dishes include rabbit and sardine and ginger paté. Closed Sun.

### MARSEILLE Toinou

*3 cours Saint-Louis, 13001* **Tel** *04 91 33 14 94*     **Road map** *C4*

Set in a lively square, Toinou is the place for seafood platters in Marseille. The restaurant started as a takeaway counter and still does a roaring trade, though many people now opt for the convenience of eating in the simple dining room. For a taste of everything, try the delicious *Toinou Spécial* for two people.

### MARSEILLE L'Epuisette

*Vallon des Auffes, 13007* **Tel** *04 91 52 17 82* **Fax** *04 91 59 18 80*     **Road map** *C4*

L'Epuisette wins favour for an excellent fish menu featuring grilled John Dory, seasonal lobster ravioli and truffle risotto. The wine list includes Cassis and Côteaux d'Aix-en-Provence. It's a popular place so reservations are recommended. Closed Sun, Mon; Aug.

### MARSEILLE Le Miramar

*12 quai du Port, 13002 Marseille* **Tel** *04 91 91 10 40* **Fax** *04 91 56 64 31*     **Road map** *C4*

One of the best places to sample the fine seafood and *bouillabaisse*. Marseille's trademark dish is prepared by chef Christian Buffa at his restaurant located beside the old port. Tables are much in demand and booking at least 48 hours in advance is mandatory. In summer, choose a table on the quayside terrace. Closed Sun, Mon.

### MARSEILLE 29 Place aux Huiles

*29 place aux Huiles, 13520* **Tel** *04 91 33 26 44*     **Road map** *C4*

The menu at this classy restaurant in the Vieux Port changes according to what ingredients are in season, but there is always something that will please calorie-conscious diners, meat-lovers and fans of Asian fusion dishes. Try the terrine of *foie gras* with cranberry chutney or the shrimp tempura. There is also an excellent wine list.

### MARSEILLE Le Petit Nice Passédat

*160 corniche Kennedy, anse de Maldorme, 13000* **Tel** *04 91 59 25 92* **Fax** *04 91 59 28 08*     **Road map** *C4*

Housed in the Belle Epoque villa of the Passédat Hotel, this restaurant has wonderful views of the Mediterranean. The menu is strong on seafood and features lobster terrine, rock lobsters with hazelnut sauce, and crab in ginger. The wine list is extensive. Closed Sun, Mon.

### MARTIGUES Le Miroir

*4 rue Marcel Galdy, 13500* **Tel** *04 42 80 50 45*     **Road map** *B4*

Facing the small fishing port of Martigues, also known as the Miroir aux Oiseaux, with its colourful wooden boats, this restaurant specializes in fish. There is plenty of space, with six dining rooms and two terraces, but for maximum charm aim to sit outside. The cooking is simple but tasty, with dishes such as mussels with fennel and saffron.

### NIMES Au Flan Coco

*31 rue du Mûrier, 30000* **Tel** *04 66 21 84 81*     **Road map** *A3*

An informal and affordable spot, with tables on the pavement on sunny days and good regional cooking prepared by a team of *traiteurs*, who use fresh ingredients and prepare your meal while you watch. The shop next door, under the same management, also sells delicious takeaway meals – ideal for picnics. Closed Sun, Mon, Tue dinner.

### NIMES Enclos de la Fontaine

*Quai de la Fontaine, 30000* **Tel** *04 66 21 90 30* **Fax** *04 66 67 70 25*     **Road map** *A3*

L'Enclos de la Fontaine, the pleasantly-modern restaurant of the classic Imperator Concorde hotel, is probably Nîmes' finest establishment. Despite that, it is affordable. The fare is both classical and inventive, with traditional dishes and newer options such as veal with fresh fig fritters. Book in advance for a table in the courtyard in summer.

### NIMES Au Plaisirs des Halles

*4 rue Littré, 30000* **Tel** *04 66 36 01 02* **Fax** *04 66 36 08 00*     **Road map** *A3*

With a particularly good regional wine list from the Languedoc, Corbières, Minervois, Provence and Herault, Au Plaisirs des Halles is decorated on clean, modern lines. Its patio is a very pleasant place to eat on a sunny afternoon or summer evening. Closed Sun, Mon; two weeks end-Oct–early Nov.

### ST-REMY-DE-PROVENCE Le Jardin de Frédéric

📋🖼 €€

*8 boulevard Gambetta, 13210* **Tel** *04 90 92 27 76*                    **Road map** *B3*

This affordable, family-run restaurant has pleasant surroundings. The imaginative menu including rack of Sisteron lamb in garlic sauce, sea bass in basil, cod soufflé flavoured with saffron, and delicious desserts. In summer, there are tables outside the pretty villa that houses the restaurant. Closed Mon in low season; Mon lunch in high season.

### SAINT-RÉMY-DE-PROVENCE Alain Assaud

📋🍴 €€€

*13 boulevard Marceau, 13210* **Tel** *04 90 92 37 11*                    **Road map** *B3*

Among the Provençal chefs resisting modern trends is Alain Assaud, whose rustic dining room with stone walls, wooden beams and an antique buffet provides the ideal setting for his classic repertoire. The focus is on top-quality ingredients in dishes such as stuffed aubergines and poached salt cod with vegetables and garlic mayonnaise.

# VAUCLUSE

### AVIGNON La Fourchette

📋🍴 €€

*17 rue Racine, 84000* **Tel** *04 90 85 20 93* **Fax** *04 90 85 57 60*                    **Road map** *B3*

Much loved locally, La Fourchette is a quirky little eating place. Antique forks and festival posters adorn the walls. The menu is traditional, with a modern take on dishes such as duck breast in garlic and a vegetable crêpe (pancake) or grilled sea bass. It has an excellent choice of cheeses. Booking is mandatory. Closed Sat, Sun.

### AVIGNON Le Petit Bedon

🧍📋🅿🍴 €€

*70 rue Joseph-Vernet, 84000* **Tel** *04 90 82 33 98* **Fax** *04 90 85 58 64*                    **Road map** *B3*

This restaurant, just inside the walls of Avignon's old quarter, has a high reputation for poached vegetables with tapenade and pistou, *bourride de loup* (sea bass), and courgette (zucchini) purée with garlic. An amiable atmosphere and a decent list of mainly Provençal wines. Closed Sun; Mon Nov–Mar; Mon lunch Apr–Oct.

### AVIGNON Christian Etienne

🧍📋🖼🍴 €€€€

*10 rue Mons, 84000* **Tel** *04 90 86 16 50* **Fax** *04 90 86 67 09*                    **Road map** *B3*

The wine list is strong on Provençal and Rhône-Valley vintages and the location in the medieval heart of Avignon, close to the Palais des Papes, is hard to beat. The food is equally unbeatable in this restaurant, with seasonal menus that emphasize local produce. Choose from set menus or à la carte. Closed Sun, Mon (except in July).

### AVIGNON La Vieille Fontaine

🧍📋🖼🅿🍴🍴 €€€€

*12 place Crillon, 84000* **Tel** *04 90 14 76 76*                    **Road map** *B3*

Housed in the 16th-century Hotel de l'Europe, today a luxury hotel *(see p202)*, La Vieille Fontaine is built around a central fountain in the courtyard. Chef Bruno d'Angelis incorporates spices and new cooking techniques into his menu that uses only the finest ingredients available.

### AVIGNON La Mirande

🧍📋🖼🍴 €€€€€

*4 pl de la Mirande, 84000* **Tel** *04 90 14 20 20* **Fax** *04 90 86 26 85*                    **Road map** *B3*

One of the best places to eat in Avignon, with tables beneath olive trees and the floodlit walls of the Palais des Papes or indoors in a grand dining room (once a cardinal's palace). The extensive menu is dazzling, the wine list equally so, and the staff are friendly. The place for a special night out; book in advance. Closed Tue, Wed.

### CARPENTRAS Chez Serge

🧍📋🖼🍴 €€

*90 rue Cottier, 84200* **Tel** *04 90 63 21 24* **Fax** *04 90 11 70 68*                    **Road map** *B3*

A surprising discovery in sleepy Carpentras. The cooking is refined, and there's some imaginative fare with lots of fresh fish and wild mushrooms. The wine list is extensive, including some from Italy and California, and the owners arrange tasting evenings where you can taste the local wines. Closed Sun Sep–Jun.

### CAVAILLON Restaurant Prévot

📋🖼🍴 €€€€

*353 av de Verdun, 84300* **Tel** *04 90 71 32 43* **Fax** *04 90 71 97 05*                    **Road map** *B3*

A gastronomic treat in the heart of the pretty market-town of Cavaillon. Chef Jean-Jacques Prévot is mad about melons – his restaurant has them as a decorative motif and there's an entire set menu dedicated to the gourd family. The melon and scallops is recommended. There's a good selection of wines as well. Closed Sun, Mon.

### CHATEAUNEUF-DU-PAPE La Mère Germaine

🧍🖼🍴 €

*3 rue Commandant Lemaitre, 84230* **Tel** *04 90 83 54 37* **Fax** *04 90 83 50 27*                    **Road map** *B3*

Surrounded by vineyards, this restaurant has an outstanding list of regional wines. The cooking is classic Provençal, servings are generous and although not cheap, La Mère Germaine offers value for money. Service is friendly and efficient. Go for lunch to make the most of the excellent view.

### CHÂTEAUNEUF-DU-PAPE La Sommellerie

🧍📋🖼🅿🍴 €€€

*Route de Roquemaure, 84230* **Tel** *04 90 83 50 00*                    **Road map** *B3*

Given its location in the heart of this prestigious wine region, it is no surprise that this hotel-restaurant housed in a 17th-century sheepfold hosts exceptional wine dinners focusing on the Côtes du Rhône. The food is no afterthought, however, as proved by the superlative, five-course, all-lobster menu for €62.

**Key to Price Guide** *see p210* **Key to Symbols** *see back cover flap*

### GIGONDAS Les Florets

*Route des Dentelles, 84190* **Tel** *04 90 65 85 01* **Fax** *04 90 65 83 80*                    **Road map** *B2*

This hotel-restaurant provides fine views of the Dentelles de Montmirail from its outdoor terrace. The seating here and in the indoor restaurant is limited, so arrive early or book ahead. Well-presented regional cooking is complemented by the fine wines of the Gigondas region. Closed Tue, Wed; Jan–Feb.

### LOURMARIN Le Comptoir d'Edouard

*Rue du Temple, 84160* **Tel** *04 90 68 06 69*                    **Road map** *C3*

One of the most respected chefs in Provence, Edouard Lubet heads this chic bistro in the luxury hotel Moulin de Lourmarin *(see p202)*. Expect to pay between €40 and €60 for set menus including dishes such as partridge cooked in a cast-iron pot with grapes and chervil root, or duck liver smoked in thyme.

### SEGURET Le Mesclun

*Rue des Poternes, 84110* **Tel** *04 90 46 93 43*                    **Road map** *B2*

Situated on the edge of the charming village Seguret, with a great view of the Rhône Valley, Le Mesclun serves surprisingly sophisticated fare that draws on Asian, Mexican and Caribbean cuisines. There are plenty of well-priced set menus to choose from, including a menu for food-loving children at €14, complete with a chocolate dessert plate.

### SEGURET La Table du Comtat

*Le Village, 84110* **Tel** *04 90 46 91 49* **Fax** *04 90 46 94 27*                    **Road map** *B2*

This hotel-restaurant has wonderful views of the Dentelles and the surrounding countryside from its terrace. The menu includes such delights as truffles, pigeon, wild boar and other game. The fine wine cellar has excellent Côtes-du-Rhône and other vintages. Also a comfortable place for a short stay *(see p203)*. Closed Tue lunch.

### SERIGNAN DU COMTAT Le Pre du Moulin

*Route de Sainte-Cécile des Vignes, 84830* **Tel** *04 90 70 14 55* **Fax** *04 90 70 05 62*                    **Road map** *B2*

Master chef Pascal Alonzo prepares delicacies such as truffle ravioli with artichokes and roast Remuzat lamb in this comfortable hotel-restaurant on a popular countryside wine-tasting route. The wine list is packed with big Rhône Valley and Gigondas vintages. Closed Mon, Sun dinner.

## ALPES-DE-HAUTE-PROVENCE

### CASTELLANE Auberge du Teillon

*Route Napoléon le Garde, 04120* **Tel** *04 92 83 60 88*                    **Road map** *D3*

This pleasant country inn, a short distance from the tourist hotspot of Castellane, offers an unpretentious bill of fare that changes seasonally. Traditional dishes are prepared with fresh ingredients. The specialities include hand-smoked "Norway" salmon and home-made *foie gras*. Closed Sun dinner, Mon; Mon lunch Jul–Aug; Nov–Mar.

### CHATEAU-ARNOUX La Bonne Etape

*Chemin du Lac, 04160* **Tel** *04 92 64 00 09* **Fax** *04 92 64 37 36*                    **Road map** *D3*

La Bonne Etape is the only real reason to stop in this nondescript market-town. This charming inn has an array of dishes and specializes in fresh local produce, especially lamb. The extensive wine list features vintages from almost every region in France. The dining room is decorated with paintings and tapestries. Closed Mon, Tue.

### DIGNE LES BAINS Villa Gaïa

*24 route de Nice, 04000* **Tel** *04 92 31 21 60*                    **Road map** *D2*

A few kilometres from the centre of Digne, this hotel-restaurant serves simple but delicious fare. Some of the dishes are made with vegetables from the garden; other recipes use such local products as Sisteron lamb, honey, game, olive oil and Banon cheese (which is wrapped in a chestnut leaf).

### MANOSQUE Les Voûtes de Mont d'Or

*43 boulevard Tilleuls, 04100* **Tel** *04 92 72 32 28* **Fax** *04 92 72 32 28*                    **Road map** *C3*

A simple yet refined cuisine with Mediterranean influences is served in a beautifully decorated, spacious dining room. There is no dividing wall between the restaurant and kitchen, allowing you to see the chef at work. Excellent value for money and a warm welcome. Closed Mon, Sun dinner.

### MANOSQUE Hostellerie de la Fuste

*Route de Valensole, 04210* **Tel** *04 92 72 05 95* **Fax** *04 92 72 92 93*                    **Road map** *C3*

An elegant country inn, 6.5 km (4 miles) from Manosque and well worth the journey. The menu features local produce and its own home-grown vegetables, served on a terrace shaded by 300-year-old plane trees. Fish and meat dominate the menu and there's a good choice of cheeses and desserts. Closed Sun dinner, Mon lunch.

### MOUSTIERS-STE-MARIE La Treille Muscate

*Pl de l'Eglise, 04360* **Tel** *04 92 74 64 31* **Fax** *04 92 74 63 75*                    **Road map** *D3*

Enjoy excellent fare such as a pistou of vegetables in this lovely bistro located in the main square of one of the region's prettiest villages. It overlooks a swift-flowing stream and has tables on the terrace. With a choice of set menus and a decent wine list, it's a great venue for a relaxed alfresco lunch. Closed Wed.

# Cafés, Bars and Casual Eating

In rural areas the world over the local bar is the centre of village life, and nowhere is this more true than in Provence. Everywhere you go you will find lively watering holes, often with outside terraces or gardens. Most bars and cafés double as lunchtime restaurants, serving straightforward daily specials at reasonable prices. Snacks are not really a part of French life but nearly all bars will make you a traditional *baguette* sandwich or a *croque monsieur* (toasted ham and cheese sandwich). Drinking is a subject close to Provençal hearts – *pastis*, the aniseed spirit synonymous with Marseille, is the region's lifeblood. In many country towns, you will see the locals sitting outside sipping *pastis* from the early morning onwards, along with strong black coffee. Lunchtime tipples include ice–cold rosé, the perfect accompaniment to a sun-filled day.

## CAFÉS

There is little distinction between cafés and bars in Provence and most serve alcohol all day. In the country, village cafés will often close around 8pm. In larger towns, many places stay open much later – popular Marseillais and Niçois bars close when the last person leaves. Many stay open all night, serving breakfast to the diehards as dawn breaks. A lot of cafés are also *tabacs* (tobacconists) selling cigarettes, tobacco, sweets and stamps.

While most Provençal cafés are simple places, where decor is restricted to the local fire brigade calendar and fashion to a hunting jacket and boots, there are several stylish exceptions. No visit to Aix is complete without an hour or two spent sipping coffee on the cours Mirabeau, one of the places in Provence to see and be seen. On the Côte d'Azur, chic cafés abound. In Cannes the **Brasserie Carlton** is the place to spot film stars during the festival. In Nice, the cafés on the cours Saleya are the hub of day and nightlife, while Monaco boasts the crème de la crème, the **Café de Paris**.

## WHAT TO EAT

Most Provençal cafés serve breakfast although, in village establishments, this will just be a couple of slices of *baguette* and coffee. More elaborate affairs are served in towns, with fresh orange juice, hot croissants and jam. Café lunches usually include a *plat du jour* (dish of the day) and a dessert, along with a quarter litre of wine. These can be great bargains, costing little more than €12. For more basic lunches, sandwiches, omelettes and salads can be ordered. Evening meals are usually the reserve of restaurants, although in rural areas, the local bar will also serve dinner, normally a varient on the lunchtime menu.

## WHAT TO DRINK

Since Roman days, when the legionnaires introduced wine to the region, drinking has been a favoured pastime in Provence. Cold beer seems to surpass the fruit of the vine in the hearts of most farmers, as village bars are filled with locals downing *pressions* (half–pint glasses of beer). More potent tipples include *pastis,* a 90 per cent proof nectar flavoured with aniseed, vanilla and cinnamon, and *marc*, a brandy distilled from any available fruits. Soft drinks such as *un diabolo* (fruit syrup mixed with lemonade) and *orange pressée* (freshly squeezed orange juice) are also popular. As in most Mediterranean lands, coffee is a way of life – *un café* is a cup of strong and black expresso. If you want white coffee, ask for *un café crème*. For filter or instant coffee order *un café filtre* or *un café américain*. Tea will always be served black unless you ask for milk or lemon. Herbal teas are also available, known as *tisanes* or *infusions*.

## BARS

In most towns you will find a handful of bars that only serve beer and miscellaneous alcohol, rather than the more diverse range offered by cafés. These bars are lively in true Mediterranean style. Student centres such as Nice, Marseille and Aix contain British–style pubs, offering a large selection of European bottled and draught beer. Some have live bands, such as **Wayne's Bar** and **De Klomp** in Nice.

More upmarket bars are found in the plush hotels of the Côte d'Azur. Here, in Belle Epoque splendour, you can sip champagne listening to jazz piano, string quartets or opera singers. Among the most impressive are the bars of the Carlton and Martinez hotels in Cannes, Le Négresco in Nice, **Somerset Maugham** at the Grand Hôtel in St-Jean-Cap-Ferrat and the Hermitage in Monte-Carlo *(see* Where to Stay, *pp194–203).*

## PICNIC AND TAKE-AWAY FOOD

You are never far from food in Provence. The traditional street food of Provence is the *pan bagnat,* a thick bun filled with crisp salade Niçoise and doused in olive oil. Pizza is a local favourite, and every small town has its pizza van, where your choice is cooked to order. A particularly Provençal form of pizza is *pissaladière,* an onion pizza coated with anchovies and olives. In Nice, the number one snack is *socca,* thick crêpes made from chickpea flour *(see pp206–7).*

The French love picnics, and the *Provençaux* are no exception. French alfresco eating is often complex – families set out tables, chairs, barbecues and portable fridges. To service this penchant for portable food, Provençal villages have specialist shops offering ready-to-eat food. *Boulangeries* and *pâtisseries* serve everything from fresh croissants to quiches and a dazzling array of cakes and tarts. Nearly all *boulangeries* provide delicious, freshly made *baguette* sandwiches.

In the main towns, specialist butchers called *traîteurs* provide ready–made dishes, such as salads, cold meats and roast chicken, sold in cartons according to weight. **Au Flan Coco** in Nîmes and **Bataille** in Marseille are fine examples. Most supermarkets also have similar delicatessen counters. *Charcuteries* specialize in pork dishes, particularly pâtés and sausages. For traditional spicy sausages much prized in the Camargue, head to the **Dorel et Milhau** in Arles.

The best place to buy picnic food is the local market. Every town in Provence has its market, some daily, like Aix-en-Provence, some just once or twice a week. No Provençal picnic is complete without French bread – the *baguette* is the mainstay of the country and Provence is no exception. The only difference is that the region boasts numerous local breads, incorporating traditional ingredients. *Pain aux olives* is found almost everywhere, often in the form of *fougasse*, a flat, lattice–like loaf. Alternatively, this may contain anchovies *(pain aux anchois)*, or spinach *(pain aux épinards)* and there is a sweet version flavoured with almonds. Wholemeal or brown bread is an anathema to the traditional Provençaux, although many bakeries now produce it – ask for *pain aux céréales*. The nearest to healthy bread is *pain de campagne*, a sturdier *baguette* made with unrefined white flour. One of the finest *boulangeries* in the region is **Le Four à Bois**, in the old quarter of Nice, where the same recipes have been used for generations.

*Boulangeries* are found in every village and usually have a good selection of *pâtisseries*, cakes and tarts. Provençal ingredients are combined to make these delights, such as honey, almonds and fruit – try those at **Béchard** in Aix-en-Provence. For those with an even sweeter tooth, these same ingredients are used in the handmade chocolates and candied fruit. *Calissons* (an almond-paste sweet) and *suce-miel* (honey–based candy) are very popular. Two of the best shops are **Puyricard** in Aix and **Auer** in Nice.

# DIRECTORY

## CAFÉS

### Aix-en-Provence
**Brasserie des Deux Garçons**
53 cours Mirabeau.
*Tel 04 42 26 00 51.*

### Cannes
**Brasserie Carlton**
58 la Croisette.
*Tel 04 93 06 40 06.*

### Eze
**Château Eza**
Rue de la Pise.
*Tel 04 93 41 12 24.*

### Monaco
**Café de Paris**
Le Casino,
place du Casino.
*Tel 00 377 92 16 20 20.*

### Nice
**Le Grand Café de Turin**
5 place Garibaldi.
*Tel 04 93 62 29 52.*

### Nîmes
**Le Café Olive**
22 boulevard Victor Hugo.
*Tel 04 66 67 89 10.*

### St-Paul-de-Vence
**Café de la Place**
Place du Général de Gaulle.
*Tel 04 93 32 80 03.*

### St-Tropez
**Café des Arts**
Place des Lices.
*Tel 04 94 97 02 25.*
**Le Café de Paris**
15 Quai de Suffren.
*Tel 04 94 97 00 56.*
**Senequier**
Quai Jean Jaurès.
*Tel 04 94 97 00 90.*

## BARS AND PUBS

### Avignon
**Pub Z**
58 rue de la Bonneterie.
*Tel 04 90 85 42 84.*

### Cannes
**Le Zanzibar**
85 rue Félix-Faure.
*Tel 04 93 39 30 75.*

### Juan-les-Pins
**Pam-Pam**
137 boulevard Wilson. *Tel 04 93 61 11 05.*

### Marseille
**Le Bar de la Marine**
15 quai de Rive Neuve.
*Tel 04 91 54 95 42.*

**La Part des Anges**
33 rue Sainte.
*Tel 04 91 33 55 70.*

### Monaco
**Flashman's**
7 avenue Princesse Alice.
*Tel 00 377 93 30 09 03.*

### Nice
**De Klomp**
8 rue Mascoinat.
*Tel 04 93 92 42 85.*
**Les Trois Diables**
2 cours Saleya.
*Tel 04 93 62 47 00.*
**Wayne's Bar**
15 rue de la Préfecture.
*Tel 04 93 13 46 99.*

### Nîmes
**La Petite Bourse**
2 boulevard Victor Hugo.
*Tel 04 66 67 44 31.*

### St-Jean-Cap-Ferrat
**Somerset Maugham**
Grand Hôtel de Cap–Ferrat, 71 boulevard du Général de Gaulle.
*Tel 04 93 76 50 50.*

### Villefranche
**Le Cosmo Bar**
11 pl Amélie Pollonais.
*Tel 04 93 01 84 05.*

## PICNIC AND TAKE-AWAY FOOD

### Aix-en-Provence
**Béchard**
12 cours Mirabeau.
**Puyricard**
7 Rue Rifle-rafle.

### Arles
**Dorel et Milhau**
11 rue Réattu.

### Marseille
**Bataille**
18 rue Fontange.
**Le Four des Navettes**
136 rue Sainte.

### Nice
**Auer**
7 rue St-François-de-Paule.
**Le Four à Bois**
35 rue Droite.

### Nîmes
**Au Flan Coco**
31 rue du Mûrier d'Espagne.

# SHOPS AND MARKETS

Shopping in Provence is one of life's great delights. Even the tiniest village may be home to a craftsman potter or painter, or you may arrive on market day to find regional produce – artichokes, asparagus, wild mushrooms – still fresh with the dew from the surrounding fields. Larger towns are packed with individual boutiques selling anything from dried flowers to chic baby clothes, and the fashion-conscious will always be

**Provençal olive oil**

able to find an avenue or two of famous names in which to window-shop. If the idea of cramming fresh foodstuffs into your luggage to take back home proves too daunting, Provence has perfected the fine art of packaging its produce, with the bottles, jars and boxes often works of art in themselves. This section provides guidelines on opening hours and the range of goods with a Provençal flavour to be found in the many stores and markets.

A butcher and a store selling household goods in a village in Provence

## OPENING HOURS

Food shops open at around 8am and close at noon for lunch, a break that may last for up to three hours. After lunch, most shops stay open until 7pm, sometimes even later in big towns. Bakers often stay open until 1pm or later, serving tasty lunchtime snacks. Most supermarkets and hypermarkets stay open throughout lunchtimes.

Non-food shops are open 9am–7pm Mon–Sat, but most will close for lunch. Many are closed on Monday mornings. Food shops and newsagents open on Sunday mornings but almost every shop is closed on Sunday afternoon. Small shops may close for one day a week out of high season.

## LARGER SHOPS

Hypermarkets (*hypermarchés or grandes surfaces)* can be found on the outskirts of every sizeable town: look out for the signs indicating the *Centre Commercial.* Among the largest are Casino, Auchan and Carrefour. Discount petrol is usually sold: you may have to pay in cash.

Department stores, or *grands magasins,* including Monoprix and Prisunic, are usually found in town centres. More up-market stores such as Galeries Lafayette and Printemps are found both in towns and at out-of-town complexes.

## SPECIALIST SHOPS

One of the great pleasures of shopping in Provence is that specialist food shops still flourish despite the new large supermarkets. The bread shop (*boulangerie)* is usually combined with the *pâtisserie* selling cakes and pastries. The cheesemonger (*fromagerie)* may also be combined with a shop selling other dairy produce (*laiterie),* but the *boucherie* (butcher) and the *charcuterie* (delicatessen) tend to be separate shops. A *traiteur* sells prepared foods. For dry goods and general groceries, you need an *épicerie.* Cleaning products and household goods are sold at a *droguerie* and hardware at a *quincaillerie.* Booksellers *(libraries)* in the main towns sometimes sell English books.

## MARKETS

This guide gives the market days for every town featured. To find out where the market is, ask a passer-by for *le marché.* Markets are morning affairs, when the produce is super-fresh – by noon the stall-holders will already be packing up and the best bargains will have been sold out hours ago. By French law, price tags must state the origin of all produce: *du pays* means local.

*Les marchés de Provence* were immortalized in song by Gilbert Bécaud, and rightly so. In a country famed for its markets, these are among the best. Some are renowned – cours Saleya (*see p84)* in Nice and the food and flower markets of Aix (*see p148),* for example, should not be missed. Others take more searching out, such as the truffle markets of the Var. Try Aups (*see p104)* on a Thursday during truffle season, from November to February.

Enjoying a drink next to a flower shop in Luberon, Vaucluse

Bags of dried herbs on display in the market of St-Rémy-de-Provence

## REGIONAL SPECIALITIES

The sunshine of Provence is captured in its distinctive, vividly coloured fabrics, known as *indiennes*. Many shops sell them by the metre; others, such as **Les Textiles Mistral** and **Souleïado** also make them into soft furnishings, cowboy shirts and boxer shorts.

Throughout Provence, working olive mills churn out rich, pungent oil, which is also used to make the chunky blocks of soap, *savon de Marseille*. Tins and jars of olives, often scented with *herbes de Provence*, are widely available, as are bags of the herbs themselves. Bags of lavender, and honey from its pollen, are regional specialities; local flowers appear in other forms too, from dried arrangements to scented oils, or perfumes from Grasse *(see p67)*.

Traditional sweets *(confiseries)* abound, using regional fruits and nuts: almond *calissons* from Aix, fruity *berlingots* from Carpentras and candied *fruits confits* are just a few.

## LOCAL WINES

Provence is not one of the great wine regions of the world, but its many vineyards *(see pp208–9)* produce a wide range of pleasant wines and you will see plenty of signs inviting you to a *dégustation* (tasting). You will usually be expected to buy at least one bottle. Wine co-operatives sell the wines of numerous smaller producers. Here you can buy wine in five- and ten-litre containers *(en vrac)*. This wine is "duty free" but, with vineyards such as Châteauneuf-du-Pape and Beaumes-de-Venise, wise buyers will drink *en vrac* on holiday and pick up bargains in fine wine to bring home.

Marseille's aperitif *pastis* is an evocative, if acquired, taste.

## ARTS AND CRAFTS

Many of the crafts now flourishing in Provence are traditional ones that had almost died out 50 years ago. The potters of Vallauris owe the revival in their fortunes to Picasso *(see pp72–3)* but, more often, it is the interest of visitors that keeps a craft alive. From the little pottery *santons* of Marseille to the flutes and tambourines of Barjols, there is plenty of choice for gifts and mementos. Many towns have unique specialities. Biot *(see p74)* is famous for its bubbly glassware, Cogolin for pipes and carpets and Salernes for hexagonal terracotta tiles.

Works by local artists sold on the harbour at St-Tropez

# DIRECTORY

**REGIONAL SPECIALITIES**

**Avignon**
**Souleïado**
5 rue Joseph Vernet.
*Tel 04 90 86 47 67.*
*One of several branches.*

**Grasse**
**Huilerie Ste-Anne**
138 route de Draguignan.
*Tel 04 93 70 21 42.*
**Parfumerie Fragonard**
20 bd Fragonard.
*Tel 04 92 42 34 34.*
**www**.fragonard.com
**Parfumerie Galimard**
73 route de Cannes.
*Tel 04 93 09 20 00.*
**www**.galimard.com

**Nice**
**Alziari**
14 rue St-François-de-Paule and 318 bd de la Madeleine. *Tel 04 93 62 94 03. Olive press.*

**Nîmes**
**Les Textiles Mistral**
2 bd des Arènes.
*Tel 04 66 21 69 57.*

**ARTS AND CRAFTS**

**Cogolin**
**Fabrique de Pipes Courrieu**
58 av G Clemenceau.
*Tel 04 94 54 63 82.*
**Manufacture des Tapis de Cogolin**
6 bd Louis Blanc.
*Tel 04 94 55 70 65.*

**Marseille**
**Ateliers Marcel Carbonel**
47–49 rue Neuve Ste-Catherine.
*Tel 04 91 54 26 58.*
**www**.santonsmarcel carbonel.com
*Santons workshop and museum.*

**Vallauris**
**Roger Collet – Poterie**
Montée Ste-Anne.
*Tel 04 93 64 65 84.*

**ENGLISH LANGUAGE BOOKSHOPS**

**Aix-en-Provence**
**Paradox**
15 rue du 4 Septembre.
*Tel 04 42 26 47 99.*

**Cannes**
**Cannes English Bookshop**
11 rue Bivouac Napoléon.
*Tel 04 93 99 40 08.*

**Marseille**
**Librairie Maurel**
95 rue de Lodi.
*Tel 04 91 42 63 44.*

**Monaco**
**Scruples**
9 rue Princesse Caroline.
*Tel (00 377) 93 50 43 52.*

**Montpellier**
**The Bookshop**
6 rue de l'Université.
*Tel 04 67 66 09 08.*

**Nice**
**The Cat's Whiskers**
30 rue Lamartine.
*Tel 04 93 80 02 66.*

# What to Buy in Provence

Best buys to be found in Provence are those that
reflect the character of the region – its geographical
blessings of bountiful produce and its historic traditions
of arts and crafts. While the chic boutiques of St-Tropez
or Cannes may rival Paris in predicting the latest fashion
trend, your souvenirs of Provence should be far more
timeless. The evocative scents, colours and flavours
they offer will help to keep your holiday memories
alive throughout the darkest winter months, and
longer – at least until your next visit.

**Lavender, one of the
perfumes of Provence**

## THE SCENTS OF PROVENCE

Provençal lavender is used to perfume
a wide range of goods, but most popular
are pretty fabric bags full of the dried
flowers. Bath times can be
heady with the scent of
local flowers and herbs,
captured in delightful
bottles, and Marseille's
famous olive oil soaps.

**Olive oil savons de Marseille**

**Orange water
from Vallauris**

**Linden-scented
bubble bath**

**Dried lavender, packed
in Provençal fabrics**

**Mallow-scented
bubble bath**

### Glassware
*Glassblowing is a
modern Provençal
craft. At Biot (see
p74) you can watch
glassblowers at work,
as well as buy examples
of their art to take home.*

### Pottery
*Look for traditional
tiles, cookware and
storage jars made
from* terre rouge,
*formal china of
Moustiers faïence
(see p186) or art-
works of* grès clay.

### Terracotta Santons
*Provençal Christmas cribs are peopled with
these gaily painted traditional figures. Most
crafts shops offer a good choice of characters.*

## Olive Wood

*As rich in colour and texture as its oil, the wood of the olive can be sculpted into works of art or turned into practical kitchenware.*

## Hunting Knives

*The huntsmen's shops of Provence are an unexpected source for the perfect picnic or kitchen knife, safe yet razor sharp.*

## Provençal Fabrics

*Using patterns and colours dating back for centuries, these traditional prints are sold by the metre or made up into fashionable items.*

## THE FLAVOURS OF PROVENCE

No-one should leave Provence without at least a jar of olives or a bottle of olive oil, but consider also easy-to-pack tins, jars and boxes of preserved fruits, scented honey or savoury purées – prettily packaged, they make ideal gifts.

Almond sweetmeats, the speciality of Aix-en-Provence

Crystallized chestnuts or *marrons glacés*

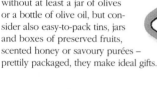

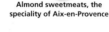

Goat's milk cheese, wrapped in chestnut leaves

Tuna packed in olive oil

Basil flavoured olive oil

Virgin olive oil

Puréed salt cod or *brandade de morue*

Almond and orange conserve

Lavender honey and hazelnut *confit*

# ENTERTAINMENT IN PROVENCE

Provence offers a wealth of cultural options to visitors. Barely a month goes by without some major festival *(see pp32–35 & pp228–9)*. Events take place all year round, with first-class dance, opera and jazz in Nice and Marseille, rock concerts in Toulon, theatre in Avignon and blockbuster art shows in Nice, Antibes, Monaco and Aix-en-Provence. Nightlife tends to be

**Actor at the Avignon Festival**

restricted to the fashionable coastal resorts, like Juan-les-Pins and St-Tropez, where clubs and bars often stay open all night. In winter, things are quieter, but the small bars and cafés of Marseille, Nîmes and Nice remain open and full of life. Provence's most common entertainment is free – locals spend much of their time enjoying the fresh air, walking and playing *pétanque*, or Provençal bowls.

## PRACTICAL INFORMATION

Information about what's on in Provence is fairly localized, with tourist offices providing listings of various events. Most large towns publish a weekly paper that outlines the best of each week's events. Local papers can also provide details of important festivals and sporting events. *Le Provençal* serves western Provence, while *Nice Matin* and its derivatives cover the east of the region. You can purchase regional newspapers and magazines at newsagents and *tabacs*.

The large English-speaking community in Provence has its own radio station, Riviera Radio, which broadcasts from Monte-Carlo in English on 106.3 FM and 106.5 FM. English-language publications such as *The Riviera Times* and *The Riviera Reporter* include event listings and websites.

## BUYING TICKETS

Depending on the event, most tickets can be bought at the

door, but for blockbuster concerts, particularly during the summer months, it is best to reserve in advance. Tickets can be purchased at branches of the **FNAC** and **Virgin Mega-store** chains in major towns.

Theatre box offices are open from approximately 11am until 7pm seven days a week and will usually accept credit card bookings over the telephone.

As a last resort, if you haven't booked in advance, tickets to popular concerts can be bought from touts at the venue doors on the night. However, they will be much more expensive and possibly counterfeit.

## OPERA AND CLASSICAL MUSIC

Music is everywhere in Provence, from small village churches to the Belle Epoque opera houses of Marseille, Toulon and Nice. The **Opéra de Nice** is one of the best in France, and the **Monte-Carlo**

**Classical cello**

Orchestra features many illustrious conductors. Classical and jazz festivals are held throughout the summer in major cities.

Every year on 21 June, the Fête de la Musique is held throughout France. Amateur and professional musicians alike set up their stages in villages and towns and perform. Take in as many different "concerts" as you can to enjoy an impressive range of genres.

### ROCK AND JAZZ

These days Provence is a major venue on most world tours, with big stadium performances at Toulon's **Zenith-Omèga** or Marseille's **Stade-Vélodrome**. The **Nice Festival du Jazz** in the Cimiez arena *(see p84)* is one of the world's best. It was here that Miles Davis gave one of his last performances among the Roman walls and olive groves. Also popular is the **Jazz à Juan** festival in Juan-les-Pins, which has seen Ray Charles and the jazz debut of violinist Nigel Kennedy.

### THEATRE

Going to the theatre in Provence can be as formal or as relaxed as you choose. A trip to a big theatre can involve dressing up, special *souper* (late dinner) reservations at a nearby restaurant and pricey champagne during the interval. On the other hand, a visit to a smaller theatre can be cheap

**Leonard Cohen performing at the Nice Festival du Jazz**

and casual, with a real feeling of intimacy and immediacy.

Marseille is the centre of theatre in Provence and boasts one of France's top theatrical companies, the **Théâtre National de la Criée**. Various smaller companies stage some of the most innovative plays in Europe, many of which end up in Paris. Avignon is also famous for its **Théâtre des Carmes**, the main venue for the **Festival d'Avignon** *(see p229)*. There is also a "fringe" festival, the **Avignon Public Off**, with its own directors and box office.

## SPECTATOR SPORTS

With its superb weather and glamorous reputation, the regions of Provence and the Côte d'Azur are ideal venues for some of France's top sporting events. The gruelling **Tour de France** passes through the area each July, while the Monte-Carlo and Nice tennis tournaments attract the best players. The **Grand Prix de Monaco** *(see p32)* is one of the highlights of the Formula 1 motor-racing season, and horse-racing enthusiasts can visit the **Hippodrome de la Côte d'Azur** track at Cagnes-sur-Mer between December and March.

Provence boasts two of the top soccer teams in France – **Olympique de Marseille** and **AS Monaco**, known as the millionaires' club. Rugby is also popular in Provence, with top-class clubs in Nice and Toulon.

The Open Tennis Championships in Monte-Carlo

## DANCE

Marseille's eclectic mixture of nationalities and styles has led to highly original and powerful dance productions.

The National Ballet Company is based at the Ecole de Danse in Marseille. Companies such as the **Bernardines** sometimes take their productions to Paris,

View over the harbour in Monaco to the glittering casino

while **La Friche La Belle de Mai**, located in an old tobacco factory, is a popular venue for experimental performance and music.

The new **Centre Chorégraphique National** in Aix-en-Provence is an exciting addition to the Provençal dance scene.

## GAMBLING

The French Riviera is famed for its opulent casinos. If you are 18 and over you can play in most resorts. Monaco has the coast's most popular casino – **Le Casino** – where you have to pay an entrance fee and show an ID card before you can start gambling. Other casinos worth visiting for architecture and atmosphere are Cannes' **Casino Croisette** and **Casino Ruhl** in Nice. Even if you are not a high-roller, there is always a dazzling array of slot machines.

## BULLFIGHTING

The annual *ferias*, or bullfighting festivals, are always dramatic occasions. The traditional bullfight of Provence is the *course à la cocarde*, which starts with an *abrivado* when the bulls are chased through the town to the local arena. The bull enters the ring with a red *cocarde*, or rosette, tied to its horns, which the *razeteurs*, or matadors, try to snatch, providing riveting but goreless entertainment. At the end of the season, the bullfighter with the most rosettes receives fame and adulation, as well as cash.

Sometimes bullfights will end in death in the full-blooded Spanish-style *corrida*, but this is usually only in the main arenas in Nîmes and Arles *(see p32)*, and it will always be advertised first. In one session there are usually six bullfights, of which two may be advertised as *mise à mort* (to the death).

**Bullfighting poster for the 1992 Nîmes *feria* by Francis Bacon**

## CINEMA

The small port of La Ciotat is where Louis Lumière shot the world's first motion picture, and Marcel Pagnol laid the foundations for modern French cinema from his studios in Marseille. The French are very supportive of *la Septième Art*, as they refer to film, and there are plenty of local, independent cinemas. If your language skills won't stretch to watching a French film, look out for cinemas that show films in their *V.O. (Version Original)* – that is, screened in their original language. *V.F. (Version Française)* denotes a dubbed screening in French.

Popcorn or other snacks are available, but it tends to be the foreigners that snack their way through a movie. However, there are some French cinemas that have bars and restaurants attached, so that you may dissect the movie over a meal afterwards.

As the fame of Cannes *(see p68)* reflects, film festivals are taken seriously by the French. Cannes itself is a maelstrom of media hype, old-school glamour and shiny new cash. It is an amazing experience if you can get tickets to any of the films or parties, but these are notoriously difficult to get as they are by invitation only.

## DISCOTHEQUES AND NIGHTCLUBS

During the summer, the main towns of Provence boogie all night long. The music is far from trend-setting, usually following styles set the previous year in New York and London, but the dancers are chic and the prices high. A handful of clubs such as **Jimmy'Z** in Monaco and **Les Caves du Roy** in St-Tropez cater for the jet set, while **Whisky à Gogo** in Juan-les-Pins and **Le Blitz** in Cannes serve a younger crowd. The dress code is usually smart, and trainers are almost always forbidden.

## CHILDREN'S ENTERTAINMENT

Provence offers the traditional attractions of beach and sea, although small children may better appreciate them in smaller resorts. Alternatives include aqua parks like **Marineland** and **Aqualand**, zoos and aquariums. There are also numerous adventure parks for rock-climbing, cycling and zip-lining, such as the **Canyon Forest** at Villeneuve-Loubet and **Coudou Parc** at Six-Fours-les-Plages. Artistically inclined children may enjoy decorating their own ceramics at **Ceramic Crea** in Antibes. In the bigger towns, museums and theatres may organize activities (ask at the tourist office). Smaller towns and villages will have playgrounds or a square where your offspring can play with other children while you relax in a café. For more action, there are plenty of sporting activities, such as biking, canoeing, tennis, horse-riding and fishing.

# DIRECTORY

### BUYING TICKETS

**FNAC**
*Tel* 08 25 02 00 20.
www.fnac.com
**Avignon**
19 rue de la République.
**Marseille**
Centre Commercial Bourse.
**Nice**
30 av Jean Médecin.

**Virgin Megastore**
**Marseille**
75 rue St-Ferréol.
*Tel* 04 91 55 55 00.
www.virgin.fr
**Nice**
15 av Jean Médecin.
*Tel* 04 97 03 09 00.

### OPERA AND CLASSICAL MUSIC

**Aix-en-Provence**
**Aix en Musique**
3 place John Rewald.
*Tel* 04 42 21 69 69.
www.aixenmusic.fr

**Marseille**
**Opéra Municipal**
2 rue Molière.
*Tel* 04 91 55 14 19.
http://opera.mairie-marseille.fr

**Monaco**
**Monte Carlo Orchestra**
Place du Casino.
*Tel* 00 377 98 06 28 28.
www.opmc.mc

**Nice**
**CEDAC de Cimiez**
49 av de la Marne.
*Tel* 04 93 53 85 95.
www.cedac-nice.org
**Forum Nice Nord**
10 bd Comte de Falicon.
*Tel* 04 93 84 24 37.
www.nicenord.com
**Opéra de Nice**
4 rue St-François-de-Paule.
*Tel* 04 92 17 40 00.
www.opera-nice.org

**Toulon – Ollioules**
**Châteauvallon**
*Tel* 04 94 22 74 00.
www.chateauvallon.com

**Festival de Musique Classique**
*Tel* 04 94 18 53 00.
**Opéra de Toulon**
Bd de Strasbourg.
*Tel* 04 94 93 03 76.
www.operadetoulon.fr

### ROCK AND JAZZ MUSIC

**Aix-en-Provence**
**Hot Brass Club**
1857 chemin d'Eguilles-Célony.
*Tel* 04 42 21 05 57.
**Le Scat**
11 rue de la Verrerie.
*Tel* 04 42 23 00 23.

**Juan-les-Pins**
**Jazz à Juan**
Office de Tourisme,
11 pl de Gaulle, Antibes.
*Tel* 04 92 90 54 26.
www.antibesjuanlespins.com

**Marseilles**
**Espace Julien**
39 cours Julien.
*Tel* 04 91 24 34 10.
www.espace-julien.com

**L'Intermédiaire**
63 pl Jean-Jaurès.
*Tel* 04 91 47 01 25.
**Le Pelle-Mêle**
8 place Huiles.
*Tel* 04 91 54 85 26.
**Stade Vélodrome**
Allée Ray-Grassi.
*Tel* 04 91 29 14 50.

**Nice**
**Bar des Oiseaux**
5 rue St-Vincent.
*Tel* 04 93 80 27 33.
**Festival du Jazz**
5 promenade des Anglais.
*Tel* 08 92 68 36 22.
www.nicejazzfestival.fr

**Toulon**
**Zenith-Oméga**
Bd Commandant Nicolas.
*Tel* 08 92 70 08 40.

### THEATRE

**Avignon**
**Avignon Public Off**
*Tel* 06 74 20 96 84.
www.avignon-off.net

## DIRECTORY

**Festival d'Avignon**
Espace St-Louis, 20 rue
Portail Baguier.
*Tel 04 90 27 66 50.*
www.festival-
avignon.com
**Théâtre des Carmes**
6 place des Carmes.
*Tel 04 90 82 20 47.*
www.theatredes
carmes.com

**Marseille**
**Théâtre du Merlan**
Avenue Raimu.
*Tel 04 91 11 19 30.*
www.merlan.org
**Théâtre National
de la Criée**
30 quai de Rive-Neuve.
*Tel 04 91 54 70 54.*
www.theatre-lacriee.com

**Nice**
**Théâtre de l'Alphabet**
10 bd Carabacel.
*Tel 04 93 13 08 88.*
**Théâtre de la Semeuse**
Rue du Château.
*Tel 04 93 92 85 00.*

### SPECTATOR
SPORTS

**Cagnes-sur-Mer**
**Hippodrome de la
Côte d'Azur**
www.hippodrome-
cotedazur.com

**Marseille**
**ASPTT Tennis**
*Tel 04 91 93 85 85.*
www.asptt.com
**Olympique de Marseille**
www.om.net

**Monaco**
**AS Monaco FC**
www.asm-fc.com
**Grand Prix de Monaco**
www.acm.mc

**Nice**
**Ligue de la Côte
d'Azur Tennis**
*Tel 04 93 18 00 95.*

**Tour de France**
www.letour.fr

### DANCE

**Aix-en-Provence**
**Centre Chorégraphique
National**
530 av Mozart.
*Tel 04 42 93 48 00.*

**Marseille**
**Bernardines**
17 bd Garibaldi.
*Tel 04 91 24 30 40.*
www.theatre-
bernardines.org
**La Friche la Belle de Mai**
41 rue Robin.
*Tel 04 95 04 95 04.*
www.lafriche.org

### GAMBLING

**Cannes**
**Casino Croisette**
Palais des Festivals.
*Tel 04 92 98 78 00.*
www.lucienbarriere.com

**Monaco**
**Le Casino**
Place du Casino.
*Tel 00 377 93 30 56 78.*
www.montecarlo
casinos.com

**Nice**
**Casino Ruhl**
1 promenade des Anglais.
*Tel 04 97 03 12 22.*

### BULLFIGHTING

**Arles**
**Arènes d'Arles**
Rond-point des Arènes.
*Tel 04 90 49 59 05.*

**Nîmes**
**Les Arènes**
Blvd des Arènes.
*Tel 04 66 21 82 56.*

### CINEMA

**Aix-en-Provence**
**Le Mazarin**
6 rue Laroque.
📶 *08 92 68 72 70.*

**Avignon**
**Utopia Cinéma**
4 rue des Escaliers
Sainte Anne.
*Tel 04 90 82 65 36.*

**Cannes**
**Cannes Film Festival**
www.festival-cannes.fr

**Marseille**
**Cinéma Chambord**
283 av du Prado.
📶 *08 92 68 01 22.*

**Monte Carlo**
**Le Sporting d'Hiver**
Place du Casino.
📶 *00 377 93 30 81 08.*

**Nice**
**Cinémathèque**
3 esplanade Kennedy.
*Tel 04 92 04 06 66.*
**Mercury Cinéma**
16 place Garibaldi.
*Tel 08 92 68 81 06.*

**Nîmes**
**Le Sémaphore**
25a rue Porte de France.
📶 *04 66 67 88 04.*

### DISCOTHEQUES
AND NIGHTCLUBS

**Aix-en-Provence**
**Le Mistral**
3 rue Frédéric Mistral.
*Tel 04 42 38 16 49.*

**Avignon**
**Les Ambassadeurs Club**
27 rue Bancasse.
*Tel 04 90 86 31 55.*

**Cannes**
**Le Blitz**
22 rue Macé.
*Tel 04 93 39 05 25.*
**Disco 7**
7 rue Rouguière.
*Tel 04 93 39 10 36.*
**Jimmy'Z**
Casino Croisette, Palais
des Congrès.
*Tel 04 92 98 78 78.*

**Hyères**
**Le Fou du Roi**
Casino des Palmiers,
1 ave Ambroise Thomas.
*Tel 04 94 12 80 80.*
**Le Rêve**
9 avenue Badine.
*Tel 04 94 58 00 07.*

**Juan-les-Pins**
**Le Village Voom Voom**
1 bd de la Pinède.
*Tel 04 92 93 90 00.*
**Whisky à Gogo**
Rue Jacques Leonetti.
*Tel 04 93 61 26 40.*

**Marseille**
**Le Circus**
5 rue du Chantier.
*Tel 04 91 33 77 22.*

**Monaco**
**Jimmy'Z**
26 av Princesse Grace.
*Tel 00 377 92 16 22 77.*
www.montecarlo
bay.com

**Le Tiffany's**
3 av Spélugues.
*Tel 00 377 93 50 53 13.*

**Nice**
**Le Grand Escurial**
29 rue Alphonse Karr.
*Tel 04 93 82 37 66.*

**St-Raphaël**
**La Réserve**
Promenade René Coty.
*Tel 04 94 95 02 20.*

**St-Tropez**
**Les Caves du Roy**
Palace de la Côte d'Azur,
av Paul Signac.
*Tel 04 94 56 68 00.*
www.lescavesduroy.com
**Papagayo**
Résidence du Port.
*Tel 04 94 97 95 95.*

### CHILDREN'S
ENTERTAINMENT

**Aqualand**
RN 98, 83600 Fréjus.
*Tel 04 94 51 82 51.*
www.aqualand.fr

**Canyon Forest**
Park des Rives du Loup,
Villeneuve-Loubet.
*Tel 04 92 02 88 88.*
www.canyon-forest.com

**Ceramic Crea**
94 Bd Beau Rivage,
Antibes.
*Tel 04 89 75 12 68.*
www.ceramic-crea.com

**Coudou Parc**
34 rue de la République,
Six-Fours-les-Plages.
*Tel 06 63 77 02 06.*
www.coudouparc.com

**Marineland**
RN 7, 06600 Antibes.
*Tel 04 93 33 49 49.*
www.marineland.fr

**Museum of
Oceanography
and Aquarium**
Ave St Martin,
Monte-Carlo.
*Tel 00 377 93 15 36 00.*

**Park Zoologique
de Fréjus**
Le Capitou, Fréjus.
*Tel 04 98 11 37 37.*

# Festivals in Provence

Festivals in Provence are very much part of the way of life. They are not staged purely for the benefit of visitors and tourism, but more to continue the seasonal celebrations that are deeply rooted in tradition. Many *fêtes* are based on pagan rites while others are celebrations of historic occasions – only a few have been hijacked by fun-loving holiday-makers on the coast. Here is a selection of the best festivals from each of the *départements*.

One of the spectacular floats in the procession at the Nice Carnival

## THE RIVIERA AND THE ALPES MARITIMES

The brilliant explosion of fireworks at the Carnaval de Nice above the Baie des Anges is one of the most popular images of Nice *(see pp84–5)*. It is the largest pre-Lent carnival in France, and crescendos on Shrove Tuesday with fireworks and the immolation of King Carnival, *Sa Majesté Carnaval.*

Carnival festivities, held in all Catholic countries, are based on the pagan celebrations of the death of winter and the birth of spring and life. It is a time of feasting (*mardi gras* means "fat Tuesday") before the fasting of Lent (*carne vale* is Latin for "farewell to meat").

Festivities begin three weeks before Mardi Gras, when the king is wheeled out into the streets. During the two weekends between then and his departure, the colourful, flower-decked floats of the procession parade along the 2-km (1-mile) route round Jardin Albert I, amid confetti battles, bands and mounted escorts.

Carnival characters in the streets of Nice

By the 19th century, the Nice Carnival had developed into little more than a chalk and flour battle. The floats did not appear until 1873, inspired by the local artist, Alexis Mossa, who also resurrected the figure of King Carnival. Since then, great effort and time has been put into making the costumes.

Meanwhile, the whole town is *en fête*, and parties and balls are held in hotels and public venues all night long. Visitors should book well in advance to secure accommodation.

## THE VAR AND THE ILES D'HYERES

A number of festivals in the region feature the firing of muskets, reminiscent of ancient witch-scaring rites. Spectacular volleys are set off into the air in St-Tropez *(see pp118–19)* for the biannual *bravade*, commemorating two significant events.

The first one takes place on May 16 and 17 and is a religious procession devoted to the town's patron, Saint Torpès, He was a Roman soldier in the service of the emperor, Nero. In AD 68, Torpès converted to Christianity and was martyred by decapitation. His body was placed in a boat along with a hungry dog and a cockerel. Miraculously, the saint's body was untouched. The vessel was washed up onto the shores of southern France, on the spot where St-Tropez stands today.

The May *bravade* honours his arrival. Celebrations begin with the blessing of a lance by the town's priest in the Eglise de St-Tropez. From here, the saint's gilded wooden bust is taken and carried around the flag-decked town in a terrific flurry of musket volleys. The procession winds down to the beach, and the sea is blessed for safely conveying the saint.

The second *bravade* takes place on 15 June and is honoured with earth-shattering fusillades and military parades. It marks the anniversary of the day in 1637, when the local militia saw off a Spanish fleet, about 22 vessels strong, after an attempt to capture four ships of the Royal French fleet.

La bravade procession in St-Tropez, honouring the town's patron saint

## BOUCHES-DU-RHONE AND NIMES

Europe's largest Romany festival, the Pèlerinage des Gitans in Saintes-Maries-de-la-Mer *(see p138)*, is a simple yet very moving occasion. At the end of May, usually 24–26, Romanies from all over the continent gather to pay their

**Procession of the saints down to the sea in Saintes-Maries-de-la-Mer**

respects to the patron saint of gypsies, Saint Sarah, known as the Black Madonna. This takes place in the picturesque town of Saintes-Maries-de-la-Mer.

The pilgrimage is a colourful occasion, brightened by traditional Arlesian costumes and *gardian* cowboys. The object of their veneration is Saint Sarah, the Ethiopian servant. As legend has it, she arrived on the shores of the Camargue by boat. Also on board was Mary Magdalene, and the saints Mary Jacobea (sister of the Virgin Mary) and the elderly Mary Salome (mother of the apostles Saint James and Saint John). Sarah and the Marys decided to stay in the town and they built an oratory on which the fortified church of Notre-Dame-de-la-Mer was built. The saints started to preach the gospel and the town became known as the "Mecca of Provence".

Saint Sarah stands serene and excessively robed in the crypt. On the two nights and days of celebration in May, she is remembered with a Mass and all-night vigil. The next day, the statues of the saints are borne down to the sea where the Camargue cowboys take their horses, neck-deep, into the water and the Bishop of Arles blesses the sea.

After the statues have been returned to the church, the great folk festival begins, with rodeos, bull-running, horse racing, Arletan dancing and all manner of entertainment. The *gardians* return for a smaller celebration of Mary Salome in October, when there is a procession around the church.

## VAUCLUSE

The Papal city of Avignon *(see pp166–8)* is a splendid setting for the foremost arts festival in Provence, the Festival d'Avignon. Theatre, music, dance and film are all covered in the month-long programme which runs from July to early August. More than a quarter of a million visitors travel to Avignon every year to attend the largest arts festival in France. It is advisable to reserve hotels and tickets in advance to avoid disappointment *(see pp226–7 for reservations)*.

**Lavender from the festival in Digne**

The festival was established in 1947 by the late Jean Vilar whose aim was to bring theatre to the masses. He devised a number of productions to be staged in the courtyard of the Papal Palace and his Théâtre National Populair still performs every year. Other venues include the theatres and cinemas, where films are shown all day, the opera house and churches.

Since the 1960s, the fringe-style Avignon Public Off, brings some 520 events to over 100 venues including many specially set-up theatres. Amateur performers can be seen for free in the main square outside the opera, the place de l'Horloge.

## ALPES-DE-HAUTE-PROVENCE

Provence's most particular flower has its festival, the Corso de la Lavande, in the mountain spa town of Digne-les-Bains *(see p180)*.

The colourful event, which lasts for four days, takes place in August and celebrates the harvesting of the crop. There are jars and pots of honey and all kinds of lavender produce for sale in the town, and events centre on the main street, boulevard Gassendi. The climax of the festival comes on the last day when the flower-decked floats, representing a variety of themes, parade through the streets, accompanied by music, dancing and cheering. Preceding the floats is a municipal truck spraying the roads with litres of lavender water leaving the whole town heady with the distinctive, sweet perfume.

**Lively street performers at the summer Festival d'Avignon**

# SPECIALIST HOLIDAYS AND OUTDOOR ACTIVITIES

Everything is on offer from sun and sea bathing to skiing and extreme sports in this extraordinarily varied region of France. Watersports are extremely popular and sailing boats can be rented in most towns. For windsurfing, the experienced will want to head for Brutal Beach, just west of Toulon, although boards can be rented at most coastal resorts. Some of the best diving in the whole of the Mediterranean is around the Iles d'Hyères. There are also plenty of opportunities for canoeing and white-water rafting in the Verdon and Gard inland. Opportunities for walking, cycling, mountain-biking and horse riding are endless. The Féderation Française de la Randonnée Pédestre publishes the widely-available *Topo Guides*, which give descriptions of the tracks with details of overnight stops and transport.

**Windsurfing in Provence**

## ARTS AND CRAFTS

The **French Institute** is a good resource for courses in learning French combined with other activities. Students can undertake a French-speaking holiday by working part time on the restoration of historic sites with **Union Rempart** (Union pour la Réhabilitation et Entretien des Monuments et du Patrimoine Artistique).

You can also learn sculpting on a weekend course in a beautiful rural setting. Contact **Provence Verte** for details.

Several specialist tour operators organize dedicated painting holidays. For information, contact the **Maison de la France** tourist board.

## COOKERY COURSES

An extensive range of gastronomic courses providing training in regional or classical cuisine is available. These courses are often combined with visits to markets to learn how to source the best ingredients. The **Hostellerie Bérard** in La Cadière d'Azur runs excellent cookery courses and workshops.

Olive oil is the lifeblood of Mediterranean cuisine and many olive oil producers offer visits to their *moulins*, such as **Château Virant** in Lançon de Provence. The Olive Tree route in Canton de Levens takes you to see oil presses in action.

For lovers of figs, the family-run specialist, **Les Figuières du Mas de Luquet**, is the perfect place to learn about this delicious delicacy.

## LAVENDER FIELDS AND VINEYARDS

The regions most associated with the growing and processing of lavender are around Le Mont Ventoux, the Lubéron and the Provençal Drôme. **Musée de la Lavende**, located in Lagarde d'Apt, organizes guided walking tours of a lavender field.

There are also plenty of opportunities in the whole of the region for *dégustations*. If you are looking to combine a trip to Les-Baux-de-Provence, Les Alpilles or St Rémy-de-Provence with a visit to vineyards, contact the **Syndicat des Vignerons des Baux-de-Provence**. For wines of the Lubéron, contact the **Section Interprofessionnelle des Côtes du Lubéron**.

A cookery course in progress at Hostellerie Bérard

## PERFUMERY AND AROMATHERAPY COURSES

In Grasse, perfume initiation courses allow perfume lovers to create their own *eau de toilette* with the help of a "master perfumer". These courses are available at **Le Studio des Fragrances** at Galimard. The **Tarinologie Workshop** at Molinard also offers courses. The other major perfumery is **Fragonard**, where aroma-synergy workshops are on offer. These courses allow participants to learn the virtues and benefits of plants and essential oils. Lessons are given by professional aromatherapists and plant experts.

## EXTREME SPORTS

The exciting new sport of snow-kiting is skiing with a stunt kite to help with the jumps. Join the best snow-kiters on the Col du Lautaret between the Grave, the Meije peak and Serre Chevalier. For an even more extreme sport, try a different kind of diving –

Beautiful, aromatic lavender fields in Châteauneuf-du-Pape

A game of *boules* in full swing, this is still a favourite pastime in the region

under ice. Other favourite sports include paragliding (*parapente*) and hang gliding (*deltaplane*). For more information, contact the **Fédération Française de Vol Libre**. Gliding (*vol à voile*) is popular in the southern regions, where the climate is warm and the thermals are also good. For details of gliding clubs, contact the **Fédération Française de Vol à Voile**.

## BIRD-WATCHING

The Camargue is a twitcher's paradise. The information centre at the **Parc Naturel Regional de Camargue** provides detailed information on bird-watching. It also organizes walks within the area and has a glassed-in section, where it is possible to observe birds through binoculars. For more information contact the tourist board in Arles (*see pp144-6*) or the tourist office in Stes-Maries-de-la-Mer (*see p137*).

## BOULES/PETANQUE

An emblem of Provençal life, this favourite game of the local men is rarely played by women. Somewhat similar to bowls, it is played with small metal balls on any dusty ground surface. Although the rules are simple, it can be very competitive with a touch of ferocity, making it interesting to watch.

## CANOEING

Canoeing is popular in the huge Lac de Ste-Croix in the National Regional Park of Verdon. The most famous route is the 24 km (15 miles) paddle down the Gorges du

Verdon from Carrejuan Bridge to Lac de Ste Croix, which usually takes two days to cover. La Palud sur Verdon is the best base for whitewater rafting and kayaking on the rapids. For less challenging canoeing, try the River Sorgue, starting from the base of the high cliffs of Fontaine-de-Vaucluse. For more information, contact the **Fédération Française de Canoë-Kayak**.

## CANYONING

The Grand Canyon du Verdon, Europe's largest canyon, can be visited by raft or on foot. It has now become a centre for adventure sports. The **Castellane Tourist Office** provides lists of companies offering canyoning, rafting and other outdoor trails.

## FISHING

Bee-eater, common in Provence

Fishing is a highly popular sport on permitted lakes and rivers. Local tourist offices and fishing shops can help you obtain a licence. You can experience bountiful sea-fishing in the Mediterranean, with catches that include bass, sardines, grey mullet, and crustaceans, such as crayfish and lobster. Night-fishing is becoming increasingly popular too.

## GOLF AND TENNIS

There's a great variety of golf in the area, from high-altitude courses to links facing the sea, or clinging to the fringes of cliffs. Overall, there are around 30 courses, mainly in the Bouches-du-Rhône and the Var and of these, over 20 are

18-hole courses. Some of the best are located at the Frégate course, St Cyr, St Raphaël's Golf de l'Esterel and, close to Avignon, the Golf De Châteteaublanc. Most offer lessons provided by resident experts.

The Provence Golf Pass gives access to 13 courses in the five departments, including five green fees. For golf addicts and occasional golfers alike, this is an excellent way to sample the courses available. For comprehensive information, contact the **Provence-Alpes-Côte d'Azur Regional Tourist Board** or the **Fédération Française de Golf**, which can supply a list of courses in France.

Most of the resorts and towns have their own tennis courts that are open to the public. Many of these are traditional Mediterranean clay courts.

Tennis lovers converge at Monte Carlo in April, when the International Tennis Championships come here for the Monte Carlo Open tournament.

Canoeing in the Gorges du Verdon, an exhilarating experience

## HORSE RIDING

Although the wetland area of Camargue is famous for its hardy white horses, said to be direct descendants of pre-historic horses *(see p136)*, the whole region – from coast to mountain to rural areas – is extremely popular with horse lovers. For a detailed list of pony-trekking and riding opportunities, contact the **Ligue Régionale de Provence de Sports Equestres.**

## NATURISM

The largest and oldest naturist colony in the region is the easternmost of the Hyères islands, the Ile du Levant. It covers half the stretch of the 8 km (5 miles) long island. For more information on baring it all, contact the **Fédération Française de Naturisme.**

## SKIING

The most important skiing areas are in the Maritime Alps, at the meeting point of the Alps and Provence. The main resorts, Auron, Isola 2000 and Valberg *(see p96)* are only a few hours from the coast, making it entirely possible to combine skiing and beach pleasures in a single day. In the north of the region in the Alpes de Haute-Provence are the ski resorts of Pra Loup and Chabanon. For more information, contact the **Fédération Française de Ski** in Annecy or the **Fédération Française de la Montagne et de l'Escalade.**

## SPA BREAKS

Set in the hilltop village of Gordes, one of France's prettiest villages, is the newly opened Daniel Jouvance spa, **La Bastide de Gordes.** It is undoubtedly an ideal spot for relaxing breaks.

In the picturesque, gastronomic village of Mougins, **Le Mas Candille** is an elegant, individual hotel, complemented by a Japanese-style Shiseido spa. For the ultimate in luxury, visit the **Thalazur** spa in Antibes.

## WALKING, CLIMBING AND CYCLING

Long-distance walking and climbing trails are known as Grandes Randonées (GR) and shorter trails as Petites Randonées (PR). Some trails are also open to mountain bikes and horses.

Parc Naturel Régional du Lubéron offers some excellent cycling and walking trails. The information centre, **Maison du Parc**, provides a list of hikers' accommodation and details of two dozen walking trails. The Camargue has many trails and walking paths. "Sentier Littoral", a splendid coastal path from St-Tropez, covers 35 km (22 miles) to Cavalaire. You can even break the journey at Ramatuelle. An excellent French book, *Promenez-vous à Pied – Le Golfe de St-Tropez* has details of 26 walks in the area.

Perhaps the most spectacular trail in the whole of Provence is the GR 9, which crosses the Lubéron range and the Monts du Vaucluse.

For tough rock climbing, try the Buoux cliffs in the Lubéron, or one of the 933 routes in the Gorges du Verdon. The creeks, *calanques*, between Cassis and Marseille are utterly picturesque. Easier ascents can be found in the Dentelles de Montmirail, despite the craggy rock faces. The area boasts excellent vineyards, such as Gigondas, Vacqueyras and Beaumes-de-Venise in which to enjoy a *dégustation* after a climb. **Comité Departemental de la Randonnée Pédestre** in Cagnes-sur-Mer, is equipped with detailed information. For details of trails in the region, contact the **Fédération Française de Randonnée Pédestre.**

Cycling tours of the lush green Lubéron in Vaucluse are great for people of all ages. In the upper Var, Figanières is famous for mountain-biking, while the Alps of Haute-Provence boast around 1,500 km (900 miles) of marked tracks. For detailed information, contact the **Fédération Française de Cyclisme.**

## WATER SPORTS

Most coastal resorts have excellent facilities for both experienced and amateur sailors. Iles d'Hyères has some top-class sailing schools, in the tiny island of Bendor and the Porquerolles, the largest of the French Riviera islands.

For windsurfing, the reliable winds of the Bouches-du-Rhône and the Var make for favourable conditions. Other good locations include the Camargue, where the lively Mistral wind blows, at Port St-Louis and Les Saintes-Maries-de-la-Mer. The windsurfing regatta in St-Tropez in July is a particularly glamorous event, which is always exciting and very well attended.

Scuba diving is popular, thanks to sparkling water, an ample sprinkling of underwater wrecks and a wealth of marine life. It is especially good in Marseille and the Iles d'Hyères and Cavalaire. The little island of Port-Cros has a special underwater "Discovery Trail". St-Raphaël is also a leading diving centre, with several World War II shipwrecks off the coast.

For more on scuba diving, contact the **Fédération Française d'Etudes et de Sports Sous-Marins** in Marseille.

The most picturesque stretch of the Rhône passes through Avignon and Arles, otherwise known as the "Cities of Art and History", and the Camargue – home to wild horses, bulls and flamingos. Several companies organize boat trips or river cruises in floating hotels. For details, contact the tourist information centres in Arles, Avignon, Les Stes-Maries-de-la-Mer or Port St Louis du Rhône.

The *calanques* can be visited by boats from Marseille and Cassis. Contact **Les Amis de Calanques** for more details.

Many beaches are privately owned and entry is by fee. Catamarans, dinghies, water-skiing and surfing equipment are all on offer.

For detailed information, contact the national sailing school, **Fédération Française de Voile.**

# DIRECTORY

## ARTS AND CRAFTS

**French Institute**
17 Queensberry Place,
London SW7 2DT.
*Tel 020 7073 1350.*
www.institut-
francais.org.uk

**Maison de la France**
Lincoln House, 300 High
Holborn, London WC1V
7JH. *Tel 090 68 244 123.*
http://uk.franceguide.
com

**Provence Verte**
Office de Tourisme,
83170 Brignoles.
*Tel 04 94 72 04 21.*
www.la-provence-verte.fr

**Union Rempart**
1 rue des Guillemites,
75004 Paris.
*Tel 01 42 71 96 55.*
www.rempart.com

## COOKERY

**Château Virant**
Route de St Chamas,
13680 Lançon de
Provence.
*Tel 04 90 42 44 47.*
www.chateauvirant.com

**Hostellerie Bérard**
83740 La Cadière d'Azur.
*Tel 04 94 90 11 43.*
www.hotel-berard.com

**Les Figuières du
Mas de Luquet**
Chemin du Mas de la
Musique, Mas de Luquet,
13690 Graveson.
*Tel 04 90 95 72 03.*
www.lesfiguieres.com

## LAVENDER FIELDS
## AND VINEYARDS

**Musée de la
Lavande**
Route de Gordes, Lagarde
d'Apt. *Tel 04 90 76 91 23.*
www.museedelalavande.
com

**Section Inter-
professionnelle des
Côtes du Lubéron**
90 boulevard Saint Roch,
BP12 La Tour d'Aigues.
*Tel 04 90 07 34 40.*

**Syndicat des
Vignerons des
Baux-de-Provence**
Chateau de Romanin,
13210 Saint-Remy-de-
Provence.
*Tel 04 90 92 45 87.*

## PERFUMERY AND
## AROMATHERAPY

**Fragonard**
Boulevard Fragonard,
06130 Grasse.
*Tel 04 92 42 34 34.*
www.fragonard.com

**Le Studio des
Fragrances**
73 route de Cannes,
06130 Grasse.
*Tel 04 93 09 20 00.*
www.galimard.com

**Tarinologie
Workshop**
60 Boulevard Victor Hugo,
06130 Grasse.
*Tel 04 93 36 01 62.*
www.molinard.com

## EXTREME SPORTS

**Fédération
Française de Vol
Libre**
4 rue de Suisse, 06000
Nice. *Tel 04 97 03 82 82.*
www.ffvl.fr

**Fédération
Française de Vol
à Voile**
29 rue de Sèvres,
75006 Paris.
*Tel 01 45 44 04 78.*
www.ffvv.org

## BIRD-WATCHING

**Parc Naturel
Régional de
Camargue**
Pont du Gau, 13460
Saintes-Maries-de-la-Mer.
*Tel 04 90 97 82 55.*
www.parc-camargue.fr

## CANOEING

**Fédération
Française de
Canoe-Kayak**
87 Quai de la Marne,
94340 Joinville-le-Point.
*Tel 01 45 11 08 50.*
www.ffck.org

## CANYONING

**Castellane Tourist
Office**
Rue Nationale, Castellane.
*Tel 04 92 83 61 14.*
www.castellane.org

## GOLF AND TENNIS

**Fédération
Française de Golf**
68 rue Anatole France,
92300, Levallois Perret.
*Tel 01 41 49 77 00.*
www.ffgolf.org

**Provence-Alpes-
Côte d'Azur
Regional Tourist
Board**
10 place de la Joillette,
Marseille. *Tel 04 91 56 47
00.* www.crt-paca.fr

## HORSE RIDING

**Ligue Régionale de
Provence de Sports
Equestres**
298 avenue du Club
Hippique,
13090 Aix-en-Provence.
*Tel 04 42 20 88 02.*

## NATURISM

**Fédération
Française de
Naturisme**
5 rue Regnault,
93500 Pantin.
*Tel 08 92 69 32 82.*
www.ffn-naturisme.com

## SKIING

**Fédération
Française de la
Montagne et de
l'Escalade**
8 quai de la Marne,
75019 Paris. *Tel 01 40 18
75 50.* www.ffme.fr

**Fédération
Française de Ski**
50, Avenue des
Marquisats, Annecy.
*Tel 04 50 51 40 34.*
www.ffs.fr

## SPA BREAKS

**La Bastide de Gordes**
Le Village, 84220 Gordes.
www.bastide-de-
gordes.com

**Hôtel Thalazur**
770 Chemin des
Moyennes Bréguières,
06600 Antibes.
*Tel 04 92 91 82 00.*
www.antibes.thalazur.fr

**Le Mas Candille**
Boulevard Clément
Rebuffet, 06250 Mougins.
*Tel 04 92 28 43 43.*
www.lemascandille.com

## WALKING,
## CLIMBING AND
## CYCLING

**Comité
Departemental de
la Randonnée
Pédestre**
4 avenue de Verdun,
Cagnes-sur-Mer.
*Tel 04 93 20 74 73.*
www.cdrp06.org

**Fédération Française
de Cyclisme**
5 rue de Rome, 93561
Rosny-sous-Bois. *Tel 01 49
35 69 00.* www.ffc.fr

**Fédération Française
de Randonnée
Pédestre**
64 rue du Dessous des
Berges, 75013 Paris.
*Tel 01 44 89 93 93.*
www.ffrandonnee.fr

**Maison du Parc
Naturel Régional
du Luberon**
60 place Jean Jaurès.
*Tel 04 90 04 42 00.*
www.parcduluberon.fr

## WATER SPORTS

**Fédération Française
d'Etudes et de
Sports Sous-Marins**
24 Quai Rive-Neuve,
Marseille.
*Tel 04 91 33 99 31.*
www.ffessm.fr

**Fédération
Française de Voile**
17, rue Henri Bocquillon,
75015 Paris.
*Tel 01 40 60 37 00.*
www.ffv.fr

**Les Amis de
Calanques**
Chemin de la Louisiane
Ceyresée, La Ciotat.
*Tel 06 09 33 54 98.*

# SURVIVAL
# GUIDE

# PRACTICAL INFORMATION

The peak holiday period for Provence runs from the middle of June until the end of August. During this time, the coastal areas in particular are very crowded. However, the region offers a range of activities throughout the year to suit all tastes: skiing slopes in the winter, golden beaches in the summer, excellent modern art museums, fine Roman ruins, traditional festivals and superb food and wine. Tourist offices are excellent sources of general information and accommodation advice (*see* Where to Stay *pp190–3*). The main branches in Provence are listed opposite. Shops and banks tend to close between noon and 3pm, so take advantage of this to enjoy a long, leisurely lunch, bearing in mind an old local saying: "Slow in the mornings, and not too fast in the afternoons."

**FNOTSI**
National logo
for tourist information

**Enjoying a relaxed lunch on a vine-shaded terrace**

## WHEN TO GO

During high season in Provence, local businesses in tourist areas hope to make their whole year's profit, and set their prices higher accordingly. The coast in particular can get very busy so to avoid the crowds, head for the wilds of upper Provence or the hills of the Var and Vaucluse.

Provence is at its best in May and September when the weather is still warm, but there are fewer visitors. The winter months can offer some sunny days, but beware of the cold mistral wind that can sweep through the area. A few festivals, such as the Nice Carnival and the Lemon Festival in Menton, are cleverly timed so as to attract off-season tourists, and skiing is usually possible between mid-November and April (*see p96*).

## WHAT TO TAKE

Apart from prescription drugs, you should find everything you need in local shops. People dress quite casually, but you should take care to be respectful when visiting churches, and some restaurants have a more formal dress code.

## VISAS AND PASSPORTS

Currently there are no visa requirements for EU nationals or for tourists from the US, Canada, Australia or New Zealand staying in France for under three months.
After that a residency permit (*carte de séjour*) is required. Visitors from other countries should ask for visa information from their local French authorities prior to departure. Like most EU countries (but not the UK and Ireland) France is part of the Schengen agreement for shared border controls. When you enter the Schengen area through any of the member states, your 90-day stay will be valid for all of them, even if you travel between several countries during your trip.

## CUSTOMS INFORMATION

Visitors from outside the European Union can claim back the sales tax (*TVA*) levied on French goods if they spend more than €175 in one shop on the same day. To claim your refund, you must obtain an export sales form (*bordereau de vente à l'exportation*) and take your goods out of the EU within three months of the date of purchase. The form should be signed by both the retailer and yourself. Hand it in to customs officials when you leave the EU, and they will give you a set of forms that you should send back to the shop. The refund will then be sent on to you or credited to your bank card. Exceptions for this *détaxe* rebate are food and drink, medicines, tobacco, cars and motorbikes.

There are no restrictions on the quantities of duty-paid and VAT-paid goods one is allowed to take from one EU country to another as long as they are for personal use and not for resale. However, you may be asked to prove that goods are for your own use if they exceed the recommended amounts: 10 litres of spirits, 90 litres of wine, 110 litres of beer and 800 cigarettes.

Non-EU nationals arriving in the European Union may bring in the following: up to 2 litres of wine and 1 litre of spirits (or 2 litres of drink less than 22° proof); 50cc of perfume; 500g of coffee; 100g of tea and up to 200 cigarettes. Visitors under 17 may not import or export duty-free alcohol or

**The tourist office at Monieux, Vaucluse**

tobacco, even as gifts. In general, personal goods (such as a car or a bicycle) may be imported to France free of duty and without any paperwork as long as they are for personal use and not for resale. A brochure called *Voyagez en Toute Liberté*, available from the **Centre des Renseignements des Douanes**, has further details on this.

Special rules apply for the import and export of plants, medicines, animals, weapons and art objects. Be sure to consult your own or French customs before travelling.

## TOURIST INFORMATION

Most large towns have a tourist office (*Office de Tourisme* or *Syndicat d'Initiative*); in smaller villages, it is the town hall (*mairie*) that provides information. Tourist offices will supply free maps and details on local events and accommodation; they will also book hotel rooms on your behalf.

## ETIQUETTE

The French rituals of politeness apply in Provence too. When introduced to a new person,

it is correct to shake hands. In shops, say *bonjour* before asking what you want, then *merci* when you receive your change and *au revoir* when you depart. In supermarkets, the cashier will not say *bonjour* to you until they have finished with the previous customer. The usual greeting among friends of both sexes is generally two or three kisses on the cheeks.

In smaller communities, any efforts made by English speakers to communicate in French and show a real interest in the area will be met with encouragement.

## OPENING TIMES

Opening hours for museums are usually 9am–noon and 2–5:30pm, but they vary according to the season, with longer hours being kept from May to September. Most museums close one day a week: national museums on Mondays and municipal ones on Tuesdays. Be advised that many museums close for the entire month of November.

Most businesses open from 8 or 9am until noon and from 2 or 3pm to 6 or 7pm. Banks

The beautifully decorated façade of the Musée Matisse in Nice

are open 8:30am–noon and 1:30–4:30pm Monday to Friday and sometimes on Saturday mornings. Department stores, supermarkets, tourist offices and some sights may remain open during the lunch break.

Restaurants often close one day a week, usually Monday; many will also close on Sunday evenings.

In winter, much of seaside Provence shuts down. Phone ahead to check what is open, because some establishments may be closed for months. Transport services may also be restricted out of season.

# DIRECTORY

## FRENCH TOURIST OFFICES ABROAD

**Australia**
25 Bligh St, Level 13,
Sydney, NSW 2000.
*Tel* (2) 9231 5244.
http://au.franceguide.com

**Canada**
1800 Av MacGill College,
Suite 490, Montreal
H3A 3J6.
*Tel* (514) 288 2026.
http://ca.franceguide.com

**United Kingdom**
300 High Holborn,
London WC1 VJH.
*Tel* (09068) 244 123.
http://uk.franceguide.com

**USA**
825 Third Ave 29th Floor,
New York, NY 10022.
*Tel* (514) 288 1904.
http://us.france
guide.com

## TOURIST OFFICES IN PROVENCE

**Aix-en-Provence**
2 Pl du Général de Gaulle.
*Tel* 04 42 16 11 61.
www.aixenprovence
tourism.com

**Arles**
Boulevard des Lices.
*Tel* 04 90 18 41 20.
www.tourisme.
ville-arles.fr

**Avignon**
41 Cours Jean-Jaurès.
*Tel* 04 32 74 32 74.
www.avignon-
tourisme.com

**Cannes**
Palais des Festivals,
La Croisette.
*Tel* 04 92 99 84 22.
www.cannes.fr

**Draguignan**
2 Blvd Lazare Carnot.

*Tel* 04 98 10 51 05.
www.dracenie.com

**Marseille**
4 La Canebière.
*Tel* 04 91 13 89 00.
www.marseille-
tourisme.com

**Monte Carlo**
2A Boulevard
des Moulins.
*Tel* 00 377 92 16 61 16.
www.visitmonaco.com

**Nice**
5 Promenade des Anglais.
*Tel* 08 92 70 74 07.
www.nicetourism.com

**Nîmes**
6 Rue Auguste.
*Tel* 04 66 58 38 00.
www.ot-nimes.fr

**St-Tropez**
Quai Jean-Jaurès.
*Tel* 08 92 68 48 28.
www.ot-saint-tropez.com

## CUSTOMS INFORMATION

**Centre des Renseignements des Douanes**
23 Rue de l'Université,
75007 Paris.
*Tel* 08 11 20 44 44.
www.douane.gouv.fr

**Marseille**
48 Av. R. Schuman.
*Tel* 04 91 26 25 25.

## USEFUL WEBSITES

**Anglo Info**
www.riviera.
angloinfo.com

**Provence Web**
www.provenceweb.fr

**Provence & Beyond**
www.beyond.fr

The striking Hôtel de Ville of Aix-en-Provence

## ADMISSION PRICES

Museum admission prices range from around €3 to €12. National museums are free the first Sunday of the month, and nearly all municipal museums offer free or discounted entry on Sundays.

The Carte Musée Côte d'Azur, which allows unlimited access to more than 50 museums in the region, can be purchased from participating museums, FNAC stores (see p226) and certain tourist offices (see p237). There is also the Nice Riviera Pass, which offers free access to many sights and has various discounts available; see www.niceriverapass.com for more information.

Churches normally offer free admission, but a small charge may be levied to visit cloisters and chapels.

## TIPPING AND TAXES

Most restaurants include a service charge of 10–15 per cent as part of the bill, so there is no need to tip. In a bar or café, leave some small change. A small amount is usually given to taxi drivers, despite service being included. Hotel porters, hairdressers and tour guides will expect a tip of around €2.

## TRAVELLERS WITH SPECIAL NEEDS

Provence's narrow streets can make it a difficult area for travellers with limited mobility.

On the plus side, disabled parking spaces are plentiful (remember to bring your international orange disc with you), and wheelchairs and other useful equipment can be hired at pharmacies. Wheelchair access is still rather limited, although newer buildings will have ramps and other facilities.

The train company SNCF has carriages designed to accommodate wheelchair users (see pp246–7), and taxi drivers are also obliged to take disabled people and guide dogs.

For more information, visit Access-Able Travel Source (www.access-able.com).

**International Student Identity Card**

## TRAVELLING WITH CHILDREN

Many hotels have family rooms, but if they don't you can ask them to add a cot or an extra bed. There may be an additional charge for this. If you are hiring a car and need child seats, be sure to book them in advance and ask for them to be fitted for you. Children are eligible for discounted train travel.

## GAY AND LESBIAN TRAVELLERS

There is a strong network of gay and lesbian venues in

Provence; this includes bars, discos and beaches. For listings of gay-friendly hotels and activities, visit the websites listed in the directory on the opposite page.

## TRAVELLING ON A BUDGET

Provence is not the cheapest region in France, but prices are much more reasonable out of season. Staying inland rather than in a seaside resort will also save money. Ask the local tourist office for advice on affordable accommodation, such as hostels and campsites. Travelling by public transport is cheaper than hiring a car, and along the coast this is a perfectly adequate option (see pp246–8 and p252). Buying carnets of tickets for travel on public transport in major towns will also save money. Visiting attractions doesn't have to be costly either, as most museums have free days. Check to see if there are cheaper family tickets too. However, most of the real pleasure of Provence can be experienced for free and consists of admiring the spectacular views of the Mediterranean and mountains, swimming in the sea, walking on the beach and hiking in the hills and national parks.

## STUDENT TRAVELLERS

Students carrying a valid International Student Identification Card (ISIC) benefit from discounts of between 25 and 50 per cent at museums, theatres, cinemas and many of the public monuments.

The region's main university is split between Aix-en-Provence and Marseille; other large universities are located in Avignon and Nice. You will find the **Bureau Information Jeunesse** (BIJ) and the **Centre Régional Information Jeunesse** (CRIJ) in all university towns. These organizations can provide a great deal of information about student life and a list of inexpensive accommodation options. For a list of hostels in the main towns see page 193.

## PROVENCE TIME

Provence is one hour ahead of Greenwich Mean Time (GMT). It is in the same time zone as Italy, Spain and other western European countries. Standard time differences between Provence and other areas of the world may vary according to local summer alterations to the time.

The French use the 24-hour military clock rather than "am" and "pm".

## ELECTRICAL ADAPTORS

The voltage in France is 220 volts. British appliances of 240 volts can be used with an adaptor, while American 110 volts appliances will need a transformer (*transformateur*).

Plugs have two small round pins; heavier-duty installations have two large round pins. Some of the more upmarket hotels offer built-in adaptors for shavers. Multi-adaptors, useful because they have both large and small pins, can be bought at most airports before departure; standard adaptors can be purchased from department stores.

Façade of the Russian Orthodox church in Nice

## RELIGIOUS SERVICES

Provence is a strong Catholic region, with many religious services and festivals dating back 500 years. In recent decades, immigrants have

brought increasing religious diversification. Regular services in English are held at the Anglican churches in Nice and Marseille.

## RESPONSIBLE TRAVEL

Throughout France there has been a rapid growth in environmental awareness. **Echoway** is one of the leading French ecotourism organizations, which encourages responsible travel. Provence has a long-running rural tourism network, with farmhouse accommodation available through the central **Gîtes de France**. There are also smaller organizations with a more defined ecological stance such as **Accueil Paysan**, which is a network of small-scale farmers practising low-impact, sustainable agriculture. Finally there are hundreds of fully equipped campsites throughout Provence (*see pp192–3*).

Information on local green tourism (*tourisme vert* or *eco*) initiatives and activities can be found through *département* and local tourist offices. Many towns have weekly markets selling only organic and traditional produce (usually called a *marché bio*), which allow visitors to give back to the local community. If a town does not have a separate market dedicated to organic produce, there are often stalls within the main market that are exclusively *bio*, as is the case at Nice's market on the cours Saleya. Market days have been provided throughout the guide.

## CONVERSION CHART

**Imperial to metric**
1 inch = 2.54 centimetres
1 foot = 30 centimetres
1 mile = 1.6 kilometres
1 ounce = 28 grams
1 pound = 454 grams
1 pint (UK) = 0.6 litre
1 gallon (UK) = 4.6 litres

**Metric to imperial**
1 millimetre = 0.04 inch
1 centimetre = 0.4 inch
1 metre = 3 feet 3 inches
1 kilometre = 0.6 mile
1 gram = 0.04 ounce
1 kilogram = 2.2 pounds

# DIRECTORY

## TRAVELLERS WITH SPECIAL NEEDS

**Association HORUS (Society for the Blind)**
Nice. **Tel** 04 92 09 03 48.
www.horus-asso.org

**Comité National Français de Liaison pour la Readaption des Handicapées**
Paris. **Tel** 01 53 80 66 44.

**Groupement pour l'Insertion des Personnes Handicapées Physiques**
Nice. **Tel** 04 93 26 77 16.
www.gihpnational.org

## GAY AND LESBIAN TRAVELLERS

**La France Gaie et Lesbienne**
www.france.qrd.org

**Gay Provence**
www.gayprovence.org

**International Gay & Lesbian Travel Association**
www.iglta.org

## STUDENT INFORMATION

**Aix-en-Provence**
BIJ, 37 bis blvd
Aristide-Briand.
**Tel** 04 42 91 98 01.

**Marseille**
CRIJ, 96 La Canebière.
**Tel** 04 91 24 33 50.
www.crijpa.com

**Nice**
CRIJ, 19 rue Gioffredo.
**Tel** 04 93 80 93 93.
www.crijca.fr

## RESPONSIBLE TRAVEL

**Accueil Paysan**
www.accueil-paysan.com

**Echoway**
www.echoway.org

**Gîtes-de-France**
www.gites-de-france.com

# Personal Security and Health

On the whole Provence is a fairly safe place for visitors, however, it is wise to take a few precautions. Extra caution is required in the larger cities and along the Côte d'Azur, especially in Nice, which has a higher crime rate than Marseille. Car crime is prevalent along the coast, so make sure you never leave your valuables in a vehicle. You should also avoid groups of innocent-looking children who may, in fact, be skilled in the art of pickpocketing. Consular offices can be good sources of help in the event of an emergency (see the directory box opposite). Rural areas are usually very safe.

Policeman              Fireman

## PERSONAL PROPERTY

Pickpockets are common in the tourist areas of the Côte d'Azur and in larger towns. In Nice, bag snatching is on the rise, but fortunately muggings are still rare. Take care of your belongings at all times. Choose travellers' cheques as the safest form of currency, and avoid carrying valuables with you when sightseeing.

Try not to park your car in remote areas, and use multi-storey car parks if you can. These are monitored by video cameras, and parking there will also remove the risk of being towed away, which is a greater everyday issue than most car crime.

It is not advisable to sleep on the beach, since robberies and attacks have been known to take place there at night.

In the event of a theft, go to the nearest police station *(gendarmerie)* with your identity papers (and vehicle papers, if relevant). The report process *(procès-verbal,* or *PV)* may take time, but you will need a police statement for any insurance claim you make. If your passport is stolen, contact the police and your nearest consulate (see opposite).

## PERSONAL SAFETY

Certain train routes – for example the Marseille-Barcelona and Marseille-Ventimiglia (Italy) lines – have dubious reputations. Stay alert and keep the compartment door shut and your valuables close to you, especially if you are travelling at night.

Some tourist visiting the area during the summer, have been victims of acts of road piracy, with their vehicle being rammed on the motorway to force them to stop. There are police stations at most motorway exits, so if you encounter any trouble, try to stay calm and keep going until the next exit.

## LEGAL ASSISTANCE

If your insurance policy is comprehensive (including a legal service in France), they will be able to help with legal advice on claims, such as accident procedure. If you are not insured, call your nearest consulate office.

## WOMEN TRAVELLERS

Women should take the usual precautions: wearing their bag strapped across the body; being careful after dark; avoiding quiet, unfamiliar areas; locking the car doors when driving; and taking care on trains, especially sleepers.

Police car

Fire engine

Ambulance

For contraceptive advice, go to a GP or a gynaecologist (no referral is necessary); to find one, ask at a pharmacy or look in the Yellow Pages *(Pages Jaunes)*. Pharmacies are also excellent sources of advice and can dispense the morning-after pill without a prescription.

## OUTDOOR HAZARDS

Forest fires are a major risk in Provence. High winds and dry forests mean that fire spreads rapidly, so be vigilant about putting out cigarette butts. Camp fires are banned in the region. If you witness a fire, contact the emergency services at once and keep well away.

The Mediterranean Sea is safe for swimming, although there can be strong currents off the Cap d'Antibes and the Camargue. Public beaches usually have a lifeguard and indicate safe areas for swimming; some display European blue flags as a sign of cleanliness. If you are stung by a jellyfish or sea urchin, seek advice from a pharmacy. If you are sailing, keep up to date with the weather reports, and carry ID and a radio or mobile phone.

Weather conditions in the mountains can change very quickly and without warning. In winter, be sure to advise the local authorities of your projected route; in summer, pack warm clothes and some provisions in case of sudden storms. Altitude sickness can occur in the southern Alps, so climb slowly, pausing regularly to acclimatize.

In the mountains behind Nice and Cannes, you may encounter the grey-brown Montpellier snake. Despite its size (up to 1.5 m/5 ft), it is very shy and will likely flee. Vipers also live in the region. Mosquitoes are common, and repellents and antidotes can be bought from supermarkets or pharmacies. The local lavender oil is an excellent repellent and a good antiseptic

treatment for mosquito bites and wasp stings if applied immediately. Occasionally hornets and scorpions can be a problem, so get into the habit of always checking shoes and clothing before getting dressed. Also check your bedding before going to sleep. Beware of the heat, especially with children, and seek immediate medical advice for heat stroke.

During the hunting season (Sep–Feb, especially on Sundays), wear brightly coloured clothes when out walking. Signs on trees usually denote hunting areas *(reserve du chasse)*.

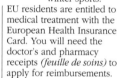

**Fire-hazard poster**

## TRAVEL AND HEALTH INSURANCE

Check that your travel insurance is valid in France, and note that you will need extra insurance to cover winter sports. EU residents are entitled to medical treatment with the European Health Insurance Card. You will need the doctor's and pharmacy receipts *(feuille de soins)* to apply for reimbursements.

## MEDICAL TREATMENT

Pharmacists can diagnose and suggest treatments for simple conditions; they can be recognized by the green cross outside. There is usually one pharmacy open at night and at weekends. Hospital accident-and-emergency units will deal with accidents and unexpected illnesses. In rural areas, the *pompiers* (firefighters) are also trained paramedics and can be called in an emergency. In major cities, a 24-hour doctor service *(médecin de garde)* is available.

## PUBLIC TOILETS

Modern automatic toilets are widely available in cities. You may also come across public toilets of the squat variety, in which case you might prefer to use the services in a café or department store.

# DIRECTORY

## CONSULATES

**Australia**
4 Rue Jean Rey,
75015 Paris.
*Tel* 01 40 59 33 00.
www.france.embassy.gov.au

**Ireland**
152 Blvd John Kennedy,
Cap d'Antibes.
*Tel* 04 93 61 50 63.

**UK**
24 Avenue du Prado,
Marseille
*Tel* 04 91 15 72 10.
www.ukinfrance.fco.gov.uk

**USA**
12 Place Varian Fry,
Marseille.
*Tel* 04 91 54 92 00.
www.france.usembassy.
gov/marseille.html

## EMERGENCY NUMBERS

**AIDS Helpline**
*Tel* 0800 84 08 00.

**Ambulance (SAMU)**
*Tel* 15.

**Centre Anti-Poison (Marseille)**
*Tel* 04 91 75 25 25.

**Drugs/Tobacco/Alcohol Hotline**
*Tel* 113.

**Fire (Sapeurs Pompiers)**
*Tel* 18.

**Police (Gendarmerie)**
*Tel* 17.

**Rape Hotline**
*Tel* 0800 05 95 95.

**SOS Médecins**
Nice.
*Tel* 08 10 85 01 01.

## HOSPITAL EMERGENCIES

**Avignon**
Hôpital Général Henri Duffaut,
305 Rue Raoul Follereau.
*Tel* 04 32 75 31 90.
www.ch-avignon.fr

**Marseille**
La Conception,
147 Blvd Baille.
*Tel* 04 91 38 30 00.

**Nice**
Hôpital St-Roch,
5 Rue Pierre-Devoluy.
*Tel* 04 92 03 33 33.

# Banks and Local Currency

Visitors to Provence may change currency in a variety of locations, but it is always wise to arrive with at least a few euros. Credit cards are widely accepted for purchases and in restaurants, but if in doubt, ask in advance. Credit cards and bank cards can also be used to withdraw money, but check the charges levied by the credit card company first.

## BANKS AND CURRENCY EXCHANGE

Banks in big towns usually open from 8:30am to noon and from 1:30 to 4:30pm Monday to Friday and Saturday morning. They are closed during public holidays.

There is no limit to the amount of money you may bring into France, but if you wish to take more than €10,000 back to the UK, you should declare it on arrival. It is wise to carry large sums of money as travellers' cheques.

You will need your four-digit PIN code (code confidentiel) to withdraw money from ATMs (but check the charges levied for this service) and for payment in shops and restaurants. ATM instructions are usually given in French, English and Italian. Note that ATMs may run out of notes just before the weekend.

Travellers' cheques can be obtained from American Express, Thomas Cook or your bank. It is recommended that you have them issued in euros. American Express cheques are widely accepted in France; if they are exchanged at an AmEx office, no commission is charged. In the event of theft, travellers' cheques are replaced at once.

The most common credit cards in France, accepted even at motorway tolls, are Carte Bleue/Visa and Eurocard/MasterCard. Because of the high commissions charged, some Provençal businesses do not accept American Express.

## DIRECTORY

### FOREIGN BANKS

**Cannes**
Barclays, 8 rue Frédéric Amouretti.
*Tel* 04 92 99 68 00
www.barclays.fr

**Marseille**
Barclays, rue de Rome
*Tel* 04 91 00 01 15
www.barclays.fr

**Nice**
American Express,
Aeroport terminal 1.
*Tel* 04 93 215 979
Barclays, 2 rue A Karr.
*Tel* 04 93 82 68 00

**Nimes**
Barclays, 20 bd Gambetta.
*Tel* 04 91 13 98 31

### LOST CARDS AND TRAVELLERS' CHEQUES

Visa.
*Tel* 0800 80 1179
Mastercard
*Tel* 0800 901 387
American Express Cards and Cheques
*Tel* 0800 832 820

## Banknotes and Coins

*Euro bank notes have seven denominations. The €5 note is grey, the €10 is pink, the €20 is blue, the €50 is orange, the €100 is green, the €200 is yellow and the €500 is purple. There are eight coin denominations: €1 and €2 coins are silver and gold; those worth 50 cents, 20 cents and 10 cents are gold, while the 5-, 2- and 1- coins are bronze.*

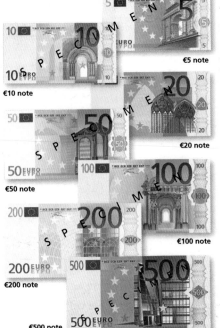

**€5 note**

**€10 note**

**€20 note**

**€50 note**

**€100 note**

**€200 note**

**€500 note**

**€2 coin**      **€1 coin**

**50 cents**      **20 cents**      **10 cents**

**5 cents**      **2 cents**      **1 cents**

# Communications & Media

**Sign for public telephone**

The main telephone company is France Télécom, while postal services are run by La Poste. Post offices *(bureaux de postes)* are identified by the blue-on-yellow "La Poste" sign. In small villages, the post office may be in the town hall *(mairie)*. Internet access is readily available via Internet cafés, hotels and WiFi.

Mail boxes throughout France are a distinctive yellow

## TELEPHONE CALLS

Public phone boxes can be found throughout Provence, and they take telephone cards *(télécartes)* and credit cards. Telephone cards can be purchased at post offices, *tabacs* and some newsagents; they come in units of 50 or 120.

**Home Direct** calling service (or *pays direct*) lets you make the call via an operator in your country, paying with a credit card or by reversing charges. Reverse-charge calls are known as *PCV*. Main post offices offer long-distance calling facilities from booths *(cabines)*.

## MOBILE PHONES

A mobile phone from another European country can be used in France, though you may need to inform your network in advance so that it can be enabled. US-based mobiles need to be tri-band to work in France.

International calls on mobile phones are expensive. As an alternative, replace your SIM card with a French card and number. Note, however, that French top-up vouchers have strict expiry periods.

## INTERNET ACCESS

Internet facilities are readily available, and many hotels also offer WiFi. The larger towns will have several Internet cafés, lists of which can be obtained from local tourist offices. The major ports in Provence are all equipped with WiFi.

## POSTAL SERVICES

Postage stamps *(timbres)* can be purchased singly or in books *(carnets)* of ten from post offices or *tabacs*.

Post office hours vary. The maximum hours are around 9am–5pm on weekdays, with a lunch break (noon–2pm), and 9am–noon on Saturdays.

To send letters from France, drop them into the yellow mail boxes. These often have three slots: one for the town you are in; the other two for the surrounding *département* and other destinations.

## NEWSPAPERS AND MAGAZINES

In main cities and airports, international papers can often be bought on the day of publication. *The Connexion* is a monthly newspaper devoted to France, and Provence also has its own English-language publications. Most major towns have an English bookshop *(see p221)*, often an invaluable source of information.

## TELEVISION AND RADIO

The subscription channel Canal+ broadcasts ABC American evening news at 7am daily. Sky News and CNN are available in many hotels. The Franco-German channel ARTE broadcasts programmes and films from all over the world, often in the original language with French subtitles. Listings indicate *vo* or *vf (version originale* and *version française)* for non-French films.

Riviera Radio broadcasts in English throughout the South of France on 106.3 and 106.5 FM stereo from Monte Carlo. The station offers music and current affairs, including BBC World Service programmes. *France Musique* (92.2 FM in Nice and 94.7 in Marseille) specializes in classical music, while *France Info* (105.2–105.8 FM) is a national rolling-news station.

*(see p221)*

## DIRECTORY

### DIALLING CODES

**Operator**
*Tel* 12.

**Home Direct**
*Tel* 0800 0900.

**International calls**
*Tel* 00 + country code.

**Mobile phones**
*Tel* 06 + number.

**Mobile phone services**
www.0044.co.uk
www.orange.fr
www.sfr.fr

### INTERNET CAFES

**Avignon**
Webzone Cybercafé,
3 rue St Jean le Vieux.
*Tel* 04 32 76 29 47.

**Cannes**
Dre@mcybercafé,
6 Rue Commandant Vidal.
*Tel* 04 93 38 26 79.

**Dignes-les-Bains**
Cyber Café Municipale,
45 avenue du Mai 1945.
*Tel* 04 92 30 87 17.

**Marseille**
Magic Café, 20 rue du Docteur
Escat. *Tel* 04 91 35 75 76.

**Monaco**
Stars 'N' Bars, 6 quai Antoine 1er.
*Tel* 00 377 97 97 95 95.

**Nice**
Cyberpoint, 10 avenue Felix Faure.
*Tel* 04 93 92 70 63.

**St-Tropez**
Kreatik Café, 19 avenue du
Général Leclerc.
*Tel* 04 94 97 40 61.

# TRAVEL INFORMATION

Situated at the crossroads between France, Spain and Italy, Provence is well served by international motorway and rail links. Nice airport is the most modern and the busiest of French airports outside Paris, handling 4 million visitors from all over the world annually. Marseille airport also welcomes daily direct flights from most major European cities. For travelling across France, the TGV train is swift *(see p246)*, while the motorail journey from channel ports takes 12 hours, but is effortless and dispenses with motorway tolls. The autoroutes are excellent, but do become crowded in mid-summer.

**Air France
Boeing 737**

## ARRIVING BY AIR

The two main airports in Provence – Marseille, and Nice Côte d'Azur, which is the second biggest airport in France – are comfortale and modern. **Marseille Provence** (or **Marseille-Marignane**) has national and international flights serving mainly business travellers, and a new low-cost air terminal, MP2. It is useful for destinations in western Provence, such as Avignon and Aix-en-Provence.

Airport taxis to the centre of Marseille cost around €40 (€50 at night and on Sundays). There is also an airport bus to the main train station in Marseille (St-Charles), which leaves every 20 minutes. Car hire companies at the airport include Avis, Budget, Citer, Ada, Europcar and Hertz. **Nice Côte d'Azur** has two terminals. The east terminal (one) takes international flights and some domestic flights on French carriers (Air Littoral and TAT). The west terminal (two) serves domestic flights only. There is a shuttle bus between the buildings, but it is best to make sure you know which terminal you will be using. Taxis to the centre of town cost €25–€30. Airport buses run to the Gare Routière station every 10 minutes, and bus No. 99 goes to Gare SNCF every 30 minutes. There are buses to Cannes every half hour and to Monaco and Menton every hour. **Héli-Air Monaco** offers regular helicopter transits to Monaco, St-Tropez and Cannes, while **Nice Helicoptères** also has many daily flights to Cannes. There are several car hire companies at Nice airport, including Avis, Budget, Europcar and Hertz.

There are three other airports in or near Provence which operate international flights; these are Montpellier, Nîmes and Toulon.

## AIRLINE DETAILS

Provence is the most easily accessible place by air in France after Paris. The vast majority of major European cities have daily direct flights. The British carriers – **British Airways**, **easyJet**, **Ryanair** and **BMI** – all run daily flights from London Heathrow, London Gatwick, Luton, Stansted or Manchester to Nice, Nimes, Marseille, Montpellier or Toulon. Other low-cost airlines include **Flybe**, which flies to Nice from Southampton and Exeter, and **bmibaby**, which flies to Nice from Birmingham. The French national airline, **Air France**, has daily flights to and from Nice to Britain, Spain, Germany, Italy and North Africa.

There is a **Delta** flight from Nice to New York several times a week, and **Emirates** also flies to Nice from Dubai five times a week. From all other international departure

The main international terminal at Nice, Côte d'Azur airport

**Departure hall at Marseille airport**

points you will be required to change planes in Paris to reach Provence.

## FARES AND DEALS

The large number of low-cost airlines flying to Provence mean that there is a wide range of prices on offer. Fares are at their highest over the Easter period and in July and August. Make sure you check which airport you are flying to when booking, as some low-cost airlines use smaller airports that may be some distance from the city centre.

## FLY-DRIVE AND FLY-RAIL PACKAGE HOLIDAYS

Air France and SNCF offer combined fares for flight and train. You fly into Paris and then catch the train south. Good deals are available for the main destinations such as Avignon, Arles, Nice and Marseille. For details on fly-drive packages see page 250.

There are also a wide variety of companies offering tailor-made package holidays in Provence, with flight, car hire and accommodation included in the cost.

## GREEN TRAVEL

Travelling in France without using high-impact flights or long car drives is easier than in many countries thanks primarily to the high quality of public transport, and above all the SNCF rail network.

The French government has introduced an "Ecomobility" programme, which aims to encourage a reduction in car use by making it easier to transfer from SNCF trains to local buses, bikes or other forms of transport (for more information, see www.sncf.com). This includes free-cycle schemes like the *Vélib* now in use in Marseille and Aix-en-Provence (*see p253*). There are cycle-hire shops in many towns and your local tourist offices will be able to provide more information on cycle hire facilities and routes in their area. There are also good facilities for taking your bikes on SCNF trains (*see p248*). If you don't hike or cycle, however, exploring the country-side will still be difficult without a car, as local buses are often slow and infrequent.

# DIRECTORY

## AIRPORT INFORMATION

**Avignon-Caumont**
*Tel 04 90 81 51 51.*
Airport to city 10 km (6 miles). Taxi €24.
**www**.avignon-airport.com

**Marseille Provence**
*Tel 04 42 14 14 14.*
Airport to city 25 km (17 miles). Shuttle bus €10, taxi €40.
**www**.mrsairport.com

**Montpellier Méditerranée**
*Tel 04 67 20 85 00.*
Airport to city 7 km (4 miles). Shuttle bus €8, taxi €15–€20.
**www**.montpellier.aeroport.fr

**Nice, Côte d'Azur**
*Tel 0820 423 333.*
Airport to city 6 km (4 miles). Shuttle bus €4, taxi €25–€30.
**www**.nice.aeroport.fr

**Nîmes/Arles/Camargue**
*Tel 04 66 70 49 49.*
Airport to city 15 km (9 miles). Shuttle bus €5, taxi €25.
**www**.nimes.aeroport.fr

**Toulon-Hyères**
*Tel 08 25 01 83 87.*
Airport to city 23 km (15 miles). Shuttle bus €1.40, taxi €40.
**www**.toulon-hyeres.aeroport.fr

## AIRLINE DETAILS

**Air France**
UK *Tel 0871 66 33 777.*
France *Tel 3654.*
**www**.airfrance.com

**British Airways**
France *Tel 0825 825 400.*
UK *Tel 0844 493 0787.*
**www**.britishairways.com

**bmibaby**
UK *Tel 0871 224 0224.*
**www**.bmibaby.com

**(BMI)British Midland**
UK *Tel 0870 6070555.*
**www**.flybmi.com

**Delta**
France *Tel 0811 640 005.*
US *Tel 0800 221 1212.*
**www**.delta.com

**easyJet**
France *Tel 0826 103 320.*
UK *Tel 0871 244 2366.*
**www**.easyjet.com

**Emirates**
France *Tel 0153 053 535.*
UK *Tel 844 800 2777.*
**www**.emirates.com

**Flybe**
UK *Tel 0871 700 2000.*
**www**.flybe.com

**Ryanair**
France *Tel 0892 232 375.*
UK *Tel 0871 246 0000.*
**www**.ryanair.com

## HELICOPTER SERVICES

**Héli-Air Monaco**
*Tel 00 377 92 050050.*
**www**.heliairmonaco.com

**Nice Helicoptères**
*Tel 04 93 21 34 32.*
**www**.niceheli copteres.com

## DISCOUNT TRAVEL AGENCIES

**Jancarthier Voyages**
7 cours Sextius.
*Tel 04 42 93 48 48.*
**www**.jancarthier.fr

**Voyages Wasteels**
67 la Canebière.
*Tel 04 95 09 30 60.*
**www**.wasteels.fr
**www**.thomascook.fr

**Trailfinders**
194 Kensington High St, London W8 6BD.
*Tel 020 7938 3939.*
**www**.trailfinders.com

# Getting Around by Train

SNCF logo

Travelling to Provence by train is fast and efficient. The French state railway, Société Nationale des Chemins de Fer **(SNCF)**, is one of Europe's best equipped and most comfortable. The train journey from Paris to Avignon is almost as quick as by air – the TGV *(Train à Grande Vitesse)* takes only four hours. The Channel Tunnel provides a fast rail link via Calais between Provence and the UK, although not all of the route is high-speed.

The interior of Avignon TGV train station

## TRAIN STATIONS

The main stations in the region are Marseille Gare St-Charles, Nîmes and Nice (Nice Ville av Thiers). All offer a range of facilities, including restaurants, shops, WiFi and secure left luggage lockers. Keep in mind that trains in France are punctual and very rarely leave late.

## MAIN ROUTES

The main train routes to Provence from Northern Europe pass through Lille and Paris. In Paris you have to transfer to the Gare de Lyon – the main Paris station serving the south of France. Tickets from London to Nice, Avignon and Marseille, via **Eurostar**, hover-craft or ferry, are all available from the **Rail Europe** office in London or on their website. The Eurostar connects at Lille or Paris with TGVs to the rest of France. Passengers arriving by sea at Calais can catch the train to Paris and transfer on to the Corail Lunéa overnight sleeper service to Nice.

From southern Europe, trains run to Marseille from Barcelona in Spain (6½ hours) and Genoa in Italy (3 hours).

Within Provence and the Côte d'Azur, the coastal route between Nice and Marseille is often crowded, so it is best to reserve tickets in advance on this and other *Grandes Lignes*. In the Var and Haute Provence, railway lines are scarce, but SNCF runs bus services. The private rail service **Chemins de Fer de Provence** runs the Train des Pignes *(see p181)*.

When purchasing a rail ticket – whether in France or abroad – it is also possible to pre-book a car *(Train + Auto)*, bike *(Train + Vélo)* or hotel *(Train + Hôtel)* to await you at your destination.

Further information on rail travel is provided on the main SNCF website.

## BOOKING FROM ABROAD

Tickets to and within France can be booked in the UK and US through Rail Europe and via www.voyages-sncf.com. Rail Europe also has information on prices and departure times. Reservations made abroad can be difficult to change once in France – you may have to pay for another reservation, or claim for a refund on your return.

## BOOKING IN FRANCE

Ticket counters at all stations are computerized. There are also automatic ticket and reservation machines (with English instructions) on the concourse of main stations. For travel by TGV, Corail and

## THE TGV TRAIN

Trains à Grande Vitesse, or high-speed trains, travel at up to 300 km/hr (185 mph). There are five versions of TGV serving all areas of France and some European destinations. The Eurostar links Paris and London, the Thalys runs to Brussels. The TGV Méditerranée to Provence leaves from Paris Gare de Lyon. Other TGVs leave from Grenoble, Geneva and Lausanne. The trains' speed, comfort and reliability make them relatively expensive. Always reserve a seat.

Paris to Marseille now takes just three hours by TGV

Motorail a reservation is essential but can be made as little as five-minutes before the train leaves, and up to 90 days in advance. Costs rise considerably at peak times. The international ticket and reservation system at Lille Europe station allows direct booking on services throughout the continent and the UK.

## FARES

TGVs have two price levels for 2nd class, normal and peak, and a single level for 1st class. The cost of the obligatory seat reservation is included in the ticket price. Tickets for other trains can be subject to a supplement and do not include the reservation charge of €3.

Discounts of 25 per cent are available for people travelling with children (*Découverte Enfant+*), for young people (*Découverte 12–25*), for the over-60s (*Découverte Senior*), for two people travelling together (*Découverte à Deux*), for return trips including a Saturday night (*Découverte Sejour*) and for advance booking (*Découverte J8 and Découverte J30*).

For those spending a bit more time on French railways, the SNCF issues a *Carte Enfant+* and a *Carte Senior* giving reductions of up to 50 per cent. Rail Europe can supply these cards.

**Inter-Rail** cards allow unlimited travel in European countries excluding the one of issue. (See the Inter-Rail website for more information.) **Eurail** passes are available to non-European residents and, in North America, France Railpass is another option.

## TYPES OF TRAIN

SNCF trains are divided into several different types. TGV trains are the flagships of the network, travelling on specially-built track at around 300 kph (185 mph). **Corail**

trains are long-distance express trains with modern carriages (Corail Téoz trains run by day, Corail Lunéa trains are overnight sleepers). Corail Intercités trains are slightly faster with fewer stops. Reservations are obligatory for all Corail services and can be made through Rail Europe or SNCF.

**Motorail** trains allow drivers to travel overnight with their car. The service runs from Calais to Nice via Avignon. Reservations are essential.

**TER** trains are regional services that usually stop at every station. Reservations are not required, and tickets are not normally available in advance. Route maps and information (in French only) are available at stations and on the TER website, see the directory box for details.

**The view from the Train des Pignes**

## SCENIC RAIL ROUTES

The private rail service **Chemins de Fer de Provence** runs the Train des Pignes, a 151-km (90-mile) ride from Nice to Dignes-les-Bains. This is a dramatic journey through tunnels and over viaducts, with magnificent views. The single-track railway from Nice to Cuneo in Italy via Peille, Sospel and Tende is also a spectacular ride through mountainous terrain. The Alpazur service runs in summer between Nice and Grenoble with a tourist steam train on the Puget-Théniers section; hikers can leave and rejoin the train after a day's walking. For more information see www.trainstouristiques-ter.com.

# DIRECTORY

## INFORMATION AND RESERVATIONS

### Autotrain
*Tel* 0844 848 4050

### Corail
www.coraillunea.com
www.corailteoz.com

### Eurail
www.eurail.com

### Eurostar
St Pancras International
Pancras Rd, London NW1
*Tel* 08705 186 186
Paris Gare du Nord, rue de
Dunkerque,75010 Paris
*Tel* 08 92 35 35 39.
www.eurostar.com

### Eurotunnel
(Off junction 11a, M20,
Folkestone)
*Tel* 08705 35 35 35
France *Tel* 08 10 63 03 04
www.eurotunnel.com

### Inter-Rail
www.interailnet.com

### Motorail
1 Lower Regent St,
London W1.
UK *Tel* 08448 484 050.
www.raileurope.co.uk

### Rail Europe
1 Lower Regent St, London
W1V 0BA.
*Tel* 08448 484 064.
www.raileurope.co.uk

### Rail Europe USA
226–230 West Chester Park,
White Plains, NY 10604.
*Tel* 888 4387 245
(freephone in US).
www.raileurope.com

### SNCF
France information 3635
Outside France 00 33 892
35 35 35
www.sncf.com

### TER
www.ter-sncf.com

## PRIVATE RAILWAY

### Chemins de Fer de Provence
*Tel* 04 97 03 80 80.
www.trainprovence.com

## BICYCLES ON TRAINS

Bicycles can be transported on the Eurostar, either as personal luggage if they fold to the size of a normal suitcase, or by advance reservation. You can transport your bike on nearly every single SNCF train, including the TGV. However, this service must be booked in advance, and in some cases your bicycle will be transported separately, and can take up to four days to arrive. Bikes may also be transported on local trains (indicated by a bicycle symbol in the timetable). The SNCF *train + velo* scheme allows you to reserve a rental bike at your destination station when you book your ticket, although be aware this option is only available on certain routes.

## TIMES AND PENALTIES

Timetables change twice a year in May and September. Leaflets for the main routes are free, and can also be checked on the SNCF website.

The Provence Alpes Côte d'Azur region has an all-inclusive TER timetable, which includes coach travel.

You must time-punch your ticket in the yellow *composteur* machine at the platform entrance or pay a penalty on the train. This is very easy to do, simply insert your ticket and (if you have one) separate seat reservation face up and the machine will date-stamp them.

## MOTORAIL

**Eurotunnel** rail shuttles vehicles between Folkstone and Calais in around 35 minutes. **Motorail** carries cars, motorbikes and passengers overnight from Calais to Provence. The journey is not cheap, but it is a practical, stress-free way to avoid the long drive south. You can reserve sleeping compartments exclusively for the people in your car. The service runs to Avignon, Nice and Fréjus/St-Raphaël between May and September. There is also the option to travel separately

**Composteur machines are found at the platform entrance**

from your car. **Autotrain** will transport your car overnight from Paris to either Frejus/St Raphael, Marseille, Nice or Toulon, while you relax on a passenger train. Tickets must be booked at least five days in advance.

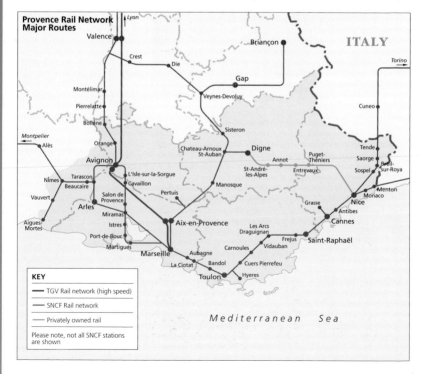

**Provence Rail Network Major Routes**

**ITALY**

**KEY**

— TGV Rail network (high speed)

— SNCF Rail network

— Privately owned rail

Please note, not all SNCF stations are shown

*Mediterranean Sea*

# Travelling by Boat

There are few more enticing sights than the glittering Mediterranean of the southern Provençal coast. Almost every city along this stretch of water has a port with boats for hire. Ferry and boat companies operating to offshore islands are easy to find, and there are trips to Corsica from Marseille and Nice throughout the year. The other main waterways in Provence are the Rhône and Durance rivers, and the beautiful Camargue wetland. It is worth noting that the best way to get to St-Tropez in summer is by boat from Ste-Maxime or St-Raphaël. The town has no train station and the roads are usually very busy.

Sailing out of a rocky inlet on the Provençal coast

## MEDITERRANEAN PORTS

Car ferries depart all year round from Marseille and Nice to Corsica (Bastia, Ajaccio and Ile Rousse), operated by **SNCM Ferryterranée**. Summer ferries run from Marseille to Propriano, and from Toulon to Ajaccio, Bastia and Propriano, often crossing overnight.

SNCM has one or two weekly sailings from Marseille and Toulon to Sardinia. There are crossings to North Africa every week from Marseille to Tunis or Algiers, and to Oran weekly in high season.

Regular ferries and boats to nearby islands operate from Bandol to the Ile de Bendor; from Tour Fondu to Porquerolles; from Port d'Hyères and Le Lavandou to Le Levant and Port-Cros; and from Cannes to the Iles de Lérins.

## CRUISES AND RIVER TRIPS

The Mediterranean is famous as a cruise destination, and numerous companies operate on the south coast of France, stopping at St-Tropez, Villefranche, Marseille and Monaco.

**Crown Blue Line** has a good range of boats for hire for weekly river trips. Day cruises to the Iles d'Hyères sail from Quai Stalingrad at Toulon.

River travel is also an option with several cruise lines operating luxury river trips on the Rhône between Avignon and Lyon. **Les Grands Bateaux de**

Some of the smaller, local boats moored in St-Tropez

**Provence-Mireio** offers lunch, dinner or sightseeing cruises from Avignon to a range of destinations. Or you can take daily cruises through the Camargue in a converted *péniche* – a traditional river cargo boat.

## SAILING

Over 70 ports along the Provence coastline welcome yachts, and mooring charges vary. The Côte d'Azur ports are particularly expensive. Contact the **Fédération Française de Voile** for information on sailing clubs and where to hire boats.

## DIRECTORY

### CAR FERRY

**SNCM Ferryterranée**
Marseille
*Tel 3260.*
www.sncm.fr

### CRUISES & RIVER TRIPS

**Crown Blue Line**
2 quai du Canal, 30800 Saint-Gilles. *Tel 04 68 94 52 72.*
www.crownblueline.fr

**La Camargue au Fil de l'Eau**
30220 Aigues-Mortes.
*Tel 04 66 53 79 47.*
www.camargue.fr

**Les Grands Bateaux de Provence-Mireio**
Avignon.
*Tel 04 90 85 62 25.*
www.mireio.net

### SAILING

**Fédération Française de Voile**
*Tel 01 40 60 37 00.*
www.ffvoile.org

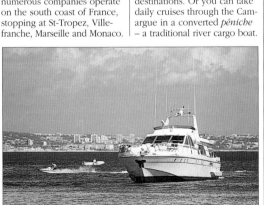

A privately owned motorboat from Cannes

# Getting Around by Road

France is a motorist's paradise and the main route to Provence is via an excellent, if expensive, autoroute (motorway) network. Provence is ideal for touring, with some of the most beautiful road routes in the world, including the stunning Grande Corniche above Nice, and the hilltop lanes of the Luberon *(see pp170–71)*. Popular routes, especially the motorway and coastal roads along the Côte d'Azur, are always busy in high season.

### GETTING TO PROVENCE

The quickest route south from Paris is the Autoroute du Soleil, the A6 motorway to Lyon, followed by the A7 to Marseille. Travellers from the UK and northern Europe should try to avoid driving through Paris, especially during the rush hour. The A26 runs from Calais to Troyes, where you can join the A5, which leads into the A6.

From Spain, the A8 motorway leads directly to Marseille and goes on to Nice and Italy.

In high season, the motorways get very crowded and if you have time it may be worth taking more minor (and attractive) roads. Try turning off the main road at Montélimar to travel to the Luberon via Nyons and Vaison-la-Romaine. Or exit at Avignon, and head into the Luberon and on to Var.

For the adventurous, the Route Napoléon (N85) leads from Grenoble south across the Alps to Digne, and continues to Grasse. From Grasse, take the scenic D3 to Cannes, or the Route de Nice, which leads to Nice and its environs.

### CAR RENTAL

Car rental in France can be expensive so it is worth checking out your options before you go. There are numerous special offers for pre-paid car rentals in the UK and USA.

Fly-drive options work well for small groups. SNCF offers train and car-rental deals with collection from several main stations *(see pp246–7).*

### INSURANCE AND BREAK-DOWN SERVICES

All car insurance policies in the EU automatically include third-party insurance cover that is valid in any EU country. However, the extent of cover provided beyond the legal minimum varies between companies, so it is best to check your policy before you travel. If you are bringing your car from outside the EU, you can purchase extra insurance cover from the **AA**, **RAC** and **Europ Assistance**. While driving in France you must carry in the car your driving licence, passport, the vehicle registration document and a certificate of insurance. A sticker showing the country of registration should be displayed near the rear number plate. The headlights of right-hand drive cars must be adjusted – kits are available at most ports.

It is advisable to organize breakdown cover. This can be arranged with your European insurance cover, or through a motoring organization such as the AA or RAC. There are also local breakdown services such as **Dépannage Côte d'Azur**.

---

## USING THE AUTOROUTE TOLL

When you join an autoroute, collect a ticket from the machine. This identifies your starting point on the autoroute. You do not pay until you reach an exit toll. You are charged according to the distance travelled and the type of vehicle used.

Gare de Péage de Fresnes

2000 m

**Motorway Sign**
*These signs indicate the name and distance to the next toll booth. They are usually blue and white; some show the tariff rates for cars, motorbikes, trucks and caravans.*

**Tollbooth with Attendant**
*When you hand in your ticket at a staffed tollbooth, the attendant will tell you the cost of your journey on the autoroute and the price will be displayed. You can pay with coins, notes or credit cards. A receipt is issued on request.*

**Automatic Machine**
*On reaching the exit toll, insert your ticket into the machine and the price of your journey is displayed in euros. You can pay either with coins or by credit card. The machine will give change and can issue a receipt.*

## RULES OF THE ROAD

Remember to drive on the right. The *priorité à droite* rule applies, meaning that you must give way to any vehicle coming out of a side turning on the right, unless otherwise signposted. On main roads a yellow diamond sign indicates where you have right of way. The *priorité à droite* does not apply at roundabouts, meaning you have to give way to cars already on the roundabout. Flashing headlights mean the driver is claiming right of way.

Seatbelts are compulsory for front and back seats. Children under ten are not permitted to travel in front seats apart from in baby seats facing backwards. Overtaking when there is a single solid centre line is heavily penalized. In case of breakdown it is compulsory to carry two red warning triangles and a luminous vest in the car. The autoroutes have emergency telephones every 2 km.

## SPEED LIMITS AND FINES

Great efforts have been made to reduce road accidents in France, and there are now speed cameras at frequent intervals. Speed limits are:
• Motorways 130 km/hr (80 mph); 110 km/hr (68 mph) in rain.
• Dual carriageways 110 km/hr (68 mph); 50 km/hr (30 mph) in towns.
• Other roads 90 km/hr (56 mph).

Instant fines are issued for speeding and drink-driving. Driving with more than 0.5g of alcohol per litre of blood can also lead to severe fines, confiscation of your license, or even imprisonment.

## FAST THROUGH ROUTES

There are three main motorways in Provence: the A7 from Lyon to Marseille, the A9 from Orange to Barcelona and the A8 from Marseille to Menton. The A54 cuts across the Camargue from Aix-en-Provence to Nîmes. The A8 is the most expensive stretch of toll motorway in France, but allows you to drive from Nice to Aix-en-Provence in under two hours.

The scenic road through the Grand Canyon du Verdon

## COUNTRY AND SCENIC ROUTES

One of the pleasures of touring Provence is turning off the main routes onto small country roads. The RN and D (*Route Nationale* and *Départmentale*) roads are good alternatives to motorways. *Bison futée* ("crafty bison") signs indicate alternative routes to avoid heavy traffic, and are especially helpful during the French holiday periods, known as the *grands départs*. The busiest weekends are in mid-July, and at the beginning and end of August when French holidays start and finish.

Apart from the busy coastal roads, Provence is a wonderful place to drive around. Some of the best scenic routes include the famous Corniche roads between Nice and Menton, with splendid sea views, or a tour of the back country of the *Massif des Maures (see pp116–17)*. The local tourist office should be able to provide you with more information and some maps.

## MAPS

The best general map of Provence is the Michelin yellow map No. 245, at a scale of 1:200,000. **IGN** (Institut Géographique National) maps are more detailed. Town plans are usually provided free by tourist offices. In large towns you may need a more detailed map, published by Michelin or **Plans-Guides Blay-Foldex**. In the UK, **Stanfords** is famous for its range of maps.

## PARKING

Parking in the big towns, particularly along the coast, is strictly regulated. If you are illegally parked, you may be towed away instantly to the police pound and face a substantial fine. Most Provençal towns have pay and display machines (*horodateurs*) and parking is often time limited. Many places offer free parking from noon to 2pm – ticket machines automatically allow for this. Ensure you have enough coins for the meter or purchase a parking card, which are available from the *tabacs*.

An *horodateur*, or pay-and-display machine

## PETROL

Petrol is relatively expensive in France, especially on autoroutes. Large supermarkets and hypermarkets sell petrol at a discount, however the pay booths may close over lunch and the automatic pumps only accept *carte bleue* (French bank cards). A map issued by French Government Tourist offices (*see p237*) indicates the cheaper petrol stations situated up to 2 km (just over a mile) from motorway exits. Unleaded petrol (*sans plomb*) and diesel fuel are found in all stations. LPG gas is also available, often on motorways.

Mountain bikes are ideal for exploring the Provençal countryside

A map of locations stocking this fuel can be obtained from any LPG station in France. Note that in rural areas petrol stations can be hard to find, so ensure you have enough petrol for your journey.

## CYCLING

Cycling is one of the most pleasant ways to see Provence. Although the French are cycling enthusiasts, there are few cycle lanes in towns in Provence. However, some cities, such as Arles, Avignon and Nîmes, have specified cycle routes. You can take bikes on certain trains – check the timetable first for the bike symbol (*see p248*). You can also reserve bicycles at several stations (*Train + Velo*). Rental shops can be found throughout the region, especially in the Luberon and in towns around the Camargue, which rent out mountain bikes (*VTT*). Bicycle theft is common along the Côte d'Azur – make sure you are fully insured before you go. Best of all, Provence is now following the initiative of Paris in introducing a free bike scheme in cities such as Marseille. Enquire at the tourist office for bike locations.

## TAXIS

Prices vary from one part of Provence to another. The charges are predictably highest along the Côte d'Azur, where

it's not uncommon to pay €30 for a 20-minute journey. Elsewhere the pick-up charge is usually around €2, and €0.60 or more for every kilometre. An extra charge will be made for any luggage. All taxis must use a meter, or a *compteur*. Hailing a taxi is not customary in Provence – you must go to a taxi rank or book by phone.

## HITCHHIKING

Hitchhiking is possible in France, although officially it is frowned upon. You are not supposed to hitch on the motorways and if you do you will be cautioned by the police. Allostop can put you in touch with cars heading south from Paris, and for region to region lifts: www.allostop.net.

## COACH AND BUS TRAVEL

Coach travel used to be the cheapest way of getting to Provence, but reductions in air fares have now made it a less competitive option. It is, however, one of the more environmentally friendly ways to travel and will take you directly from city centre to city centre. **Eurolines** (*see p251*) coaches depart all year round from London to Nîmes, Toulon, Marseille, Aix-en-Provence and Avignon. The journey to Marseille takes about 23 hours from London.

Larger towns have a bus station but, otherwise, the bus services are limited. SNCF runs bus lines in northern Provence, and private companies run along the major motorways between towns and on some minor routes, such as the coastal road between Toulon and St-Tropez. Local bus services are notoriously erratic.

Eurolines long-haul coach

# Travelling in Cities

Apart from Marseille, which competes with Lyon for the title of second city of France, the towns and cities of Provence are small. The best way to get around is generally on foot, parking in most towns is strictly regulated, and in the summer months traffic can be very heavy. Marseille and Nice both have excellent public transport systems that are efficient and easy to use. Marseille and Aix-en-Provence also have bike rental schemes that are similar to the *Vélib* in Paris.

## METRO

The fastest way to get around Marseille is by **Métro**. The system has two lines, which meet at Gare St-Charles and Castellane stations. Métro 1 goes from the main hospital La Timone in the east to La Rose in the northeast, passing through the Vieux Port on the way. Métro 2 runs roughly north to south, connecting the shipping port with Notre-Dame-de-la-Garde and Ste-Marguerite. Tickets can be bought from Métro stations, on buses or in *tabacs*. Trains run from 5am–10:30pm daily.

## TRAMS

A new tram network is under construction in Marseille; when completed in 2011 it will consist of three tram lines. Two lines are already open linking the centre to the northwest and east of the city. The lines meet at Noailles near Gare St-Charles. The Marseille fare system is called *Reseau Liberté*. Tickets are valid for Métro, tram and buses with free transfers within a one-hour period.

In Nice part of the long-awaited tramway system is operational. The u-shaped Line 1 connects the northern and eastern neighbourhoods to the city centre, passing through Place Massena and the main railway station. Tickets can be bought from machines or tram operators.

## BUSES

Although bus routes between towns in Provence can be slow and inadequate, within the towns the service is usually good. In Marseille an extensive bus network covers all of the city. Long distance buses and airport shuttle buses leave from the *gare routière* (bus station) behind the main train station Gare St-Charles. There is a useful left-luggage facility *(consigne)* at both stations.

Nice has a good network of city buses including night buses. The Sunbus is a tourist service that runs daily and has multiple stops throughout the city. Tickets can be bought on board buses or from *tabacs*. Check the website of **Lignes d'Azur** for timetables.

## TAXIS

There are taxi ranks on most main squares in towns and cities. You can also telephone for taxis; enquire at the tourist office or your hotel for local numbers. It is not usual practice to hail a taxi in the street.

**Bicycles can be hired through the Le Vélo scheme in Marseille**

## CYCLING

Whether you bring your own bicycle, or rent one, most of Provence's towns are small enough to cycle around. Marseille and Aix-en-Provence have introduced bike-sharing schemes for inner city transport. Ask at a tourist office for further details and locations.

## WALKING

Explore the towns on foot as much as you can. Apart from Marseille and Nice the main city-centre sights of Nîmes, Avignon or Aix-en-Provence can easily be seen in a walking tour. Even in Marseille with its louche reputation the crime rate is no higher than any other French city, so the usual precautions should be adequate to stay safe.

**Marseille tram travelling along the Boulevard Longchamp**

# General Index

Page numbers in **bold** type refer to main entries

# Acknowledgments

Dorling Kindersley would like to thank the following people whose contributions and assistance have made the preparation of this book possible.

## Main Contributor

Roger Williams is a writer and editor who was for many years associated with the *Sunday Times* magazine. He has written two novels and a number of guide books, on places ranging from Barcelona to the Baltic States, and was a contributor to *Over Europe*, the first aerial record of the united continent. He visits France regularly, and has been writing about Provence for more than 30 years.

## Contributors

Adele Evans, John Flower, Robin Gauldie, Jim Keeble, Anthony Rose, Martin Walters.

## Additional Photography

Demetrio Carrasco, Andy Crawford, Lisa Cupolo, Franz Curzon, Philip Freiberger, Nick Goodall, Steve Gorton, John Heseltine, Andrew Holligan, Richard McConnell, Neil Mersh, Ian O'Leary, Clive Streeter.

## Additional Illustrators

Simon Calder, Paul Guest, Aziz Khan, Tristan Spaargaren, Ann Winterbotham, John Woodcock.

## Cartographic Research

Jane Hugill, Samantha James, Jennifer Skelley, Martin Smith (Lovell Johns).

## Design and Editorial

MANAGING EDITOR Georgina Matthews
DEPUTY EDITORIAL DIRECTOR Douglas Amrine
DEPUTY ART DIRECTOR Gaye Allen
PRODUCTION CONTROLLER Hilary Stephens
PICTURE RESEARCH Susan Mennell
DTP DESIGNER Salim Qurashi
MAP CO-ORDINATORS Simon Farbrother, David Pugh
MAPS Uma Bhattacharya, Kunal Singh, Jennifer Skelley, Samantha James (Lovell Johns Ltd, Oxford)
RESEARCHER Philippa Richmond
Azeem Alam, Vincent Allonier, Rosemary Bailey, Shahnaaz Bakshi, Laetitia Benloulou, Josie Bernard, Tessa Bindloss, Hilary Bird, Kevin Brown, Margaret Chang, Cooling Brown Partnership, Guy Dimond, Joy Fitzsimmonds, Lisa Fox-Mullen, Anna Freiberger, Rhiannon Furbear, Vinod Harish, Victoria Heyworth-Dunne, Jackie Grosvenor, Annette Jacobs, Stuart James, Laura Jones, Nancy Jones, Erika Lang, Delphine Lawrance, Francesca Machiavelli, James Marlow, Helen Partington, Sangita Patel, Katie Peacock, Alice Peebles, Carolyn Pyrah, Philippa Richmond, Ellen Root, Kavita Saha, Sands Publishing Solutions, Baishakhee Sengupta, Sailesh Sharma, Bhaswati Singh, Catherine Skipper, Priyanka Thakur, Amanda Tomeh, Daphne Trotter, Janis Utton, Conrad Van Dyk, Dora Whitaker, Irina Zarb.

## Special Assistance

Louise Abbott; Anna Brooke, Manade Gilbert Arnaud; Brigitte Charles, Monaco Tourist Board, London; Sabine Giraud, Terres du Sud, Venasque; Emma Heath; Nathalie Lavarenne, Musée Matisse, Nice; Ella Milroy; Marianne Petrou; Andrew Sanger; David Tse.

## Photographic Reference

Bernard Beaujard, Vézénobres.

## Photography Permissions

Dorling Kindersley would like to thank the following for their assistance and kind permission to photograph at their establishments: Fondation Marguerite et Aimé Maeght, St-Paul-de-Vence; Hotel Négresco, Nice; Monsieur J-F Campana, Mairie de Nice; Monsieur Froumessol, Mairie de Cagnes-sur-Mer; Musée Ephrussi de Rothschild, St-Jean-Cap-Ferrat; Musée Jean Cocteau, Menton; Musée International de la Parfumerie, Grasse; Musée Matisse, Nice; Musée National Message Biblique Marc Chagall, Nice; Musée Océano-graphique, Monaco; Musée Picasso/Château Grimaldi, Antibes; Salle des Mariages, Hôtel de Ville, Menton, and all other churches, museums, hotels, restaurants, shops and sights too numerous to thank individually.

## Picture Credits

t = top; tl = top left; tc = top centre; tr = top right; cla = centre left above; ca = centre above; cra = centre right above; cl = centre left; c = centre; cr = centre right; clb = centre left below; cb = centre below; crb = centre right below; bl = bottom left; b = bottom; bc = bottom centre; br = bottom right; bla = bottom left above; bca = bottom centre above; bra = bottom right above; blb = bottom left below; bcb = bottom centre below; brb = bottom right below.

Every effort has been made to trace the copyright holders and we apologize in advance for any unintentional omissions. We would be pleased to insert the appropriate acknowledgments in any subsequent editions.

Works of art have been reproduced with the permission of the following copyright holders:

© ADAGP, Paris and DACS, London 2006: 26tr, 27tr, 27b, 30tr, 74tl, 76t, 76cla, 76bl, 77tl, 77cr, 78c, 78b, 85bl, 99tr, 107cr, 119crb, 120ca, 120bc, 121cra, 121crb, 144ca; ©ARS, NY and DACS, London 2006: 59tl, 76clb; © DACS, London 2006: 132tl; © Estate of Francis Bacon/DACS, London: 225bl; © Succession H.Matisse/DACS, London 2006: 27cr, 82tr, 82bl, 83tc, 83ct, 83br; © Succession Miro/ADAGP, Paris and DACS, London 2006: 77cra; © Succession Picasso/DACS, London 2006: 26br, 73cl, 73cr, 73clb, 73bl, 73br.

The publisher would like to thank the following individuals, companies and picture libraries for permission to reproduce their photographs:.

ALAMY IMAGES: Neil Juggins 240clb; Justin Kase zeightz 240cl; Justin Kase zfourz 54tl; Barry Mason 247c; Pictures Colour Library 246cla, 251tc; Pixonnet.com/Goran Strandsten 240bl; Travelshots.com 238tl; Dave Watts 231c; Gregory Wrona 236br; ALVEY & TOWERS: 246b; ANCIENT ART AND ARCHITECTURE COLLECTION: 39t and cb, 40bl, 43t; ARCHIVES DE L'AUTOMOBILE CLUB DE MONACO: 52ca; ARTEPHOT, PARIS: Plassart 27c; ASSOCIATED PRESS LTD: 29cb.

LA BELLE AURORE: 32b, 37t; HOSTELLERIE BÉRARD: 230cr; BRIDGEMAN ART LIBRARY: Christie's, London 47crb, 50–51; Giraudon 47t, 48bl; Schloss Charlottenburg, Berlin 179t.

CAMPAGNE, CAMPAGNE!, PARIS: Jolyot 92br; JL Julien 31bl; Meissonnier 159b; Meschinet 138c; Moirenc 245; Pambour 171t, 172t; Picard 159t; Pyszel 90t; CEPHAS: Mick Rock 208br, 209ca and br; JEAN-LOUP CHARMET, PARIS: 28cl; © Antoine de Saint-Exupéry/Gallimard 29cla; 37b, 42bl, 46ca and cb, 49t and cla, 50tl and tr, 52t, 53t, 132cl, 140t, 153t, 160cl; BRUCE COLEMAN: Adrian Davies 114bl; JLG Grande 136bca; George McCarthy 19tl; Andrew J Purcell 115cb and bl; Hans Reinhard 137t, 171bl, bc and br; Dr Frieder Sauer 114c; 136bra; CORBIS: Sophie Bassouls 29cr; Owen Franken 231t; John Hicks 11br; Chris Lisle 11tl; Robert Harding World Imagery/Angelo Cavalli 205ca; JOE CORNISH: 23tr, 188, 234; JULIAN COTTON PICTURE LIBRARY: Jason Hawkes aerial collection 13, 56–7; Culture Espaces, Paris: 86t and ca; Véran 87t.

Photo Daspet, Avignon: Musée du Petit Palais, Avignon 44t, 45bc; Palais des Papes, Avignon 44crb and b; Diaf, Paris: J-P Garcin 33cb; J-C Gérard 228 t and b, 151b; Camille Moirenc 162c; Bernard Régent 26t; Patrick Somelet 158b; Direction Des Affaires Culturelles, Monaco: 91c.

European Commission: 241; Mary Evans: 9 inset, 28t, bl and br, 28crb, 45br and t, 46b, 57inset, 189inset, 235inset; Jane Ewart: 22cb, 23c, 24tl, 25cb, 58tl, 76cb, 127b, 163ca and cb, 203b, 237b, 244b; Explorer Archives, Paris: L Bertrand 38cb; Jean-Loup Charmet 67t, 124c, 147b; Coll. ES 42t, 46cb and bl; Coll. Sauvel 15t; G Garde 33ca; J P Hervey 64t; J & C Lenars 39c; J-P Lescourret 165c; M C Noailles 65b; Peter Willi 40ca; A Wolf 43clb.

FNOTSI: 236ca; Fondation Auguste Escoffier, Villeneuve-Loubet: 74c; Fondation Maeght, Saint-Paul-de-Vence, France: Claude Germain 77t and c; Coll. M et Mme Adrien Maeght 77b; Frank Lane Picture Agency: N Clark 170b; Fritz Polking 18tr; M B Withers 136bla.

Galerie Intemporel, Paris: Les Films Ariane, Paris 54–5; Editions Gaud, Moisenay: 70bl, 86b, 87bl and br, 142t, 181c; Getty Images: Peter Adams 220cla; AFP/Valery Hache 224bl; Hemis/Bertrand Rieger 16c; Hemis/Jose Nicolas 220br; Slow Images 154c; The Image Bank/Peter Adams 16tl; The Image Bank/Remi Benali 32cl; WireImage/Tony Barson 55br; Giraudon, Paris: 27t, bl and br, 28cr, 32t, 36, 40br, 48ca and br, 133b, 145b, 172c; Lauros-Giraudon 38ca, 45cb, 46tr (detail), 46–7, 49clb, 51clb, 53clb (all rights reserved), 73tl and tr, 110bl, 125b, 134t, 144t, 146t; Musée de la Vieille Charité, Marseille 38tr; Musée de la Ville de Paris, Musée du Petit Palais/Lauros-Giraudon 26bl; Musée des Beaux-Arts, Marseille 48–9, 49b, 152b; Musée du Louvre, Paris 8–9; Musée du Vieux Marseille, Marseille 48cb, 50ca; Gîtes de France: 193ca; Grand Hôtel Du Cap Ferrat: 191t; Grottes de St-Cézaire: 65c.

Robert Harding Picture Library: 35b, 244t; Hemispheres Images: Bertrand Gardel 253tr; Hotel Eden Roc, Cap D'antibes: 191b; Hulton-deutsch Collection: 28c, 29bl, 52br; Keystone 94t.

Illustrated London News Picture Library: 50b.

Catherine Karnow, San Francisco: 110c; The Kobal Collection: United Artists 71tl.

Daniel Madeleine: 183b; Magnum Photos: Bruno Barbey 228c; René Burri 55clb; Robert Capa 82c; Elliott Erwitt 91br; Mairie de Nîmes: Jean-Charles Blais 132t (all rights reserved); Francis Bacon 225b (all rights reserved); Mansell Collection: 39b, 42br, 43b, 51cla, 52bl; Editions Molipor, Monaco: 94b; courtesy of SBM 51crb, 94c; Musée De L'Annonciade, St-Tropez: E Vila Mateu 119b, 120–21; Musée D'anthropologie,

Monaco: J-f Buissière 38tl; Musée Archéologique De La Vaison-la-Romaine: Christine Bézin 41clb; Musée D'art Moderne Et D'art Contemporain, Nice: 54br, 85b; Musée Fabre, Montpellier: Leenhardt 135b; Musée De La Photographie, Mougins: 66b; Musée Matisse, Nice: © Service photographique, Ville de Nice 82t and b, 83t, c and br.

Reproduced By Courtesy Of The Trustees, The National Gallery, London: 26c; Nature Photographers: Carlson 16ca; michael gore 16b; Network Photographers/Rapho: Mark Buscail 184t.

L'oeil Et La Mémoire/Bibliothèque Municipale d'Avignon: Atlas 24, folio 147 42cb; OTC Marseille: HAUER 253; Oxford Scientific Films: Mike Hill 136blb; Tom Leach 160br; Frank Schneidermeyer 136brb.

John Parker: 21bl, 24b, 58tr, 108t, 157; Photolibrary: SGM 236cl; Photo Resources: Cm Dixon 41cbr; Pictures Colour Library: 185b; Planet Earth Pictures: Richard Coomber 136bcb; John Neusch-wander 114br; Peter Scoones 19b; Popperfoto: 29t, 29cb, 72b.

Range: Bettmann 28cb, 29crb and br; Retrograph Archive, London: © Martin Breese 30tr, 69b; Roger-viollet, Paris: 47cla, 51t, 52cb, 163b.

SA Aéroports de la Côte d'Azur: J Kelagopian 244bc; Service de Presse de la Ville de Cagnes-sur-mer: 78c and b, 79b; Roger Smith, Eze: 86cb, 87c; SNCF – Societe National des Chemins de Fer: 55b, 246 tl, 248tr; Frank Spooner Pictures: Robin 67b; P Siccoli 54cb; Gamma/T Pelisier 38b; Gamma/Christian Vioujard 67cra and clb; STA Travel Group: 238c; Sygma: 75t; 68b; H Conant 54bl; J Donoso 67crb; Keystone 52–3; 53cla and b; Leo Mirkine 55cl.

Editions Tallendier, Paris: Bibliothèque Nationale 42–3; Terres du Sud, Venasque: Philippe Giraud 2, 44clb, 45c and bl, 46tl and br, 64b, 70br, 81ca, 105b, 166t, 167cb, 168b; Tony Stone Images: Joe Cornish 14; Travel Library: Philip Enticknap 93t and br.

Wallis Phototheque, Marseille: Clasen 55t, 67cla; Constant 182b; Di Meglio 115ca; Giani 96t, 225t; Huet 185t; LCI 31br, 176t; Leroux 16b; Poulet 96cl; Royer 96cr and b; Tarta 193b; Roger Williams: 101, 138b, 165t, 170c, 181b, 185ca.

Front endpaper: all commissioned photography.

Jacket: Front - Corbis: Owen Franken main image; DK Images: bl. Back - John Parker: cla; The Travel Library: Philip Enticknap bl; Wallis.fr: © ILICO tl; Leroux clb. Spine - Corbis: Owen Franken t; DK Images: Kim Sayer b.

All other images Dorling Kindersley. For more information see www.DKimages.com

# Phrase Book

## In Emergency

| | | |
|---|---|---|
| Help! | **Au secours!** | oh se**koor** |
| Stop! | **Arrêtez!** | aret-**ay** |
| Call a | **Appelez un** | apuh-**lay** uñ |
| doctor! | **médecin!** | med**saũ** |
| Call an | **Appelez une** | apuh-**lay** oon |
| ambulance! | **ambulance!** | oñboo-**loñs** |
| Call the | **Appelez la** | apuh-**lay** lah |
| police! | **police!** | poh-**lees** |
| Call the fire | **Appelez les** | apuh-lay leh |
| brigade! | **pompiers!** | poñ-**peeyay** |
| Where is the | **Où est le** | oo ay luh |
| nearest | **téléphone le** | tehleh**fon** |
| telephone? | **plus proche?** | luh ploo prosh |
| Where is the | **Où est l'hôpital** | oo ay l'**opee**tal |
| nearest hospital? | **le plus proche?** | luh ploo **prosh** |

## Communication Essentials

| | | |
|---|---|---|
| Yes | **Oui** | wee |
| No | **Non** | noñ |
| Please | **S'il vous plaît** | seel voo **play** |
| Thank you | **Merci** | mer-**see** |
| Excuse me | **Excusez-moi** | exkoo-**zay** mwah |
| Hello | **Bonjour** | boñ**zhoor** |
| Goodbye | **Au revoir** | oh ruh-**vwar** |
| Good night | **Bonsoir** | boñ-**swar** |
| Morning | **Le matin** | matañ |
| Afternoon | **L'après-midi** | l'apreh-**meedee** |
| Evening | **Le soir** | swar |
| Yesterday | **Hier** | ee**yehr** |
| Today | **Aujourd'hui** | oh-zhoor-**dwee** |
| Tomorrow | **Demain** | duh**mañ** |
| Here | **Ici** | ee-**see** |
| There | **Là** | lah |
| What? | **Quel, quelle?** | kel, kel |
| When? | **Quand?** | koñ |
| Why? | **Pourquoi?** | poor-**kwah** |
| Where? | **Où?** | oo |

## Useful Phrases

| | | |
|---|---|---|
| How are you? | **Comment** | kom-moñ tal**ay** |
| | **allez-vous?** | **voo** |
| Very well, | **Très bien,** | treh byañ, |
| thank you. | **merci.** | mer-**see** |
| Pleased to | **Enchanté de** | oñshoñ-**tay** duh |
| meet you. | **faire votre** | fehr votr |
| | **connaissance.** | kon-ay-**sans** |
| See you soon. | **A bientôt.** | byañ-**toh** |
| That's fine. | **Voilà qui est** | vwalah kee ay |
| | **parfait.** | par**fay** |
| Where is/are...? | **Où est/sont...?** | oo ay/soñ |
| How far | **Combien de** | kom-**byañ** duh is |
| is it to...? | **kilomètres** | keelo-**metr** |
| | **d'ici à...?** | d'ee-**see** ah |
| Which | **Quelle est la** | kel ay lah |
| way to...? | **direction** | deer-ek-**syoñ** |
| | **pour...?** | poor |
| Do you speak | **Parlez-vous** | par-**lay** voo |
| English? | **anglais?** | oñg-**lay** |
| I don't | **Je ne** | zhuh nuh |
| understand. | **comprends pas.** | kom-**proñ** pah |

## (continued)

| | | |
|---|---|---|
| Could you | **Pouvez-vous** | poo-**vay** voo |
| speak slowly, | **parler moins** | par-**lay** mwañ |
| please? | **vite, s'il** | veet seel |
| | **vous plaît?** | voo play |
| I'm sorry. | **Excusez-moi.** | exkoo-**zay** mwah |

## Useful Words

| | | |
|---|---|---|
| big | **grand** | groñ |
| small | **petit** | puh-**tee** |
| hot | **chaud** | show |
| cold | **froid** | frwah |
| good | **bon** | boñ |
| bad | **mauvais** | moh-**veh** |
| enough | **assez** | as**say** |
| well | **bien** | byañ |
| open | **ouvert** | oo-**ver** |
| closed | **fermé** | fer-**meh** |
| left | **gauche** | gohsh |
| right | **droite** | drwaht |
| straight on | **tout droit** | too drwah |
| near | **près** | preh |
| far | **loin** | lwañ |
| up | **en haut** | oñ **oh** |
| down | **en bas** | oñ **bah** |
| early | **de bonne heure** | duh bon**urr** |
| late | **en retard** | oñ ruh-**tar** |
| entrance | **l'entrée** | l'on-**tray** |
| exit | **la sortie** | sor-**tee** |
| toilet | **les toilettes,** | twah-let, |
| | **les WC** | vay-**see** |
| unoccupied | **libre** | leebr |
| no charge | **gratuit** | grah-**twee** |

## Making a Telephone Call

| | | |
|---|---|---|
| I'd like to | **Je voudrais** | zhuh voo-dreh |
| place a long- | **faire un** | fehr uñ |
| distance call. | **interurbain.** | añter-oorbañ |
| I'd like to make | **Je voudrais** | zhuh voo**dreh** |
| a reverse- | **faire une** | fehr oon kom- |
| charge call. | **communication** | oonikah-**syoñ** |
| | **PCV.** | peh-seh-veh |
| I'll try again | **Je rappelerai** | zhuh rapel**eray** |
| later. | **plus tard.** | ploo tar |
| Can I leave a | **Est-ce que je** | es-**keh** zhuh |
| message? | **peux laisser** | puh leh-**say** |
| | **un message?** | uñ meh**sazh** |
| Hold on. | **Ne quittez pas,** | nuh kee-**tay** pah |
| | **s'il vous plaît.** | seel voo play. |
| Could you | **Pouvez-vous** | poo-**vay** voo |
| speak up a | **parler un** | par-**lay** uñ |
| little please? | **peu plus fort?** | puh ploo for |
| local call | **la communi-** | komoonikah- |
| | **cation locale** | **syoñ** low-kal |

## Shopping

| | | |
|---|---|---|
| How much | **C'est combien** | say kom-**byañ** |
| does this cost? | **s'il vous plaît?** | seel voo play |
| Do you take | **Est-ce que vous** | es-**kuh** voo |
| credit cards? | **acceptez les** | zaksept-**ay** leh |
| | **cartes de crédit?** | kart duh kreh-**dee** |

| | | |
|---|---|---|
| Do you take travellers' cheques? | **Est-ce que vous acceptez les chèques de voyage?** | es-**kuh** voo zaksept-**ay** leh shek duh vwa**yazh** |
| I would like ... | **Je voudrais...** | zhuh voo-**dray** |
| Do you have? | **Est-ce que vous avez?** | es-**kuh** voo zav**ay** |
| I'm just looking. | **Je regarde seulement.** | zhuh ruh**gar** suhl**moñ** |
| What time do you open? | **A quelle heure vous êtes ouvert?** | ah kel urr voo zet oo-**ver** |
| What time do you close? | **A quelle heure vous êtes fermé?** | ah kel urr voo zet fer-**may** |
| This one | **Celui-ci** | suhl-wee-**see** |
| That one | **Celui-là** | suhl-wee-**lah** |
| expensive | **cher** | shehr |
| cheap | **pas cher, bon marché** | pah shehr, boñ mar-**shay** |
| size, clothes | **la taille** | tye |
| size, shoes | **la pointure** | pwañ-**tur** |
| white | **blanc** | bloñ |
| black | **noir** | nwahr |
| red | **rouge** | roozh |
| yellow | **jaune** | zhohwn |
| green | **vert** | vehr |
| blue | **bleu** | bluh |

## Types of Shop

| | | |
|---|---|---|
| antique shop | **le magasin d'antiquités** | maga-**zañ** d'oñteekee-**tay** |
| bakery | **la boulangerie** | booloñ-**zhuree** |
| bank | **la banque** | boñk |
| book shop | **la librairie** | lee-**brehree** |
| butcher | **la boucherie** | boo-**shehree** |
| cake shop | **la pâtisserie** | patee-**sree** |
| cheese shop | **la fromagerie** | fromazh-**ree** |
| chemist | **la pharmacie** | farmah-**see** |
| dairy | **la crémerie** | krem-**ree** |
| department store | **le grand magasin** | groñ maga-**zañ** |
| delicatessen | **la charcuterie** | sharkoot-**ree** |
| fishmonger | **la poissonnerie** | pwasson-**ree** |
| gift shop | **le magasin de cadeaux** | maga-**zañ** duh kadoh |
| greengrocer | **le marchand de légumes** | mar-**shoñ** duh lay-**goom** |
| grocery | **l'alimentation** | alee-moñta-**syoñ** |
| hairdresser | **le coiffeur** | kwa**fuhr** |
| market | **le marché** | marsh-**ay** |
| newsagent | **le magasin de journaux** | maga-**zañ** duh zhoor-**no** |
| post office | **la poste, le bureau de poste, les PTT** | pohst, booroh duh pohst, peh-teh-teh |
| shoe shop | **le magasin de chaussures** | maga-**zañ** duh show-**soor** |
| supermarket | **le super-marché** | soo pehr-**marshay** |
| tobacconist | **le tabac** | tabah |
| travel agent | **l'agence de voyages** | l'azhoñs duh vwayazh |

## Menu Decoder

| | | |
|---|---|---|
| **l'agneau** | l'anyoh | lamb |
| **l'ail** | l'eye | garlic |
| **la banane** | banan | banana |
| **le beurre** | burr | butter |
| **la bière** | bee-**yehr** | beer |
| **le bifteck, le steack** | beef-**tek**, stek | steak |
| **le boeuf** | buhf | beef |
| **bouilli** | boo-**yee** | boiled |
| **le café** | kah-**fayle** | coffee |
| **le canard** | kanar | duck |
| **le citron pressé** | see-**troñ** press-**eh** | fresh lemon juice |
| **les crevettes** | kruh-**vet** | prawns |
| **les crustacés** | **kroos**-ta-say | shellfish |
| **cuit au four** | kweet oh foor | baked |
| **le dessert** | deh-**ser** | dessert |
| **l'eau minérale** | l'oh **meeney**-ral | mineral water |
| **les escargots** | leh zes-kar-**goh** | snails |
| **les frites** | freet | chips |
| **le fromage** | from-**azh** | cheese |
| **les fruits frais** | frwee freh | fresh fruit |
| **les fruits de mer** | frwee duh mer | seafood |
| **le gâteau** | gah-**toh** | cake |
| **la glace** | glas | ice, ice cream |
| **grillé** | gree-**yay** | grilled |
| **le homard** | om**ahr** | lobster |
| **l'huile** | l'weel | oil |
| **le jambon** | zhoñ-**boñ** | ham |
| **le lait** | leh | milk |
| **les légumes** | lay-**goom** | vegetables |
| **la moutarde** | moo-**tard** | mustard |
| **l'oeuf** | l'uf | egg |
| **les oignons** | leh zon**yoñ** | onions |
| **les olives** | leh zol**eev** | olives |
| **l'orange pressée** | l'oroñzh press-**eh** | fresh orange juice |
| **le pain** | pan | bread |
| **le petit pain** | puh-**tee** pañ | roll |
| **poché** | posh-**ay** | poached |
| **le poisson** | pwah-**ssoñ** | fish |
| **le poivre** | pwavr | pepper |
| **la pomme** | pom | apple |
| **les pommes de terre** | pom-duh **tehr** | potatoes |
| **le porc** | por | pork |
| **le potage** | poh-**tazh** | soup |
| **le poulet** | poo-**lay** | chicken |
| **le riz** | ree | rice |
| **rôti** | row-**tee** | roast |
| **la sauce** | sohs | sauce |
| **la saucisse** | soh**sees** | sausage, fresh |
| **sec** | sek | dry |
| **le sel** | sel | salt |
| **le sucre** | sookr | sugar |
| **le thé** | tay | tea |
| **le toast** | toast | toast |
| **la viande** | vee-**yand** | meat |
| **le vin blanc** | vañ bloñ | white wine |
| **le vin rouge** | vañ roozh | red wine |
| **le vinaigre** | vee**naygr** | vinegar |

## Eating Out

| | | |
|---|---|---|
| Have you got a table? | **Avez-vous une table libre?** | avay-**voo** oon tahbl leebr |
| I want to reserve a table. | **Je voudrais réserver une table.** | zhuh voo-**dray** rayzehr-**vay** oon tahbl |
| The bill, please. | **L'addition, s'il vous plaît.** | l'adee-**syoñ** seel voo **play** |
| I am a vegetarian. | **Je suis végétarien.** | zhuh swee vezhay-**tehryañ** |
| Waitress/ waiter | **Madame, Mademoiselle/ Monsieur** | mah-**dam,** mah-dem wah zel/muh-**syuh** |
| menu | **le menu, la carte** | men-**oo,** kart |
| fixed-price menu | **le menu à prix fixe** | men-**oo** ah pree feeks |
| cover charge | **le couvert** | koo-**vehr** |
| wine list | **la carte des vins** | **kart**-deh vañ |
| glass | **le verre** | vehr |
| bottle | **la bouteille** | boo-**tay** |
| knife | **le couteau** | koo-**toh** |
| fork | **la fourchette** | for-**shet** |
| spoon | **la cuillère** | kwee-**yehr** |
| breakfast | **le petit déjeuner** | puh-**tee** deh-**zhuh-nay** |
| lunch | **le déjeuner** | deh-**zhuh-nay** |
| dinner | **le dîner** | dee-**nay** |
| main course | **le plat principal** | plah prañsee-**pal** |
| starter, first course | **l'entrée, le hors d'oeuvre** | l'oñ-**tray,** or-duhvr |
| dish of the day | **le plat du jour** | plah doo zhoor |
| wine bar | **le bar à vin** | bar ah vañ |
| café | **le café** | ka-**fay** |
| rare | **saignant** | say-**noñ** |
| medium | **à point** | ah **pwañ** |
| well done | **bien cuit** | byañ **kwee** |

## Staying in a Hotel

| | | |
|---|---|---|
| Do you have a vacant room? | **Est-ce que vous avez une chambre?** | es-kuh voo-**zavay** oon shambr |
| double room | **la chambre pour deux personnes, avec** | shambr ah duh pehr-**son**avek |
| with double bed | **un grand lit** | un gronñ lee |
| twin room | **la chambre à deux lits** | shambr ah duh lee |
| single room | **la chambre pour une personne** | shambr ah oon pehr-**son** |
| room with a bath, shower | **la chambre avec salle de bains, une douche** | shambr avek sal duh bañ, oon doosh |
| porter | **le garçon** | gar-**soñ** |
| key | **la clef** | klay |
| I have a reservation. | **J'ai fait une réservation.** | zhay fay oon rayzehrva-**syoñ** |

## Sightseeing

| | | |
|---|---|---|
| abbey | **l'abbaye** | l'abay-**ee** |
| art gallery | **la galerie d'art** | galer-**ree** dart |
| cathedral | **la cathédrale** | katay-**dral** |
| church | **l'église** | l'ayg**leez** |
| garden | **le jardin** | zhar-**dañ** |
| library | **la bibliothèque** | beeb**leeo**-tek |
| museum | **le musée** | moo-**zay** |
| railway station | **la gare (SNCF)** | gahr (es-en-say-ef) |
| bus station | **la gare routière** | gahr roo-tee-**yehr** |
| tourist information office | **les renseigne-- ments touristiques, le syndicat d'initiative** | roñsayn-**moñ** too-rees-**teek,** sandee-ka d'eenee-syateev |
| town hall | **l'hôtel de ville** | l'oh**tel** duh veel |
| private mansion | **l'hôtel particulier** | l'ohtel partikoo-**lyay** |
| closed for | **fermeture** | fehrmeh-**tur** |
| public holiday | **jour férié** | zhoor fehree-**ay** |

## Numbers

| | | |
|---|---|---|
| 0 | **zéro** | zeh-**roh** |
| 1 | **un, une** | uñ, oon |
| 2 | **deux** | duh |
| 3 | **trois** | trwah |
| 4 | **quatre** | katr |
| 5 | **cinq** | sañk |
| 6 | **six** | sees |
| 7 | **sept** | set |
| 8 | **huit** | weet |
| 9 | **neuf** | nerf |
| 10 | **dix** | dees |
| 11 | **onze** | oñz |
| 12 | **douze** | dooz |
| 13 | **treize** | trehz |
| 14 | **quatorze** | ka**torz** |
| 15 | **quinze** | kañz |
| 16 | **seize** | sehz |
| 17 | **dix-sept** | dees-**set** |
| 18 | **dix-huit** | dees-**weet** |
| 19 | **dix-neuf** | dees-**nerf** |
| 20 | **vingt** | vañ |
| 30 | **trente** | tront |
| 40 | **quarante** | karo**ñt** |
| 50 | **cinquante** | sañko**ñt** |
| 60 | **soixante** | swaso**ñt** |
| 70 | **soixante-dix** | swasoñt-**dees** |
| 80 | **quatre-vingts** | katr-**vañ** |
| 90 | **quatre-vingts- dix** | katr-vañ-**dees** |
| 100 | **cent** | soñ |
| 1,000 | **mille** | meel |

## Time

| | | |
|---|---|---|
| one minute | **une minute** | oon mee-**noot** |
| one hour | **une heure** | oon urr |
| half an hour | **une demi-heure** | oon **duh-mee** urr |
| Monday | **lundi** | luñ-**dee** |
| Tuesday | **mardi** | mar-**dee** |
| Wednesday | **mercredi** | mehrkruh-**dee** |
| Thursday | **jeudi** | zhuh-**dee** |
| Friday | **vendredi** | voñdruh-**dee** |
| Saturday | **samedi** | sam-**dee** |
| Sunday | **dimanche** | dee-**moñsh** |

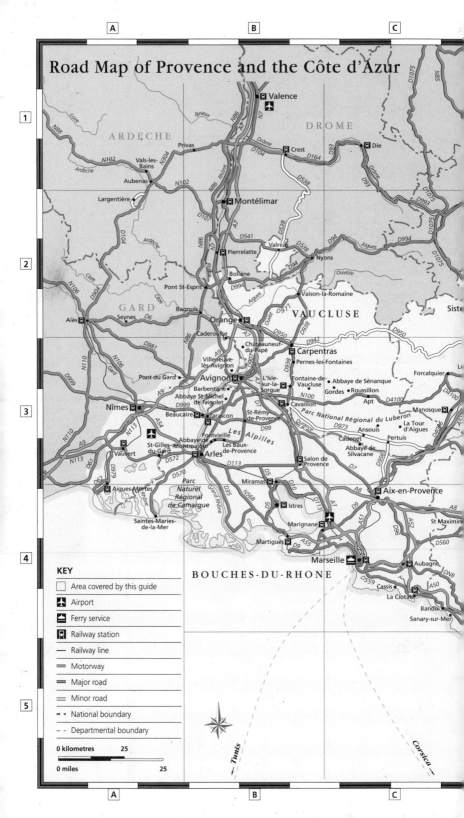